The Barcelona Reader
Cultural Readings of a City

The Barcelona Reader

Cultural Readings of a City

EDITED BY

Enric Bou AND *Jaume Subirana*

LIVERPOOL UNIVERSITY PRESS

First published 2017
Liverpool University Press
4 Cambridge Street
Liverpool, L69 7ZU

in collaboration with Ajuntament de Barcelona
Direcció d'Imatge i Serveis Editorials
Passeig de la Zona Franca, 60
08038 Barcelona
barcelona.cat/barcelonallibres

Copyright © 2017 Liverpool University Press,
unless stated otherwise in the text

The right of Enric Bou and Jaume Subirana to be identified as the editors of this book has been asserted by them in accordance with the Copyright, Designs and Patents Act 1988.

All rights reserved. No part of this book may be reproduced stored in a retrieval system, or transmitted, in any form or by any means, electronic, mechanical, photocopying, recording, or otherwise, without the prior written permission of the publisher.

British Library Cataloguing-in-Publication Data
A British Library CIP Record is available.

ISBN 978-1-78694-032-2

Typeset by Carnegie Book Production, Lancaster

Contents

List of illustrations vii
Notes on contributors xiii

Introduction: Barcelona: Cultural readings of a city
 Enric Bou and Jaume Subirana 1

I City, history, and territory

1 Barcelona: The siege city *Robert Davidson* 21

2 Barcelona as an adaptive ecology *Ferran Sagarra* 43

3 A present past, Barcelona street names, from Víctor Balaguer to Pasqual Maragall *Jaume Subirana* 71

4 'The asylum of modern times': Barcelona and Europe *Felipe Fernández-Armesto* 91

5 A fragile country *Colm Tóibín* 131

II City and society

6 Barcelona and modernity *Brad Epps* 145

7 Football and identities in Catalonia *Alejandro Quiroga* 163

vi   The Barcelona Reader: Cultural Readings of a City

8   The family and the city: Power and the creation of
    cultural imagery *Gary Wray McDonogh*   185

9   Memory and the city in Barcelona's cemeteries
    Elisa Martí-López   209

III Art, architecture, and the city

10 Picasso among his fellows at 4 Gats: Beyond
    Modernisme? *Jordi Falgàs*   243

11 Gaudí: Poet of stone, artistic hedgehog
    Marià Marín i Torné   265

12 El Poble Espanyol / El Pueblo Español (1929)
    Jordana Mendelson   295

IV The Olympics and the city

13 Barcelona: Urban identity 1992–2002 *Donald McNeill*   323

14 From the Olympic torch to the Universal Forum of
    Cultures: The after-image of Barcelona's modernity
    Joan Ramon Resina   347

V Literature, cinema, and the city

15 *La Gran Encisera*: Three odes to Barcelona, and a film
    Josep Miquel Sobrer   383

16 The deceptive dame: Criminal revelations of the
    Catalan capital *Stewart King*   395

17 A *Biutiful* city: Alejandro González Iñárritu's filmic
    critique of the 'Barcelona Model' *Benjamin Fraser*   417

Illustrations

1.1 MANGO apparel label with Barcelona brand added *c.*2009 — 39
2.1 Cerdà's 1/500 topographical plan of 1855 with the addition of partial 1/1200 surveys (Idelfons Cerdà: Plano de los alrededores de ciudad de Barcelona levantado por orden del Gobierno para la formación del proyecto de ensanche. 19 November 1955. Ink on 'canson' paper, 270 × 168 cm. Municipal Archives of Barcelona) — 48
2.2 Miquel Garriga's 1/2000 version of the topographical plan of the city with its 'project of reform' (Miquel Garriga i Roca: Plano topográfico-geométrico de la ciudad de Barcelona. Proyecto de Reforma General. Ink on canvas, 135 × 173 cm, scale 1/2000. 15 August 1962. Municipal Archives of Barcelona) — 49
2.3 One of Garriga's 118 partial 1/250 surveys (Miquel Garriga i Roca 1858. Ink on 'canson' paper, scale 1/250. Set of 118 drawings covering the survey of the entire city of Barcelona. 65 × 45 cm approximately each. Municipal Archives of Barcelona) — 50

2.4 Garriga's 1858 'pre-project' proposal for the city extension (Project approved by the Municipal Council the 6 April 1858. Printed. Undated version)   52

2.5 Preparatory draft for Garriga's 1858 city extension (Miquel Garriga i Roca: This is one of the six different drafts of the 'Proyecto de ensanche de la ciudad de Barcelona sobre la topografia de dicha ciudad y sus afueras'. 28 November 1857. Ink on canvas and watercolour, 160 × 90-100 cm. Project approved by the Municipal Council 6 April 1858)   53

2.6 Cerdà's 1959 'Plano de Ensanche' with, added in, the three axes cutting through the Old City (Arxiu Històric de la Ciutat de Barcelona)   55

2.7 Sheet of the handwriting of Cerdà: 'Synthetic part, Spaces of public use' in *General Theory of the cities' construction applied to the case of Barcelona. April 1859* (Cerdà 1859)   56

2.8 Sheet of the handwriting of Cerdà: 'Synthetic part, Spaces of public use' in *General Theory of the cities' construction applied to the case of Barcelona. April 1859* (Cerdà 1859)   57

2.9 Sheet of the handwriting of Cerdà: 'Synthetic part, Spaces of public use' in *General Theory of the cities' construction applied to the case of Barcelona. April 1859* (Cerdà 1859)   58

2.10 Thomas Mitchell's suggested treatment of street intersections as urban squares in his 1829 plan for a town extension (Mitchell Library, Glasgow)   61

2.11 Garriga's Boulevard, as a reformulation of the contact between Cerdà's grid and the old city, 1861 (Miquel Garriga i Roca: Proyecto para un Boulevard, 19 d'abril 1861 colour ink on canvas. 'Box n. 7 Garriga-Fontseré' Arxiu Administratiu de l'Ajuntament de Barcelona)   63

2.12 Cerdà's proposal of 1863 interpreted by the author (Sagarra 1993)   64

2.13 Cerdà's proposal of 1863 interpreted by the author (Sagarra 1993)   65

2.14	Cerdà's 1863 proposal for rail connections interpreted by the author (Sagarra 1993)	65
2.15	Section 'Theorie' from the *Revue Générale de l'Architecture et des Travaux Publics*, Paris	67
2.16	Section 'Pratique' from the *Revue Générale de l'Architecture et des Travaux Publics*, Paris	67
2.17	Cross-section of Cerdà's 1859 project (Teoria de la construcción de las ciudades, Cerdà y Barcelona, Ministerio para las Administraciones Públicas, and Ajuntament de Barcelona, 1991. ISBN 84-7088-583-9)	68
2.18	Carrer Aragó before the covering over of the railway (Arxiu Fotogràfic de Barcelona)	68
3.1	Plan of the project for the remodelling and extension of Barcelona by Ildefons Cerdà (1859) (Arxiu Històric de la Ciutat de Barcelona)	74
3.2	The new district of Vila Olímpica (Institut Cartogràfic de Catalunya)	84
9.1	A mausoleum in the Recinte dels panteons, Cementiri de Poblenou (Cementiris de Barcelona, S.A.)	213
9.2	Commemorative monument for the deceased buried in the communal grave at the Cementiri de Poblenou in 1862 (Cementiris de Barcelona, S.A.)	215
9.3	Cementiri de Poblenou. 'Paz a los muertos' (Arxiu Històric de la Ciutat de Barcelona)	219
9.4	Cementiri de Poblenou (Cementiris de Barcelona, S.A.)	221
9.5	Sepulture of the Família Patxot (1858). *Cementiri de Poblenou* (Cementiris de Barcelona, S.A.)	222
9.6	Family tomb in the Cementiri de Montjuïc (Cementiris de Barcelona, S.A.)	229
9.7	Cementiri de Poblenou (Arxiu Històric de la Ciutat de Barcelona)	230
9.8	'Resurrection', a 1920 sculpture by Enric Clarasó adorning the sepulchre of Jaume Brutau in the *Cementiri de Montjuïc* (Cementiris de Barcelona, S.A.)	231
9.9	Mausoleum (1894) of the Riva family. Architect: Antoni	

x   The Barcelona Reader: Cultural Readings of a City

M. Gallisà. Sculptor: Eusebi Arnau. Cementiri de Montjuïc (Cementiris de Barcelona, S.A.)   233

9.10 Mausoleum of José Olano Iriondo, 1896. Architect: Claudi Duran i Ventura. Sculptor: Eusebi Arnau. Cementiri de Montjuïc (Cementiris de Barcelona, S.A.)   234

9.11 El Jardí americà, Cementiri de Collserola (Cementiris de Barcelona, S.A.)   237

10.1 Ramon Casas, *4 Gats* (1900), colour lithograph on paper, 58.2 × 34.4 cm (Museu Nacional d'Art de Catalunya, Barcelona)   245

10.2 Ramon Casas, *Aux aguets* (c.1891), oil on canvas, 58 × 47.5 cm (Fundació Institut Amatller d'Art Hispànic, Barcelona)   247

10.3 Santiago Rusiñol, *After the War. The Sad Home* (c.1898), conté crayon, ink, pastel, and colour pencil on paper, 42.8 × 34.6 cm (Museu Nacional d'Art de Catalunya, Barcelona)   248

10.4 Ramon Casas, *Portrait of Pablo Picasso* (1900), charcoal and pastel on paper, 69 × 44.5 cm (Museu Nacional d'Art de Catalunya, Barcelona)   249

10.5 Ramon Casas, *Portrait of Ramon Pichot* (c.1897–1899), charcoal, pastel, gouache and ink on paper, 62.9 × 29.8 cm (Museu Nacional d'Art de Catalunya, Barcelona)   250

10.6 Carles Casagemas, *A Couple* (c.1899), ink and coloured crayon on paper, 21.5 × 14.5 cm (Artur Ramon Collection, Barcelona)   253

10.7 Isidre Nonell, *At the Boqueria's Meat Stands* (1894), conté crayon and charcoal on paper, 28.9 × 21.5 cm (Museu Nacional d'Art de Catalunya, Barcelona)   254

10.8 Xavier Gosé, *Meditation* (1900), graphite and conté crayon on paper, 25 × 25 cm (Museu d'Art Jaume Morera, Lleida donation from Maria Teresa Barrio (Llobet widow), 1985)   256

10.9 Xavier Gosé, *Throwing the Tackle*, cover for *Quatre Gats: publicació artística–literària*, no. 6 (16 March 1899) (Barcelona), magazine, 30.5 × 25.4 cm (Universitat de Barcelona, CRAI, Biblioteca de Lletres)   257

10.10 Pablo Gargallo, *En Nogueras* (1900), charcoal and pastel on Ingres paper, 49.9 × 47.5 cm (Museo Pablo Gargallo, Ayuntamiento de Zaragoza)   259

10.11 Isidre Nonell, *Consuelo* (1901), oil on canvas, 131 × 90 cm (Museu de Montserrat. Donation from Josep Sala i Ardiz)   260

11.1 The four columns which support the ceiling of the crypt of the Colònia Güell and symbolize the four evangelists are made with basalt pieces from Castellfollit de la Roca combined with lead. Gaudí always used local materials or materials from nearby areas, which is now a popular concept. The crypt was the first construction to make use of parabolic structure resistance (© Pere Virgili 2014)   273

11.2 Model to scale 1:25 of the church of the Colonia Güell, which Gaudí never finished, produced by the Chair of the History of Construction and Architectural Heritage of Innsbruck University (© Pere Virgili 2014)   276

11.3 Inverted polifunicular model – based on ropes or chains – in the church of the Colonia Güell, a system for calculating forces which inaugurated the Gaudian architectural revolution (© Vicens Vilarrubias c.1898)   277

11.4 The crypt of the Colònia Güell under construction in the year 1910. The architect invented a cheap, efficient and easy-to-assemble scaffolding system, based on the recycling of materials (© Vicens Vilarrubias 1910)   279

11.5 Sketch – drawing and painting on photography – by Gaudí for the initial studies for the design of the church of the Colònia Güell (*c*.1910). Public domain.   280

11.6 A corridor which goes through the entire lower part of the crypt of the Colònia Güell, built in the shape of a hyperbolic paraboloid which Gaudí created as a resonance box for the organ and which also contributes to the climatization of the building (© Pere Virgili 2014)   286

11.7 Bars made with pieces repurposed from textile machinery from the Colònia Güell (© Pere Virgili 2014)   289

12.1 Francesc d'Asís Galí, *D'Ací i d'Allà*, special number (December 1929): cover   297

17.1 The Torre Agbar and Sagrada Família as seen from Uxbal's hospital window (pan–left) (© *Studies in Latin American and Spanish Cinemas*)   426

Notes on contributors

Enric Bou is Full Professor of Spanish and Catalan literature at the Università Ca' Foscari di Venezia. Previously he taught at Brown University. His teaching and research interests cover a broad range of twentieth-century Spanish Peninsular and Catalan literature but particularly involving poetry, autobiography, city and literature, and Spanish film. His latest books are *Daliccionario. Objetos, mitos y símbolos de Salvador Dalí* (2004), the edition of Pedro Salinas' *Obras Completas* (3 vols, 2007) and an essay about space and literature: *Invention of Space. City, Travel and Literature* (2013). He directs MELILF (Migration and Everyday Life. Iberian Literature and Film), and is the editor of *Catalan Review* and *Rassegna Iberistica*.

Robert Davidson is Associate Professor of Spanish and Catalan, and holds a PhD from Cornell. He teaches Modern Peninsular Literature and Culture and his current research interests include theories of space and cultural theories of food and hospitality. He is the author of *Jazz Age Barcelona* (2009) and is currently completing *The Hotel: Space Over Time*. He is the co-editor of UTP's TorontoIberic book series and has published on different aspects of the Castilian and Catalan avant-gardes, cultural theory and film. Prof. Davidson has served on the editorial boards of *Revista Canadiense de Estudios Hispánicos, Diacritics* and *Catalan Review.*

Brad Epps holds the Chair in Spanish at the University of Cambridge, where he is also Head of the Department of Spanish and Portuguese and Professorial Fellow at King's College. For over two decades, he was Professor of Romance Languages and Literatures and the Committee on Degrees in Studies of Women, Gender, and Sexuality at Harvard University, for which he also served as Chair. He has published over a hundred articles on modern literature, film, art, architecture, urban theory, queer theory, and immigration from Spain, Latin America, Hispanophone Africa, and Catalonia, and is the author of several books on Juan Goytisolo, Pedro Almodóvar, Spanish literary history, and immigration and sexuality. He has been a visiting professor or scholar in Spain, Germany, France, Chile, Cuba, the Netherlands, Sweden, China and the United Kingdom, and is the new series editor for Hispanic Studies at Routledge.

Jordi Falgàs, PhD, is an art historian and since 2008 directs the Fundació Rafael Masó in Girona. He is also museology consultant for Gaudí's Casa Vicens in Barcelona and project coordinator for a new Museum of Modern and Contemporary Art in Girona. He was Cleveland Fellow in Modern Art at the Cleveland Museum of Art (2004–2007) and Assistant Executive Manager at the Fundació Gala-Salvador Dalí (1996–2003). He has published extensively, edited several books and curated numerous exhibitions on Catalan modern art. His latest books are *Masó: Interiors* (2016) and *Dalí: Acadèmia neocubista i altres obres* (forthcoming from Abadia de Montserrat).

Felipe Fernández-Armesto occupies the William P. Reynolds Chair for Mission in Arts and Letters at the University of Notre Dame. From 1969 he was an undergraduate, graduate student and teacher at Oxford, where he was a Fellow of St Antony's College. In 2000 he moved to be Professor of Global Environmental History at Queen Mary, University of London, and, from 2005 to 2009, Prince of Asturias Professor at Tufts University. Awards he has won include the John Carter Brown Medal, the World History Association Book Prize (for *Pathfinders,* 2007) and Spain's national prizes for geographical research and food writing. He is the sole author of 23 books (of which the most recent are *Our America* (2014) and *A Foot in The River* (2015) and over fifty major published papers, chapters and articles. His work has appeared in 27 languages.

Benjamin Fraser is Professor of Hispanic Studies and Chair of Foreign Languages and Literatures in the Thomas Harriot College of Arts & Sciences at East Carolina University. He is the executive editor of the *Journal of Urban Cultural Studies*, co-editor of the *Hispanic Urban Studies* book series, an associate editor of *Hispania* and a senior editor of the *Arizona Journal of Hispanic Cultural Studies*. His recent scholarship on urban themes has been published in the monographs *Toward an Urban Cultural Studies* (2015) and *Digital Cities* (2015), as well as the *Journal of Spanish Cultural Studies*.

Stewart King is Senior Lecturer in Spanish and Catalan Studies and coordinates the International Literatures programme at Monash University, Australia. He has published extensively on contemporary Spanish and Catalan narrative and on crime fiction as a form of world literature. He is the author of *Escribir la catalanidad. Lenguas e identidades en la narrativa contemporánea de Cataluña* (2005) and has edited or co-edited *The Space of Culture: Critical Readings in Hispanic Studies* (2004), *La cultura catalana de expresión castellana* (2005), and a special issue of the *Bulletin of Hispanic Studies* (2017) on memories in contemporary Spain with Alison Ribeiro de Menezes.

Marià Marín Torné is a historian and cultural manager. He graduated in Geography and History from the University of Barcelona. He was director of the Visual Arts and Book Area at the Catalan Cultural Industries Institute. He teaches advanced classes on art and cultural industries for masters and postgraduate courses at the University of Barcelona, Pompeu Fabra University and the Open University of Catalonia. He has written on the publishing industry, digital environment and research papers of artistic studies. He is cofounder of The Gaudí Research Institute, promoter of Gaudí World Congresses and curator of exhibitions on Antoni Gaudí.

Elisa Martí-López is Associate Professor of Spanish at Northwestern University. She is the author of several articles and a monograph (*Borrowed Words: Translation, Imitation, and the Making of the Novel in Nineteenth-Century Spain* [2002]) where she addresses the processes of cultural production and consumption in mid-nineteenth-century

Europe and the role of translations and imitations of foreign literary models in the development of the bourgeois novel in Catalonia and Spain. As part of her project 'The Urban Spaces of Death: Cemeteries as Narratives of the Modern City 1780–1918', she has published articles and two monographs: *Un passeig pel Cementiri de PobleNou* (2004) and *Somnis de Barcelona: El Cementiri de Montjuïc, 1883–1936* (2008). She is also currently working on death, money and painting in the narrative of Narcís Oller.

Gary McDonogh is Helen Herrmann Professor and Chair of the Department of Growth and Structure of Cities at Bryn Mawr College. An urban anthropologist by training, he has worked in Barcelona for four decades in projects involving the financial-industrial elite, the culture of planning, the myth and lives of Barcelona's Raval/Barrio Chino and the meanings of immigration in the city, especially with regard to Chinese. He is the author of *Good Families of Barcelona: A Social History of Power in the Social Era* (1987). He also has published widely on African-American life and religion in the United States and society, culture and media in Hong Kong. He is currently completing a long-term comparative study on global Chinatowns.

Donald McNeill is Professor of Urban and Cultural Geography at Western Sydney University. His doctoral research on political identity and urban space in post-transition Barcelona was published as *Urban Change and the European Left: Tales from the New Barcelona* (1999). He continues to research on architecture, urban design and cities, and his subsequent books include *The Global Architect: Firms, Fame and Urban Form* (2009) and *Global Cities and Urban Theory* (2016).

Jordana Mendelson is Associate Professor in the Department of Spanish and Portuguese, New York University. She is the author of essays on Spanish modern art, photography and the illustrated press and is curator or co-curator of several exhibitions: *Margaret Michaelis: Photography, Vanguard and Politics in Republican Barcelona* (1998), *Magazines and War 1936–1939* (2007), *Other Weapons: Photography and Print Culture during the Spanish Civil War* (2008) and *Encounter with the 1930s* (2012). She is the author of *Documenting Spain: Artists, Exhibition Culture, and the Modern Nation 1929–1939* (2005) and co-editor of *Postcards: Ephemeral Histories of Modernity* (2010).

Alejandro Quiroga is a Reader in Spanish History at Newcastle University. He specializes in the study of national identities and nationalisms. His most recent book is *Football and National Identities in Spain* (2013). He is also the author of *The Reinvention of Spain. Nation and Identity Since Democracy* (2007, with Sebastian Balfour), *Making Spaniards. Primo de Rivera and the Nationalization of the Masses, 1923–1930* (2007) and *Los orígenes del Nacionalcatolicismo* (2006). He has edited *Right-Wing Spain in the Civil War Era. Soldiers of God and Apostles of the Fatherland, 1914–45* (2012) and *Católicos y patriotas. Religión y nación en la Europa de entreguerras* (2013).

Joan Ramon Resina is Professor in the Department of Iberian and Latin American Cultures and the Department of Comparative Literature at Stanford University, where he directs the Iberian Studies Program at the Europe Center. He holds a PhD in Comparative Literature by U.C. Berkeley and a PhD in English by the University of Barcelona. He has been visiting Professor at the Humboldt University in Berlin, Universidad Iberoamericana in Mexico D.F., Universidad de Murcia, Universitat de València, the CUNY Graduate Center, and Columbia University. Awards include the Donald Andrews Whittier Fellowship at the Stanford Humanities Center, the Fulbright fellowship, the Alexander-von- Humboldt fellowship, a Wien International Scholarship, a DAAD grant, fellowships at the Simon Dubnow Institute in Leipzig and at the Internationales Kolleg Morphomata in Cologne, the Serra d'Or prize for literary criticism, the Omnium Cultural award (Ex Aequo with the TV channel Arte), and the Literary Criticism Award of the Institució de les Lletres Catalanes. He has published one hundred and fifty essays in professional journals and collective volumes. Between 1998 and 2004 he was general editor of *Diacritics* and coordinated a special issue of this journal titled 'New Coordinates: Spatial Mappings, National Trajectories'. Select books include: *Barcelona's Vocation of Modernity: Rise and Decline of an Urban Image* (2008), *Del Hispanismo a los Estudios Ibéricos. Una propuesta federativa para el ámbito cultural* (2009) and *El postnacionalisme en el mapa global* (2005).

Ferran Sagarra Trias was awarded a degree in Architecture from Escola Tècnica Superior d'Arquitectura de Barcelona (ETSAB) in 1976 and a PhD from Universitat Politècnica de Catalunya in 1991. From 2006 to 2013 he was Dean of the ETSAB. He is a member of the Institut d'Estudis Catalans, IEC (Catalan Academy of Sciences). He is the author of articles and chapters on the transformation of Barcelona. He is scientific advisor for publications such as *El Carrer* (1995–2008 FAVB, Barcelona), *3ZU Journal of Architecture* (Barcelona) and *Urbanistica* (Milan). He was the Director of *Visions* (2007–2012, ETSAB).

Josep Miquel Sobrer (Barcelona 1944–Bloomington 2015) taught at the University of Puget Sound, at the University of Michigan, and finally at Indiana University, where he retired as Professor emeritus in 2009. An expert of Spanish and Catalan culture, he was the author of many articles, books and editions of Catalan medieval and contemporary literature. He was interested in presenting his country to an Anglo-Saxon audience as he did in *Catalonia. A self-portrait* (1992). A poet and essayist, he was very proud of the English version of his *Book of Oracles* (1988), and of the Catalan *Desfer les Amèriques. Contradiccionari* (2006). He translated *A Broken Mirror* by Mercè Rodoreda into English. He served as President of the North American Catalan Society and editor of *Catalan Review*.

Jaume Subirana is Associate Professor at Universitat Oberta de Catalunya, UOC, where he coordinates the research group IdentiCat. Language, Culture and Identity in the Global Age. He holds a PhD in Catalan Language and Literature and a BA in Arts by Universitat Autònoma de Barcelona. He has been Visiting Scholar at Duke University, and Visiting Professor at the University of British Columbia, Brown University and Università Ca' Foscari Venezia. His books include *Josep Carner, l'exili del mite 1945–1970* (2000), *Barcelona acròstic* (2003), *BarcelonABC. A City Alphabet* (2013) and *Funcions del passat en la cultura catalana contemporània. Institucionalització, representacions i identitat* (2015), edited with J.A. Fernàndez.

Colm Tóibín is an Irish novelist and essayist. He studied at University College Dublin and lived in Barcelona between 1975 and 1978. Out of his experience in Barcelona he produced two books, the novel *The South* and *Homage to Barcelona*, both published in 1990. Tóibín is currently Irene and Sidney B. Silverman Professor of the Humanities at Columbia University, and succeeded Martin Amis as professor of creative writing at the University of Manchester.

INTRODUCTION

Barcelona:
Cultural readings of a city

Enric Bou and Jaume Subirana

In 1972 an independent filmmaker, Jordi Lladó, collaborated with a few actors from Els Joglars company to shoot *Aullidos*, a short film that tried to stage the beauties of Barcelona. Franco's dictatorship was still very much alive, a greyness (the colour of the uniforms of the repressive police, the air, the mood) filled everything. The result was a hysterical portrait of things to visit in a depressed city, among others scuba diving in Barcelona's sewer system, buying postcards picturing a slump, and picnicking at Montcada's *turó* [hill] near a cement factory. It was 40 years before a Mexican filmmaker made a similar move and portrayed a poignant image of a 'beautiful' city unfriendly to immigrants and poor people alike. It was also 40 years before the city became, much to the dismay of many of its inhabitants, one of the most popular tourist destinations in Europe. The city's 1.6 million residents have seen the number of visitors skyrocket from 1.7 million in 1990 to more than 8.2 million in 2015. Barcelona, 'la Gran Encisera' (the Great Enchantress) as defined by Joan Maragall, one of her greatest poets, has constantly delivered a dual yet contradictory message: *la rosa de foc* [the rose of fire] for the anarchists and *ciudad de ferias y congresos* [city of fairs and conventions] during the dictatorship; pickpocket trap and tourist paradise.

The aim of this book is to provide an in-depth overview of Barcelona through texts written by a selected group of scholars who have devoted much time and energy to studying the city. We have drawn together published and unpublished work that best illuminates a wide-ranging selection of critical perspectives of Barcelona, ways of reading the city from complementary cultural approaches, stressing the negatives, but also the glowing aspects of the city. The book provides scholars, students, journalists, and visitors looking for a more comprehensive approach to Barcelona than tourist guides can deliver with an overview of the central issues about Barcelona. We have included both strictly scholarly and non-scholarly writings, thus enabling a wider range of perspectives.

The seeds of this book were sown a few years ago, when we started a discussion about how to present Barcelona to a foreign audience. For the last 30 years now a number of colleagues have been teaching courses on different aspects of Barcelona. These took place around the time (and particularly after) the Olympic impulse that, for good or for worse, changed everything in the city. The first idea we had was to put together a stylish version of a course pack that some of us had prepared at one point or another, which would include noteworthy scholarly essays on Barcelona. These might coincide with the materials we were using in our current courses. But early in the process this possibility was dismissed: we thought it would be better to address the book to a wider range of readers, including students, the general public, and, particularly, visitors in need of some thorough explanations about the city that is and that has been, thus going beyond the hollow explanations one can read in a commercial tourist guide. At an early stage in our project we considered a map of topics and different kinds of approaches – architecture, history, literature, art, film – and started looking for good texts. *The Barcelona Reader: Cultural Readings of a City* includes scholarly essays that can be of interest both to the student and the general public. We focus on cultural representations of the city: the arts (including literature) provide a complex yet discontinuous patchwork portrait of it. The authors together create a kaleidoscope of views and voices, thus presenting a diverse yet inclusive picture.

Our book owes its greatest debt to the authors whose work we have reprinted and those who have written new material. In addition to these, a number of people and institutions have crucially contributed to making this volume possible. We would like to thank the Universitat Oberta de Catalunya and Università Ca' Foscari Venezia, who have supported the project. We are also grateful to Sara Antoniazzi for her practical support. Thanks are also due to Barcelona's City Hall, for providing financial support and the cover photograph.

*

Over the last 20 years there has been a growing international interest in the city of Barcelona. This has been reflected in the academic world through a series of studies, courses, seminars, and publications. *The Barcelona Reader: Cultural Readings of a City* hinges together a selection of the best academic articles, written in English, about the city, and its main elements of identity and interest: art, urban planning, history, and social movements. During this period, interest in Catalan studies has grown exponentially due to the initiative of single individuals and universities, or, in some cases, to contributions from the Institut Ramon Llull. In the UK and Ireland alone Catalan is taught in 23 universities. Moreover, Catalan is also taught in more than 27 universities in the USA, Canada, and Australia. Yet there are currently very few books available in English that can be used as a thorough introduction to Catalan culture. Most of them fill partial gaps, but none of them addresses the specific issues we deal with. Many titles are no longer available or have extremely out-of-date approaches. One could mention, for instance, Joan Triadú's *Anthology of Catalan Lyric Poetry*, edited by Joan Gili (Oxford: Dolphin, 1953), Dominic Keown and Tom Owen's *Joan Salvat-Papasseit: Selected Poems* (Anglo-Catalan Society, 1982), Albert Balcells' *Catalan Nationalism: Past and Present* (New York: St. Martin's Press, 1996), and Josep R. Llobera's *Foundations of National Identity* (New York: Berghahn Books, 2004). Closer to our aim are books such as Josep Miquel Sobrer's, *Catalonia, A Self-portrait* (Bloomington: Indiana University Press, 1992), Arthur Terry's, *A Companion to Catalan Literature* (Rochester, NY: Tamesis, 2003), Helen Graham and Jo Labanyi's *Spanish Cultural Studies. An Introduction: The Struggle for Modernity* (New York: OUP, 1995), and Barry Jordan and Rikki Morgan's *Contemporary Spanish Cultural Studies* (London and New York: Arnold and OUP, 2000).

The book that gets closer to what we wanted to achieve is Dominic Keown's *A Companion to Catalan Culture* (Woodbridge, UK, Tamesis Books, 2011), which, in 268 pages, encapsulates a first port of entry for general information about Catalan culture for the English reader. The salient theme uniting the essays is that of identity: each contribution in that volume illuminates some aspect of Catalan identity, linking cultural expression with *catalanitat* [Catalan-ness]. The editor has assembled essays that address contemporary culture, medieval culture, political history from the nineteenth century to the twenty-first, the notion of Barcelona as 'siege city', language, sport, music, cinema, festival and cuisine – manifestations of both 'high' and 'low' culture. Keown claims coherence for these disparate cultural expressions with the observation that their best-known proponents (Gaudí, Dalí, among others) 'did not emerge from a vacuum but are merely distinguished exponents of a cultural choir whose fellow protagonists, through repression, inaccessibility or just plain ignorance – have been denied the opportunity of the reception they so richly deserve'. Other volumes worth mentioning are a special issue of *Catalan Review*, 'Barcelona and Modernity' edited by Brad Epps in 2006, Joan Ramon Resina's *Barcelona's Vocation of Modernity: Rise and Decline of an Urban Image* (Stanford, CA: Stanford University Press, 2008), and Edgar Illas' *Thinking Barcelona: Ideologies of a Global City* (Liverpool, UK: Liverpool University Press, 2012). At the international level, this reader follows the example (with very different goals) of similar publications, most notably *The Berlin Reader: A Compendium on Urban Change and Activism (Urban Studies)*, edited by M. Bernt, B. Grell and A. Holm (Bielefeld, Germany: Transcript Verlag, 2013). As happens with other books of this nature, critics may claim that there are thematic gaps and that the selection of material and authors can be called into question. A comprehensive, complete and balanced presentation of all issues that are to be discussed in relation to Barcelona exceeds the frame of an ordinary reader.

*

The Barcelona Reader: Cultural Readings of a City focuses on one single city, a centre of attention for students and cultivated tourists alike. It presents a plural and in-depth introduction and reflection about the most relevant aspects of the city of Barcelona. Our selection includes some of the best published approaches to each aspect of the city and its society (in so far as copyrights and permissions have made this possible), and a few articles written for this volume. We hope that a work of this kind will be an invaluable aid for programming new courses on the Catalan capital and on Catalan culture in universities around the world, and it will provide a supplementary guide for sophisticated visitors.

We have two complementary experiences of explaining Barcelona to foreign people. One is that of living abroad and trying to make the city comprehensible to a foreign regard. Another is writing from Barcelona thinking of a foreign audience. Many years ago, when one of us was still living in the USA, he was once asked the inevitable 'where are you from?' When he replied 'from Barcelona', the questioner stared at him and asked, with a notable look of surprise: 'So, what are you doing here?' That must have been back in 1998. It happened in Wellesley, a town outside Boston, MA, not the worst city in the country, just a provincial, snobbish one, as a writer in *The New Yorker* once depicted it, 'a retiring community for the newly wed'. The question epitomizes the surprise felt by anyone unable to understand how one of the editors could have lived so far away from the marvellous, prodigious, exciting, attractive city of their dreams. A few years before 1992, his questioner might have asked if he was Mexican.

Not far away from Wellesley, in Durham, NC, and around that time, the second editor of this book was also asked 'Where are you from?' This well-intentioned question is part of the ritual of small talk. It happens at parties, in the line at the supermarket, in the corridors of the department if you are a visiting scholar: 'Where are you from?' But the trivial question, with such an apparently simple answer for many people, contains all the ambiguity and complexity of self-definition relevant to the situation of Catalans. How does one suppose that we should answer the question 'Where are you from?' if you come from Barcelona? The official response is obvious: 'I am Spanish'. That is what our passport and national identification document state. But it is not what many us feel and these are not the exact words we would use, if we could reply – shall we say – 'freely'. In the last 100 years of history, with short parentheses, for many Catalans the adjective 'Spanish' excludes any reality distinct from centralist, 'Castilian' and, typically, *castizo* or *flamenco*. Most Catalans accept the Spanish flag and national anthem without emotion, if not to say with a certain reticence. Letting us be carried away by sentiment, the second response would be 'I am a Catalan'. But then, no matter how sincere we feel, grave problems of comprehension arise for a large number of average Americans and Europeans: 'Catalan? Where is Catalan?' There is still, however, a third possible option, 'I am from Barcelona'. It is recognizable that the 1992 Olympic Games and the architecture of Antoni Gaudí have put our city on the map and, therefore, the majority of interlocutors will make a gesture of understanding by nodding their head, even if they do not simply say: 'Oh, Messi!'. Yes, Messi, or Gaudí: there's where we live. In many ways these book is a multifaceted response to the question 'where are you from?'

As we all well know, there was a basic transformation in the perception of Barcelona abroad before and after the 1992 Olympic Games, and its subsequent transformation into an international tourist destination. Ten days of Olympic competitions, with swimmers diving into the Montjuïc pool against the backdrop of the city, beautiful images that captivated TV audiences worldwide, did much to attract international attention towards the city. And the image remains, despite the notoriety the city has earned itself in the tourist rankings as the world capital of pickpockets, though the authorities seem none too concerned about that. Back in 1992, the number of television programmes, books, special magazine issues (on food – on tapas, something that had previously never existed in Barcelona), did a lot to attract interest in a city off the radar of international travellers until then.

Woody Allen's 2008 infomercial, or publicity documentary, added further reasons for Barcelona's attraction and promoted the mirage of exoticism for foreigners keen to visit the city. The growing interest in the city turned into courses on Barcelona and modernity, taught by ourselves and our many colleagues, invariably arousing great interest in people, promoting slightly more cultivated tourists and raising the number of enrolled students, which is of the utmost concern to departmental deans and directors in the North American university system, governed as it is by the relentless laws of supply and demand.

All this happened after the Olympics. The situation before 1992 is well known: Barcelona was a grey city that tourists spending a few days in Lloret de Mar or Salou tried to avoid. The Catalan capital did not have any particular appeal to the modern visitor, except for those looking for the underground, as attested by some old novels picturing aspects of the red light district or 'Barri Xino' (Chinatown).[1] No one – apart from Carles Soldevila, the author of an original guide in 1929, *L'art d'ensenyar Barcelona* [The art of showing Barcelona] – could have suspected what would happen a few decades later, in the early twenty-first century. Though Barcelona had received some international attention on the occasion of the world fairs, in 1888 and 1929, they did not have any significant lasting effect in terms of attracting a steady influx of tourism.

The 'Barcelona Brand'

A good amount of the interest generated today about Barcelona can be linked to the success of the branding of this city. When we talk about a city's 'brand' we are talking about associating that city with an image. About imagining it in the sense of forming a mental image, representing it in our mind. We might say 'adjectivizing' the city, or re-baptizing it, or even tuning it, but we are in any case ostensibly dealing with conceptual images (figures: symbols, allegories, metaphors) and are therefore talking about imagination. Through 20 centuries of history Barcelona has been given countless nicknames.

The art historian Salvatore Settis argues that all significant cities aspire to strengthen and to grow their power of attraction: all important cities want to be better than the others, they want to feel unique or special, and they do this by displaying their symbolic capital. The way to distinguish yourself today in a highly competitive world is by emphasizing your uniqueness, and this uniqueness is often associated with a name and/or a nickname, words usually linked to the original name of the city. At a time when the words 'branding' and 'brand' are on everyone's lips (as if they were thoroughly modern) and are applied to so many things, including countries and cities, it might

---

1 Paul Morand's *Ouvert la nuit* (1922), Francis Carco's *Printemps d'Espagne* (1929), Henry de Montherlant's *La Petite infante de Castille* (1929), Jean Genet's *Journal d'un voleur* (1949), Peyre de Mandiargues', *La Marge* (1967) or even George Orwell's *Homage to Catalonia* (1938).

be worthwhile recalling that 'brand' actually comes from Old English and first surfaced in *Beowulf* circa the year 1000 (as *brond*), literally meaning something burnt, marked by fire. What we mean is that the discussion goes a long way back, and that the kind of brand referred to – although it has been known extensively over time to Barcelona (thanks to people like Al-Mansur (in the year 985); by the Duke of Berwick (in the siege of 1713–1714); by general Espartero, the man who said that for things to go smoothly in Spain you had to bomb Barcelona every 30 or 40 years... and he did so in 1842; and by another general, Francesco Pricolo, from the Italian Air Force, in 1938...) is neither easy nor sweet to relate to a city.

Today, from the old mark engraved through fire and bombs on the streets or the bodies of people, we have moved to the search for a brand that might be easily and pleasantly recorded in the memory of the hundreds of millions of potential visitors scattered around the world, precisely those who are not living in the city we refer to. When we talk about the 'Barcelona Brand' we are talking about associating the city (or the place) with an image. We are talking about imagining a place in the sense of the first meaning cited in the dictionary: forming a mental image of it, representing it in our mind.

Through a long history of more than 20 centuries, Barcelona has not only been given different names (Barcino, Barchinona, Barshiluna), and heard them pronounced in different ways, but it has also seen how whatever was tacked on to its core name changed according to the circumstances: the parallel adjectives, nicknames or names associated with the city's name. Of all the nicknames that in one way or another are still with us, perhaps the oldest is *Cap i Casal*, from the Middle Ages, from the times when the city was the headquarters of the County of Barcelona, and was added to reassert its importance (the same name was used in the Kingdom of Valencia for the city of Valencia). The times when the City Council (Consell de Cent, one of the oldest protodemocratic bodies in Europe) would tell the king, when swearing his oath of allegiance: 'We, who are as good as you, swear to you, who are no better than us, to accept you as our king and sovereign lord, provided you observe all our liberties and laws – but if not, not'....[2] One of the most common nicknames still in use for Barcelona also

---

[2] Unless otherwise indicated, all translations are by the editors.

comes from this period (or perhaps from the reference to the period): namely the 'Ciutat comtal' [City of the Counts], which through mental sovereignty has the drawback of turning the capital into, so to speak, a mini-capital. Although, we just learned: 'if not, not'... and it has been like this again and again. And somehow we are still there, struggling. Subsequently, in the early seventeenth century, Miguel de Cervantes set a long episode of the second part of *Don Quixote* in Barcelona, where the city is evoked as an 'archivo de cortesía', a 'repository of gentility' ('that repository of gentility, refuge of wayfarers, asylum of the poor, homeland of the brave, avenger of the wronged, and home of harmonious and lasting friendship, a city unique in its setting and beauty'): the formula went down well, with a clear preponderance in the times when Spanish was the official language of those who wished to refer to the city of Agustina de Aragón and Juan Antonio Samaranch – and is, in fact, still used to this day.

Come the nineteenth century and industrialization, Catalonia was sometimes referred to as the 'factory of Spain', although many of the leading lights in that economic and cultural recovery preferred for Barcelona the ring of the 'Paris of the South' (a stroll through the Eixample district shows that this was not merely an abstract idea). Nevertheless, for a Parisian of the ilk of Prosper Merimée (the librettist of *Carmen*), at that time Barcelona was little more than 'a city that masquerades as a capital and is the spitting image of a provincial industrial city' The truth is that the skyline of Barcelona showed then a forest of chimneys and the Eixample, the plan for the urban expansion designed by Ildefons Cerdà, approved in 1859, was to take years to become a reality, with innumerable empty spaces, unpaved streets, etc. Hence, from this came another name (in this case, a nickname): at the very beginning of the twentieth century the journal *L'Esquella de la Torratxa* published many jokes about *'la ciutat del fang'* [city of mud], and here was born the nickname *'can Fanga'*: a not very polite way for Catalans from outside the capital to refer to Barcelona and to those who come from there.

In any event, industrialization did lead workers to get organized, sparking heightening social tension which, at the turn of the century (and well into the twentieth century), turned the city's streets into the reason why Barcelona, when Sant Jordi's Day was not yet a holiday, was also called *'la Rosa de foc'*, 'the rose of fire'. Or, if you want a brighter and more literary version (penned by the poet Joan Maragall in his 'Oda nova a Barcelona' ['New ode to Barcelona'], in the same year as the Tragic Week), 'the Great Enchantress', an image chosen by the art critic Robert Hughes as the title of one of his books about the city.

After the Spanish Civil War Barcelona was for decades Franco's (and Porcioles') *ciudad de ferias y congresos*. Perhaps even into the merry 1980s, when a poster by an illustrator, Mariscal, and a song by Gato Pérez joined forces to conjure up, in the broken-up 'Bar Cel Ona' [Bar Sky Wave], a way of defining a cheery/cheesy seaside summer holiday destination years before the Olympic Games were to open up the city's waterfront for us to rediscover that the city actually had beaches... reachable, to boot, by underground or bus. These were the years when Eduardo Mendoza retrospectively novelized the era of modernism, talking about 'la ciudad de los prodigios' ['the city of marvels'], the title of his novel of 1986. In that year the City Council launched the 'Barcelona, posa't guapa' [Barcelona, get pretty] rehabilitation campaign, a popular, successful and long-lived initiative (three characteristics that rarely come together in politics, not even at the local level), and a campaign that played with picturing Barcelona as a woman (in Catalan and Spanish, 'ciutat' is a female noun). These initiatives coloured the years just before the 1992 Olympic Games bequeathed us Cobi, the Olympic mascot, and the idea of a compelling and attractive city, along with the 'power' which, perhaps divested of real arguments ('Ella tiene poder, ella tiene poder / Barcelona es poderosa, Barcelona tiene poder' [She has power, she has power / Barcelona is powerful, Barcelona has power]) was attributed to it by Peret and Los Manolos ('romántica reina, la que nos parió') [romantic queen who gave birth to us all] as Olympic excitement peaked.

At the turn of the century Barcelona's municipal government exalted the city as 'the best shop in the world', underlining the importance, attractiveness and diversity of its trade, seen as an asset already related to the burgeoning boom of international tourism. Because Barcelona is now officially a huge, beautiful shop. A large number of guidebook writers think so, and repeat it, as well as hundreds of media people and investors, millions of football fans worldwide and many of Barcelona's citizens, too. Not all of them, however: in recent years the crisis and some of the changes of the so-called tertiarization – the development of a tertiary (i.e. service) sector of an economy – have led to the quite sporadic birth of new nicknames such as 'Brandcelona' (initially ironic, then integrated and turned into something fancy), 'Farsalona' (proposed by the anthropologist Manuel Delgado) or 'Karcelona'. What this last nickname implies is that the city has become (or may become) a jail for its inhabitants.

Barcelona vs *Barcelonas*

Barcelona's many nicknames have referred to its being a capital (albeit a minor one) of gentility, hard work, enchantment, explosive appeal, sun, and beaches, shops, and a relatively unfounded and self-satisfied power (but nevertheless quite convincing, at least on the inside). When all is said and done, if taken together these attributes might not amount to such a bad general description of the city, although obviously the question about the identity of the target still remains, not to mention the telling detail that all these nicknames have never worked as a sum, but rather as tags like the ones people used to stick on luggage long ago, always over the previous one, replacing it.

Which Barcelona might be imagined from each one of the nicknames the city has had and from each and every one of the different proposals that have recently appeared on the scene? One of the latest, the title of the film that Woody Allen came to shoot among us (*Vicky Cristina Barcelona*), was an original but ultimately laughable attempt at a new moniker crafted from wooliness and many of the clichés of crossover success in globalized times. What metaphor and nickname might we give Barcelona now, post-Cobi, to put the image of a pretty, powerful and sensational shop behind us? What we have now is certainly the triumph of a city (more than a model) without a clear nickname or unambiguous image, but which has undeniably become an international tourist destination.

The names given to Paris, the 'Ville Lumière' (actually coined in London almost two centuries ago), New York, the 'Big Apple' (through a campaign sponsored by the city in the late seventies), or Rome, the 'Eternal City', neither help nor hinder them. These are not random examples: Harold Bloom holds that Barcelona is a 'city-of-cities', like the three above, and that it is like them because they are cities of the imagination. The question is whether Barcelona is in the same league as Paris, New York and Rome – and can therefore hold its own with or without a brand – or whether it desperately needs a revamped brand as a motor or lever and subsequently run the risk of getting stuck with this would-be happy (and inevitably one-dimensional) brand forever, like a piece of chewing gum or a stain (just as Avignon is the 'City of the Popes' or Dubrovnik 'the Pearl of the Adriatic'). In 30 years, Barcelona has gone from living to be shown to living off being shown (with many citizens subsequently feeling as if they were mere extras in some parts of the city, rather than the main characters). This process has needed no brand, only the excellent work of the Barcelona Tourism consortium, created in 1993.

The difficulty of finding a single likeable slogan that would summarize the Barcelona brand stresses the fact that the capital is a multifaceted place. In 1990 Manuel Vázquez Montalbán published *Barcelonas*, a commanding survey of Barcelona over the centuries from a multifaceted perspective including history and politics, art, literature, architecture. This book was summarized in *Publisher's Weekly* as 'less a guide than a cultural resource for Barcelona-bound visitors'. Montalbán deplored an Olympic Games-inspired, four-year speculative frenzy of uncoordinated implacable destruction and construction. The city thus changed forever. A change that had been more than a century in the making had finally found its raison d'être. Montalbán claimed that his book was not 'poetic', or 'historical' but a 'subjective documented chronicle'. He also stressed that he 'wanted to highlight a few choir soloists so far unheard and contribute to a different memory of a multidimensional city'. This book was published in English in 1992. That was a remarkable year in the diffusion of an idea of Barcelona in the English-speaking world: besides the translation of *Barcelonas*, Robert Hughes published his *Barcelona*, a personal homage to the city that followed a historical chronological approach. Similar to Vázquez Montalbán, the Australian art historian had a personal relationship to the city. Finally, in that same year Thelma Kaplan's *Red City, Blue Period. Social Movements in Picasso's Barcelona* focused on episodes of the transformation of a conflictive society that emphasize the input of gender, class, and ritual.

Our selection, in line with Vázquez Montalbán approach, examines Barcelona not as one single city but as a city of cities. Geographical and cultural markers have shifted to accommodate, in each instance, the 'refashioning' and 'repackaging' of the city. Thus in *The Barcelona Reader: Cultural Readings of a City* we offer a multifaceted assessment that will enrich the city's experience of cultivated readers. It also suggests further reading for the culturally inclined. Some of the articles are brand new, commissioned for this volume, others are reprints (most of them updated) from recent publications in journals or volumes. A third group are much older texts. But they are not old: we consider that their vintage quality provides another look at the city that enriches the reader. They are witnesses to a growing interest in the study of Barcelona through the years, and they present from a diachronic perspective not only the transformation of the city but also how the ways of studying it have changed.

*

We have divided the volume into five sections. In the first one, 'City, history, and territory', we include articles that depict the intimate relationship with space. They deal with the way space has been modified by politics and urbanism. Robert Davidson in 'Barcelona: The siege city' rightly points to the fact that Barcelona's particular difference is based on the fact that modernity (and even postmodernity), with its social practices and strategies of development, have been conditioned intimately by the experience of siege. This explains why the 'Barcelona brand' has become so potent today: it is because inherent in Barcelona's aesthetic and spatial distinction are the tensions of centuries of struggle for cultural survival as the main urban element of what constitutes Catalonia. Ferran Sagarra, in 'Barcelona as an adaptive ecology', examines the so-called 'Barcelona Model' (of urban regeneration) as a 'model of urbanism' deserving the name of 'adaptive ecology' because its form and urban system have been able to correspond to the increasingly complex reality, both cultural and social, of contemporary times. Architecture and modern urban design have shaped its urbanism, because designing systems in architecture has to do with 'territoriality'. Special attention is devoted to the nineteenth-century transformation that has had a deep impact on the contemporary urban fabric of Barcelona and on its layout. Jaume Subirana's 'A present past. Barcelona street names, from Víctor

Balaguer to Pasqual Maragall' elaborates on the idea that street names tell a kind of story, a narrative of varying degrees of coherence that is often a 'message' on the part of planners. We can study how successful it has been in its incorporation into the imaginary of the city and its citizens, thus analysing the 'christening' of the streets in the Eixample, in the second half of the nineteenth century, and of the Vila Olímpica at the end of the twentieth century. If the 'living chronicle' of the Eixample tells of what has been (honouring and legitimating the city as a capital and Catalonia as a country), the living chronicle of the Olympic areas in Poblenou and Vall d'Hebron tells of what we would like the country and the city to have been.

Felipe Fernández-Armesto's '"The asylum of modern times": Barcelona and Europe' starts by discussing the notion of a 'European Barcelona' which he considers to be a truism redeemed by a mistake: it relies for its force on a presumed distinction between Barcelona and the rest of Spain — or, at least, the rest of Spain, without Catalonia. He analyses Barcelona's assumption of a European identity through relevant architectural examples from the last two centuries. He concludes 'Yet despite the admirable resilience with which the Barcelonese, for more than a thousand years, have made an adventure of every adversity and wrung an achievement from every disaster, none of the city's historic ambitions has been fulfilled'. Colm Tóibín's 'A fragile country' is a vivid personal account of visits to Barcelona (and Catalonia) that have taken place during the last week of April through the years. The writer reflects on festivities such as Sant Jordi, the meaning of Montserrat mountain and the relationship between Catalonia and the rest of Spain, the art scene, thanks to the opening of a Tàpies show, and the many local implications of football.

In the second section, 'City and society', we include a few symbolic readings of the city and some of its elements. Brad Epps's 'Barcelona and modernity' offers a swirling flood of precise comments on Barcelona's main themes. He provides a glimpse into the promises and problems, achievements and challenges, of modern Barcelona. Going beyond what many have pointed to: the wealth of the city's commercial and cultural offerings, its art and industry, its openness, as a port, to the business of the world, he examines with outstanding subtlety interactions between literature and urban space. Alejandro Quiroga's 'Football and identities in Catalonia' examines the issue of dual patriotism and the use of football as an instrument to transmit national identities that has remained central in Catalan society since the death of Franco in 1975. In particular, he analyses the role of FC Barcelona as the alternative national team of Catalonia; the recreation of Catalonia's national football team; and the dialectic between Catalan and Spanish national narratives via soccer reporting. Gary McDonogh's 'The family and the city: Power and the creation of cultural imagery' focuses on an institution that embodied an elite 'sociology' of industrial society: the Gran Teatre del Liceu (Barcelona's Opera House). Built in the nineteenth century under the aegis of the emergent elite, it was a dynamic construction whose physical structure and interpretation have been sensitive to shifting power relations. It continues to stand in modern Barcelona as a historical monument to class differentiation and the cohesion of the city's 'Good Families'. Thus, this building is key to past and present world views of the power groups that dominated Catalan industrial society. Elisa Martí-López's 'Memory and the city in Barcelona's cemeteries' explores Barcelona's cemeteries as one of the principal loci, material or immaterial, in which memory had become embodied and which remained their most specific representations and most dazzling symbols. As *lieu de mémoire* Barcelona's cemeteries exemplify wonderfully that 'the community's idea of itself in history cannot be disentangled from the ways it represents death'.

In the third section 'Art, architecture, and the city' we have included articles focusing specifically on some of the best-known artists and architects that have shaped an image of Barcelona. Jordi Falgàs, 'Picasso among his fellows at 4 Gats: Beyond *modernisme?*' studies Picasso's presence at the 4 Gats tavern, a place that served to catapult Picasso to fame. This happened thanks to an intergenerational setting, the fact that this was an interdisciplinary space where painters interacted with sculptors, illustrators, architects, musicians, and, especially, writers of various genres. It was also a place where travellers met on their way to and from Paris, then the capital of Western culture. The article covers Santiago Rusiñol and Ramon Casas, but also other figures whose works visitors can see at the Museu Nacional d'Art de Catalunya (MNAC). Marià Marín's 'Gaudí: Poet of stone, artistic hedgehog' uses new research to confirm that Gaudí was a pioneer, well ahead of his time, creator of innovative work processes in addition to the new architectural forms that we all now know. His abilities as a creator, inventor and innovator, beyond his identity as an architect, and based on his matchless style, brings us a legacy that can be applied to many current disciplines, from ergonomic design to business management. Jordana Mendelson's 'El Poble Espanyol / El Pueblo Español', analyses a construction built for the 1929 World Exhibition, the Poble Espanyol (Spanish Town), that was both an ideal dreamscape in which rituals of citizenship and nationality were performed, and an obvious construction in which the balance of harmony and fragmentation was constantly in danger of coming undone. She pays attention to the use of photography, which provided the necessary foundation for architects to construct the realistic illusions on which Primo de Rivera's dictatorship depended to build a coherent vision of nationality.

The fourth section, 'The Olympics and the city' deals with two major events that have had a remarkable impact on Barcelona, the 1992 Olympics and the Universal Forum of Cultures. Donald McNeill's 'Barcelona: Urban identity 1992–2002' explores how Barcelona has been catalanized, globalized, informationalized, gentrified, redesigned, and Europeanized. He pays attention to issues of urban identity, and how interventions in the urban landscape are intimately political, particularly the changing nature of the old town, the growing dogma of a technologically modernized city, the impact of deterritorialization on the city's icons, primarily its football club, the 1992 Olympics and the 2004 Forum. In turn Joan Ramon Resina's 'From the Olympic torch to the Universal Forum of Cultures. The after-image of Barcelona's modernity' critically scrutinizes policies and policymakers that have affected recent transformations of the city, starting with Oriol Bohigas' 'Mediterranean' predilection for the street as 'living space' that generated a politics of 'urbanization' of open spaces, the turning over of potential park sites to the architectural establishment; Barcelona's coming of age as a world city in the Olympics and the revitalization of the waterfront with the Forum event committed to a bland, undialectical image of diversity and with little attention paid to memory and the past. It is outspoken against the political forces that have turned Barcelona into the theme park of its past. Resina ends his essay by referring to 'the after-image of a people divested of their history, language, and sensory culture and the repertoire of related concepts – stripped, that is, of their raison d'être as people'.

The fifth and last section, 'Literature, cinema, and the city', briefly summarizes literary and cinematic versions/visions of the city. Josep Miquel Sobrer's 'La Gran Encisera: Three odes to Barcelona, and a film', examines three odes to Barcelona, written by Jacint Verdaguer, Joan Maragall, and 'Pere Quart' [Joan Oliver] respectively, that make clear the changing faces of the city. They roughly correspond to three generations and offer a poetic history of the city. The section also addresses Barcelona at the turn of the twentieth century as seen by Pedro Almodóvar in his 1998 Oscar-winning film, *Todo sobre mi madre*. Stewart King's 'The deceptive dame: Criminal revelations of the Catalan capital' studies the ways in which writers use crime fiction set in Barcelona to reveal what one character in Manuel Vázquez Montalbán's *El delantero centro fue asesinado al atardecer* (1988) calls the 'palabras que [cada época] necesita para enmascararse' [words that each era needs in order to mask itself]. King analyses both Catalan- and Castilian-language crime novels, as well as works written in English. Benjamin Fraser's 'A *Biutiful* city: Alejandro González Iñárritu's filmic critique of the "Barcelona Model"' launches an urban reading of the 2010 film *Biutiful*. He makes the case that the film functions as a complement to theoretical critiques of urbanism such as that of Lefebvrian theorist Manuel Delgado. The article helps to contextualize the struggles of immigrant and marginalized characters against the widespread, triumphant image of Barcelona as a 'model' European destination city in extra-filmic discourse.

*

At the beginning of this introduction we stated that the discussion that brought us here started a few years ago. As a matter of fact, it started decades, maybe centuries ago, and could go on forever. Ours is a small contribution to a reflection on Barcelona that follows the steps of many others. Contributors to the volume have helped us to show the richness and the ambitions (sometimes illuminating, sometimes irrational) of the city, and its ways 'of making leaps of civic and architectural faith against all odds, and winning' (Robert Hughes's words at the close of his 1992 guide, *Barcelona*). Hughes refers to Gaudí's Sagrada Família and, quoting Joan Maragall, calls it 'boastful and treacherous and vulgar'. In this book we have tried to refocus both quotations to talk about and discuss not a building but the city, this city of ours, yesterday's rose of fire and today's international attraction: 'Our Barcelona, the Great Enchantress'.

PART I
City, history, and territory

CHAPTER ONE

Barcelona:
The siege city*

Robert Davidson

Barcelona is a metropolis for which the concept of siege has specifically modern connotations. Captive in various forms for much of its history following the comprehensive defeat of Catalonia in 1714, what was to become the economic motor of Spain would learn to live under the watchful eyes, cannon and restrictive centrist policies of the Spanish state for the bulk of its modernization. What is more, around the turn of the twentieth century, a foundational period both in cultural and political terms, this external vigilance was supplemented in the Catalan capital by periods of brutal class warfare among its own citizens. The fact that this time of growth was inflected by urban violence only heightened the city's understanding of what it meant to be under prolonged attack as both working – and ruling-class Barcelona felt besieged from without and from within.

 The city persisted and survived these trials. It withstood, as well, two military dictatorships in the twentieth century totalling some 43 years. In terms of urban expansion and growth the period of transition

---

* Reproduced with permission from Boydell & Brewer Ltd, 'The Siege City' by Robert Davidson, in Dominic Keown (ed.), *Companion to Catalan Culture* (Woodbridge, Suffolk: Tamesis Books, 2011), pp. 97–116.

to democracy in 1975 would come to rival the latter half of the 1800s. As had happened during the first modern Catalan renaissance, Barcelona was able to slough off its overt prison garb as it built and developed frenetically. This process of revitalization culminated in the hosting of the 1992 Olympics. The ostensible success of those Games as a performance of urban possibility and renewal has resonated around the world ever since. Even though critics are increasingly questioning the ultimate consequences of this period, urbanists now point to a 'Barcelona model' – especially in terms of waterfront revitalization – as a way of helping urban centres connect not only to their citizenry but also to the built environment and their natural geographies as well.

Barcelona's arrival as a sought-out destination - an 'in' city - on the world's map, though, has been a mixed blessing. Among its valued attractions Gaudí and his contemporaries' *modernista* architecture has helped confer upon Barcelona 'must-see' status for travellers to Europe. At the same time, the celebrated urban renewal has brought the holiday beach experience to within steps of the city proper. Similarly, the image of Barcelona has become one not of a specifically Catalan conurbation but rather of a cosmopolitan/sensorial experience that one consumes. As a result of these multiple dynamics, the city is a local city less and less and a 'world' metropolis more and more: a style, a surface to be admired or a brand, as Andrew Smith has suggested (Smith: 398–423).

The flip side of this success is that the city is also, increasingly, a difficult place to live. Mass tourism and its desirability for the potential expatriate are changing Barcelona, with the wide-ranging consequences of both having been felt in a relatively short period of time. Not surprisingly, this rapid ascension after years of repression has had unintended results; and now, as in the past, the Catalan capital is once again facing a siege. The walls and conflicts of old have been replaced by new threats to social cohesion, but the effects are just as serious. Real estate speculation, top-down urban planning and the promise of a unique urban experience projected by the postmodern brand image have all had deleterious consequences.

Perversely, the city's strong design-based foundation has contributed to the current danger. The perspective offered in this chapter engages the topic of Barcelona as a historically besieged city with its own continuing dynamic of blockade by critiquing the increasingly mainstream reading of Barcelona as a place that is a very deliberately 'designed' city on the one hand and that is a now pre-eminent 'city of design' on the other. The cleavage between these two entwined Barcelonas is becoming as increasingly patent as the Barcelona *brand* and invites an examination of the Catalan capital through the lens of what may be termed its own siege modernity.

An exploration of these facets of the urban experience and its packaging is especially appropriate now that the idea of what an urban siege entails has been literally and figuratively internalized with the advent of the postmodern global city. What is more, the insistence on *look* has also been fundamental to forced evolutions in the city's *sound*: a telling yet under-appreciated aspect of how the Catalan capital has changed through external and internal pressures such as densification, immigration and the consequences of mass tourism.

Phase 1: A city squeezed

Geography, forts, and a wall

The city of Barcelona lies on a seaside plain contained by the Collserola massif and its emblematic Tibidabo peak on the west, the Besòs river to the north and, to the south, the Llobregat river and the imposing Montjuïc mountain, which looms over the old city. This geography would come to figure prominently not only in the way that Barcelona would develop but also in how it would experience the various forms of siege that were to await it. The city has its roots in the Roman colony of Barcino, which was established in the first century BC, and this natural setting was advantageous for future development. Fortified in the third century AD, the city suffered subsequent conquests by Visigoths in the fifth century, Moors in 711 and then a reconquest by the Franks under Louis the Pious in 801. This last event saw Barcelona converted into a literal buffer zone or Hispanic Marchland between the Franks and the Umayyad Moors of Al-Andalus.

The urban nucleus of the city was consolidated during the Middle Ages, and it was Jaume I who moved to reinforce the existing walls, a process that took more than 100 years to finish. With the establishment in the twelfth century of a Catalonia with similar borders to those of today, Barcelona began to flourish, reaching its apex as the capital of the western Mediterranean under the Crown of Aragon, which controlled areas such as Sardinia, Corsica, Naples and the Roussillon.

Catalonia's - and hence Barcelona's - early modern moment of 'what if?' occurred with the defeat of their forces at the end of the War of Spanish Succession in 1714, the geopolitical repercussions of which would persist into the twenty-first century. Catalonia's capital, a Mediterranean port and former centre of an important mercantile empire, would be metaphorically cut off from the openness of the sea, as well as literally restricted in terms of growth and development. Rather than projecting outwards and creating its own destiny as a capital, Barcelona would be cast into second-city status by a hostile proto-state and would see the force of a centralist Spain thwart its ambitions while actively seeking to snuff out Catalan cultural difference in public discourse.[1] Thus began a period of cultural and literal siege that included various crackdowns on teaching, business and other dealings in Catalan, the banning of cultural production in the vernacular and other limitations on Catalan culture in the public sphere that stretched out until almost the end of the twentieth century.

When the Spanish military established its presence in Barcelona following the events of 1714, it used the city's own geography against it. Cannons were placed on the stronghold of Montjuïc mountain and trained not towards the sea to fend off external foes, but rather down on the city to keep the citizenry in line. To the north, a massive army barracks and military citadel - the Ciutadella - was constructed. Its location at the edge of the old city facilitated the quick response of infantry and cavalry in the event of any more local revolts against Madrid's authority. These two bases of operations - above, the always-visible Montjuïc and its army-held castle; below, the bulky and ominous Ciutadella - anchored the first sense of siege in the modern consciousness of Barcelona.

It would be hard to underestimate the psychological impact of such twin threats on the population; even more so given the fact that at two dark junctures, first in 1842 and then again a year later, the threat of lethal force passed from potential to actual as the regents of Barcelona decided to teach their rebellious city a lesson. The second occasion

---

1 Ainaud de Lasarte's *El llibre negre de Catalunya* (1996) provides a comprehensive compilation of these attacks on Catalan culture from 1714 onwards.

was especially fierce and punishing as a barrage was ordered that saw more than 4,800 projectiles fired on the city during a military siege that lasted 81 days.

One of the prime reasons for the revolt of 1843 was the level of poverty and suffering in the city caused by sheer overcrowding. That Barcelona's old walls still stood in the middle of the nineteenth century was a primary reason for this dangerous congestion. From ancient times to the point when modern munitions rendered them obsolete, walls were cities' primary fortifications. Intended to help a populace repel invaders and control entry and egress, in the case of modern Barcelona the massive barriers came to function in precisely the opposite manner. The city did not control how they were managed and had no say in when they might be demolished so as to allow the burgeoning urban centre to expand.

That authority was held by Madrid, and because it did not serve the central government's political purposes to permit the Catalan capital to develop, the walls kept their latent military charge: that of containing Barcelona, pinning it to old dimensions even as industrial growth occurred and population density increased to hazardous and unsustainable levels. In this way, the walls became their own form of siege engine, a cordon around the populace to regulate and restrict it while maintaining the strategic capacity of the Ciutadella and Montjuïc to impose military authority and punishment should the need arise.

Rebirth and the designed city

Barcelona's modern rebirth was sparked by Madrid's eventual capitulation on the issue of the city's walls. The old barricade started to come down in the early 1850s and once it was demolished, the city could finally expand. Even though a radial project was preferred by the Catalans, Madrid imposed the now-famous grid system devised by Ildelfons Cerdà. Cerdà's plan was to literally urbanize the rural and ruralize the urban by creating a series of octagonal blocks, with half of each being dedicated to green space. In this way, Barcelona would encroach on the meadows separating it from its closest neighbours but would still maintain an important trace of rural character by incorporating land into the city's modern expansion zone or Eixample.

This utopian vision along the lines of Howard's Garden City was not to be. Cerdà had not counted on the relentless power of the nascent bourgeoisie's desire to maximize space - and thereby increase profit - during the decades that would then lead to Catalonia's famous Gold Fever. Thus, rather than maintain the green spaces, the grid filled in and buildings and flats were constructed to a height of five or six floors. Given that the original idea was to have parks at every corner, with the elimination of this facet, the new district would over time find itself bereft of any substantial urban green space. What is more, the construction of buildings on all sides of the grid's octagons and the abundant spaces that Cerdà presaged for traffic usage would come to have a large impact on sound pollution in the city in the twentieth century.

Part and parcel of the architectonic dynamics at work was the fact that the nouveaux riche had economic power but lacked the history and tradition that gave Barcelona's old aristocrats their social and cultural pedigree. The businessmen compensated for this by relying on spectacle and design, contracting the city's architects to create buildings of increasing grandeur and style. Of course, these barons also competed among themselves through this conspicuous consumption of architecture as they jockeyed for individual standing while, at the same time, seeking as a group to consolidate the sea-change that had occurred in social terms relating to the concentration of political and economic power in Barcelona. Of course, this interest in city-building and civics was never totally philanthropic; it was also a sound investment in bricks and mortar that would appreciate even more quickly given the artistic supplement attached.

As the city's manufacturing and industrial capacity grew, new money came to trump old; the metaphorical centre of Barcelona shifted from the labyrinthine Gothic City, bastion of the old aristocratic families, to the Eixample's young turks. The main artery of this new sector, the Passeig de Gràcia, became the grand boulevard of a city that was living a period of intense growth and change, when mercantile expansion and speculation were rife and the city was awash in new money, construction projects and the allure of getting rich quick.

Appearances are key to social status and reputation and, as such, surface appeal emerges as an important aspect of bourgeois aesthetics. This consideration is especially marked in the case of

Catalan *modernisme*, the artistic movement that coincided – and flourished – along with the rise of the new upper class in Barcelona. The architectural phase of the experience was spearheaded by such luminaries as Domènech i Muntaner, Puig i Cadafalch and Antoni Gaudí, whose reputation would become world-renowned and whose work has come to epitomize the *modernista* architectonic strain.

The buildings are elaborate, detailed and, in many cases, spectacular. Works such as Gaudí's Casa Milà and Casa Batlló, which incorporated new building techniques while also speaking to the local vernacular architecture and Catalan natural environment, have since become globally renowned. Likewise, Domènech i Muntaner's Simon Editorial (now the Tàpies Foundation) and Puig i Cadafalch's Casa Amatller and Edifici Terrades (Casa de les Punxes) contributed to the concentration of impressive *modernista* buildings in the area. So while, on one hand, the new rational, grid-based Eixample, which represented Barcelona's liberty from the confinement of the old city's walls, grew according to practical concerns regarding the maximization of space and profit, an aesthetic mandate governed by *look* was also key to its development. This is the part of the Eixample's foundation that would become an important basis for future tourist interest.

Catalan architectural *modernisme* occurred around the same time as other European styles of a similar mien, such as Arts and Crafts and Art Nouveau, and while it integrated vernacular models and influences the overall result was to draw Barcelona closer to the European centre that it had long admired and wanted to join. Integration into European circuits - even though state power still resided in Madrid - was also of interest to those who had contracted the building of the Eixample. Catalonia and its capital were looking towards Paris, backs turned on the Spanish capital, which was in full decline after undertaking disastrous military campaigns to suppress revolts in its colonial holdings in the Americas and North Africa.

One of the results of this political and cultural orientation was the decision to hold an International Exposition in 1888, some 30 years after Paris and London had set the vogue in motion and which has persisted into the twenty-first century. In terms of the siege mentality of Barcelona, the Universal Exposition was especially important because it marked the city's reclamation of the hated Ciutadella. The military fortifications were demolished over the course of the 1870s and the land on which they had stood was earmarked first for a much-needed park and, subsequently, for the world's fair, an event that would serve as the coming-out party not only for the bourgeoisie who sought to consolidate their power and influence but for the modern metropolis itself.

Even though the 1888 Expo failed to make a profit and sparked a firestorm of recriminations, it was an important event for the dominant class that had organized it. The international exposure it provided was a validation of the social advances made during the Renaixença, Catalonia's linguistic and cultural reawakening. For while Castile was engaged in profound soul-searching as its moribund empire disintegrated further, Catalonia found itself on the upswing both culturally and economically.

The Expo empowered the local bourgeoisie to continue to think big, served as a precursor to the *modernista* period proper and, importantly, saw the first large-scale influx of tourists to Barcelona. From an architectural perspective, the fair contributed fine new buildings to the city's stock, but the most important edifice may well be one that was demolished at the end of the event. Domènech i Muntaner's impressive - yet temporary - 1,600-room Hotel Internacional was built in order to address the serious shortage of tourist beds in the city, and its construction took place in an astonishing 63 days, using prefabricated modular bricks set up around a massive iron frame. A hotel of such a category placed Barcelona within an international network, closer to the European centrality that it coveted. Thus, while the fair's most important legacy was arguably the city's recuperation of an urban zone that had been a centre of oppression, its subsequent transformation into a cosmopolitan space would whet the urban appetite for more engagement beyond Spain's borders.[2]

The fact that it was through a first foray into mass tourism that this revitalization marked the symbolic removal of another part of Barcelona's past as a besieged city cannot be ignored; for in eliminating the civic memory of one oppressive element, the city was unknowingly taking its first steps into a world that would see it transformed and besieged even further more than a century later.

---

2 For more on the cosmopolitan aspect of the fair and the temporary Hotel Internacional in particular, see Davidson 228–43.

Phase 2: From social war to dictators

A new siege: The social war

To speak only of the Catalan bourgeoisie's role in the articulation of modern Barcelona and Catalonia is to tell only part of the story. An intensely militant syndicalism also helped forge the modern city and the way that the citizens would relate to it. Rigged electoral processes of the Restoration period excluded huge parts of the population from the decision-making formula. This political disenfranchisement - especially in the case of the new Catalan proletariat - led inevitably to the excesses of extra-parliamentary activity. The counter-weight to non-representative government and bourgeois economic might adopted by the immensely powerful anarchist trade union, the CNT, was 'direct action'.

This taking of matters into one's own hands often took the form of bombings and the targeted assassinations of business leaders. This social war between factory owners and workers was fought mainly over working and living conditions. It was contested in the streets and claimed many lives while terrorizing the citizenry. It is perhaps epitomized by the spectacular outrage at the Liceu opera house in 1892 where, with the building full to capacity, the anarchist Santiago Salvador threw two bombs down from the gods into the expensive, bourgeois seating. Twenty-two people died in the resulting explosion. A ruthless police round-up of presumed anarchists was ordered and 400 were detained. Salvador and six others were among them and were executed for their roles in the outrage.

The spiral of violence continued into the next century with the Tragic Week of 1909 when angry mobs rioted in response to the call-up of reservists to fight in North Africa. A state of war was declared in the city after numerous churches and convents were sacked and razed, and the military ruthlessly quelled the disturbances after seven days of conflict. The event left an indelible mark on a city that continued to experience social violence, with its ferocity increasing as both sides of the ideological divide became bolder. Faced with workers' militancy, industrialists created their own *Sindicats Lliures* (Free Unions), essentially the cover for death squads, to find and eliminate trade union leaders and others sympathetic to the anarchist cause. Between 1919 and 1923, the death toll caused by this conflict stood at 246, of which around 200 were workers or union leaders, marking another phase in the escalation of a battle between two diametrically opposed classes bent on 'defending' their own visions of Barcelona's future.

The dictatorship of Miguel Primo de Rivera

By 1923, uncontrolled warfare on the streets of Catalonia, the sham political system of the Restoration, the post-war recession and military disasters in Africa created a crisis the government was unable to resolve. The 'solution' was provided by the military coup of General Primo de Rivera. While the Catalan elites appreciated the stability that military rule brought they would quickly come to realize that the General had no interest in safeguarding the cultural gains that Catalonia had made in the previous decades. Instead, Primo de Rivera followed in the footsteps of those who had come before him and clamped down on the Catalan culture. Under his seven-year dictatorship the Catalan capital was once more an occupied city and saw such varied acts of cultural repression as a comprehensive system of press censorship, restrictions on the sardana and even the closing down for six months of FC Barcelona after supporters had dared to boo the Spanish anthem.

The Roaring Twenties came to end in spectacular style, however, as Barcelona played host once more to an international exhibition. The 1929 edition, the Exposición Internacional de Barcelona, initially stated to have been a showcase for Catalan culture, was reorientated under the centralist dictatorship to be a platform for Spanish cultural identity. The manner in which this was accomplished left little doubt that minority cultures such as Catalan and Basque were but folkloric parts of a greater Spanish whole. From the exposition of *Spanish* art in the gaudy and neo-Baroque Palacio Nacional, to the architectural inscription of Spain as a diverse yet ultimately single unit in the eerie Pueblo Español (Spanish Village - an amalgam of reproduction buildings from all over the state that can still be visited today as a tourist attraction), the 1929 Exposición sought to bring a modernizing, europhile Barcelona back within the symbolic sovereignty of Spain. And if the metaphors of unity were not clear enough, then the presence of Spanish warships in the harbour on the Expo's inaugural day served to underline the point.

While the co-option of the fair meant that it played as a specifically *Spanish* spectacle for the international audience, the fall of Primo de Rivera and the monarchy in early 1930 gave the city some breathing space after this cultural siege. An important symbolic move occurred in the wake of the dictatorship: the ceding to the city of the despised castle on Montjuïc. A story in the Catalanist journal *Mirador* attests to both the ideological importance of such a move and the peculiar social situation in which Barcelona found itself at the time: 'The handing over of Montjuïc Castle to the city represents the beginning of a new era of individual and social liberty for Barcelona. And it is natural that this process will not be realized until freedom is guaranteed' (Anon. 1930: 1).[3] Unfortunately, for Barcelona and Catalonia at large, this new era of personal and social liberty would be stillborn during the tensions of a short-lived Republic that segued directly into the Spanish Civil War and, subsequently, the Francoist dictatorship.

The Spanish Civil War and the Francoist dictatorship

With the proclamation of the Second Spanish Republic in 1931, the city was once again ostensibly free. Rising political tensions in the run-up to the Spanish Civil War, however, meant that it was hardly a tranquil place; street fighting and political polarization were endemic again as official endorsement for autonomy was granted, withdrawn and reconceded virtually every two years. Street fighting broke out once again during the war itself, especially in its initial phase when, after suppressing the military coup, internecine battles on the Republican side led to Barcelona being carved up by competing groups. George Orwell's *Homage to Catalonia* paints an especially clear picture of the way in which the city became a collection of separate fiefs identifiable only to the informed local:

> What the devil was happening, who was fighting whom, and who was winning, was at first very difficult to discover. The people of Barcelona are so used to street-fighting and so familiar with the local geography that they knew by a kind of instinct which political party will hold which streets and which buildings. A

---

3 Unless otherwise stated, all translations are by the author.

foreigner is at a hopeless disadvantage. Looking out from the observatory, I could grasp that the Ramblas, which is one of the principal streets of the town, formed a dividing line. To the right of the Ramblas the working-class quarters were solidly Anarchist; to the left a confused fight was going on among the tortuous by-streets, but on that side the PSUC and the Civil Guards were more or less in control. Up at our end of the Ramblas, round the Plaza de Cataluña, the position was so complicated that it would have been quite unintelligible if every building had not flown a party flag. (Orwell: 126)

The Civil War dragged on and Barcelona was subject to aerial bombardments by Nationalist forces in the spring of 1938. Then, when a Republican defeat became more and more inevitable, refugees streamed towards the French border. On 26 January 1939 the city was captured by the advancing Francoist army. It would be occupied for over 36 years.

Under Franco's dictatorship Barcelona was a militarily besieged city once more. Reprisals in the form of torture and executions were carried out against suspected Republicans and Communists. The Modelo prison filled up and the stronghold of Montjuïc once again became a place of death while summary executions were carried out on the outskirts of the city. Catalan culture in general was also targeted, tainted as it was with the 'separatist' brush that had so enraged Spanish nationalists. The Catalan language was prohibited and any remaining signs of Republican rule were eliminated. Strictly confined to the private realm, the Catalan fact was erased in public and the semiotics of the city were altered, most apparently in the renaming of streets so as to reflect the imposed centrist ideology.

By the 1950s, post-war Barcelona still showed signs of the Civil War conflict as many bombed buildings had still not been fully reconstructed. Amid the post-war economic disaster the tensions of living in an occupied city that functioned poorly in conditions of rationing and electricity restrictions provided only sporadic acts of resistance. The campaign to erase Catalan difference also entailed massive immigration and Barcelona received thousands of Castilian-speaking migrants from rural areas throughout the Peninsula. The Francoist government's intention was to homologize Catalonia within Spain. And while the immediate effect was to exacerbate the acute housing shortage in the city as huge shanty towns appeared on the outskirts, this influx would have an important impact on the social make-up of the metropolis and on linguistic politics for decades to come.

Phase 3: The postmodern siege

From the Transition to the Olympics

With the death of Franco and the transition to democracy in the late 1970s, Catalonia entered a new phase. Now relieved of the weight of overt right-wing derision, Barcelona started a rapid and steady process of change and revitalization headed by architect and critic Oriol Bohigas. Even though, as Joan Ramon Resina points out, 'Bohigas favored monumentalization of open spaces through architectural design of a markedly avant-garde character [and with] his blessing, his disciples inflicted the unpopular *places dures* on a city that was starved for green space' (Resina: 209) there is no denying the radical nature of the changes that the city was about to experience.

This type of comprehensive and interventionist urbanism was not new. Urban design as policy had begun as early as 1953, with the Francoist administration's official plan for the city, and continued through this scheme's revision in 1964, and the 'Plan General Metropolitano' developed and approved in principle in the 1970s under Enric Massó, the last mayor to be named by the Generalísimo. But now multiple projects, expansions and developments occurred around the city, with all the excitement that could be expected by a new era of domestic executive planning.

It was around this time that International Olympics Committee chief Juan Antonio Samaranch announced that Barcelona had been awarded the 1992 Olympic Games, a decision that meant the Catalan capital was to enter a new phase of its history. Barcelona would now gear itself up not only for the world's premier sporting event but for its largest celebration of mass spectacle and image production. The idea of city-as-image would propel Barcelona into the global imaginary, but it would do so at a great cost. If the technocratic development principles of the city planners had initiated the estrangement between citizen and city, it was this element of spectacle that would ultimately contribute to a new sense of siege as the legacy of Barcelona's modernist past combined with new endeavours to maximize the city's potential as an image of cosmopolitan urbanity and progress.

The success and panache of the 1992 Games, with their groundbreaking opening ceremony, the drama-cum-acrobatics of the Comediants and Fura dels Baus, and the compelling venues, played off Barcelona's intrinsic architectural beauty and style while underlining the tremendous transformative potential (from a capitalist perspective) of such a global media event. Indeed, in addition to the spectacular choreographed theatricality of the opening ceremony, one of the most suggestive - and repeated - images, as Smith observes, was that of Olympic divers in full flight while framed against the city's skyline at the Picornell complex (Smith: 411).

The ostensible subject may have been the athletes soaring freely above the metropolis; but the placement of the pool and the diving towers when combined with the ingenious camera angles ensured that more often than not Barcelona's most recognizable building and epitome of its look, the Sagrada Família, would figure in the background. The fact that Gaudí's masterpiece was (and still is) unfinished and flanked by massive cranes served as an ironic reminder of the continuous construction project that Barcelona had become - both literally and in terms of how its image would continue to be built as its renown grew in the post-Olympic years.

Barcelona's Olympic transformation was so acute and so visible that ever since, urbanists, architects and politicians from around the world have sought to duplicate it. While the specifically Mediterranean context of the city is often suppressed in the transfer and application of this model, it has become, nevertheless, both a powerful template for innovative change at home and a vehicle for Catalan architects and urbanists to succeed abroad. This interchange - consolidation and planning at the local level, projection and distribution of form and technique overseas - has been celebrated worldwide.

A charitable interpretation would be to read this dynamic as a natural, yet postmodern, evolution of Barcelona's status as a port and a city to and from which people, ideas and goods have long flowed - even if that exchange has often been restricted. However, the notion that the Barcelona Model has mostly served planners, political elites and property developers is one that has begun to gain greater traction.

That said, in the wake of such an ostensibly successful Games and Spain's full entrance into the EU - which Catalan nationalists initially saw as a way to further escape Madrid's influence - it seemed that the siege experiences of the past were finally over.

Olympic consequences

There is no doubting that 1992 was a watershed year as Barcelona finally achieved the international prominence that it had sought when it hosted the World Fairs of 1888 and 1929. With the Olympic Games focusing the world's attention on the city, the Catalan capital tried to make the most of its global media close-up by portraying itself as a vibrant, economic and cultural hub. Nevertheless, while Catalan was one of the official languages of the Games, the Spanish state was determined to incorporate the event into the larger 1992 celebrations going on in the country and prevent it becoming a rallying point for Catalan national sentiment.

These tactics recalled the treatment of Barcelona during the 1929 Exposición. And the further emptying of the city of its political charge as a capital of a stateless nation abetted its growth as an international image while, at the same time, contributing to the alienation experienced by its citizens. The timing for the presentation of a depoliticized urban image of city-as-spectacle was propitious in that Barcelona's ascension coincided with a general shift in style and tourism trends. The 1990s saw a rise of superficial 'specificity' as travellers looked beyond traditional packaged trips and more at tailored travel experiences that would become increasingly mainstream by the 2000s.

A concurrent general gentrification and democratization of architecture and design spearheaded by star architects such as Frank Gehry, Enric Miralles and I. M. Pei also contributed to the attractiveness of Barcelona. New monumental and trophy architecture in cities around the world helped make Gaudí's early twentieth-century work even more known and immediately recognizable. Buildings such as the Casa Batlló, the Pedrera and especially the Sagrada Família, helped confer 'must see' status not only on Gaudí's *modernista* oeuvre but also, through the metonymy that the built environment can engender, on the entire city itself. These dynamics contributed to the growing stream of international tourists 'doing' Barcelona by consuming the city's surface appeal - its distinctive *modernista* look - often with only the briefest of historical or cultural contexts provided by their *Lonely Planet* or *Let's Go* travel guide. With the must-sees checked off during the day, nights would be free to enjoy the city's increasingly vibrant entertainment culture.

The image production that arises from the Barcelona Model is, on the one hand, a product of technocratic desire - development, speculation, transformation, etc. - and, on the other, predicated on the promise of experience. This potential for sensation is where the look, feel and taste of the city come into play. Unfortunately for those residents of Barcelona who aspire to a normal urban existence, this focus on sensation as both a side-effect and progression of the Barcelona brand image has had deleterious effects as regards quality of life in the city.

In response to the changes that Barcelona's international success has wrought, many neighbourhood groups have sprung up in order to protest at both public and private initiatives. For these, the Barcelona Model is flawed in that it privileges capital over community. Undeniably, Barcelona's ascendance to world city status has come at the expense of a further erosion of its own Catalan specificity, but that notwithstanding, the local areas, neighbourhoods and communities that make up the greater city of Barcelona have all been caught up in consequences of the city's wider move towards spectacle and image production whether they like it or not. It is here that this latest phase of the city's experience of siege comes to the fore. For while mass tourism may pour millions of euros into municipal coffers, the effects on daily life have been far from negligible.

This siege may be unlike those previously suffered, but the attention given to large-scale developments that emphasize the city's international reputation and image have come at the expense of investments in making the city a viable place to live for its citizens. Electrical blackouts, water problems, as well as chronic delays in local train services and stunted airport growth all underline the growing disjuncture between Barcelona, the imagined city of style and design and Barcelona, the city where citizens live and work.[4]

---

4 In July 2007, Barcelona suffered a prolonged blackout that affected more than 100,000 households, a major hospital and the metro network. Three days later, some people and businesses were still without power. Infrastructure deficiencies

The negative perception of top-down urbanism and its triumph of style over substance have been exacerbated by the rampant property speculation of the 1990s and early 2000s. This speculation has not only affected individuals: the irony of the economics is patent, too, in the changes in the nature of businesses that exist in what have become prime tourist areas of the city. High amounts of visitor traffic have contributed to a general loss of specificity as chain stores that can afford high rents gradually push out the small family and independent businesses that contributed to the character of the Gothic Quarter or the Ramblas.

Of course, these increasing flat rents and prices have had a serious impact on the local populace across the city in that people through the age spectrum found it impossible to afford to live in the city proper. Barcelona has become too expensive for the Barcelonese. Where walls and cannons once kept citizens in, economic forces now conspire to blockade many out. The replacement of the natives with an army of foreign tourists is no doubt ironic but shows no sign of abating as trips to the Catalan capital - and their nature - have been transformed by the proliferation of cheap inter-European airlines.

The Barcelona experience

The cosmopolitan Barcelona brand is made out to be part museum and part beach, with bits of discothèque and restaurant thrown in for good measure. The physical alterations to the city's seafront have reacquainted the city with the sea and are the direct result of the rehabilitation projects of the 1980s and 1990s. As a result of the massive investment in remodelling the zone from the base of the Ramblas to the Olympic Port, the holiday beach experience has been brought literally to within steps of Barcelona proper. The knock-on effect has been to make the city even more attractive for a wide range of tourists and emigrants from Northern Europe.

As in other areas, however, this development has occurred much to

also caused problems for commuters, as works on high-speed train links wreaked havoc on local and regional travel. During the same period, the airport had to fight to increase intercontinental flights, allowing the city to assume the mantle of European hub and permit travellers to bypass Madrid airport.

the chagrin of locals. In this case, those in the proletarian Barceloneta neighbourhood have seen their waterfront radically redesigned for purposes incompatible with the needs of small-scale fishers and port workers who were once the area's primary residents. What is more, property speculation has gone hand in hand with beach development and has meant that, as elsewhere in the city, flats have been priced out of reach for many locals as property is bought up to service a growing tourist trade and expatriate community. Once again, residents are faced with a future in which their children will not be able to afford to live in the area where they grew up.

The economic question is a constant and, for tourists, the Catalan capital is still a relatively affordable city. This is especially so for the British who, up until the economic crisis of 2008–2009, had seen their money go much further in Catalonia than in their own cities, particularly London. The combination of easy access through cheap flights and this basic affordability has given rise to masses of invasive weekenders - among them travelling 'stag' and 'hen' parties - who treat the city as a fun park for wild outings of binge drinking.

Neighbourhoods such as the Gothic Quarter and Gràcia, where homes, bars and restaurants are often found in very close proximity, have seen a reduction in quality of life as noise and general rowdiness encroach on formerly quiet residential areas. Frustrated by inaction at the City Hall, residents have formed a variety of groups to protest and lobby the local government for more stringent laws. Here is where one sees the intersection of the effects of Barcelona's look and the changes in Barcelona's sound.

The metropolis is increasingly loud, so much so that in 1998 L'Associació Catalana Contra la Contaminació Acústica was founded specifically to combat noise pollution. Residents have found themselves literally besieged by noise as nightlife proliferates, discothèques multiply, and flats are transformed into illegal guest apartments where tourists noisily stay during their brief sojourns. This acoustic contamination tied to the tourist trade is but one example of how life is becoming more unpleasant for the local citizenry. What is more, as Espadaler astutely observes, one of the more insidious consequences of a city becoming such a tourist magnet is that citizens 'lose' parts of their metropolis to the hordes (such as the Ramblas, in the case of Barcelona) and come to see it as a stereotype (Espadaler: 5).

Conclusion

Barcelona is different. Capital of a stateless nation, Mediterranean port city, the place where anarchism triumphed, the site of the rebirth of the Olympic movement in an orgy of spectacle and urban potential... Barcelona is all of these things at once. When one considers the metropolis as both an aesthetic entity/experience and as a built environment - as spatial practice and geographic place with a history of enduring siege situations - its singularity becomes even more apparent. Indeed, such is the power of the image of this lived and constructed Barcelona that one now speaks of the city's brand. This process, in which meaning is collapsed into an image or a feeling that can then be managed and manipulated, relies on patent difference in order to function effectively.

As regards the possibility of urban branding, Smith points out rightly that 'city re-imaging is the deliberate (re)presentation and (re)configuration of a city's image to accrue economic, cultural and political capital' (Smith: 399). In the case of Barcelona this practice or dynamic has taken place at various levels: as a result of innovative urbanism and, most pointedly, in municipal campaigns geared towards increasing tourism and promoting the city as a stylish, sensual locale.

Image and marketing are no strangers to one another in the promotion of the Catalan capital, and a recent change in labelling practices by a Catalan company reflects this most fittingly.

Figure 1.1
MANGO apparel label
with Barcelona brand
added, c.2009

From the company's perspective, the addition of the city's name to its apparel logo (Figure 1.1) taps into the stylish aura of the place as, say, with Burberry of London. Jordi Hereu, Barcelona's mayor, explains the advantage to the city:

the signing of this agreement is another step towards linking the Barcelona brand with international references of renowned prestige and innovation. For Barcelona, fashion is an important aspect of its economy and culture, since our city is a reference in training and development for fashion. Through this initiative, the city is delighted to institutionalize the link between the Barcelona name and a Catalan company like MANGO, which is internationally renowned for its innovative character. It is further proof of the projection and guarantees offered by the city of Barcelona, undoubtedly a valued asset. (Anon. 2009)[5]

This mutually beneficial relationship is predicated on the special character of Barcelona as a 'sure bet' of quality and distinction. But, that said, how does one adequately engage with the difference exhibited by a city such as the Catalan capital if the process of branding is itself a generic process - one that literally commodifies variation and reifies the supposedly intangible elements of urban life that make the city unique and 'authentic'? If branding - or re-imaging - has become part of the modern capitalist condition and touches everything from the smallest consumer item to how cities and even nations imagine and market themselves, what sets Barcelona apart? If the easy and interchangeable symbols that come to be metonyms for cities looking to proclaim their difference do not indicate distinction, where then does it lie?

Barcelona's particular difference - and thus its inherent brand, so to speak - is powered by a motor that has not received the specific attention that it deserves: the fact that Barcelona's modernity - its social practices and strategies of development - and now its postmodern period as well, have been conditioned intimately by the experience of siege. If the Barcelona brand has become so potent today, it is because inherent in its aesthetic and spatial distinction are the tensions of centuries of struggle for cultural survival as the main urban element of the Catalan fact.

If Barcelona's hook to the world has become the intoxicating *potential* or *possibility* for transformation that it represents - which MANGO president Isak Andic points to directly when he states that the link

---

5 See http://news.mango.com [accessed 15 May 2009]. The following reference to the comments of the Mango chairman is at the same web page.

between his company and the metropolis 'is a way of not forgetting where we started and of projecting the potential of the city across all continents' - it must be recognized that this root of the city-as-brand goes even deeper and touches the concomitant potential inherent in the thing *to not be*.[6] For it is in the experience of siege, both literal and metaphoric, that Barcelona's potential *to not be* has been made patent or enforced on so many occasions. The city's brand becomes, then, more than surface appeal: it is a question of bellicose resonance, of echoes of cannon shots and of deeper meaning for the 'consumer' who is open to its message. Barcelona is different, yes. It is popular, exciting, fun. Unfortunately, for many it is also increasingly becoming a zombie - a city with 'dead' parts that still move - animated by tourist dollars and multinational leases. It has become a burden for many residents and, as a result of the negative potentiality inherent in the city's history of oppression, has contributed to the latest manifestation of the siege rubric in which Barcelona, the seemingly indomitable capital of Catalonia, has finally been drained of its authenticity.

Works cited

Agamben, Giorgio (1998). *Homo Sacer: Sovereign Power and Bare Life* (Stanford, CA: Stanford University Press).
Ainaud de Lasarte, Josep Maria (1996). *El llibre negre de Catalunya* (Barcelona: Edicions La Campana).
Anon. (1930). 'La cessió a la cituat del Castell de Motnjuïc' (*sic*). *Mirador*, 73: 1.
— (2009). 'L'Ajuntament de Barcelona i MANGO promocionen la marca Barcelona', http://news.mango.com [accessed 15 May 2009].
Davidson, Robert (2005). 'Observing the City, Mediating the Mountain: *Mirador* and the 1929 International Exposition of Barcelona', in Susan Larson and Eva Woods (eds), *Visualizing Spanish Modernity* (Oxford: Berg), 228–43.
Espadaler, Anton M. (2009). 'La ciudad y el tópico', *La Vanguardia*, 'Vivir', 2 June: 5.

---

6 Agamben explains the phenomenon in the following way: 'what is potential can both be and not be' (45).

Orwell, George, (1975) [1938]. *Homage to Catalonia* (Harmondsworth, UK: Penguin).

Resina, Joan Ramon (2008). *Barcelona's Vocation of Modernity: Rise and Decline of an Urban* Image (Stanford, CA: Stanford University Press).

Smith, Andrew (2005). 'Conceptualizing City Image Change: The "Re-Imaging" of Barcelona', *Tourism Geographies* 7.4: 398–423.

CHAPTER TWO

Barcelona as an adaptive ecology

Ferran Sagarra

[Barcelona] as a successful adaptive ecology [..] example of an urban development where the visionary postulation of a city fit for the future tallied with a corresponding level of technical invention and achievement. [..] limit[ing] the risk of the divide between design speculation and material capability. (Marc Burry 2013: 316)

As Mark Burry's statement in the quotation above, Barcelona fits in the concept of 'adaptive ecology' as defined by Theodor Spiropoulos. This is a 'model of urbanism' corresponding to the fact that 'recent architecture has found itself having to cope with new social and cultural complexities that demand networked systems that are time-based, reconfigurable and evolutionary', that is to say 'a notion of architecture that looks towards designing systems that seek higher ordered goals emerging through an intimate correlation of material and computational interaction' (Burry 2013: 3).

The expression 'Barcelona Model' has been promoted by the local tourist boosters helped by some scholars and takes profit of the fact that Barcelona can be considered a 'model of urbanism' deserving the title of 'adaptive ecology' because its form and urban system have been able to correspond to the increasingly complex cultural and social realities of contemporary cities. Architecture and modern urban design have shaped Barcelona's urbanism, perhaps because this city assumes that one of the 'higher ordered goals' to which the designing systems of architecture should respond is 'territoriality'. With that apparent tautology I mean that for a long time Barcelona's plans and projects have coped with 'social and cultural complexities' to produce the present urban territory as its outcomes, allowing high quality in buildings and urban spaces. This resulted from a widely shared consciousness among citizens of a common territory, as well as the urban projects mentioned above.

Crucial modern plans and projects for Barcelona had always been achieved by recently invented new systems of representation that changed the way of seeing the world and new systems for materially producing that vision. It is a general assumption that the Renaissance was an outstanding example of a time of unprecedented achievement, when humanism and the invention of perspective led to the emergence of the architect as a figure specialized in imagining and designing buildings and spaces, and providing technical explanations to the master masons responsible for realizing them. Similarly, at the end of the eighteenth century and at the beginning of nineteenth century, the invention and diffusion of the level curves system enabled the accurate design of water channels and, later on, the very precise construction of railway lines by newly created specialists: civil engineers. The coetaneous refinement of the physical sciences, descriptive mathematics, and geometry resulted in greater precision in the calculation of resistances and behaviour of materials and the stereotomy that led to the birth of the academician architect, a professional who was skilled at producing institutional buildings and spaces, with the new tools produced by industrial methods. New systems for representing the Earth and of locomotion transformed the colonial experience and promoted the formation of an industrialist society, with new 'capital cities' having the potential for unlimited growth.

This article analyses the effectiveness of the implementation of the urban project in the case of the transformation of Barcelona during the nineteenth century, recognizing the important part played by nineteenth-century patterns and urban forms on Barcelona's contemporary urban fabric and on its layout. Notwithstanding the increasing acceleration of urban complexity since the industrial revolution, new design layers (some of striking quality) have been added to those nineteenth-century ones that are still acting as a binder for its urban community.

This and other meaningful periods of the urban history of modern Barcelona always coincide with the advent of new professions that arise as part of the changes in building production systems. Which new professionals will be needed once the era of analogical aerial photography, systemic abstraction, standardization and 'scientific planning' is over? Which new disciplines will take the baton and replace the engineers and architects in the complex urban conurbation of the future? We can ask how urban design products are responding to effectiveness in implementation and how design research is helping us to understand local and global reality. Have the new professionals, so knowledgeable about the tools of computational visualization and realization, any relationship with the tangible realities of work organization in order to be able to shape meaningful and sustainable buildings, urban spaces, and interesting, resilient territories?[1]

In this article, I argue that the result of the urban project of the nineteenth century, which can be considered a time when Barcelona was re-founded, is ecologically adaptive due to three conditions: first, the fact that the project to re-found the city has a rich history; second because the technicalities of implementation multiplied as part of the project from the first stirrings as a result of the capability and commitment of the new architects and engineers; and third, because a logical urban narrative (a theory) has been built for these new architects and engineers in order that they might interweave and network with the other disciplines involved in the project, and be understood and accepted by them.

---

1 In this respect, the timely warning of Mark Burry – when talking about 'adaptive ecologies' – should be taken seriously by architects. In his words: 'Computation and visualization progressed far more than computation and realisation' (Burry 2013: 5). An unintended consequence could be 'the possibility that designers will be relegated to a back-seat role in the teams shaping the urban environment of the future' (2013: 5).

To be adaptive, an urban project has to have a rich collective history; a genius like Cerdà does not emerge from nothing. The transformation of Barcelona in the mid-nineteenth century included the expansion and the renewal of the city and was motivated by far more complex reasons than the pressure of population growth due to commercial and industrial development. The demolition of the city walls would help, of course, to move the number of steam-driven factories located inside them, outward, together with the conspicuously dense crowds of the populace. The people in the 'Spanish Manchester', as Barcelona was known at the time, so miserable were the unhygienic conditions in which they lived, nevertheless throbbed with energy. But, more importantly in the view of Catalan industrialist bourgeoisie, its subsequent enlargement could change the role of this city and would allow its conversion into the new Spanish capital. Regardless of its battered condition, they considered Barcelona the only possible Spanish future competitor of Paris and London, as was said in the lavish literature of the period 1840–1860. Indeed, the modernization of Barcelona as a cultural capital was a crucial part of the general design to build the infrastructure necessary to develop a Spanish industrialist economy centred on Catalonia. The idea of the new industrialist capital city as a luxurious cultural hub – absolutely distinct from other cities devoted to production or designated to be main transport nodes in a national system – came, needless to say, from the followers of the French utopian socialists, Charles Fourier and the comte de Saint-Simon, who were diffusing the idea, applied to Paris, in their influential periodical *Revue Générale de l'Architecture et des Travaux Publics* published by César Daly from 1842 until the 1880s (Saboya 1991; Jenkins 2006; Roncayolo 2002).

Nevertheless, that was not the point of view of Spanish governments, which were extremely reluctant to accept the industrialist system that was arising in the western world and, subsequently, adjudged the city of Barcelona to occupy the more humble role of the main modern industrial harbour in the Spanish model. This was the territorial face of the economic debate between the Spanish free traders and the Catalan protectionists about the process of industrializing a 'late-comer' country. The dichotomy of becoming the main port or the capital city of the new nation-state explains the main issues and most of the changes in the shaping and infilling of the new street grid for the city. Free-trader Cerdà's proposal was to add a brand new 'warehouse' township or logistic city. Protectionist Garriga i Roca was thinking in terms of transforming the old centre into a more 'hip' central hub and of organizing progressive growth.

The issue had been discussed in Barcelona since the 1840s, in newspapers and through applications to the central government asking for the demolition of the walls and the transformation of the city, which was considered an urgent matter for the whole of Spain. The responses being very poor, in 1853 the Mayor created a Commission of the Corporations of Barcelona, which included important cultural and entrepreneurial personalities, to study ways to promote the enlargement of the old city, stepping back from its former pretensions to be a capital city, but stressing the need to use the enlargement as an opportunity to enhance the old city and provide it with all the facilities and attributes of a modern one.

Whether or not this has any relation with the Commission, in 1855 a new liberal government conceded, insistently set about the demolition – if only provisional and partial – of the fortresses, and entrusted to Ildefons Cerdà – a Catalan civil engineer employed by the state – the task of surveying the outskirts of the city (the plain surrounding it); the survey of the inner city was given to the Municipality, who commissioned the architect Miquel Garriga i Roca. In both cases the resulting topographical surveys are extraordinary documents that can be considered benchmarks of scientific thoroughness. Both surveys were to include a plan for future layout and development.

Miquel Garriga i Roca, a municipal architect, made an extremely precise survey of all the buildings, streets, and infrastructure (water supply, sewers, pavements…) of the city by drawing 118 maps at a 1:250 scale (monuments were designed at a scale of 1:100), then assembling them at a scale of 1:1250 and 1:2000 respectively (figures 2.2 and 2.3). He did not submit a draft or a finished plan until a few years later, but the year before he had proposed a plan for the renewal and simultaneous first steps for the enlargement of the land that had been occupied by the old city walls, as had been done in Paris and other European cities. His proposal included three boulevards that he

48   City, history, and territory

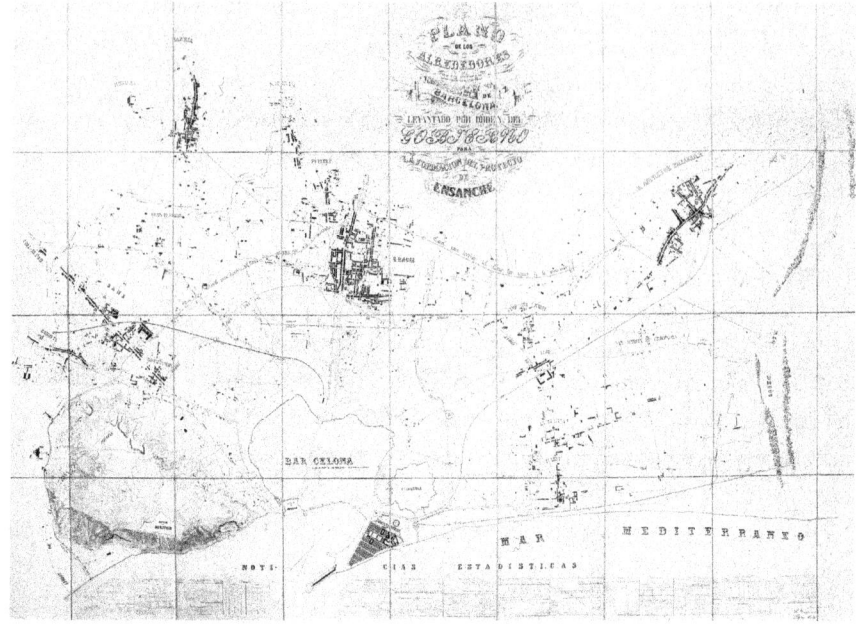

Figure 2.1 Cerdà's 1/500 topographical plan of 1855
with the addition of partial 1/1200 surveys

Idelfons Cerdà: Plano de los alrededores de ciudad de Barcelona levantado
por orden del Gobierno para la formación del proyecto de ensanche.
19 November 1955. Ink on 'canson' paper, 270 × 168 cm.

Municipal Archives of Barcelona

had already proposed in former drafts. They were the link with the enlargement, together with a square furnished with monuments.

Ildefons Cerdà drew up a topographical map at a scale of 1:5000 (Figure 2.1), by laying out maps of parts of the entire plain and the different townships at a scale of 1:1250, and projected a 'new city' in the form of an unlimited grid, which he called 'Anteproyecto de Ensanche' [Draft of Enlargement] between the city and the other outer subrubs that had been growing in the first part of the century. The document was based on an enormous amount of statistical data about the city provided by the most innovative foreign examples. The main emphasis is on the shapes of rectangular blocs and houses for a city that was to be clean and hygienic, and these were presented as a varied repertoire of examples. He identified three main axes: the

Barcelona as an adaptive ecology 49

Figure 2.2
Miquel Garriga's
1/2000 version of the
topographical plan of
the city with its
'project of reform'

Miquel Garrriga i Roca:
Plano topográfico–
geométrico de la ciudad
de Barcelona. Proyecto
de Reforma General. Ink
on canvas, 135 × 173 cm,
scale 1/2000. 15 August
1962.

Municipal Archives of
Barcelona

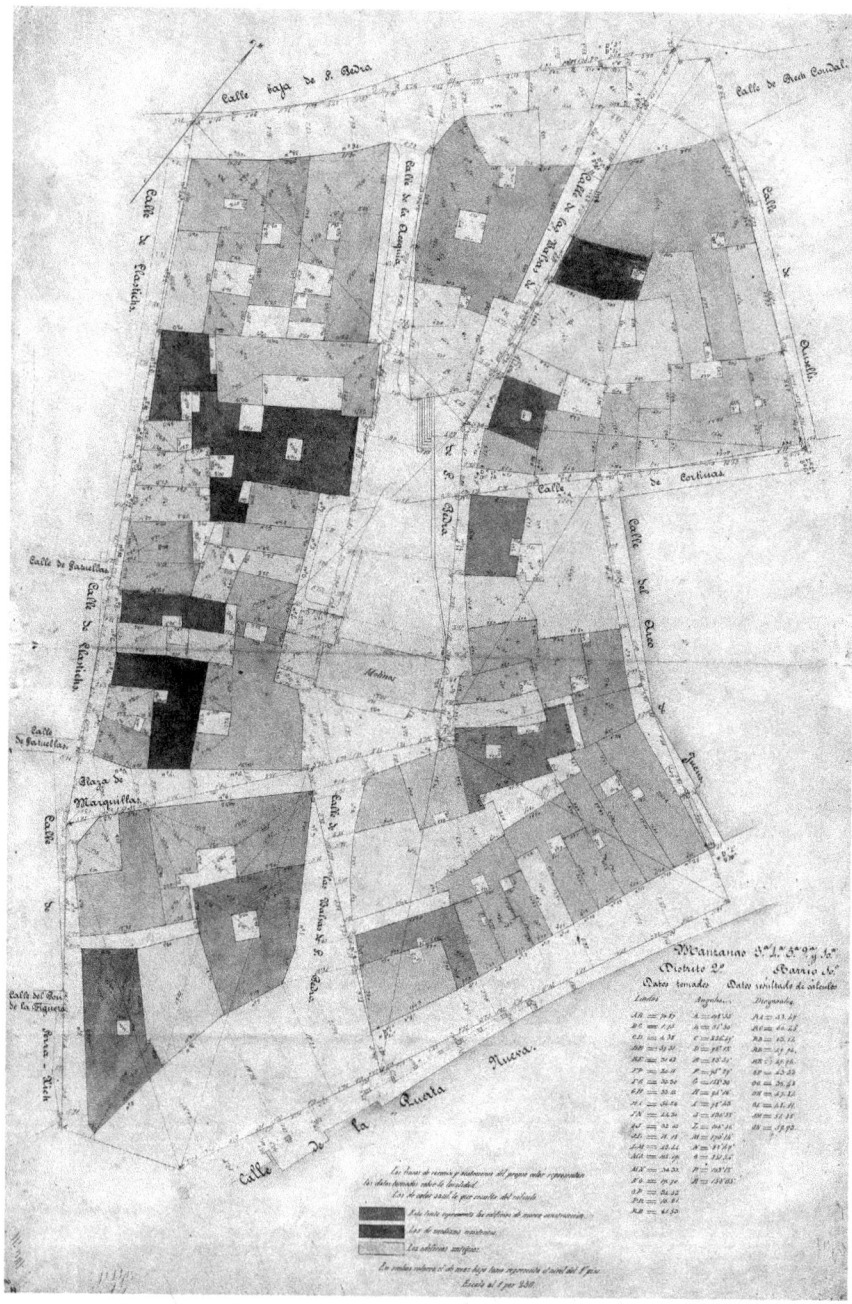

Figure 2.3 One of Garriga's 118 partial 1/250 surveys

Miquel Garriga i Roca 1858. Ink on 'canson' paper, scale 1/250. Set of 118 drawings covering the survey of the entire city of Barcelona. 65 × 45 cm approximately each. Municipal Archives of Barcelona

Parallel, the Meridian, and the Gran Via ('Great Way'), surrounding the old city as boulevards, but extended them towards the accesses to the plain, crossing the future new city.

It was unclear whose responsibility were the huge public venues of the fortresses – their ownership had been discussed in previous years in court hearings between the Municipality and the State – but in any case they were important sites for the Municipality to locate the new 'monuments' of the city – the significant facilities and commodities related to cultural, administrative, commercial, and industrial ruling institutions – as well as to transfer residential density from the inner city. They were also crucial for the government and important to Cerdà – who was not interested in monuments and public representation – as real estate development, which was needed to partially finance his project for a large-scale city extension.

A ministerial task force (Commission) was created the same year – 1855 – to study these documents and to decide about the question of the 'Eixample' – the enlargement – of Barcelona, but after the fall of the Liberal ('progressista') government, the question was again bogged down by the conservatives. For this reason, proprietors of outer venues near the publicly owned city ramparts terrains made the proposal to acquire a huge and highly remunerative strip of them in order to put simultaneously their ownership into play. Right away, another group of entrepreneurs related to the railways offered to finance the new urbanization, taking the walls as a guarantee from the government. Their initial interest was to enlarge all the small lines leading to the city by connecting them through the future grid. All these plans may finally have convinced the central government about the importance and land value of Barcelona's fortresses and interested it in the possibility of an 'Enlargement'.

In 1857, concerned by governmental stagnation and a wave of speculation, the municipality prepared a competition for the 'Eixample' or 'Enlargement' project by publishing a proposal called 'Bases for the Enlargement' with the annexed 'pre-project' carried out by its architect, Miquel Garriga i Roca, covering the central part of the future extension, linking the city with the suburb of Gràcia, and 'feeding' it by lengthening the main axes or cutting new ones through the old fabric. These documents were thoroughly studied by a New Commission, which produced an in-depth work covering design, economic, and legal and managerial issues.

52   City, history, and territory

Figure 2.4 Garriga's 1858 'pre-project' proposal for the city extension
Project approved by the Municipal Council 6 April 1858.
Printed. Undated version

Meanwhile Cerdà had rushed to finish his project, developing his previous draft for the unlimited extension, and presented it to the Ministry. But before this plan for the extension was considered by the Ministry, the competition was finally launched in a rush by the Municipality and was judged just a few months later, but not before the government had approved Cerdà's plan.[2] The conflict between the two institutions appeared publicly, since a project was approved when the competition was still under way. Nonetheless, to calm everybody down and put aside any suspicions, they agreed to wait for the contest to be over and the projects, including Cerdà's, exhibited.

The winner of the municipal contest was the project by Antoni Rovira i Trias, which presented the most extreme reincarnation of the

---

2 Cerdà's plan was entitled: 'Ildefons Cerdà: *Teoría de la construcción de ciudades, aplicada al proyecto de reforma y ensanche de Barcelona.* Barcelona 1859', The original document is in the Spanish state archives: Archivo General de la Administración del Estado Legajo R.41.808, Simancas. There is a copy in the archives of COAC, Col·legi Oficial d'Arquitectes de Catalunya, Barcelona.

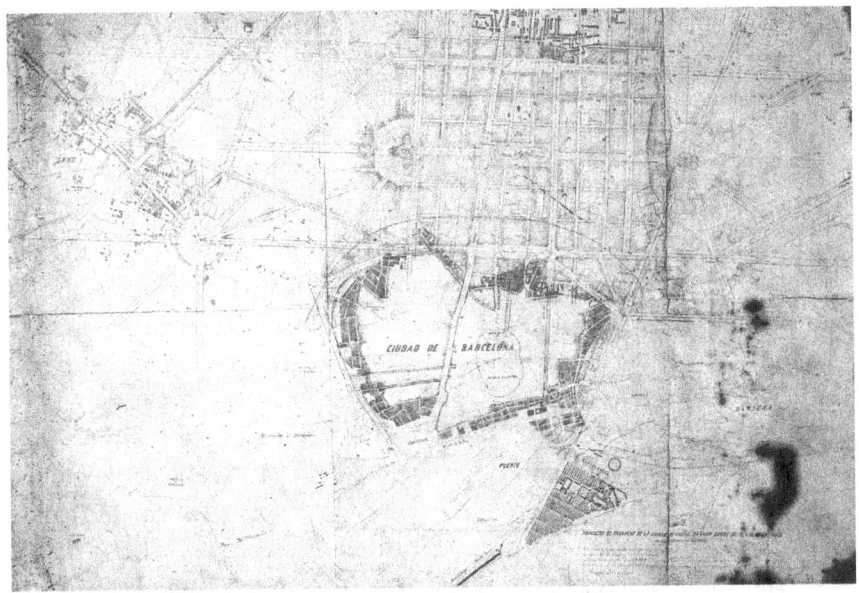

Figure 2.5 Preparatory draft for Garriga's 1858 city extension
Miquel Garriga i Roca: This is one of the six different drafts of the
'Proyecto de ensanche de la ciudad de Barcelona sobre la topografia de
dicha ciudad y sus afueras'. 28 November 1857.
Ink on canvas and watercolour, 160 × 90-100 cm.
Project approved by the Municipal Council 6 April 1858

old idea of a bourgeois capital. Rovira's main concern was to control the process of growth in an orderly fashion by establishing a series of rings of urban fabric development around the old city, defining future stages of growth and spreading outwards from a sumptuous and enormous central square. It also included a zoning of the city, corresponding to the growth of each part (industrial, commercial, cultural, and business), and allocated special uses to different areas, such as large-scale industries, hospitals, and cemeteries.

Interestingly enough, the motto chosen by the author to identify the competition entry was 'Le trace d'une ville est oeuvre du temps plutôt que d'architecte' [City layout is the work of time rather than an architect's[3]] – a literal quotation of the first statement of the new chapter on cities that had been added to the last edition of a treaty

---

[3] Unless otherwise stated, all translations are by the author.

published in Paris a month or two before. Its author, Léonce Reynaud, was a collaborator on the *Revue Générale de l'Architecture* published in Paris, so that these references, unveiled, are convincing evidence of the sources of the Catalan architects' ideas. Reynaud's treatise was on 'urban architecture', and this last chapter tried to establish some 'scientific' criteria for the location, form, and development of urban settlement, based on a historical reading. He was against the 'chessboard' urban layout and advocated for more 'organic' solutions resulting from the processes of growth of a historic centre. Applied to Paris, all those questions had been discussed previously in the *Revue* (Reynaud 1850–1858).

Reynaud was professor of architecture at the École Polithécnique and in 1830, with his philosopher brother Jean, he took part in a fascinating 'querelle' between the two most knowledgeable French naturalists, Cuvier and Geoffroy, about the meaning of molluscs. The discussion, on the basis of the genetics of form, was extremely inspiring to some architects. As these zoologists explained, the dialectics between shell and body in the growth of the molluscs had strong similarities with architecture, and urban growth and the inhabitation of architectural heritage. These debates paralleled and mingled with the properly architectural debate between the classicist Quatremère de Quincy and the neo-Greek Labrouste about the historical interpretation of Greek monuments and the idea of 'type' in architecture. It is quite surprising for us to learn nowadays that this debate also had deep political implications about the working class masses as the new protagonists of history (Lee 1998).

This sour French debate is of major interest if we want to create a genealogy of 'adaptive ecologies' in general and for its relationship to architectural debates in the nineteenth century. And it is highly appropriate in the case of Barcelona.

We will cross paths again later with Paris the thinkers. We now need to stress the idea of growth as a process that should be controlled from a former central point that has to be enhanced to avoid the danger of the new city, growing without limit, becoming lost in the new open territory.

Cerdà knew Reynaud's treatise, but conversely, the only central place that Cerdà recognized was the port, which from his point of view was the city's 'engine'. The city should therefore be transformed

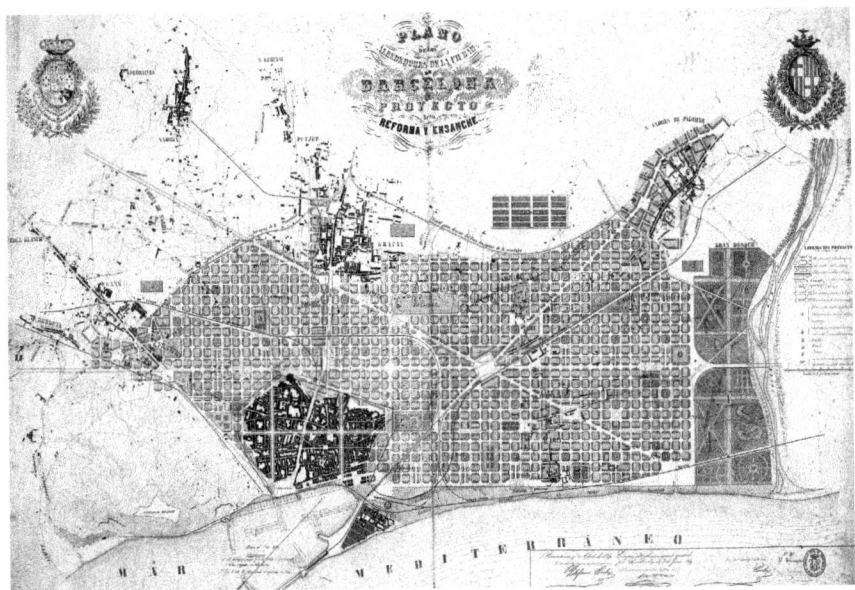

Figure 2.6 Cerdà's 1959 'Plano de Ensanche' with, added in, the three axes cutting through the Old City

Arxiu Històric de la Ciutat de Barcelona

into what we would now call a 'logistical platform'. That approach would convince traders, who formed the majority of the bourgeois of Barcelona. Cerdà's proposal ought also to be more than acceptable to the landlords of the city outskirts because the large size of the planned blocks allowed for fast growth, and the plan's clear geometry permitted the free colonization of the plain without needing much control, regardless of the eventual disordered landscape resulting from the urbanization process.

In his proposal, Cerdà specified all the technical aspects of urbanization and construction and also added a recently approved Project of the Port and a Reform of the Old City. These comprised a drastic extension of three streets, cutting through his 'Eixample' (Figure 2.6), which was meant to link the new city with the port, overcoming the existing 'old and deaf' urban fabric. This, in fact, was a radical reinterpretation of a previous proposal of Garriga. In the general layout Cerdà introduced a new main axis, the Diagonal, as a direct connection between suburbs and in response to criticisms of the grid's rigidity.

56   City, history, and territory

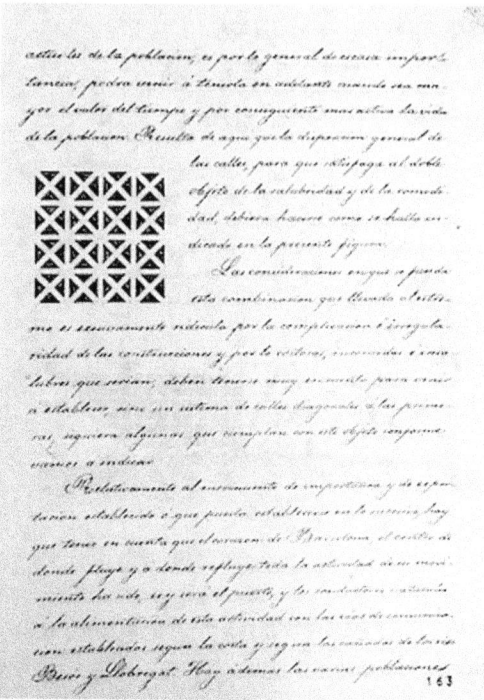

Figure 2.7 Sheet of the handwriting of Cerdà: 'Synthetic part, Spaces of public use' in *General Theory of the cities' construction applied to the case of Barcelona. April 1859*

Cerdà 1859

He adjusted the dimensions of the blocks and the streets by carrying out some calculations of their capacity, but also fitting them into the topography of Barcelona in a regular distribution, and he distributed urban facilities into regular bases, defining neighbourhoods, as in the earlier draft by Garriga. In general, therefore, it can be said that the project established a deep conversation with all the previous works carried out by commissions or individuals.

Furthermore, the document, which Cerdà had been elaborating for years, was accurately executed. His discussions of the earlier documents in the 'Barcelona conversation' (figures 2.7, 2.8, and 2.9) had clearly enriched his first plan, so that it was no longer merely a simple project or a 'township plan' – even an unlimited one – as it was in the draft of 1855. It was extensive and comprehensive. It included an 'analytical' part' and a 'synthetic' part, besides the 'construction

Barcelona as an adaptive ecology 57

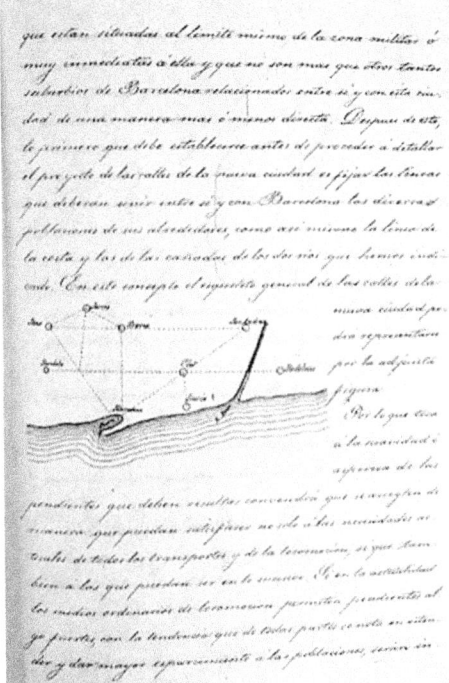

Figure 2.8 Sheet of the handwriting of Cerdà: 'Synthetic part, Spaces of public use' in *General Theory of the cities' construction applied to the case of Barcelona. April 1859*
Cerdà 1859

norms' and 'economic bases'. It is therefore a comprehensive and complete example of what can be considered a modern urban plan.

This plan was titled by his author 'Teoría de la construcción de ciudades, aplicada al proyecto de Reforma y Ensanche de Barcelona' [Theory of the Construction of Cities, Applied to the Project for the Renewal and Spread of Barcelona] – a formal theory being required to counter the one proposed by French architects in the *Revue* and by their Catalan followers. It is for this reason that Cerdà included as an annexe to his plan an 'Examination of Old and Modern Cities', in which there first there appeared, as the basis of his theory, an embryonic classification of cities according to their origin and modes of transport. It is also why he thought it necessary to include the procedural thinking of his plan's adversaries (a theory must be based on history), but used historical reality to claim the need to resolve the problems presented

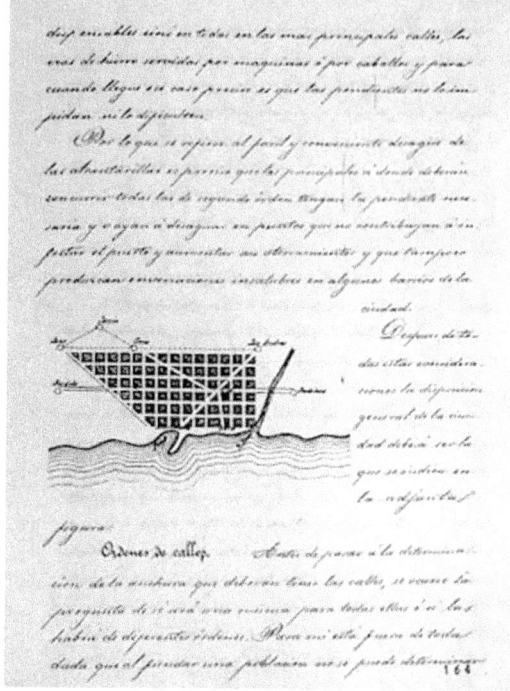

Figure 2.9 Sheet of the handwriting of Cerdà: 'Synthetic part, Spaces of public use' in *General Theory of the cities' construction applied to the case of Barcelona. April 1859*

Cerdà 1859

by history, in order to correct erroneous practices that had become the norm in European cities and to invent new schemes with which to replace them. This was used to justify the grid, and the breakthrough of the old town to link the new city to the new port.[4]

Cerdà also presented three long, theoretical contributions or 'discussions', deviating from his earlier arguments pertaining to cleanliness and hygiene, together with a section about 'vías de comunicación' [communication routes]. His 'moral or social' discussion, his 'industrial or economic' and his 'political' discussion dealt with the

---

4 That is why he included the question of the 'reform' or renewal of the Old Town in his project, which then became a theory: *'Teoría de la construcción de ciudades, aplicada al PROYECTO DE REFORMA Y ENSANCHE de Barcelona* por D. Ildefonso Cerdà, ingeniero de caminos, canales y puertos', emphasis added.

most characteristic subjects of the nineteenth-century modern city: industrial localization and working class housing in a context of unlimited growth; the centre–periphery relationship; and the shape of the city related to the tools to implement it in a radical free market context. He advocates the spread of the city as the solution to the housing problem in terms of its potential to overcome the monopoly of urban landlords in a fortified city and so avoid the establishing of a ceiling for rents, or the conversion the entire expanse of urban land into public property, 'as had been done by some governments'. In an 'open city' a map depicting public streets and squares and land in private use should suffice. As stated in Cerdà's political discussion, he was convinced that his proposal would have a revolutionary value as a solution for every social pain, especially for the integration of the working class if every worker became a holder of shares in a 'Society of the Enlargement'. This fragment echoes the economist Jean-Baptiste Say (1767–1832) and the libertarian philosopher Pierre-Joseph Proudhon (1809–1865), both French, in making explicit Cerdà's ideological and economic presumptions. He reveals an endearing faith in urbanism as an instrument of social reform for the working class through the ownership of single detached family houses.

Cerdà considered workers' neighbourhoods placed far away from the urban centre as 'inconvenient and unpolitic' because they separated the classes. And furthermore, workers should live near the factories, which would be located all round the city. Cerdà believed that the system of 'factory towns' shaped like convents or barracks that had received much current publicity was inimical to governments as much as to workers. He considered such schemes dangerous.

Cerdà saw movement as the distinctive element of the new society: movement of people, merchandise, air, and also capital. His subsection on roads drafts what would become the bases of Cerdà's theory: locomotion as the engine of urban transformation. Previous historical processes had left a heterogeneous set of streets that all in all did not meet the needs of modern traffic. He dedicated a deep analysis to crossroads, through a Baudelairean dramatic narration of diverse interacting movements to discuss the working of the grid and the role of diagonals. In this interesting section, Cerdà responds to Reynaud's statements and to Garriga's designs, who in his final projects had drawn up a draft for the enlargement of the city with a triangular grid, and justifies the addition of the new Diagonal axis for Barcelona crossing the entire grid, defended by the French author, but in a less 'organic' way.[5]

The introduction of the characteristic Barcelona's octagonal corners in the design of blocks could be also considered to have been inspired by a design included in Reynaud's book as an example of a square. Nevertheless it is more plausible that Cerdà had known Thomas Mitchell's suggested treatment of the street intersections as urban squares published in 1829 (Figure 2.10), which he used literally.[6]

The next subsection, entitled 'Examination of Old and Modern cities' presents a first classification of cities based on movement systems used in its origin in a theoretical effort that had as its immediate aim the justification of the need to reform the city in order to adapt it to new routes created by the railway stations and the port: 'In a word, the ports or stations of the seaways should be in immediate contact with the stations or ports of the land routes, and dependent one on the other as is most suited to the greater comfort and economy of both forms of transport'.[7]

Once the winner of the competition was announced, all the entries were exhibited in the room where the Cerdà plan was also displayed. The conversation, until then kept largely underground, became a

---

5 'Así es cosa de ver en todos los cruceros mezclados en torbellino los peatones con y sin carga, las caballerías ligeras y pesadas llevando ó arrastrando diferentes cargas, cruzarse en diferentes direcciones. Todo con atropellos, encontrones, pisadas y sustos hasta que se ha escapado del crucero. Es verdad que en presencia del inminente peligro que se corre disminuyen todos los transeuntes la velocidad del movimiento pero esta misma disminución ocasiona una perturbación general en las cuatro avenidas del crucero en términos de haber siempre en ellas mayor condensación de transeuntes. El campesino que de repente se encontrara en uno de estos cruceros no diría que está en una población civilizada, se creería transportado en la probervial torre de Babel ó en una verdadera anarquía' (Cerdà 1859: 306).

6 Thomas Mitchell was an English engraver who published the Darling Regulations drawn up by the Governor of New South Wales, Sir Ralph Darling, in Sydney in 1829.

7 'En una palabra el puerto o estacion de las vias marítimas debiera hallarse en contacto inmediato con las estaciones ó los puertos de las vias terrestres, y las dependencias de unas y otras con la contiguidad conveniente á la mayor comodidad y economía de los transportes' (Cerdà 1859: 306).

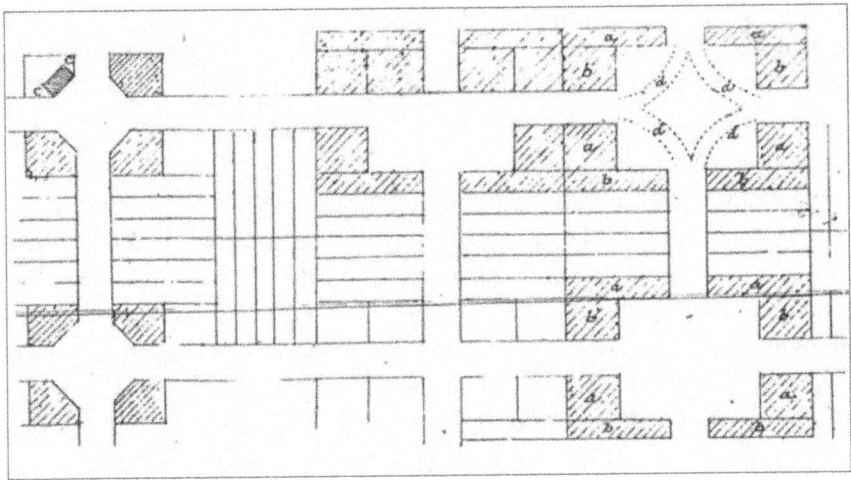

Figure 2.10 Thomas Mitchell's suggested treatment of street intersections as urban squares in his 1829 plan for a town extension
Mitchell Library, Glasgow

quite violent public discussion known as 'Battle of Enlargement'. The debate was varied and many different issues were discussed, mostly related with city centrality ('centers of movement' as it was said then) that included the role of civic monuments as well as the proper venues for locating them. They also defined urban spaces or how to deal with the factories, defining the less inconvenient way to place them and its workers (they were supposed to go together) whether it has concentrated in one sector or sprawled across different areas of the city. The housing types, buildings, and neighbourhoods related with the diversity of streets and passages were another of the main subjects. In brief, the debate was about urban standards and control of growth dynamics for the new city. In this respect, the most controversial question was the layout of the railway tracks throughout the city.

In relation to the centrality question, the introduction of the Avenue Diagonal conspicuously reinforced the crossing point of two other main axes – Meridiana and Gran Via – consequently everyone regarded this point as the future central square and considered it to be too far away from the current city centre. Its author saw it as just an infrastructural junction... but Barcelonians are still discussing the positioning of this space.

The project of Cerdà, approved provisionally in 1859, was passed definitively by the government in 1860 as a simple 'Proyecto de Ensanche'. That is to say, only the layout of the streets of the extension would be regulatory, the *ordenanzas* were to be excluded, as were the 'economic bases'.

What was left somehow undefined was whether the land surface formerly covered by the city walls was in the approved plan and if the three new streets, crossing (and disemboweling) the old inner city were as well. Other doubts were about the affectation of the urban fabric of the Old City. The Municipality passed the plan of the inner city that Garriga had been working on for some years and split it into three different files to be sent to the government for approval: the inner city renewal plan; the project for the 'boulevards'; along the terrains of the old walls of the fortresses' venues and the renewal plan for the port neighbourhood of Barceloneta. The objective of the Barceloneta plan was to protect it from Cerdà's demolition project by converting it into an enormous, and *avant la lettre* intermodal area, which Garriga called the 'Intercambio Marítimo Terrestre' [Maritime–Terrestrial Interchange]. These three proposals were intended to complement the approved extension 'project', the comprehensive transformation plan.[8]

Both Cerdà and the municipal architect both continued for years to reformulate their projects in response to the each other's moves. Meanwhile, Cerdà was keeping many initiatives the go: he was directing the actual location of milestones at every future crossing of the Gran Via, which was the longest tangential axis and his reference for the implementation of the new urban grid, while studying other related tasks such as the preparation of a system to make it economically and legally possible to make inroads into the old town, in order to obviate the problems that had hampered the acceptance of his earlier plans.

This inevitably led to another public discussion in the city, as a tense continuation of the earlier discussions of the plans for the

---

8 From Garriga i Roca's *Proyecto de Reforma de la Barceloneta*. See also Sagarra 1993; Cerdà 1859. A first modification of the grid had already been made to retain the Passeig de Gràcia – the most popular promenade, built in the 1820s – and the Rambla Catalunya (a former stream that caused extensive flooding when the walls were demolished), which the recently approved grid had ignored.

Barcelona as an adaptive ecology 63

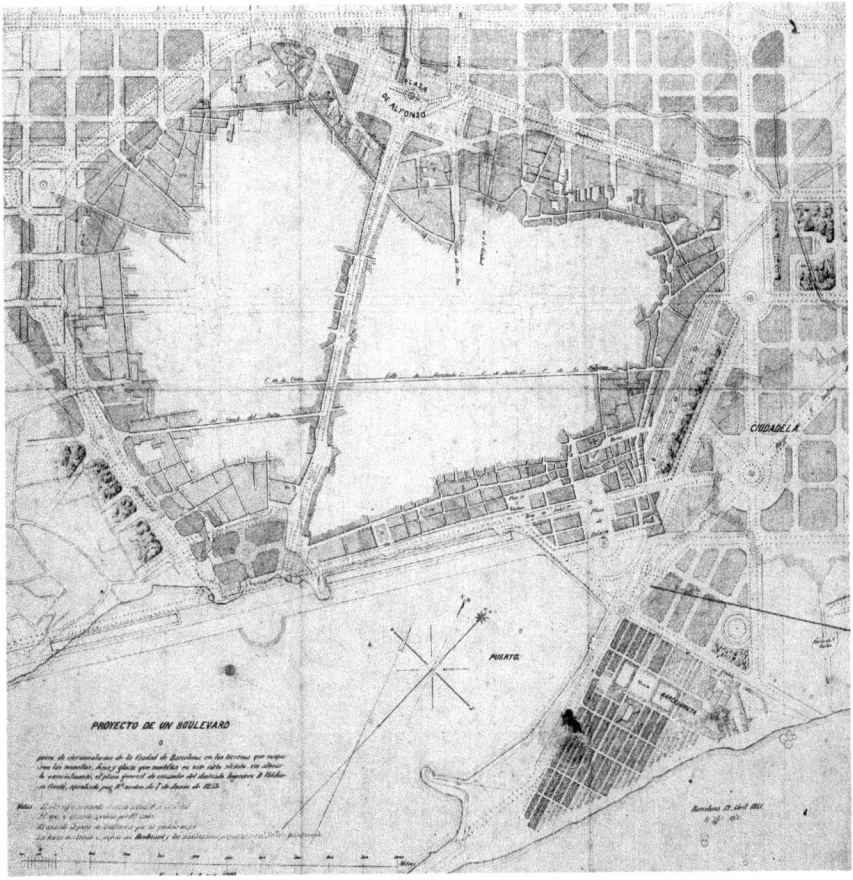

Figure 2.11 Garriga's Boulevard, as a reformulation of the contact between Cerdà's grid and the old city, 1861

Miquel Garriga i Roca: Proyecto para un Boulevard, 19 d'abril 1861 colour ink on canvas. 'Box n. 7 Garriga-Fontseré' Arxiu Administratiu de l'Ajuntament de Barcelona

enlargement. Garriga introduced the question of tramways into the conversation, and redesigned the boulevards to link the approved grid with the old city. These boulevards could never have been achieved because Cerdà was, meanwhile, selling the land beneath the walls, where the government had commissioned them to be constructed.

Cerdà's new reformulation of the grid in 1863 (Figure 2.11) deserves special mention. He envisaged a 'Scottish' network, meaning a double mesh alternating specialized streets of railway track with urban

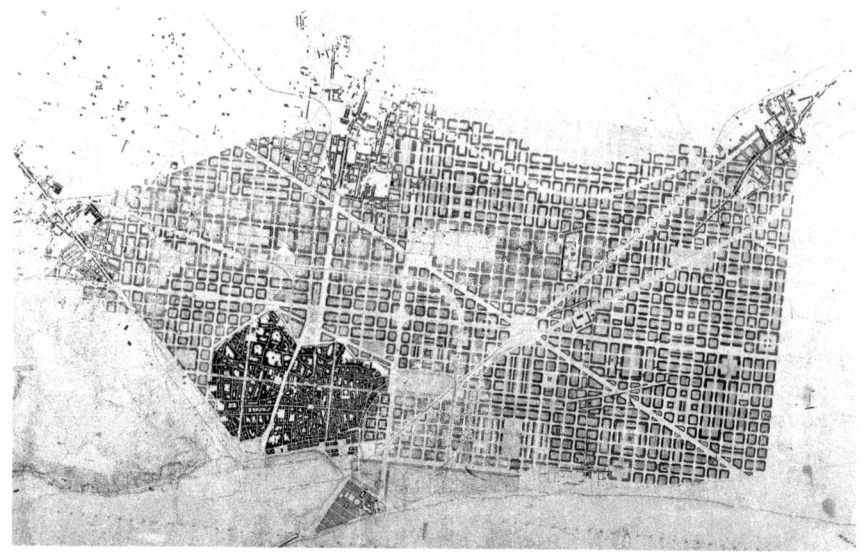

Figure 2.12 Cerdà's proposal of 1863 interpreted by the author
Sagarra 1993

streets in a longitudinal street. One of every two longitudinal streets of the former design is converted into a sunken path along which an open-air railway track would pass below ground level, under a bridge every other street and blocking the others. This would define a new pattern of 'superblocks' by merging four of the former current blocks. The interior area of those superblocks was intended for industrial and logistics, and its periphery, following urban streets, to housing and commercial purposes. This produced three lines that crossed the entire city as a part of his scheme for a 'Maritime–Terrestrial Interchange'. The issue of the lengthening of railways; was a major concern of the railway companies throughout the implementation of the new urban grid; as the principal landlords in the enlargement area of the city, they were deeply interested in connecting the coast with its hinterland, while speculating with the land.

All these projects – although the foundations of a rich planning culture in the city – remained shelved and were never approved, due to the arrival of the 1863 economic crisis. This outcome was partially related to the failure of railway companies and, not surprisingly, to the land speculation bubble that dogged Barcelona's enlargement, and to

Barcelona as an adaptive ecology 65

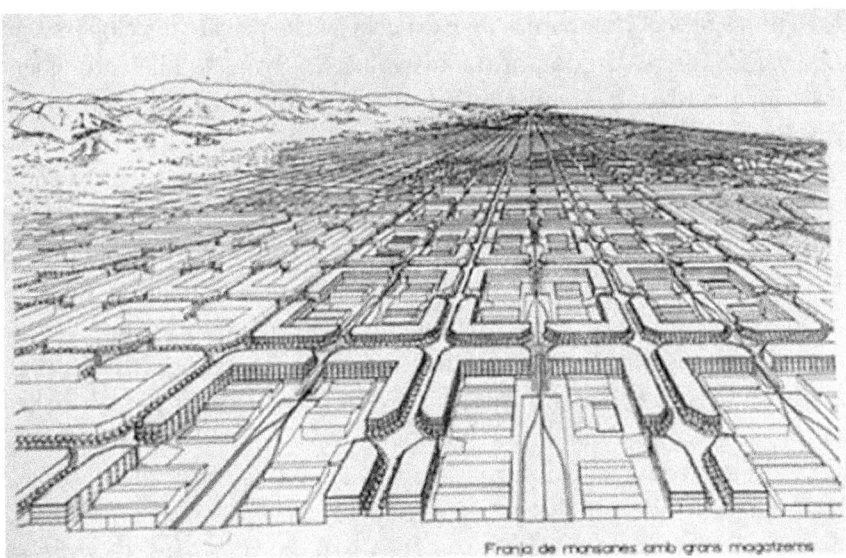

Figure 2.13 Cerdà's proposal of 1863 interpreted by the author
Sagarra 1993

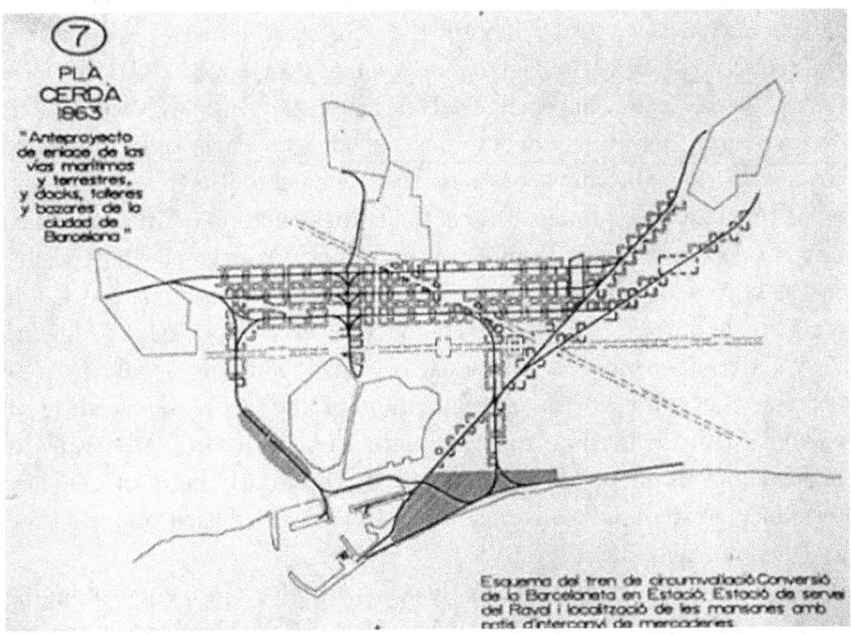

Figure 2.14 Cerdà's 1863 proposal for rail connections
interpreted by the author
Sagarra 1993

the failure of the 'Compañías de Ensanche' – the private developers that undertook the realization of the urbanization project. The subsequent economic recession eventually led to a big political crisis and to the revolution of 1868.

Also in 1863, four years after the first three 'discussions', which, as is explained above, Cerdà referred to in his 1859 proposal, Cerdà finished his *Teoría General de la Urbanización* [General Theory of Urbanization]. In it, he presented urbanization as a 'transition' towards an ideal city – thus adopting the leading argument of his counterparts: that history is the key to reading the city; however Cerdà's urban history was generic and unspecific. Cerdà's theory was not published until 1867. We do not know whether it is a coincidence that just a year before Cerdà's completion of his *Teoría General*, in 1862, César Daly had established the principles and themes of what would be a new discipline in an article in the 20th issue of the *Revue Générale de l'Architecture*, in which he analysed the transformation of Paris.[9]

It was in the early 1860s, therefore, coinciding with the conversations in Barcelona and the radical transformation of Haussmann's Paris, and a few years before the 'German fathers' – Reinhard Baumeister (1833–1917), Hermann Stübben (1845–1936), Camilo Sitte (1843–1903) – could have achieved the same, the first two elaborations of an urban planning theory were produced: Paris and Barcelona would be the laboratories where the limits and the possibilities of what this new discipline could be: the transformation of an established city inside the framework of a new territory. Coincidences are visible in the chronology and in the topics dealt with. Haussman and Cerdà treated the problems they encountered very differently, following very different principles. The goal of urban planning would in time become the analysis and manipulation of the processes leading to this city transformation, together with the definition of the ways of influencing those processes adopted in these two hubs of the new territorial system. Urbanism can only exist if it is based on structural and historic ideas.

As we know, Cerdà built his theory in three stages, corresponding to the 1855 draft for the expansion, the 1859 project for expansion

---

9 My studies of this is available in *Barcelona ciutat de transició* (1993). See also Papayanis 2006.

Barcelona as an adaptive ecology 67

Figure 2.15 Section 'Theorie' from the *Revue Générale de l'Architecture et des Travaux Publics*, Paris

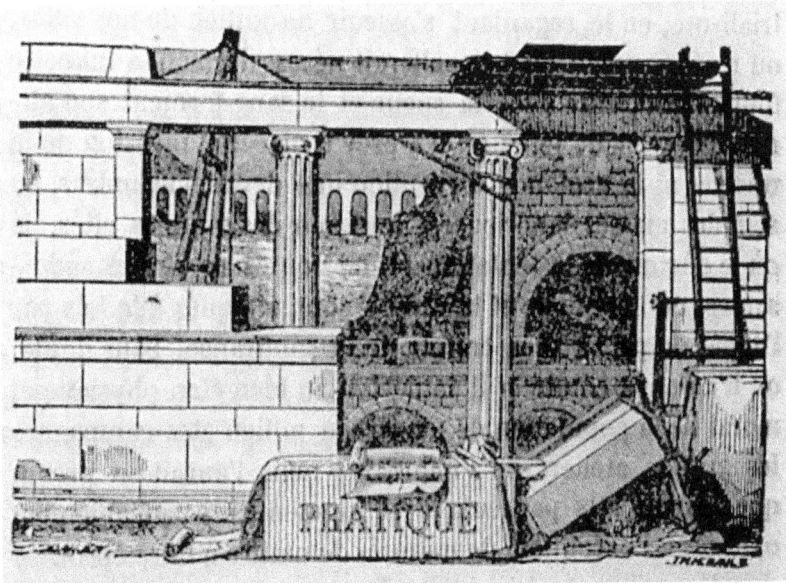

Figure 2.16 Section 'Pratique' from the *Revue Générale de l'Architecture et des Travaux Publics*, Paris

68   City, history, and territory

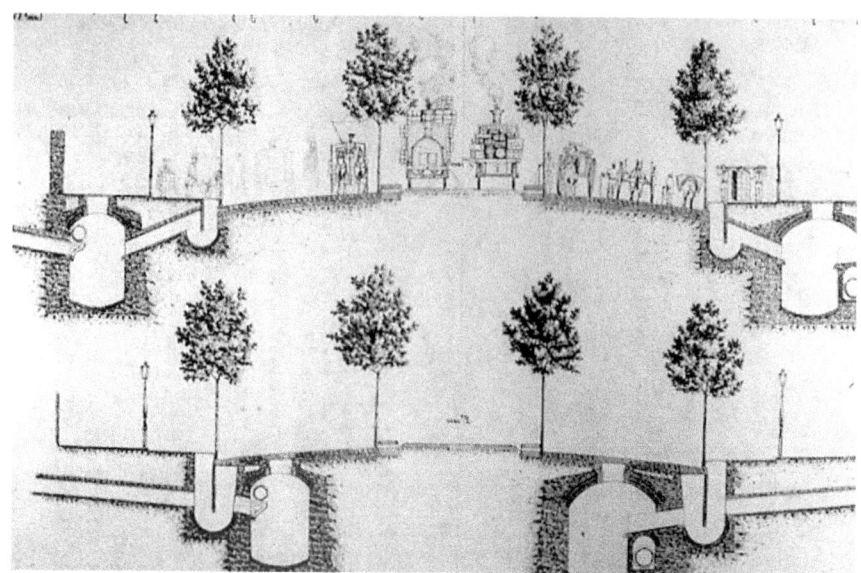

Figure 2.17 Cross-section of Cerdà's 1859 project
Teoria de la construcción de las ciudades, Cerdà y Barcelona, Ministerio para las Administraciones Públicas, and Ajuntament de Barcelona, 1991. ISBN 84-7088-583-9

Figure 2.18 Carrer Aragó before the covering over of the railway
(Arxiu Fotogràfic de Barcelona)

and renewal, and the plan of 1863, with the eventual introduction of railways and tramways into the city, together with the recognition of the values of centrality. Initially centred on the grids, roads, blocks (or 'inter-roads', as Cerdà liked to call them) and on urban growth, he had been progressively adding to his initial impetus towards a 'clean and hygienic city, ideas based on a deepening reflection on urban growth and locational issues.

In this time-lapse he set aside what was one of its initial leading preoccupations: the working-class housing problem. In his 1859 plan Cerdà nevertheless, unwittingly introduced the consideration of structural problems related to industrial location or urban renewal, and incorporated the important Diagonal axis. All these issues were local wishes proposed by the municipality, and were the results of taking into account the higher value of the centrality of the existing city in the modern process of deploy and growth. In 1863, after so many years of controversies, Cerdà tried to respond to these aspects, which were, actually, the object of the new discipline of Urban Planning, going on to refine his model for a new city fabric.

As well as having a rich history and a logical narrative, the resulting Barcelona grid is also adaptive because the construction's 'technicalities' were not a simple post-added value but grew with the project. It looks as if the protagonists of this story knew from very early on what tasks they would have to face and consequently prepared themselves. The depth of their knowledge of foreign examples and experiences was surprising, as was their experience of the practices and systems necessary to realize their projects.

The technical and economic feasibility of the projects had been entwined at any stage with the design issues but in the 1880s, when the double economic and political crisis was over, a complex system of urban taxes and *ordenanzas* (regulations governing land division and building), and time programming was put in place after a process of trial and error. For many years, the system was under the control of the Comissió d'Eixample, a public/private commission basically under the control of landlords, who administrated the pro-growth policy of taxes released from the state until a new cycle of thinking about urban issues began in the first third of the twentieth century.

The direct 'genealogical' path from the first so-called 'Bases de l'Eixample' and the first modern urban code, both dating from 1856, and tens (or hundreds) of other documents that enlightened this collective work, created an urban culture of participatory procedures that have led to the best moments of the adaptive ecology that is Barcelona. These are the times when designers venture to take part in the international debate while acting with greater transparency towards the wider public.

Works cited

Burry, Mark (2013). 'Ideas and Computation in Contemporary Urban Design: Addressing the Disconnects', in Theodore Spyropoulos (ed.), *Adaptive Ecologies: Correlated Systems of Living.* (London: AA).

Cerdà, Ildefons (1859). *Teoría de la construcción de ciudades, aplicada al proyecto de reforma y ensanche de Barcelona por Ildefonso Cerdà, Ingeniero de caminos canales y puertos.* (Barcelona: Archivo General de la Administración AGA- Educ. y Cienc).

Jenkins, Lloyd (2006). 'Utopianism and Urban Change in Perreymond's Plans for the Rebuilding of Paris', *Journal of Historical Geography*, 32.2: 336–51.

Lee, Paula Young (1998). 'The Meaning of Molluscs: Léonce Reynaud and the Cuvier-Geoffroy Debate of 1830, Paris', *The Journal of Architecture*, 3.3: 211–40.

Papayanis, Nicholas (2006). 'Cesar Daly, Paris and the Emergence of Modern Urban Planning', *Planning Perspectives*, 21: 321–46.

Reynaud, Léonce (1850–1858). *Traité d'Architecture contenant des notions générales sur les principes de la construction et sur l'histoire de l'art* (Paris: Carilian-Goeury et V. Dalmont).

Roncayolo, Marcel (2002). 'Prélude à l'haussmannisation. Capitale et pensée urbaine en France autour de 1840', in Marcel Roncayolo, *Lectures de villes* (Paris: Parenthèses), 55–70.

Saboya, Marc (1991). *Presse et architecture au xixe siècle: César Daly et la Revue générale de l'architecture et des travaux publics* (Paris: Picard).

Sagarra, Ferran (1993). *Barcelona ciutat de transició. El projecte urbà a través de l'obra de l'arquitecte Miquel Garriga i Roca. 1848–1868* (Barcelona: Institut d'Estudis Catalans).

CHAPTER THREE

A present past, Barcelona street names, from Víctor Balaguer to Pasqual Maragall*

Jaume Subirana

In his essay, *The Idea of Europe*, the critic George Steiner writes:

> The streets, the squares walked by European men, women and children are named a hundredfold after statesmen, military figures, poets, artists, composers, scientists and philosophers. [...] The European schoolchild, urban men and women, inhabit literal echo-chambers of historical, intellectual, artistic and scientific achievements. [...] Cities such as Paris, Milan, Florence, Frankfurt, Weimar, Vienna, Prague or Saint Petersburg are living chronicles. To read their street-signs is to leaf through a present past. (Steiner: 41–42)

---

* An earlier version of this text was published in the *Journal of Iberian and Latin American Studies* 19(3), 2013. © Jaume Subirana. Previously, I presented excerpts at the 2013 Toronto Colloquium of the North American Catalan Society and in the seminar 'Ideational and Imaging Labour: Power and Collective Entities' at the Università Ca' Foscari Venezia. I would like to thank lecturers Massimiliano Bampi, Jaume Claret, Itamar Even-Zohar, Thomas Harrington, Elisa Martí-López and Rakefet Sela-Sheffy for their comments and contributions.

Steiner writes that in Europe, unlike in America, there is a real 'sovereignty of remembrance', and that the continent defines itself as a *lieu de mémoire*, using Pierre Nora's expression. This was the affiliation (the genealogy) of the city as a living chronicle and as a place of memory that was aspired to in the latter half of the nineteenth century by the Barcelona that had recently approved the major urban planning reform of the Eixample; the Barcelona, too, of the Jocs Florals (Floral Games, reinstated in 1859) and the imminent 1888 Universal Exposition. And it was also largely this affiliation, as we shall see, to which the Catalan capital aspired on the occasion of the changes at the end of the twentieth century, bringing about the return of democracy and the awarding to the city of the organization of the Summer Games of the XXV Olympiad. This article analyses the 'christening' of the streets in the Eixample, in the second half of the nineteenth century, and of the Vila Olímpica at the end of the twentieth century.

Naming a city's streets is a semiotic and political operation (Azaryahu) and a 'performative practice that produces a contested space of political utterances' (Rose-Redwood: 890). Street names tell a kind of story, a narrative of varying degrees of coherence that is often a 'message' on the part of planners, and we can study how successful it has been in its incorporation into the imaginary of the city and its citizens. In *City of Glass* (1985), one of Paul Auster's characters spends two hours walking around New York, tracing out an itinerary in the form of a huge letter on a plan of Manhattan Island, and the sum of the days and the letters is a message with a meaning. If we look at a plan of the city of Barcelona and, more specifically, of the Eixample district, and read and make note of the names of the streets, we realize that the map is also a written page, and that the list of the street names pieces together a kind of story, a coherent discourse and a 'message'. What is this message? How long has it been there? Who wrote it? How has it been passed down to us, and how can we or should we still read it today?

List of street names for the new Eixample

In Barcelona, the names of most of the streets in the Eixample district are due to a proposal made by historian, politician and writer Víctor Balaguer to the city council that was approved in 1863. The proposal was obviously associated with the great planning operation that was Ildefons Cerdà's project for the Eixample. Though known to specialists, this is a distant fact in the memory or the consciousness of most local people (let alone visitors). As with popular art, for many of the city's inhabitants the streets of the Eixample seem always to have been there and always to have been called just as they should be.

To extend a Barcelona that was smothered by its medieval walls, in 1859 the City Council appointed a special commission to organize a project competition. Although the winner of the competition was the architect Antoni Rovira i Trias, a Royal Order of the Ministry of Public Works approved the project of Ildefons Cerdà, a civil engineer who in 1855–1856 had drawn the topographic map of the Barcelona Plain, further extended by several demographic and urban planning studies of the city. Cerdà was a Saint-Simonian utopian (Grau) and a specialist in progressive (and, later, republican) ideas, concerned with the living conditions of workers and with achieving, by means of urbanism, the ideals of equality and fraternity. The implementation of his urban planning project, based on a regular, egalitarian grid stretching from the river Besòs to the mountain of Montjuïc (Figure 3.1), envisaged the construction of much longer, broader streets than those in the old town, but rather than names, the streets on the engineer's plan had letters or numbers. This is where Víctor Balaguer came in; since 1852 'Chronicler of the City' and, in February 1859, appointed member of an advisory board for the task of advising the Municipal Eixample Committee, Balaguer was commissioned in 1863 by Section Four of the City Council (responsible for urban planning issues) to propose a list of names for the 50 or so new streets initially envisaged, closest to the old town.

Víctor Balaguer was certainly a remarkable character: Josep M. Fradera (2001) awards him the status of giant. Born in 1824 in Barcelona's Carrer de Sant Pau, son of a doctor of liberal ideas, he, too, was a liberal politician with his roots in Romanticism, a lover of literature and a dilettante historian, according to some a Mason,

74 City, history, and territory

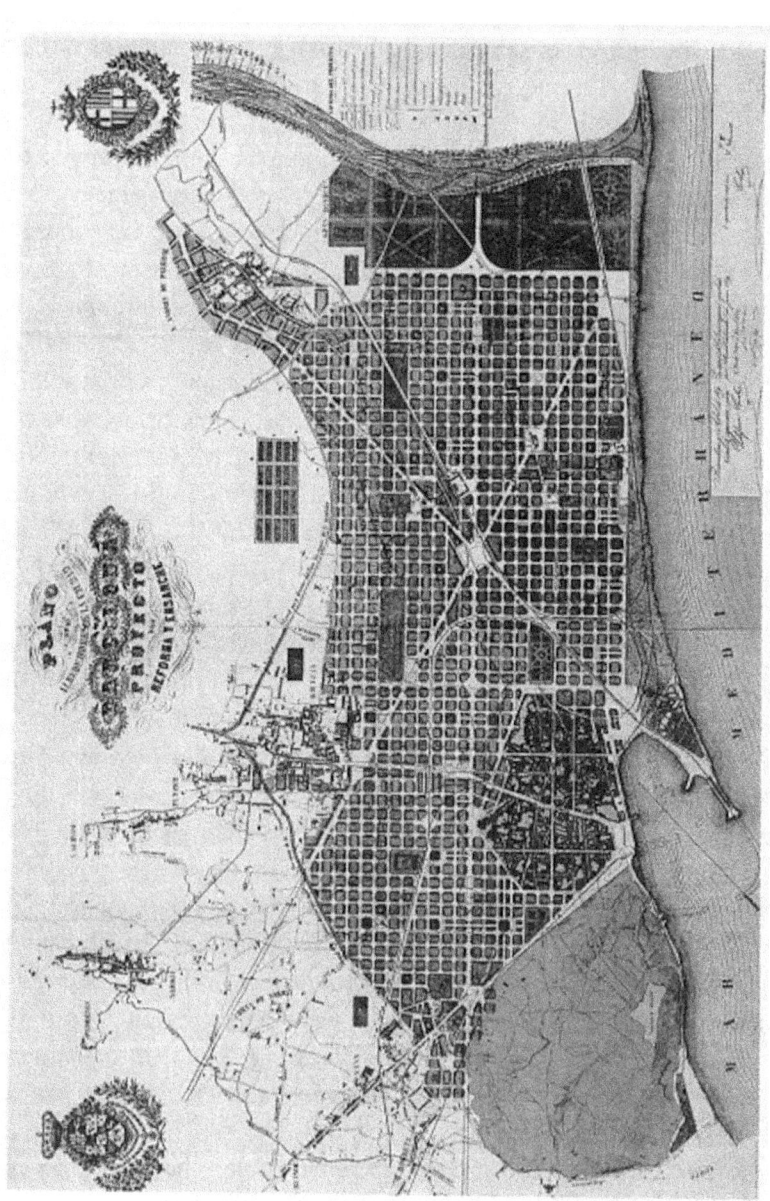

Figure 3.1 Plan of the project for the remodelling and extension of Barcelona by Ildefons Cerdà (1859)
Arxiu Històric de la Ciutat de Barcelona

an untiring activist, first a contributor to and then founder of liberal newspapers and publications ('radical', at the time), and foremost participant in the restoration of the Jocs Florals literary event. He soon devoted himself above all to politics: he made his first visit to Madrid in the 1940s, went into exile in France (from 1865 to 1867) for his participation in the General Prim conspiracy (in France he met the writer and lexicographer Frederic Mistral and collaborated with the Felibritge, of which he became vice president), and returned to Spain when his party came to power to take up various important positions, such as Minister of Economic Development and Overseas under the reign of Amadeo I of Savoy, then with the First Republic (1871), and once again in 1886.[1] In 1899, when he was near death, Balaguer wrote in *Historias y leyendas*: 'A mí, viejo revolucionario, sólo me place y halaga ser constante en mis ideas, y soy, mal que pese a mis años, romántico en literatura y progresista en política' (Balaguer 1899: 490).

In Barcelona, the central years of the nineteenth century were fast-paced and exciting from the viewpoint of political events of and economic and social change: in 1835 Spain had decreed the confiscation of Church property (in July several convents were burned down in Barcelona and other cities in Catalonia); in 1840 the Cotton Industry Workers Mutual Benefit Society was set up, the first Catalan workers' association; in September 1843, the capital saw the revolt of La Jamància; in 1848 the Peninsula's first train made its maiden voyage between Barcelona and Mataró; in 1854, after years of discussion, work finally began (under a progressive civil governor, Pascual Madoz) to demolish the medieval walls; July 1855 saw the first general workers' strike in Catalonia; on 1 May 1859 (the same year the winner of the Eixample projects competition was announced), the city recovered its medieval Floral Games, and, that summer, Narcís Monturiol

---

1 According to Josep M. Fradera, he was 'the only Catalan, with the unfortunate exception of Prim, who had been able to forge a political career in Madrid and in Barcelona (or in the constituency of Vilanova i la Geltrú, which amounts to the same). He was a versatile personality and a dabbler: poet, playwright, novelist, and historian, a scholar of Italian and Philippine language and culture, with confidants and contacts everywhere. Balaguer was not an author of the first order in any of these activities but nor was he superfluous in any of them, taken against the general context of the country' (2009: 144; my translation).

carried out the first trials with his submarine *Ictineu* in the waters of Barcelona's harbour; in 1868 there was the uprising against the regime of Isabel II, known as 'La Gloriosa', and, soon after, the first elections with universal suffrage (for men over the age of 25). In this socially and politically vibrant context, on 28 October 1863 Víctor Balaguer wrote a letter to the City Council that was at once a proposal and a request:

> Según se dice, se aproxima el momento de tener que dar nombre a varias calles de las que han de formar la nueva Barcelona, y ninguna ocasión mejor que la presente para remediar el olvido en que por mala aventura han caído ciertas empresas gloriosas, ciertos nombres célebres, que lo han sido, y serán siempre de gloria para Cataluña. Segurísimo estoy que no hago sino interpretar los deseos de V. E. y anticiparme a su voluntad suplicándole se digne bautizar las calles que se van a abrir con nombres que recuerden algunos de los grandes hechos de valor, de nobleza, de virtud, de abnegación y patriotismo que por cierto abundan en nuestra historia y pueden presentarse como ejemplo y como modelo a generaciones posteriores. Así se cumplirá en parte con el deber que tiene cada pueblo de recordar la memoria de sus pasados, mayormente cuando estas memorias son tan ilustres y memorables como las nuestras. (quoted in Carreras y Candi: 877)

Just two months later, the Municipal Plenary Session of 19 December 1863 unanimously passed the proposed names for the new Eixample presented by Balaguer,[2] some slight changes having been made by 'Section Four'. What was, in essence, the proposal presented by Balaguer?

---

2 Arxiu Municipal Administratiu de Barcelona, fol. 366r and 366v. The minutes of the meeting are reproduced in Quintana: 56–58. For a summary of the relationship between Balaguer and Barcelona Council, see the opening pages of Cuccu: 147ff.

Víctor Balaguer's proposal

The intention of the historian and writer with his proposal, combining (as in other aspects of his life) the recovery and dissemination of Catalan history, is plainly reflected in a few lines from *Las calles de Barcelona*, the book he was to publish a few years later: 'cuando el autor de estas líneas se encargó de poner nombre a todas las calles del ensanche, concibió el plan de que todos fuesen acomodados a hechos, glorias e instituciones pertenecientes a la historia de Cataluña, a fin de formar un conjunto general, histórico y armónico' (Balaguer 1865: 434). As Stéphane Michonneau explains (2001), a great modern city, as well as being rational, had to be significant in terms of symbolism and public instruction: the nineteenth century was, in much of urban Europe, the time of new town extensions, but it was also the time of great monumentalizing fervour.

The streets of Barcelona's Eixample were, in their own way, to be a life-sized history book, in which it was possible (and still is today) to read the mental and identitary 'map' of one of the emblematic representatives of the nineteenth-century Catalan Renaixença. A map based on history, on the past. Although, as we will see, Balaguer was to act more as a director or organizer of ideas than an actual historian. To summarize, the names of the streets in the Eixample contain:

- horizontally, from the sea to the mountain, first of all the principal Catalan political and administrative institutions: Corts catalanes (Gran Via), Diputació, Consell de Cent;

- next, the principal territories that belonged at various times to the Crown of Aragon: Aragó, València, Mallorca, Provença, Rosselló, Còrsega, as well as Catalunya itself (Plaça) and, running vertically, Nàpols, Sicília, and Sardenya (also, on the other side of Passeig de Gràcia, Calàbria);

- foremost personalities from the past in different areas (Ramon Llull, Ausiàs Marc, Ramon Muntaner, Jeroni Pujades, Arnau de Vilanova, Alí Bei, Antoni Viladomat);

- a series of great Catalan soldiers and sailors, with particular emphasis on those related to medieval Mediterranean expansion

(Roger de Flor, Berenguer d'Entença, Bernat de Rocafort, and Roger de Llúria, Conrad de Llançà, Bernat de Vilamarí);

– the origins of the motherland: the counts of Urgell and Villena (the latter also a writer, though his name was one that did not gel), and figures linked to the principal episodes (according to Balaguer) of Catalan resistance to the loss of liberties (fifteenth century: Hug de Pallars; seventeenth century: Pau Claris, Joan Pere Fontanella, and Francesc Tamarit; eighteenth century: Rafael Casanova and Antoni de Villarroel; nineteenth century: Bruc, Girona, and Tarragona for their links with the Peninsular War). Also Wad-Ras (spelled 'Gualdrás', an episode of the war in Africa involving the Catalan volunteer corps commanded by General Prim); and, finally,

– some contemporary references: Aribau (economist) and Balmes (philosopher), but particularly the triad that formed the basis of economic activity as it was conceived at that time: Marina, Comerç, and Indústria.³

So we have institutions, territories, men and feats (of arms), and the foundations of modern economic activity. Víctor Balaguer developed his list of street names for the city according to a logic that was historicist (at a time of all-pervasive historicism), medievalizing, Catalan nationalist and liberal, with a clear bias towards the tradition of the struggle for freedom. And he did so at a time that he perceived as pre-revolutionary ('Barcelona está llamada a figurar en los grandes acontecimientos que se acercan y que no pueden tardar en conmover a la nación con estrépito. [...] El espíritu altamente liberal que reina en esta ciudad es una

---

3 It is important to note (because failure to do so could result in erroneous interpretations of Balaguer's ideological proposal) that some alterations were made. Balaguer notes that 'el plan dejó de realizarse por completo a causa de no haber sido aprobados todos los nombres' (1865: 434), and there also seems to have been the addition of Bailén, Bergara (where the end of the Carlist Wars was signed), Casp (after the Compromise of 1412), Pelagi (now Pelai) and Trafalgar. In any case, Lluís Quintana points out that Casp could well respond to Balaguer's own particular logic and that 'in the text of *Las calles...*, where Balaguer had the freedom to comment on these decisions, he does not explicitly say that these names are not his' (39).

garantía de que, cuando lleguen sucesos, hoy de todos previstos, sabrá mantenerse a la altura de su heroico pasado' [Balaguer 1865: 19–20]). Having said that, I find it interesting to point out some absences. We have seen that Balaguer sums up or presents the country in terms of territories (historic territories), institutions (historic institutions) and characters (historic characters). It is curious that such a radically historic list of names should feature nothing prior to the Middle Ages (neither Barcino nor Arabs nor Visigoths, nor even the first count of the Marches, up to Borrell) – nothing, then, prior to the moment at which Balaguer situates the start of a separate identity. It is also noteworthy that there is no reference to language (for us, today, a key element in any definition of Catalan identity), and that the Industrial Revolution might never have happened. On the other hand, there is a preliminary supposition that is not emphasised but is, nonetheless, highly significant: the equation of Barcelona and Catalonia. Balaguer 'writes' on the streets of Barcelona as he would write on the country; the history they contain is that of the country rather than strictly of the city (which is, then, equated with the country).

I mention a couple of significant absences and an a priori supposition in the plan. I will now add three operations that are complementary, though less discussed than the lesson in liberal Catalan nationalist history that is my initial conclusion. All three are underlying operations. The first is the radical secularization of the proposal (leaving behind, or to one side, the old town with its reams of saints and churches): the only religious street name in the Eixample area christened by Balaguer was Passeig de Sant Joan, which (like Passeig de Gràcia) is a name that existed beforehand. In the lengthy entry he devotes to this avenue in *Las calles de Barcelona*, the author includes not a hagiography but the chronicle of the events of 1714 and the construction of the Citadel that Balaguer had always fought, and that he was fighting to have demolished as a member of parliament at the time of writing his book. Second underlying operation: the powerful elegy to freedom that permeates the proposal. The moments and institutions chosen are those of the struggle for Catalan rights and for freedom; indeed, the history of Catalonia is identified with this fight for freedom. In Balaguer's words,

> la capital del Principado catalán, la antigua cuna y corte de los condes, conservó aun gran parte de su esplendidez y poderío

mientras le fueron conservadas sus insignes libertades. El día que estas cayeron rotas y destrozadas por la mano del verdugo, cayó con ellas Barcelona, como si esta ciudad no pudiera vivir más que respirando aires de libertad. (1865: 12)[4]

The third operation, as opposed to the defence made by others of a degree of concession to topography and a more clearly local reality, was an equally radical arbitrariness, in a magnificent example of top-down revolution, or late enlightened despotism (there again, what else was the approval of Cerdà's project?).

This is, then, a lasting lesson in toponymy, which has, interestingly, survived through thick and thin, including Francoism: as Joan Palomas writes, of the 48 street names attributable to Balaguer, a century and a half later, all remain except one, Wad-Ras, today Doctor Trueta; or two, if we include Enric Granados (renamed after the composer died in a tragic shipwreck, in 1916) instead of the former Universitat, the only name to refer to a nearby building (138). It is, then, a long, everyday lesson in history and self-assertion: a project in community cohesion put forward by a single individual, a new symbolic repertory based essentially on the past for a city and a society that aspired to be new.

Names that come and go

After the great urbanistic operation that was Ildefons Cerdà's project for the Eixample, the history and orography of Barcelona meant that there were few planned initiatives of the same scope until the 1992 Olympic Games. There were, however, major initiatives that involved giving new names to streets and squares that did not previously exist or that had no name, rather than changes of name for primarily political reasons: of this sort of change (also fascinating to study; see, for example, Fabre and Huertas), between 1863 and 1993 the city experienced a few. Though not the focus of this article, an emblematic

---

[4] In *Bellezas de la historia de Cataluña* Balaguer records his aspiration to recover the history 'de todo un país, la de toda una nación, la de toda una monarquía [...]. La historia de Cataluña es también la de Aragón, la de Valencia, la de Mallorca... y es también, no hay que dudarlo, la historia de la libertad de España' (1853: 3).

case of the influence of political circumstances on street names is that of the square at the junction of Diagonal and Carrer d'Urgell, on the outer edge of the Eixample. While still being developed, this square was named Alcalá Zamora (first president of the Second Spanish Republic) in 1932; next, in 1937, Plaça dels Germans Badia (Estat Català militants killed in April 1936); then, for a few months (when the Nationalist troops arrived), it was 'Plaza del Ejército Marroquí', and, from that same year, 1939, up until 1979, it was called 'Plaza de Calvo Sotelo'. Since the restoration of democracy it has borne its present-day name, Plaça de Francesc Macià.

As we know, the Francoist side 'purged' many of the street names in Catalan towns and villages of any suspected collusion with liberalism, Catalan nationalism or republicanism, as well as any words in Catalan, but it did not have an exclusive right to changes for ideological reasons: in November 1936, after the death of revolutionary syndicalist Buenaventura Durruti, an anarchist hero, his name was given to Via Laietana (built in 1908 in Ciutat Vella), which was then called Via Durruti. The Republican City Council then made the change official, and it remained until January 1939. But the city already had a Carrer Carles Marx, approved by the Republican Council in February 1931, alongside others dedicated to Salvador Seguí, Voltaire, and Francesc Ferrer i Guàrdia (Fabre and Huertas: 111). Nor were these fluctuations dependent solely on revolutions and dictatorships: at the time of writing, in 2016, Barcelona City Council has publicised its intention to erase or at least reduce the presence of monarchical (Bourbon) references in the city's list of street names.

The opportunity of Barcelona '92

Leaving to one side this excursus through the changes in existing street names for ideological reasons, we return to the city's second major urban planning operation involving the naming of a considerable number of 'new' streets. We take a leap of 130 years after the Eixample design, to the 1992 Olympic Games. The Games – which Pasqual Maragall called 'the Olympic catalyst' (165), in addition to opening the city up to the sea and making it possible to create the Ronda ring roads, involved the demolition and new construction of large areas of Poblenou and Vall d'Hebron and, in both cases, the City Council had to find names for the newly designed streets and squares.

In the last 25 years of the twentieth century, after the death of General Franco, the expected approval of the Metropolitan General Plan for Barcelona took place, in 1976. After the first democratic municipal elections in 1979, the city had a socialist council (Partit dels Socialistes de Catalunya). And there was an undisputed protagonist of much of what was to happen: Pasqual Maragall i Mira (born in 1942, grandson of Joan Maragall),[5] mayor of Barcelona from 1982 (after the resignation of Narcís Serra, who had been appointed Minister of Defence of Spain's first socialist government of democratic times) to 1997, when it was Maragall who stepped down to spend a sabbatical year in Rome before standing as candidate for the presidency of the Generalitat de Catalunya. Here was a mayor who was re-elected by the city people in 1983, in 1987, in 1991 and in 1995.

In Barcelona, street names are now decided by the Ponència del Nomenclàtor [Street Name Commission], a body that meets bimonthly, presided by a councillor and made up of a series of council experts. Until 1991, the president was councillor (and writer) Maria Aurèlia Capmany, who was succeeded on her death by the councillor (and historian) Joan Fuster i Sobrepere,[6] who had previously formed part of the Commission.

In autumn 1986, Barcelona was chosen to host the 1992 Summer Olympic Games. The amenities proposed in its candidature outlined four areas of urban planning intervention in the city: Montjuïc, Diagonal, Vall d'Hebron and Vila Olímpica (in Poblenou), the latter two requiring demolition and new street layouts, particularly in the case

---

5 The poet and thinker who called Barcelona 'the Great Enchantress' (in his 'Oda nova a Barcelona'). But who also in the same year – remember: the year of the Tragic Week – wrote 'La ciutat del perdó' [The city of pardon]. For the people of Barcelona, the Olympic Games, as Enric Bastardes points out, marked the shift from the mayor who was the grandson of Joan Maragall to the poet who was the grandfather of Pasqual Maragall (87).

6 Joan Fuster Sobrepere (Barcelona, 1955), graduate in Philosophy and PhD in History, editor of the magazine L'Avenç (1985–1988) and director of the Barcelona history seminar of the Arxiu Històric de la Ciutat (1999–2000). Between 1989 and 1999 he was a councillor of Barcelona City Council. He currently lectures at the Department of Arts and Humanities at the Universitat Oberta de Catalunya.

of the Vila Olímpica.[7] What criteria did the Ponència del Nomenclàtor apply to decide on new names? According to Fuster Sobrepere, in the case of the Vila Olímpica, the issue was whether to continue

> the outline of the Eixample and, accordingly, extend the names of the streets in the Eixample, or should we have a christening process like Víctor Balaguer's? And what the Mayor says is: 'Wow, this is an opportunity for our generation that we'll never have again. Listen, to hell with the names in the Eixample, let's use street names to explain things'. But the proposal comes from the Commission. So, what is the idea behind it? [..] The idea is to commemorate the generation that was the missing link in the chain of Catalan culture after the war. (Fuster Sobrepere interview, 2013)[8]

Let us see how this idea took form on the map of the new district of Vila Olímpica (Figure 3.2), erected where, not long previously, warehouses and factories had stood, and very close to where, in an ironic twist of fate, in 1846 a small group of followers of Étienne Cabet had settled to live in community (for them, for some time, Poblenou was called Icària; and for them, the old Camí del Cementiri was Avinguda d'Icària, a name that Francoism replaced with Avenida del Capitán López Varela and which the democratic City Council restored in 1978).[9] Returning to the Vila Olímpica, a Mayor's Decree of 2 December 1992 approved the names of Plaça dels Voluntaris

---

[7] 'Some major decisions that had to be taken to make the Olympic bid possible have been taken. Starting with the urban development planning of the Poble Nou area in keeping with the project for the Vila Olímpica. The Spanish government, the Generalitat, the City Council, RENFE and the companies affected have been able to agree on an urban design which would not otherwise have had this drive and this specific timeframe' (Maragall: 173).

[8] All the citations of Joan Fuster Sobrepere are taken from an interview with him conducted on 4 April 2013. I would like to thank him for his availability, his comments and his help.

[9] Cabet's utopian corner of Barcelona was assigned names such as those of Anselm Clavé, Abdó Terrades and Narcís Monturiol (who in 1847 signed the translation of *El viaje a Icaria*, with F. J. Orellana, and was responsible for the weekly publications *La Fraternidad* and *El Padre de Familia*, organs of the self-proclaimed social revolution).

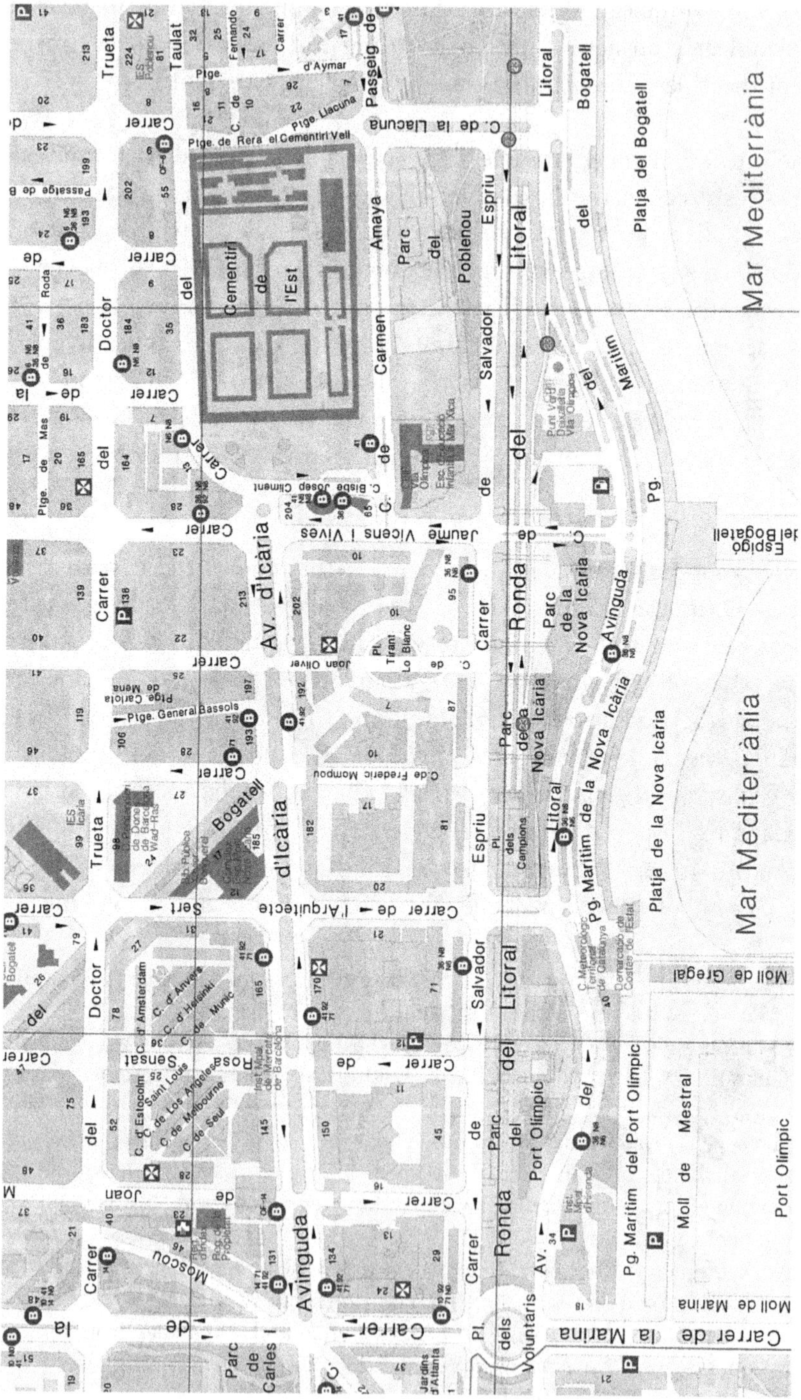

84   City, history, and territory

Figure 3.2 The new district of Vila Olímpica
Institut Cartogràfic de Catalunya

Olímpics, Carrer del Doctor Trueta, Carrer de Salvador Espriu, Carrer de l'Arquitecte Sert, Carrer de Joan Miró, Carrer de Joan Oliver, Carrer de Rosa Sensat and Plaça dels Campions. Shortly afterwards, a Mayor's Decree of 19 January 1993 approved the names of Carrer de Jaume Vicens Vives, and Moscou, Estocolm, Amsterdam, Anvers, Hèlsinki, Munic, Sant Louis, Los Angeles, Melbourne, and Seul (all, except Moscou, concentrated in the double city block bounded by Joan Miró, Arquitecte Sert, Avinguda Icària and Doctor Trueta): the ten Olympic cities that did not yet have a Barcelona street named after them. Subsequently, on 24 March 1994, Carrer de Frederic Mompou was approved (an extension of Carrer d'Àlaba, parallel to Arquitecte Sert, heading towards the river Besòs).

This left the district of Vall d'Hebron, where the number of new streets to be named was much less. Specifically, on 8 February 1993 the Municipal Council approved three (Jordi Rubió i Balaguer, Joan Cornudella and Josep Pallach) and, on 10 March 1993, Arquitecte Moragas. When I interviewed him, former councillor Joan Fuster i Sobrepere told me there was no strong political opposition to the proposed names for the Vila Olímpica (the Partit Popular municipal group was then headed by Alejo Vidal-Quadras but led de facto by Alberto Fernández Díaz), partly because the names were well chosen, but some were left over, which were then 'taken to' Vall d'Hebron.[10]

10 In the interview, Joan Fuster Sobrepere says: 'this is where we brought in Rubió Balaguer, who we hadn't been able to "fit in" at the bottom... It's also true that he would have been harder to explain, because he was less known than those other names we mentioned, less universal. Antoni de Moragas, Moragas the architect, who was the foremost personality of Grup R (well, perhaps not the foremost: the foremost was Coderch, but Coderch was a Falangist): Moragas was someone who, as President of the Architects' Association, was in La Caputxinada and a liberal, a figure in the resistance to Francoism and someone who picked up the ideas of the GATCPAC [Grup d'Arquitectes i Tècnics Catalans per al Progrés de l'Arquitectura Contemporània]. He was a man of the opposition: he was at the lock-in at Montserrat, he was fined as president of the Association... Then the other one is Joan Cornudella. We made the most of the occasion to put in two politicians of the resistance, the biggest: Pallach and Cornudella. Why Pallach and Cornudella? Because they were the ones who were dead. Cornudella was secretary general of Estat Català during the war. Estat Català had broken away from Esquerra, and he is someone who in the year '40 came back as secretary of Estat Català and founded the Front Nacional de Catalunya.

Both the formulation of the approach ('an attempted manifesto of the names that kept Catalan culture alive in those 40 years') and the choice of the specific names for the new streets in the Vila Olímpica, with the remainder for Vall d'Hebron, are due to the councillor Joan Fuster i Sobrepere:

> For me, what comes to mind is La Caputxinada.[11] I think of that presidency of La Caputxinada with Doctor Rubió i Espriu. Don't ask me why. It's really obvious: the presidency of La Caputxinada. Initially, that's what I think, but then there's an evolution of the idea that led to 'It has to represent culture in its various forms'. This is a bit eclectic, because ultimately it's not the generation of '36, either; some are older, some are younger, but there's a poet (that's Espriu), there's a historian and then some (because Vicens is an influence, he's important as a historian but he's more important as the last person to have conceived of a 'Greater Catalanism', so to speak); there's a musician, that's Mompou; there's a visual artist, that's Miró; there's an architect, that's Sert, all of them with an international component, and there's a scientist, that's Trueta. I think that's it… Oh, sorry: then of course there's Rosa Sensat. There weren't any women, and also education had been a central aspect, the movements of educational reform were as important to cultural resistance as Espriu, as Miró, as a symbol… (Fuster Sobrepere, interview with the author, 4 April 2013)

And working for the British, he's someone who throughout the war, from '40 to '45, was the lifeblood of a network to get British pilots who made it into French territory out to Gibraltar, get them over the Pyrenees. He was in contact with British intelligence services. But apart from that, he's someone who spent time in prison, he was back in the country by 1940 […]. And then Pallach was Pallach. He was the other person in the resistance who also came back to Catalonia in '43, and in '44 he founded the Moviment Socialista de Catalunya. So then, two activists, two people who very quickly returned to rebuild the resistance, the two leaders of the Consell de Forces Polítiques de Catalunya of 1974–1976 who, by then, had died'.

11 Constituent assembly of the Democratic Students Union held in March 1966 in the Capuchin convent in Sarrià, Barcelona, attended by a large number of students, lecturers, intellectuals, and activists of the opposition to Francoism. It ended with a police raid and hundreds of arrests.

According to the former councillor's explanations, the choice was broad-based (with no ideological bias) and circumstantial (associated with the window of opportunity offered by Olympic construction). This seems to hold fairly true for the case of Vila Olímpica, but there is more of a bias in the case of Vall d'Hebron. And a review of the names approved in previous years for spaces not always directly linked with the Olympics, though sometimes with infrastructures that might be associated with the Games, serves to relativize this broad-based approach: as far back as 1984, the controversial Plaça de Karl Marx had been approved (accompanied, however, by another, smaller square, in memory of John F. Kennedy); in 1990, Plaça de Buenaventura Durruti (we have seen how he briefly had a street named after him during the war) and Carrer de Víctor Jara and Carrer de l'Abat Escarré; in 1991, Plaça de Palestina, 'Plaça Roja' [Red Square] in Ciutat Meridiana (in this case to consolidate a name used by local residents) and streets named after Pablo Iglesias, Batista i Roca, Rafael Campalans, and the Madres de Plaza de Mayo; in 1992, Plaça d'Olaff Palme and Carrer de Haifa (there was also, it should be noted, Plaça del Tirant lo Blanc – to mark the fifth centenary – and carrers de Robert Gerhard and Ricard Zamora). I asked Joan Fuster i Sobrepere whether Carrer de Carmen Amaya (the southern boundary of Poblenou cemetery, approved on 3 December 1993), was part of the Olympic package, and he said no, that was a different operation.

Continuities of Catalan culture

We have seen how the naming of streets generated by the construction of Olympic Barcelona responds to institutional planning and to the idea (as with Víctor Balaguer) of using the list of street names to write a manifesto. What, precisely, was this manifesto? It was the manifesto of the continuity of Catalan culture. Fuster Sobrepere further links it to a vision which, for Pasqual Maragall, went beyond the city:

> The political project that he had at that time, which was a project to regenerate Catalan nationalism, because he thought that Pujolism had not, for whatever reason, according to his diagnosis, been that inspiration. So he thought: 'This is the country!'

Somehow, it's the country we'd have wanted, it represents the country we'd have wanted to have. Of course, the reality is always a little less than the symbols, but if in '79 or '78 or '77, they'd asked us 'What country would you like to build?', we'd have said 'The country of these people'. (Fuster Sobrepere interview with the author, 4 April 2013)

This analysis and declaration of intentions coincides fully with Donald McNeill's 'What had to be re-asserted after the hiatus of the dictatorship was this role [of Barcelona] as a citadel and promoter of democratic values, so important to Maragall's vision of how the city fitted into Catalonia, Spain and Europe' (146). We must not forget that we are talking about the same mayor (and the same municipal team) who, in the course of these years, was to promote the reconstruction of Mies van der Rohe's Germany Pavilion for the 1929 Barcelona International Exposition (unveiled on Montjuïc, practically in situ, in 1986) and of the Pavilion of the Spanish Republic for the 1937 International Exposition in Paris, designed by Josep Lluís Sert and Luis Lacasa (inaugurated in Vall d'Hebron in 1992). For Pasqual Maragall, the city (which he regarded as a space of experimentation) is key to communitarian cultural and political identity: 'The citizen – as a part of his or her social contract with the state – is entitled to be able to "read" the city, rather than being "lost in a landscape you cannot understand". In other words, a responsibility of the state is to provide legibility' (McNeill: 145). But Maragall wanted to do this at municipal level, because he considered that the problems of poor urban quality were unlikely to be resolved by the state: 'The kind of urban planning problems that involve careful stitches and invisible mending can only be addressed at ground level, can only be carried out from the bottom' (Bastardes: 100).

In this way, the city seen as a monumental slate, as a symbolic and educational echo chamber, takes the form, in the case of Maragall and Fuster Sobrepere, of a lesson about recent history, a lesson in resisting and overcoming (Francoism and exile), in resilience and excellence. Furthermore, it turns out that this naming of streets in the late twentieth century – and this is important to note – repeats the three underlying operations outlined in the case of the Eixample and Víctor Balaguer: secularization, an elegy of freedom and arbitrariness. Accompanying it was the reproduction of an imaginary which, obviously, no longer corresponded to the Renaixença, but to the country that Barcelona's socialists, with Maragall at the forefront, would have wanted to have or to build if the Civil War, followed by the long, long post-war years, had not happened.

The idea expressed by former councillor Joan Fuster i Sobrepere, that the choice of the street names for Vila Olímpica (and also Vall d'Hebron) was a decision to write the 'manifesto of the continuity of Catalan culture', may be closer to the truth than he thought: the streets named after Doctor Trueta, Salvador Espriu, Arquitecte Sert, Joan Miró, Joan Oliver, Rosa Sensat, and Frederic Mompou (and Jordi Rubió i Balaguer, Arquitecte Moragas, Josep Pallach, and Joan Cornudella) speak to us of the continuity of Catalan culture after the hiatus of Francoism, but they speak too of the continuity of the *renaixentista* gesture, of the preservation (a long century and several currents of thought later) of a determination to build, on the map, a new 'conjunto general, histórico y armónico' seen as a celebration and recognition of recent examples of collective dignity, 'como si esta ciudad no pudiera vivir más que respirando aires de libertad'. It is the echo chamber and the 'present past' referred to by George Steiner, with a twofold resonance, immediate and mediated. If the 'living chronicle' of the Eixample tells of what has been (honouring and legitimating the city as a capital and Catalonia as a country), the living chronicle of the Olympic areas in Poblenou and Vall d'Hebron tells of what we would like the country and the city to have been: a *meta-chronicle* pieced together, in this case, by some of the names that allowed Catalan culture to survive, once more, with a degree of dignity.

Works cited

Auster, Paul (1985). *City of Glass* (London Faber & Faber).
Azaryahu, Maoz (1996). 'The Power of Commemorative Street Names'. *Environment and Planning D: Society and Space* 14(3): 311–30.
Balaguer, Víctor (1853). *Bellezas de la historia de Cataluña* (Barcelona: Imprenta de Narciso Ramírez).
— (1865–1866). *Las calles de Barcelona. Origen de sus nombres...*, 3 vols (Barcelona: Salvador Manero).
— (1899). *Historias y leyendas. Obras de Víctor Balaguer*, XXXVII (Madrid: Imprenta de la viuda de M. Minuesa de los Ríos).

Bastardes, Enric (1987). 'Entrevista a Pasqual Maragall: de la ciutat dels prodigis a la ciutat del futur'. *L'Opinió Socialista. Revista Política i de Pensament*, 5: 87–100.

Carreras y Candi, Francesch (1916). *Geografia general de Catalunya. La ciutat de Barcelona* (Barcelona: Albert Martín).

Cuccu, Marina (2008). 'Las calles de Barcelona de Víctor Balaguer', *Barcelona Quaderns d'Història*, 14: 147–61.

Fabre, Jaume, and Josep Maria Huertas (1982). *Carrers de Barcelona, com han evolucionat els seus noms* (Barcelona: Edhasa).

Fradera, Josep Maria (2001). 'Visibilitat i invisibilitat de Víctor Balaguer', *L'Avenç*, 262: 19–26.

— (2009). *La pàtria dels catalans. Història, política, cultura* (Barcelona: La Magrana).

Grau, Ramon (2009). 'El saintsimonisme: horitzó ideològic d'Ildefons Cerdà', in Teresa Navas, *La política pràctica, Cerdà i la Diputació de Barcelona* (Barcelona: Diputació de Barcelona), 73–80.

Maragall, Pasqual (1986). *Refent Barcelona* (Barcelona: Planeta).

McNeill, Donald (2005). *Urban Change and the European Left. Tales from the New Barcelona* (London: Routledge).

Michonneau, Stéphanne (2001). *Barcelona: memòria i identitat. Monuments, commemoracions i mites* (Vic: EUMO Editorial).

Palomas i Moncholí, Joan (2004). *Víctor Balaguer. renaixença, revolució i progrés* (Vilanova i la Geltrú: El Cep i la Nansa).

Quintana, Lluís (2006). 'Una proposta historiogràfica en pedra: las calles de Barcelona de Víctor Balaguer', in Ramon Panyella and Jordi Marrugat (eds), *L'escriptor i la seva imatge. Contribució a la història dels intel·lectuals en la literatura catalana contemporània* (Barcelona: L'Avenç), 34–61.

Rose-Redwood, Reuben S. (2008). '"Sixth Avenue is now a Memory": Regimes of Spatial Inscription and the Performative Limits of the Official City-text'. *Political Geography*, 27(8): 875–94.

Steiner, George (2015). *The Idea of Europe* (New York: Overlook Duckworth).

CHAPTER FOUR

'The asylum of modern times': Barcelona and Europe*

Felipe Fernández-Armesto

Veig allà el Pirineu amb ses neus somrosades
i al davant Catalunya tota estesa als seus peus,
i m'en vaig.
[I see the Pyrenees, the gilded peaks of snow,
and all of Catalonia, stretched out at their feet,
And I feel drawn.]
(Joan Maragall, 'Oda Nova a Barcelona')

Africa begins at the Pyrenees.   (Attributed to Pascal)

---

* This is an abridged version, approved by the author, of a chapter in Felipe Fernández-Armesto, *Barcelona. A Thousand Years of the City's Past* (Oxford University Press, 1992). © Felipe Fernández Armesto.

Europe and Spain

'You could say that Barcelona does not belong to Spain', wrote Jaume Balmes, 'but is more like something imported from Belgium or England' (972–73[1]). Balmes was an arch-conservative who distrusted northern Liberalism and his remark was not entirely complimentary, but it reflected a perception of Barcelona as a 'European city' which almost every citizen would have shared by the mid-nineteenth century, when the remark was made. It remains an almost universal assumption about Barcelona - practically a badge of Barcelonese identity - to the present day. Yet the notion of a 'European Barcelona' is a truism redeemed by a mistake: it relies for its force on a presumed distinction between Barcelona and the rest of Spain - or, at least, the rest of Spain, less Catalonia. Barcelona is deemed to be European because Spain is thought of as an extra-European culture. If 'Africa begins at the Pyrenees', or if Spain is 'Europe's Tibet' - if, in short, in the words of the old tourist-board slogan, 'Spain is different' - then Barcelona's assumption of a European identity gives the city a peculiar status and a special role. Events in our own time, however, seem to be exposing the notion of the 'differentness' of Spain as a historical myth.

The conviction that Spain does not 'belong' to European culture began - though like any similar thesis about another European country it can be justified by reference to earlier texts - in the nineteenth century. It may originally have been a foreign conceit. The cult of the picturesque peddled abroad the vision of romantic engravers, in which Spain was an exotic and archaic land, peopled by swart gypsies inhabiting Moorish ruins. Spanish intellectuals peered with delight into the supposed cultural cleft. For those on the political right a 'different' Spain was a vindication of distinctively Spanish virtues, which the materialists and heretics beyond the Pyrenees threatened to pollute. For those on the left, the image was equally welcome as an explanation of Spain's 'backwardness' and hostility to progress. The world of Spanish intellectual debate became divided between *europeizadores*, who clamoured for more European influence, and *hispanizadores*, who defended Spain's impoverished chastity. Adored by one party, abhorred by the other, the myth was believed by both. It

---

1 Unless otherwise stated, all translations are by the author.

became entrenched in Spanish historiography as historians confronted the most conspicuous problem of the Spanish past: that of why the makers of the world's first great maritime empire - a captive market of unparalleled dimensions as well as an achievement of breathtaking prowess - should largely have failed to share in the commercial and industrial revolutions that accompanied 'the expansion of Europe'. This problem - called or confused with 'the decline of Spain' - could be 'solved' by a nice bit of semantic magic; if commerce and industry were classified as European activities, and Spain were docketed as a non-European land, the demonstration could be regarded as neatly complete. As Barcelona rapidly became Spain's major industrial centre, the same reasoning fed Barcelonese convictions and political claims, culminating in Almirall's exasperated cry for Catalonia to leave Spain in the interests of progress.

What made Spain different was a matter of debate, but three elements of her historical experience have commonly been alleged in explanation. The first two rely on the effects of the Moorish presence, which has often been represented as so pervasive and so enduring as to make Spain an honorary oriental land which has somehow got washed up on the wrong shore of the Mediterranean. Moorish settlement is commonly envisaged as carpeting Spain, at least to the Duero and the Ebro, like the dense pile of an oriental rug. Moorish culture is thought of as 'superior' to anything the Christians could produce; and Spain's beauties, as well as her vices, are frequently attributed to oriental influence. I have encountered scholarship which attributes almost every innovation in Spanish art, from Romanesque sculpture to hispano-flemish architecture, to Moorish inspiration or craftsmanship. The learned editor of a 1909 edition of Richard Ford's *Gatherings from Spain* found evidence of the exotic strain in the Spanish character in the fact that the trains failed to run on time. For a long time, it was foreigners, not Spaniards themselves, who detected this eastern flavour. It probably originated in early-modern Italian abuse, reproaching Spaniards' alleged impurities of blood. In the last century, it was popular with travellers who judged Spain on the basis of an acquaintance with Andalusia, where most Moorish survivals are concentrated. Since 1942, however, when Américo Castro published an impressive version of the fabric of Spanish history, woven, as it were from three equal strands - Christian, Moorish and Jewish - a veritable school of Spanish historians, supported from America, France and Britain, has devoted itself to the search for the Moors' cultural legacy (Castro; Gómez-Martínez).

There was a time when I was of their persuasion. As a young researcher working in the Archivo General de Indias in Seville in 1972, I lived in a piece of folded corrugated tin on top of a pension in the old Jewish quarter. From there I could look out at night over the tangled street plan of the old *aljama* to the Almohad minaret, below the cathedral belfry, and the flying buttresses of the vast cathedral that aggressively proclaims the success of the Christian Reconquest. I could feel that these three ingredients of Spanish culture - Jewish, Moorish and Christian - were spread before me: the three strands of Spanish history, woven into the texture of a city. Long study and experience have now convinced me that the Moorish contribution is conspicuous only by its paucity. The magic carpet of Moorish settlement was patchy and threadbare. Moorish Spain clung to the eastern and southern coasts, to the Ebro and Guadalquivir valleys and to a few inland towns and uplands. The Moors were a disparate crowd whose numbers have never been convincingly calculated nor their composition clearly analysed. They included Islamized natives and the assimilated descendants of east European slaves. The Berbers may have been a smaller category than either of these. Pure Arabs were a tiny group - perhaps 50,000 strong - whose immigration was confined to the eighth century and who disappeared thereafter into the mélange of natives and migrants. There was never a census of the Moors until the expulsion of their last identifiable descendants in the early seventeenth century; this yielded an unreliable tally of about 275,000, which cannot be projected back because of the chequered demographic history of communities which seem to have declined from the mid-thirteenth century onwards, then to have surged ahead in the sixteenth. It would be rash to suppose that the Moorish population of Spain was ever very numerous - perhaps as little as five per cent, probably no more than ten per cent at its height, though all assumptions are risky.

The enduring Moorish presence was, moreover, narrowly circumscribed. In most parts of the peninsula Moorish communities lasted no longer than in Sicily or Apulia. Only Granada and Valencia remained in any sense Moorish lands for longer, and they were important but peripheral kingdoms, whose places in Spain suggest comparison with those of Turkmenia, say, or Kazakhstan in Russia. Until 1578, when Morisco communities were resettled all over Spain, most Spaniards probably never saw a Moor, except in the romantic versions offered by novelists and poets. Demographic importance can be ascribed to the Moors only by an act of imagination, and cultural superiority only by a subjective judgement. Caliphal art was cannibalistic and that of the Nasrids - from some points of view - decadent. Until the rather phoney Mauresque revival of the last century, which was as strong in Barcelona as anywhere, most patrons of art in Christian Spain avoided Moorish taste - except in the form of some decorative arts where the Moorish legacy is not peculiar to Spain but common to much of the Mediterranean. Spanish languages - especially their poetic and technical vocabularies - have inherited a lot of Arabic terms, which are evidence of the scale of Moorish contributions to particular fields but are not on their own enough to justify the traditional generalizations.

The second explanation of Spain's 'differentness' treats the Moor as other, rather than brother, but still exaggerates his importance. In this traditional Spanish reading of the Spanish past, Spain's distinctive historical experience was the Reconquest and Spanish identity was forged in the white heat of a long crusade, begun almost at the moment of Moorish invasion in 711 and sustained, with checks and interruptions, of course, but without essential mutation or substitution of 'spirit', until the fall of Granada in 1492 (Sánchez-Albornoz). In reality, conquests from the Moors were the work of widely interspersed bouts of phrenesis in the tenth, eleventh, thirteenth and fifteenth centuries. No ideological continuity underlay these fitful and hesitant encounters, though the idea of 'reconquest' of unjustly usurped lands can be found as a source of legitimation in some texts. Nor did the occasional violence normally depend on awareness of differences of religion, though at a late stage the example of the crusades may have spawned some real odium. In most encounters, there were Muslims and Christians on both sides. The conventional hero of the Reconquest myth, El Cid, spent as much time, after his exile from Castile, fighting for Muslims as for Christian masters. It would be no more convincing to portray Spain as the product of conflict between Christians and Moors than, for instance, to see Britain as the result of the struggle between Saxons and Celts, or Germany of that between Teutons and Slavs. The conflictive model of the Spanish Middle Ages was invented in modern times, when the Moor became the epitype of the enemy. He was never the prototype.

The third explanation of the supposed distinctiveness of Spain attributes it not to any historical experience but to autochthonous national 'character' inherited from a pre-Celtic 'Iberian' population (Sánchez-Albornoz, I: 131–33; cf. Castro: 135–41). This theory seems to belong to the context of nineteenth-century nationalism, animated by a desire to emphasize distinctions, which were often feeble and usually invidious, between racial or linguistic groups. Apart from its inherent improbability, it suffers from two main defects: lack of evidence that the 'Iberians' ever existed, and lack of means by which their legacy, if any, might be supposed to have been transmitted. The evidence in favour of the Iberians consists of mentions of the name in Roman texts and some cultural peculiarities, mainly detectable in art forms, at some pre-Roman peninsular sites. But the Romans were glib taxonomists and it is not clear what meaning they attached to the term or whether, in Roman times, 'Iberians' were thought of as belonging to a different classification from 'Celts'. Evidence of a distinctive 'Iberian' room of the Archaeological Museum of Madrid leaves the visitor dazzled by the splendours of a lost civilization, which produced the elaborately coiffured and attired female stone figures of Baza and Elche, the lions and tapering 'pyramid' of Pozo Moro, the delicately wrought gold candlesticks of Lebrija. But these effects could have been produced by the interplay of eastern Mediterranean influences on indigenous culture. They are all very late, of the sixth to the third centuries BC. No evidence has yet been found that Spanish cultures developed any features that distinguish them from those of other western European peoples before the first millennium BC.

However the 'differentness' of Spain is characterized, it looks like an increasingly unhelpful description today, when the syncopations that made Spanish history seem out of step with that of other western European countries in the last century are over and done with. All the big historic communities of which western Europe is composed now seem to have gone through similar historical experiences, though without perfect synchronisation. In as much as one can talk about a 'typical' western European past, Spain has had it: a pre-Roman Celtic culture; a Roman conquest; an impressively thorough Romanization; barbarian invasions which led to the creation of sub-Roman states by relatively small migrant élites, who included the Moors; medieval *Staatsbildung* by means of the dynamic expansion of initially small political centres; the 'unification' of what was to become 'national' territory within frontiers which were determined by a combination of geography and dynastic accident with the limitations imposed by the formation of other strong states nearby; the creation of what was in effect a single and unitary state in tension with separatist or devolutionist tendencies at the periphery; colonial expansion overseas, followed by the traumatic severance of empire; the conflict of 'constitutionalist' and 'absolutist' politics, ending at last in the triumph of the former; industrialization; and the rise of parliamentary democracy.

These experiences have not necessarily happened in the same order or at the same times all over western Europe: Spain's imperial experience came relatively early; her industrialization took relatively long. But all the other states in the area have had their own departures from the same general pattern: England's constitutional conflicts were resolved relatively early; Germany and Italy took a relatively long time to develop unitary states. Spain looked odd in the nineteenth century because of her banana politics and backward economy; progressive constitutional development was frequently sent out of line by violent interventions and coups; periods of stability were dominated by cliques and bosses. In the last century Spain continued for a long time to appear out of step, because of her neutrality in the world wars, her exclusion from the post-war democratic clubs and her late seduction by consumerism. Now, however, it is hard to detect any 'differentness' greater than that which distinguishes other member-states of the European Community from one another. What one might call the 'normalization' of Spain has not been suddenly contrived, but was anticipated by much of previous Spanish history. General Franco, the self-proclaimed guardian of 'Hispanic' values, probably did as much to perfect it as any individual in his lifetime, by hectically promoting industrial activity and consumer habits while committing Spain to a future of partnership with western democracies. In partial consequence, Spain's democratic institutions today are not only abreast of those of other member-states of the European Union, but actually ahead: Spain's devolved system of regional government could become a model for the constitutional development of states, like the United Kingdom, which enclose a number of historic ethnicities or regions with divergent interests; it could even be the blueprint for a European super-state of the future.

Where does this 'European' Spain leave Barcelona? In the past, Catalans have seemed to see themselves as happy observers on a European shore, while the rest of Spain drifted off, perhaps to some Atlantic destiny as part of an imagined Hispanic identity, perhaps back to supposed African or oriental origins. That is no longer a convincing perception. Most Barcelonese intellectuals, however, could never be satisfied with the knowledge that they are European only or chiefly by virtue of being Spanish. They can take some comfort from the prospect that in a future 'Europe of regions', Catalonia's distinct identity could be enhanced as a result of Spain's assimilation by a super-state. For the loss of her claim to a uniquely European heritage in Spain, Barcelona could be compensated with the status of a European regional capital. If that proves insufficient, the Barcelonese can reformulate their historic claim; Barcelona can be seen as unique, not in having a European character - for that is common to the whole of Spain - but in always having embraced European identity with enthusiasm and conviction.

The Gothic tradition

Barcelona certainly has a convincingly European look. Part of this comes from the grandeur of scale and geometrical precision of the urbanizations of the late nineteenth and early twentieth centuries, which remind the reader of the rationalizations and extensions of the street plans of Paris and Vienna. A further contribution to the same impression is made by the copious surviving modernist ornament that clothes the streets in the first great international style of the twentieth century. Anyone who has entered a Parisian Metro station under Horta ironwork or sat in Glasgow on a Mackintosh chair, or taken coffee in an art nouveau café in Brussels or a Secessionist *Konditorei* in Vienna, would have been able to feel at home in Barcelona before the First World War. Few other Spanish cities have much of this sort of finery, and Barcelona's 'European' character must therefore be explored through her architectural traditions and her decorative arts.

Of the various international styles that have captivated Barcelonese architects and adorned the streets, Gothic has contributed most, perhaps, to the look and reputation of the city and has done as much as any other, until the present century, to give Barcelona a European air. For though it is commonly asserted - with the architect Gaudí it was virtually a faith - that Barcelona's Gothic is of a special 'Mediterranean' kind which contrives dim interiors and dramatic external shadows, the fact is that Gothic is a trans-Pyrenean style, transmitted to Spain from France. It never took root in Italy, except in the consciously 'European' Milan, and in Spain the great High Gothic cathedrals of Burgos, León and Toledo were all created by the imaginations of patrons who had studied in Paris. Barcelona is known in Spain as the Gothic city par excellence and is uniquely Gothic in two respects: nowhere, in so concentrated a space, are High Gothic buildings so numerous; nowhere did the Gothic tradition last so long or undergo so many faithful revivals. The survival and revival of Gothic in Barcelona is particularly conspicuous in the Catalan setting, because Catalonia's greatest medieval buildings, in the rest of the principality, are Romanesque.

The durability of Barcelona's Gothic look was accompanied by resistance to periods of neo-classicism. No writer of eighteenth-century Barcelona was more loyal to the Enlightenment than Antoni de Capmany; yet none was more eloquent in the defence of Gothic architecture. His aesthetics were projected directly from the streets and shapes of his native city. Gothic was superior to 'Greek' for height and sense of space. It created spaces suited to meditation and 'secret reverence'. Neo-classical buildings, however mature, always seemed brash; by Gothic alone a sense of the past could be conveyed - 'a sort of delicious sorrow [...] best for the noble seriousness of a place of worship' (Capmany: 918–21). Like Capmany, the Valencian Antoni Ponz (1725–1792) made his career in Madrid, where he was secretary of the painters' academy. When he visited Barcelona in maturity to inventory the property of the expelled Jesuits, he was disgusted by the intrusion of Baroque altars into the aisle chapels of Barcelona Cathedral. 'It would have been better not to have made them, since, as far as artistic criteria are concerned, the money spent on them was wasted and the church uglified' (Duràn i Sanpere: 362; Ponz: 14). His dislike of the altars was in part a neo-classical reaction in favour of stylistic chastity and restraint, but his main concern was for the unity of the Gothic building. Barcelonese fidelity to Gothic is more remarkable when one recalls how it went on in defiance of prevailing taste. Within a few years of the publication of Ponz's description, Milan Cathedral, which had survived the Renaissance with its Gothic character not just preserved but enhanced, was defaced with neo-classical architraves on the west front for Napoleon's coronation as King of Italy.

Loyalty to Gothic tradition was threatened with suspension in the early nineteenth century, when Barcelona's enthusiastic espousal of a struggle for constitutional liberties seemed to demand 'enlightened' townscaping. In 1823, when the French invaded in support of absolutism, it was an act of political defiance to drive the carrer de Ferran through the old town to link up with one of Barcelona's three other straight streets. To name the new street after the king, whom constitutionalists had temporarily adopted, willy-nilly, as the figurehead of 'national' resistance, seemed ironic when he abolished the constitution for the second time. From the Rambla, the street led to the civic centre, the plaça de Sant Jaume, where the façade of the town hall looks down at a neo-classical enclave in the Gothic empire of the old town. At the time the façade was built, between 1830 and 1855, Barcelona was fighting Carlism - Spain's Jacobite-like movement of romantic reaction - as well as centralization; liberalism was too strong, for the moment, for traditional taste to prevail. A church and a cemetery made way to improve the view. Even here, however, antiquarianism triumphed over progress and the Gothic over the neoclassical. A lobby led by Piferrer and Pi i Margall saved the Gothic interiors and north-side façade from destruction; the niches intended for Hercules and Minerva were occupied instead by statues of Jaume I - a reminder of the imperial power of medieval Barcelona - and Joan Fiveller, a semi-legendary town councillor of the fifteenth century whose intransigence had supposedly compelled a king of Castilian origin to pay a municipal tax on fish consumed by his retinue (Duràn i Sanpere: 288–89).

The reaction against classicism began as soon as the new city hall was built. In 1845, the most promising young talent among the architects of Barcelona, Elies Rogent, burned his copy of Vignola's classical manual of instruction. Influenced by the wider European romantic movement, inspired with the idealization of the Catalan past by the Renaixença writers and the poets of the Jocs Florals, he immersed himself in the study of medieval architecture. Out of his work on the restoration of the monastery of Ripoll emerged the idea for his neo-Romanesque university building of 1860, where the harmony of the inspiration of tradition with the ideal of progress was symbolized by the exposed cast-iron columns of the library. In Barcelona, though Romanesque and Mauresque styles were also cultivated, medieval models necessarily meant Gothic ones. When, for example, a competition was held for a design for the west front of the cathedral in 1882, a Gothic design was decided on in advance. Tortosa and Girona had classical façades, but Barcelona was to remain true to its Gothic tradition and self-perception. Conservatism was the chapter's only criterion in selecting the successful design. Josep Oriol Mestres and August Font won the competition because their project most closely resembled the unexecuted fifteenth-century designs of a French master, though the public seems to have preferred Joan Martorell's florid conception, which was very high and omitted the rose window (Duràn i Sanpere: 332–33). When Gaudí was invited to take over the church of the Sagrada Família in 1884, a Gothic design had already been decided on.

A Gothic idiom therefore dominated the language of Barcelonese architecture when Elies Rogent began to gather a team of young architects to design the buildings for the great exhibition of 1888. The most influential member of the team was Lluís Domènech i Muntaner (1850–1923), a major figure in Catalanist politics - he became President of the Lliga and was twice elected to parliament - as well as the designer of some of the most original buildings of his day in Barcelona. His contribution to the designs for the exhibition was inspired by the 'search for a national architecture' which he had announced some years before; his formula for achieving this involved mixing Gothic structures and Romanesque details with fairly bold Mauresque decoration. The grandest of the temporary edifices of 1888, the Hotel Internacional, had florid castellations, square corner towers with tall clerestories and, on the ground floor, a glazed arcade of arches of Mughal flavour. The only permanent building was the café known as the Castell dels Tres Dragons, to which Domènech gave a strongly Mauresque appeal in the splayed battlements and romantic minaret: the bleak façades probably owe less to 'functionalism' than to lack of time and money for Domènech's usual reckless use of ornament; its future as a home for a collective workshop of art and crafts ensured that the building would be something of a cynosure for artists into the new century. It now houses part of the zoo.

The effect of the work for Rogent and Domènech was to open Barcelonese architecture, in a period of prolific building, to a comprehensive range of medieval influences. The Gothic tradition remained strongest, however; Puig i Cadafalch was a faithful successor to Rogent and Domènech - the historian of Catalonian Romanesque, the presiding genius of the Catalan movement. In the years when art nouveau and Expressionism were bending the forms of Barcelonese building out of the Gothic line, he punctured the Barcelona skyline with spikes and angles, spires and pinnacles and battlements. In the period after the First World War, a fashion for Mediterranean traditions interrupted the era of Gothic predominance, but Gaudí's perseverance with the Sagrada Família ensured that the most conspicuous monument of the period - with the cluster of fantastically elongated, slightly concave spires that became the indelible symbol of Barcelona - would fix a Gothic image of the city in the minds of all educated people. Gaudí's pupil, Joan Rubió i Bellver, who built the Gothic bridge of sighs over the carrer del Bisbe in 1926, actually proposed a remodelling of the city centre to enhance its Gothic flavour.

Creative bad taste

Rubió was a Gothic purist, but most of the other leading figures in Barcelona's Gothic revivals were interested in other historic vocabularies that had elements in common with Gothic: Romanesque, because it was a style of enormous regional importance represented by the most admired monuments of rural Catalonia; Mauresque because it was a Spanish form, legitimized in Barcelona by Domènech i Muntaner and Gaudí. Gothic also had a further property as an international style characteristic of northern Europe rather than the Mediterranean: a link between the Spanish 'national' architecture proclaimed by Domènech and the 'European' look which the patrons and architects wanted their city to wear. To the northern heartlands of Gothic, Barcelonese architects now looked for new influences that would enrich their traditions. In the 1880s, the most influential imported models came from the Arts and Crafts Movement: the collaborative studio of decorative arts Domènech established in the Castell dels Tres Dragons had the feel of an urban Kelmscott; enthusiasm for 'total' design and for the revival of medieval crafts was probably owed to the same source. Barcelonese followers never adopted the anti-industrial commitment of Morris and his friends; Gaudí left some exposed steel girders even amid the luxury of the Palau Güell and designed the first block of flats with an underground car park. Although he hated material values, he relied, until his late, reclusive years, on enterprising patrons and joined in the collective enterprise of the Barcelonese architects of the era: to produce an architecture that grew, out of tradition, into the ways of the modern world. In the 1890s art nouveau seemed to offer a suitable vocabulary: it was another international style, whose heartlands overlapped with those of Gothic, whose main schools were in centres of European tradition; its forms had the subversive boldness of 'superbly creative bad taste'; and it was unashamedly 'modern'. Its influence helped to produce the art and architecture of the movement known in Barcelona as 'Modernism'.

The term is unsatisfactory because its secular connotations were rejected by some of the greatest practitioners, especially Gaudí himself, who anticipated the movement, or produced what might be considered its first building, in the Palau Güell of 1885–1888. One way of dating the much-debated inception of Modernism could be to trace it to the moment when Gaudí rejected his first, rigidly angular design for the palace and introduced the parabola as its defining and unifying shape. Gaudí was also the author of the two buildings in Barcelona in which aversion from the straight line is taken to its wildest extremes: the Casa Batlló, where interior ceilings swirl like ridged whipped cream, and the notorious Casa Milá of 1906–1910, where there is no straight line in the entire composition. The intended effect of the Casa Milá was to give an impression of organic growth, of symbiosis between building technology and nature. Decoratively, it is barnacled and seaweed-draped, as if submerged in primal life forces - a *cathédrale engloutie*, eroded into curves. In the middle of the city, it provides an impact similar to that of a mighty ruin overgrown, say, by the jungles of Yucatán. Its critics found it unstable and grotesque. A typical caricature published in ¡*Cu-cut!* showed a podgy boy in bolero and gaiters saying to his elegantly dressed mother as they hurried past the exterior, 'Mummy, do they have earthquakes here, too?' (¡*Cu-cut!*, 21 January 1909). These asperities, by acknowledging the building's 'unbuilt' look, testified to its success.

The Casa Milá came, if not at the cusp of Gaudí's career, certainly at a turning point, when the dandyism of his early work and early appearance was buried under an avalanche - slowly gathering, suddenly falling - of religious sensibility. By all accounts, the young Gaudí, who arrived in Barcelona in 1869 as a seventeen-year-old provincial *ingénue*, had no very strong religious feelings; his sympathies were with liberal politics and, therefore, secular values. Much of the impact of his work, until well into middle age, derived less from depth of feeling than from technical brilliance, capricious invention and, above all, love of display, which made him the perfect architect for his showy bourgeois patrons. The façade of the Casa Batlló expresses this best, perhaps, clad in the shimmer of iridescent spangles, like a pop waistcoat, and topped with a conceit so outrageous as to threaten reverence with mockery: a scaly dragon's hump of a roof, pierced by the lance of the patron saint of Catalonia. The conquest of dandyism by Catholicism is a fairly well-established theme of the history of the last hundred years. An attraction based, perhaps, on some form of affinity - the panoply of the sanctuary, the drama of the liturgy, the 'superbly creative bad taste' of traditional Catholicism - has won thousands of such souls from Wilde to Waugh. The conversion of Gaudí had begun by 3 November 1883. On that day he had a spiritual experience which, as far as we know, he never precisely described but which convinced him that a miracle of St Joseph had brought him the commission to complete the church of the Sagrada Família. This was intended to be a sort of Catalan equivalent of a tractarian church, a vessel to gather in the godless and a monument to the doctrine of salvation by grace through works. It was to be offered as an expiatory sacrifice for the sins of the city and to be built entirely on the proceeds of alms. 'Come with me and build something for God', said Gaudí to an assistant whom he took to view the site. The intensity of his conversion was made ferociously apparent in 1894, when his Lenten fast imperilled his life. But religion did not come to monopolize his values or exclusively inform his art until the events of 1909 caused a crisis in his work on the Casa Milá.

The rioters who burned houses of religion in the disturbances of the Tragic Week unnerved the proprietor of the Casa Milá, who decided to dispense with the great statue of the Virgin that was to have dominated the façade, in case she proved a provocation to future secularist violence. Gaudí, disgusted by the pusillanimous evasion, virtually withdrew from the project. At the same time, the sacrilege of the Tragic Week seemed to make the expiatory purpose of the Sagrada Família all the more urgent. Gaudí made an anchorite's cell of his studio in the crypt of the church and worked on little else after 1911. When the former dandy was killed by a tram, in 1926, he died barefoot in his shoes, with his jacket held together by safety-pins and a gospel book in his hand. During his long, reclusive afterlife in this world, he had continued to attract adulation and to entertain the great amid the rising bones of his church or under the dangling baroque busts and primitive casts that decorated his cell. His funeral procession was half a mile long and mourners lined every inch of the two-and-a-half mile route. But people forgot that he had once been not just in the mainstream but in the forefront of Modernism, and the myth of a Gaudí who had always been withdrawn and isolated came to dominate even his fellow-artists' image of him.

Nor was the uniqueness of the Sagrada Família produced by hermetically sealing the architect's genius. Gaudí had always affected to find fault with Gothic, which was 'incompletely evolved' and 'industrial'. Yet the classical and Baroque architecture, which he claimed to admire more, was never an informative influence in his own work in the way that Gothic was; and although a Gothic conception was imposed on the plan for the Sagrada Família before he assumed responsibility for the project, it was typical of the work Gaudí was doing on other commissions at about the same time - like the pavilions of the Compañía Transatlántica in the early years of the project, or later, the Teresian College and the chapel of the Güell estate. Almost from the first, Gaudí's Gothic had two distinctive features: he modified its straight lines and acute angles with paraboloid shapes; and he interpreted it as a source of 'natural' rather than 'rational' patterns. This made his Gothic buildings inside Barcelona - he applied rather different rules when he built beyond the city - look strikingly different from, say, the historically accurate and angular work of Puig or the functionally austere frameworks erected by Domènech. For example, he always dispensed with flying buttresses, substituting bowed, angled struts which wrenched the buildings into curvilinear forms: in the interior of the chapel of the Colonia Güell, the supporting pillars are like vast tree trunks, recalling the origins of Gothic in Abbot Suger's search for suitably shaped trees in the forests round Saint-Denis. The corridors of the Teresian College are formed of recessive paraboloid arcades, like fluttering ranks of angels' wings. In both cases, the effect is eerie, terrible and beautiful.

The Sagrada Família was produced by the same cross-fertilization between Gothic and Modernist ideas. The building's symbolism is densely, even ludicrously, complex, but the basic conception is simple. The dominant clusters of long, concave spires rise like giant tubers from the grotto–shrine which encloses the crypt and floor; from them the multi-coloured, ceramic-smothered sunburst finials which crown the composition sprout like flowers. It makes a deeper impression than other Gaudí buildings because of its intense passion, its utter solemnity - though even this is muted, to some onlookers' taste, by the bland naturalism of the sculptures of the finished façade. But it is not of a different kind from the rest of Gaudí's oeuvre, nor unrepresentative of its time. It seemed old-fashioned, by the time of Gaudí's death, or soon after, because it had been so long a building and had little in common with the severities of rationalist thinking which were then becoming fashionable. Yet it captivated Barcelona's leading rationalist, Josep Lluís Sert, not least because, like all Gaudí's work, it was not merely dazzlingly imagined but also carefully planned to suit its function. Today, when it is still far from completion, it seems in every way a more far-sighted building than anything created by rationalism. 'Post-modernism' - which is, in some ways, a return to architectural dandyism and a celebration of frenziedly ludic values - has rehabilitated the early Gaudí, too.

All the leading architects of the city borrowed from art nouveau and Secessionism, and acknowledged the cult of natural form, in buildings of the first and second decades of the twentieth century. Even Puig i Cadafalch, whose angles and spikes made rather unsuitable settings, introduced art nouveau stained glass into the Casa Amatller. Domènech i Muntaner blended Modernism with Mauresque and Byzantine elements in the Casa Lleó Morera, only a few doors from the Casa Amatller in the passeig de Gràcia; it won him the city's prize for the best building of 1905 and seems to have emboldened him to embark on his most imaginative building ever, the effusive Palau de la Música Catalana, of 1905–1908. Structurally, this lavish concert hall in the carrer de Sant Pere més alt, looks ahead to functionalism, even rationalism, with its steel diaphragm, structural glazing and acoustic efficiency. Its underlying forms remain in the Gothic tradition. But the big, pointed arches are almost totally submerged by riotous décor which makes the building a sort of lexicon of Modernist vocabulary. Outside, tumescent turrets smothered in livid mosaics surmount a deep entablature decorated in mosaic with scenes of song and dance, appropriate to the society which commissioned the work, the Orfeó Català. Below that, palm-like arcades, supported on colourful pillars in floral motifs, with deeply carved capitals adorned with leaves and flowers, enclose bulging, sinuous balconies. The arcades continue inside the auditorium, giving the upper circle the feel of the deep triforium of a pilgrim cathedral. The proscenium is swirled in curves, the defining lines smothered by gigantic mouldings of horsemen and trees emerging from the living rock and of Orpheus, Eurydice and Pegasus; the effect suggests an urbane grotto, like that of Horace's Pyrrha. Every pillar and every recess seem to be splattered by the bright palettes of two brilliant men whom Domènech employed as mosaicist and stained-glazier, Lluís Bru i Salelles and Antoni Rigalt. With his next great building, the Hospital de Sant Pau in the neighbourhood of the Sagrada Família, Domènech returned to austerely Gothic principles, but still used selectively the rich, even riotous effects of his Modernist period.

Domestic interiors of this period, as well as shop fronts and fittings, were executed with the same lack of inhibition as the Orfeó Català. The minor arts, where turnover was quick, were more easily and quickly conquered by fashion than architecture. The leading figure in interior decoration was Caspar Homar i Mezquida (1870–1953), who worked with Domènech on the Casa Lleó Morera and produced influential marquetry furniture, inlaid with willowy geishas. Eusebi Arnau i Mascort (1863–1963), another protégé of Domènech, was a versatile sculptor who made a speciality of sculptural contributions to decorative schemes; his grandest work was done for the Palau de Música, but he also carved capitals and fireplaces for houses built by Domènech and Puig i Cadafalch, treating the fireplaces with the same bulging arcs, like distended bubbles or half-lily pads, that *modernista* designers favoured for sofa- and mirror-backs and shop windows.

The world of Els Quatre Gats

There were cafés which looked more aggressively Modernist. The Café Torino of 1902, for instance, in the Gran Via, was a riot of art nouveau extravagance, with hardly a straight line in the place. In the plaça de Catalunya, the Café de la Luna of 1907 dripped with stylized frondeur and a theatrical clientele. These, however, were the resorts of high fashion and high prices. They had Modernist décor but little Bohemian ambience. For that, one went to the places the artists not only designed but also frequented - above all, to the café which, from its opening in 1897 to its demise in 1903, was the art world's creation and club, housed in a building of Puig i Cadafalch, Els Quatre Gats (Jardí).

Here, in contrast to the swirling exoticism of the Torino and the Luna, the decoration was almost homely. Ascetic and eclectic, it evoked an artist's studio of the time, full of incoherent clutter. The main saloon had broad, low, Gothic windows, a ceiling of heavy, machined, dark beams, tile-hung lower walls and hard, sturdy furniture. From a presiding position hung one of the vast, ersatz-medieval chandeliers without which no Barcelona domestic interior of the time seems to have been considered complete: Ramon Casas once sketched Santiago Rusiñol sitting in one. The upper walls were bespattered with select kitsch bric-à-brac - all on a small scale but for the huge, dominant oil sketch of the owner, Pere Romeu, with the painter, Ramon Casas. They sat together on a tandem bicycle, good-naturedly straining for progress, with doubled backs and set teeth, in cycling socks and jodhpurs. The painting hung there until a car replaced the bicycle and a more up-to-date image went up.

Though Romeu and Rusiñol were the most creative forces in the world of Els Quatre Gats, Casas seems in retrospect its most distinguished member. Like Rusiñol, but more so, he was a child of privilege. His father was a nabob who had made a fortune in the Indies; on his mother's side, he was heir to a textile mill. His fortune thus combined two typical sources of the wealth of Barcelona in his day. Artists had formerly relied on grants from a city council that accepted unquestioningly an art patron's role for study trips to Rome. Casas and Rusiñol, however, preferred - and could afford - to go to Paris instead. There, with Romeu and Miquel Utrillo, who was to become the fourth of the 'cats' of Els Quatre Gats, and other Barcelonese artists who were attracted by their example, they selectively absorbed the lessons of Impressionism and equipped themselves to challenge the realistic, historical and anecdotal conventions still dominant in the art schools of their native city. When they returned, they brought their spending power with them, and used it to create and promote a self-consciously radical circle of artists. Outside that circle, they had more admirers than customers, except for their commercial graphics; so money of their own was necessary. It helped to pay for the indulgences of the life of Els Quatre Gats - the shaky finances of the café, the succession of ephemeral publications, the exhibitions and poetry readings.

No Barcelonese painter has ever excelled Ramon Casas in technical mastery or faithfulness to the idea of beauty. Yet he created a new and challenging style. He had every qualification to be an amateur dabbler - in his self-portraits, with a fat cigar always stuck into the bowl of a pipe, he is the image of the rich eccentric - and yet he dedicated himself to painting and the graphic arts with single mind and full heart. His finest works are genre-scenes which capture fleeting moments - usually of a story which is dramatic and tragic in varying degrees. Their subject matter covers a wide range of human experience from intimate secrets to public conflicts. In *Plein Air* (1890) - a work admired enough to be bought by the city council in 1891 in spite of its heavy Parisian flavour - a young woman seated alone in an open-air café observes a man in the distance, framed by an impressionistic townscape. In a portrait of the artist's sister and brother-in-law at coffee (1892), the charm and languor of the scene conceal pointed personal and social commentary; the man's attitude of spineless ennui inversely balances his wife's purposeful and upright pose. The most memorable canvases are those in which the social commentary is most overt. *Barcelona 1902* is an extraordinarily dynamic composition, in which a mounted civil guard is about to trample a sprawling, dramatically foreshortened worker in the foreground, while the crowd is cleared by the cavalry from a space which seems to grow before the onlooker's eyes. It was in fact painted in 1899, apparently without any intention of documenting a specific incident, but renamed after a violent strike in the later year (Mendoza: 138). Patriotic scruples led the Spanish committee to reject it for the Paris Exhibition in 1899, but in 1902 it was acclaimed in Madrid.

Casas' most famous - and, in his day, most popular - work was *Garrote Vil* (1893), recording the public execution in that year of a nineteen year old who had cut the throats of his victim and accomplice for a gold watch. Some aspects seem ironic: the clergy are a corpulent contingent under an enormous crucifix; the penitents' black conical caps prod towards the centre of the canvas like pitchfork prongs. The main purpose of the painting, however, seems to be simply to document with fidelity a scene of extraordinary emotional power at which the painter was a witness. The public loved its engaging horror more than they feared its social import. It belongs to a well-established genre of horror paintings in Barcelona, always popular and frequently connected with the traditions of public scourging, common until the early nineteenth century, and public execution, which continued until 1908.

Casas' reputation as a rebel against his class seems exaggerated. He was a shrewd and critical observer rather than a rebel. He never forsook a bourgeois way of life or abandoned its comforts. He was more at home in his time, perhaps, than almost any other artist of his generation; while Gaudí, in the depths of his tortured soul, rejected the values of industrial society, Casas was one of the first men in Barcelona to own a motor car. While Nonell found his models in the gutters and the suburbs, Casas got them from the cafés. He was invited to paint a portrait of the king. While Apel·les Mestres fled to the clericalist extreme right, Casas remained in the mainstream of Catalanist politics. He shared the concern of the Barcelonese middle class for practical applications of art, and produced a huge corpus as an illustrator and commercial artist. Most conspicuous among this output is a haunting poster for Dr Abreu's syphilis cure, in which a rather raffish prostitute extends a flower in one hand and holds a serpent behind her back; characteristically of Casas' ability to puzzle us, we are left uncertain which of these symbols denotes the curse, and which the cure.

Casas was the finest, Rusiñol the most effective talent of the world of Els Quatre Gats. Soon after his return from Paris Rusiñol erupted into the seaside village of Sitges, just outside Barcelona, and turned it into a theatre of his ideas and a playground of his friends. It was already a haunt of painters when Rusiñol discovered it, apparently by accident, in 1891. He bought property there and, from 1893 to 1899, was the impresario for a series of what he called 'Festivals of Modernism', at which he made speeches defining Modernism in imprecise but potent language. The highlight of the first - bafflingly called the Second Festival - was a performance of Maeterlinck's *L'Intruse*, of the next a parade through the streets of two canvases by El Greco which Rusiñol had bought in Paris and exhibited alongside his own. He cultivated the idea, and attempted the practice, of total art, illustrating his own books, criticizing his own pictures, writing the publicity for his own plays and libretti, meticulously 'designing' his art and his life in detail. His influence and his energy helped to make Barcelonese art talkative, even declamatory, and self-justificatory, and to make a cult of novelty. If his showmanship was of the very highest order, his painting ran it close in quality. He was not quite such a consummate technician as Casas but he produced genre scenes and human studies of stark beauty and nicely judged restraint, which seemed to exemplify the 'sincerity' he extolled as the aim of art.

The name of Els Quatre Gats was coined in tribute to Le Chat Noir of Paris; but it was also a self-proclamation of the founding friends as a small band of outsiders. It is now a commonplace to point out that Modernism was a minority taste in Barcelona even in its heyday. Casas and Rusiñol sold little to private patrons; the brilliant but more avant-garde members of the circle, like Nonell, Picasso, and Joaquim Mir, even less. Within a few years of the turn of the century, Modernism was under attack from proponents of an anti-Parisian, anti-Impressionist reaction known as *Noucentisme*. By the time of the Great Exhibition of 1929, the decorative excesses of Modernism were regarded with horror in a world of functional aesthetics. A guide of that year bewailed the 'misfortune' that brought so much building to Barcelona during the Modernist supremacy (Mendoza: 158). The Café Torino, on which the leading Modernists had collaborated in design and decoration, was demolished to make room for the Joieria Roca of 1934 by Josep Lluís Sert, its curves raped by the incisive lines of rationalism. But despite the sacrifice of much Modernist art to revolutions of taste - especially the interior decorations and the shop fronts, two forms which are notoriously fragile and yet were modernist specialities - Barcelona is still splashed with the motley of its own eccentric art nouveau. The bullring is sandwiched between a vast mosaic butterfly and a circus of ornamental flowerbeds in art nouveau patterns. The spires and stained glass of the Casa de les Punxes lead towards the sunflower ornaments that crown the spires of Sagrada Família. Gawpers gather under the mosaic mushroom forest of the Parc Güell. The jaws of the Casa Milá drip; the jowls of the Casa Batlló bulge; the dozens of shops - pharmacies, especially, but also bakeries, restaurants, bars, haberdasheries - still wear their fin de siècle finery, their gaudy curves, with pride. Images that identify Barcelona with that era are indelible. They are impressed on every visitor's mind. Barcelona would have no distinctive 'profile' as a city without them.

The new centurions

In the early years of the new century artists began to gather in a new group, presided over by the columnist Eugeni d'Ors. He seems to have fancied himself as a sort of Spanish Oscar Wilde, photographed with long hair, a centre parting, an abstracted countenance, an expansive manner and a lavish buttonhole. In the time of his influence, however, he was an energetic reagent against fin de siècle decadence. Adopting his lead, the innovators called themselves *noucentistes*: the term was coined to distinguish them from 'Modernists' - a name which embarrassed or outraged the Modernists themselves. Noucentism was the product of a generation gap, devoted to a cult of youth, proclamatory - a little late, it must be said - of new values for a new century, and noisily rejecting the art of the academics of the Llotja and the Modernists of the cafés. D'Ors was its pontiff. The acolytes on whom he laid hands by naming them in his column, 'Glosari', from 1906 or publishing their names and work in the *Almanach dels noucentistes* in 1911 became its priests. Like all such brotherhoods, intellectually esoteric, personally exclusive, it was defined as much by who was left out as by what was admitted. Still, it was a genuine movement with positive, distinctive and coherent features. It continued or renewed the search for a peculiarly Catalan art. D'Ors' novel of 1912, *La ben plantada*, symbolized the indomitability of Catalanism. Nogués illustrated the subject as a tall, upright female; poor but pious; as indifferent as a statue to the rage of the mean, crabbed figures - plutocratic and militaristic - who dance around her frenziedly, stones in hand. Noucentism looked to the Mediterranean for the sources of a Catalan heritage, away from the Paris that had influenced or engendered Modernism, to 'these immortal daughters on the other side of our sea'. It responded to the call of the writer of the first personal artist's 'manifesto' of twentieth-century Barcelona, J. Torres García, 'to turn to the tradition of art which belongs to Mediterranean lands' instead of 'alien' Impressionism, pre-Raphaelitism and Symbolism. Finally, and in consequence, Noucentism was a classicizing movement. The Roman excavations of Empúries influenced Barcelonese artists of the era of the *Almanach* as those of Italica had influenced the early Sevillian Baroque; they sought simple structural principles and, with contempt for the decorative, the recovery of form.

The most characteristic art of Noucentism was, perhaps, talk; but sculpture ran it a close second. Enric Casanovas sculpted solid Mediterranean women in granite-like stone: his Majorcan peasant woman was an Iberian goddess; his *Youth* a rather *Männlich* Minoan. Josep Clará embodied everybody's idea of Noucentism in his muscular representations of Teresa, the heroine of *La ben plantada*. Any of these sculptures, dropped from even a moderate height, would have shattered the fragile, drooping, *modernista* nudes of a sculptor like Josep Llupinol, who, despite his avowed contempt for the style, found the over-studied and therefore rather uncommunicative eroticism of Rodin irresistible in his own work. For most of the painters who belonged to the movement, Noucentism was a haven, rather than a home, on their way to more radical and avant-garde styles, but it helped for a time to produce some of the more brilliant and luminous works of Torres García and Joaquim Mir, who, in Majorca and Tarragona, captured Mediterranean light as faithfully as any painter has ever done.

Architecture, always slower to respond to fashion than quicker, cheaper art forms, took a long time to absorb Noucentism. A few buildings of before the First World War seemed to anticipate or reflect Noucentism, but were perhaps only continuing the tradition of nineteenth-century neo-classicism. In the carrer Ample, for instance, the building of the Societat del Crèdit Mercantil, of 1896–1900, has a masonic feel, with its low pediment and the central bay of its third storey, formed by a tympanum-like eye enclosing a window. The architect Joan Martorell i Montells also built a Gaudiesque Modernist–Gothic pastiche, at about the same time, in the form of the Collegi Sant Ignasi de Loiola. In the carrer de Balmes J. Torres i Grau built the outstanding Foment d'Obres i Construcció in an early *noucentista* or *pre-noucentista* style, but the neighbouring numbers 81 and 169 in the same street, constructed at about the same time, between 1908 and 1910, are Modernist with historical references - Hispano-Flemish and Gothic-Mauresque respectively. Not until after 1913, when J. Torres García published *Notes sobre l'art* with a Greek portico on the cover, did Noucentism begin to take over the way Barcelona looked; today, though *noucentista* buildings are less identifiable and less conspicuous than those of Modernism, they are probably more numerous. J. Folch i Torres (1886–1963) built villas of a rustic Italian flavour with Palladian entrances, recessed and colonnaded. J. Goday (1882–1936) was responsible for slightly Baroque palazzi and the acclaimed school buildings, such as those of the carrer del Carme, which embodied Barcelona's commitment to public education in elegant form. Francesc Folguera (1891–1960) was influenced by the Florentine Renaissance, designing façades which strongly echoed Brunelleschi, as did Nicolau Rubió (1891–1981) and Raimon Duran Reynals (1895–1966) whose humanistic composition, the church of Maria Reina de Montserrat on Pedralbes, of 1922, could have been transplanted from the Tuscan countryside. Antoni Puig i Guiral (1887–1955) was an accomplished architect of the same generation who built Italianate tower-villas, like the Casa Guarto, and Mediterranean pastiche, like the Valencian- or Andalusian-looking carrer Ample number 46.

The apogee of the *noucentista* era was the International Exhibition of 1929, and in some ways the best memorial to the period is still the exhibition site on Montjuïc. The event had been long planned and often deferred, first projected in 1901, scheduled for 1917 and almost scrapped because of the First World War, then held up by the political uncertainties of the twenties and competition from other international fairs. This long gestation meant that when the exhibition at last opened, it was clad in the finery of bygone hand-me-downs, housed in buildings which looked fusty by comparison with the effortless rationalism of some of the foreign pavilions - especially of the German pavilion of Mies van der Rohe. The characteristic new constructions by Barcelonese architects for the fair were: Goday's Pavelló de la Ciutat - by Herrera out of Helsinki Station; the Olympic Stadium by Pere Domènech i Roura, with its spiky tower with the look of an elongated Bramantesque tempietto; the loggia and gardens of the

'Greek temple' by R. Raventós (1892–1976); the Pavelló de les Arts Gràfiques by Pelai Martínez Paricio (1898–1978) and Raimon Duran (now the Archaeological Museum), which has the form of a Florentine Renaissance octagon with round windows, mathematically disposed, and a recessed entrance, pilastered and pedimented; and the former hotels which line the plaça de Espanya, gaunt, heavily clock-towered and monastic in appearance, by Nicolau Rubió. These relics, scattered down the slopes and at the foot of Montjuïc, like the debris of a battle, testify to Barcelona's last bid to project the image of a Mediterranean *polis*. In the light of the exhibition, Noucentism seemed an ill-judged architectural adventure, thrown into shadow by the rays of rationalism, which conquered Barcelona for a new style in the new decade.

The bonds of the Fatherland

When I first visited Barcelona as a little boy in the 1950s, the most durable sight of the 1929 exhibition was the Pueblo Español, a collection of buildings on Montjuïc, modelled on examples of medium-scale regional and vernacular architecture from all over Spain. It is still a tourist attraction, under the Catalanized name of 'Poble Espanyol', as pointless as any such 'theme park'. It seemed bizarre when I first saw it, and seems tawdry now. When new, however, it was both hugely esteemed and highly significant. Variegated and archaic, it seemed to offer a town-planning model that was refreshingly different from the monotony of the Eixample (Bohigas: 105–121). Escape from the tightly woven net of the Cerdà plan had been the aim of Barcelona's town planners, ever since 1903, when a new competition for a further enlargement of the town produced a series of entries designed to link the Eixample to the outlying towns with a rich new texture of streets. The Pueblo Español seemed a harmless, even laudable *divertissement*, which would provide attraction for visitors and recreation for citizens. All the intellectuals interviewed by the press at its inauguration liked it. Ortega spoke for the lot when he said he thought it would give 'all foreigners a clear and representative idea of what Spain is' (*Diario oficial de la Exposición Internacional de Barcelona*, 22 January 1929).

The terms of that praise betrayed the deeper significance of the Pueblo Español in the Barcelona of 1929. It demonstrated that the exhibition was a Spanish event, not merely Barcelonese and not at all Catalan. By implication, Barcelona was stamped as a Spanish city. In the introduction to the official catalogue, the Duke of Berwick sketched a historical panorama of Spain, with emphasis on her links with European-wide movements, without mentioning Catalonia (Berwick 1931–1933). The evasion with which Catalonia was treated, the intrusion which the Pueblo Español represented, were politically determined. General Primo de Rivera had seized dictatorial power in 1923 partly because of the disgust with which, as military governor of Barcelona, he beheld the separatism of some Catalan extremists. He proclaimed that he had taken office 'without any proposals to shoot anybody' but with the warning that 'the bonds of the fatherland are not even to be questioned'. Hostility to the idea of Spanish unity was, he opined, 'sick, abandoned, criminal and abominable' (*La Vanguardia* 1923).

Primo's repression, always tempered by inefficiency, was directed against the Catalanism of the urban middle class. The workers were bought off with policies of cheap food and full employment, to which, in Barcelona, the preparations for the 1929 exhibition made a major contribution. Paternalism - the language of Primo's politics, which, like many forms of rhetoric, gradually influenced and therefore increasingly reflected the behaviour of the regime - also blunted the edge of repression, which was just effective enough to stimulate an indignant reaction in favour of Catalanism without succeeding in inhibiting its spread. The ban on the Catalan flag, the extrusion of the Catalan language from public life and education, the abolition of the Mancomunitat and the dissolution of the Catalanist political parties created grievances and garbed Catalanism with the romance of a fugitive creed, celebrated in catacombs and fed on exiles' bread. The most incurably romantic of all Catalanist spokesmen, Francesc Macià, was transformed from a marginalized dreamer into an effective symbol of national resistance. In 1926, his attempt to launch a comic-opera 'invasion' of Catalonia in the cause of liberation was turned back at the frontier by French border guards, with all the advantages of bloodless martyrdom for its leaders. Yet while no anti-Catalanist regime could ever be entirely successful in Barcelona, much of the rest of Primo's language and ethos were close to Barcelonese sympathies. In the adulation of industry, the espousal of protectionism, the effort to combine full employment with cheap labour, the advocacy of values of high production and hard work, Primo echoed the economic and moral priorities of a community he knew well from his days in Barcelona as captain-general of the province. At the level of talk, the passion to 'galvanise' society could be indulged in to ludicrous extremes, as in the dictator's plan to abolish the siesta and introduce 'a fork lunch at 10.30 or 11.00' in the morning (*La Vanguardia*, 9 October 1929). The emulation of Europe was seen by the regime, as by many of the Catalanists, as a matter of the abolition of Spanish traditions and the adoption of frantic 'foreign' habits of hustle and bustle.

In the Ruritanian world of Primo's Barcelona, where two types of unreality, represented by Primo and Macià, were locked in a conflict both solemn and ludicrous, the most progressive spirit was, perhaps, that of Josep Lluís Sert i López. Born into comfortable circumstances in 1902, he grew up with a strong sense of the social obligations of his class. His gifts were constructive rather than creative; he was a great organizer, administrator and teacher, but as a practical architect he tended to need the shelter of collaborative projects; his designs were derivative and dependent on the example or inspiration of heroes like Le Corbusier. He was a genie rather than a genius, responding to needs rather than imposing his own vision; popping out of the context rather than defying his times. Yet despite his limitations, he became one of this century's most influential Spaniards, marking the face of Spain through his work as a propagandist of rationalist architecture, and later, after the Civil War, when he fled to a chair at Harvard, helping to define and spread the notions on which the urban planning of the fifties was conceived worldwide. His solutions suffered from all the arrogance of the modern planning tradition, but were not dogmatically inspired. The unprecedented problems of rapid urban growth in an era of global economic instability impelled the sort of dramatic response which Sert articulated. Blended with the paternalistic traditions of the Barcelonese bourgeoisie, his genuine anxiety to ameliorate the conditions in which ordinary people lived produced the magnificent orthodoxies of his day, which have since come to seem abominable heresies: 'slum clearance' that swept away human-scale housing; intimidating 'leisure zones'; uniform, minimalist estates; tower blocks; all the instant detritus of the 'functional city'. Until his exile, Sert was that rare type of intellectual: the prophet honoured in his own country.

The 'ample horizon'

Though the rationalist solutions advocated by Sert are now out of fashion, they represented at the time the most radical and promising approach to the problems of Barcelona's rapid growth: into a megalopolis of over a million registered inhabitants in 1930. Because they are architectural - and therefore, in a sense, apolitical - solutions, they could be allowed to incubate freely under the Primo regime. Because they were the work of Catalanist intellectuals, and because they had a utopian flavour, and because they seemed a means of redistributing happiness in favour of the underprivileged, they could flourish from 1931 when the regime was replaced by a republic in which leftist and Catalanist tendencies were strong. Rationalist architecture had, in some measure, the power of reuniting the workers' movement with the Catalanist movement after Primo had wedged them apart. The rationalists' plan for the development of the city was, for sentimental reasons, called the 'Macià Plan'.

Just as, in the 1890s, the last reception in Barcelona of the major international style of architecture had been anticipated by indigenous experiments, so the reception of rationalism in the thirties was preceded by a surprisingly long tradition. The basic ingredients of rationalist thinking in architecture - the aesthetics of function, the determination to exploit technology to the full - had animated the work of Domènech i Muntaner and even Gaudí. Under the functional simplicity of Gaudí's school buildings for the Sagrada Família or the wine vaults designed at Garraf by his pupil Berenguer was a beacon for 'modern architecture' and, perhaps, a direct source of inspiration for Le Corbusier. A feature of rationalism as advocated by Sert and practised in Spain was its concern with the environment of mass housing, in which every outlook would be sunlit towards an 'ample horizon', this recalls Gaudí's concern that his dwellings should enjoy access to the sun and be surrounded by a palette of light.

In Barcelona modern architecture, as the term is now understood, began just when Noucentism was at its height and the buildings of the 1929 exhibition were going up. This was not only because of the impact of the foreign pavilions - German, Swedish and Yugoslav - designed on rationalist principles. Barcelonese architects had already begun new departures from Modernism and Noucentism in the direction of functional, rational buildings. In 1928 - while Le Corbusier was being diverted to lecture in Barcelona by a telegram from Sert on his way to Madrid - the Myrurgas factory by Antoni Puig i Gairalt (1887–1935) was begun, starkly innovative, as was a coldly functional block of flats by Ramon Raventós (1892–1959) on the corner of the carrer de Lleida. These examples seemed to show that rational simplicity and decorative austerity were natural developments within Noucentism, on which these architects had been nurtured. The same possibilities were even more strikingly manifest in Francesc Folguera's Casa de Sant Jordi on the corner of the carrer de Casp and via Laietana, begun in 1929, a building so maturely representative of modern architecture that it would be ascribed to the fifties or sixties by an impartial observer (Mackay: 61). In the same year Sixt Yllescas built what might be called a pre-rationalist house in Gràcia, the Casa Vilaró. In 1930, in collaboration with Yllescas, he put up a revolutionary block of duplex flats in the carrer de Muntaner in which the visual relief on the outside derived from the eccentric (but functionally determined) geometry of the disposition of the windows, the boldness of the ship's-railing balconies and the delicacy of the pale green render.

Modern architecture was formally incorporated into a 'movement' or, at least, a club in Barcelona in March 1931, when Sert and Torres i Clavé organized their friends in GATCPAC. Decoded, the elaborate acronym signified 'Group of Catalan Artists and Technicians for the Progress of Contemporary Architecture'. The group's interest in rationalism was confirmed in October of the same year when, at a meeting in Saragossa, it was altered to GATEPAC - the *Spanish* Group for the same purpose - under the presidency of García Mercadal, the Aragonese architect normally credited with the first rationalist buildings in Spain. Most of the group's collective energy went into publicizing the ideas of Sert and Torres, which were closely based on those of Le Corbusier, on town planning. Planning was a form of gospel which would save the urban masses from eternal immolation in the rubble of pandemonium or under its detritus. The demons' breeding grounds in tenements, gloomy courtyards and narrow streets would be abolished; new housing would be of modest dimensions, low cost and limited variety, but it would be open to light, space, 'pure air' and the 'ample horizon'. Work would benefit from planned amenities for leisure and health; efficiency would be improved by planned communications with the city; the needs of progress and civilization would be paired. The solutions to the problems of the developing city were attainable by study and thought. Planning would deliver the just polity almost as a by-product of the civilized city, supplying the 'vital elements that every human being needs and which society has no right to deny' (*Actividad contemporánea*, iii (1933), no. 11). Ironically the only purely rationalist building to survive from the Gatepac era is a jeweller's shop on the Gran Via; thus the utopian ideal is to be found beyond a threshold crossed only by the rich. The Gatepac vision can, however, be seen embodied in two entirely characteristic examples: the Casa Bloc, built to house workers in 1932–1936, and the Dispensari Central Antituberculós of 1934–1938. Both show the depth of Bert's discipleship of Le Corbusier. The Casa Bloc lurches around a series of right angles through a green space, hoisted aloft on ground-floor stilts. The clinic is built around a lecture room based on Le Corbusier's rejected design for the assembly hall of the League of Nations.

Fortunately, perhaps, the plan Macià, except for a few experiments, remained on paper. Its destructive potential was terrible in a city whose charm arose largely from the picturesque decay of a slummy centre. Torres Clavé's mock-up is a futuristic nightmare, with the old town dominated by gaunt towers, flimsy and precarious, like cardboard pop-outs. All that the Prince of Wales abhors in London could have been realized, had the Republic had more time and the city more money, 50 years ago in Barcelona.

The cockpit of a European conflict

The Spanish Civil War, which began in July 1936, subverted the rationalists' plans and dispersed their personnel. Sert took refuge in Harvard; Torres i Clavé died on the battlefield. Within the plan of the existing streets, the workers of Barcelona created in the early days of the war a utopia of their own. The revolt of part of the regular army garrison was successfully countered by a rising of 'popular militias' organized by anarchists, anarcho-syndicalists and left-Marxists. Behind their barricades a social revolution was enforced by armed gangs. When George Orwell arrived to join the revolutionary militia in the hope of being sent to fight 'fascism' at the front, he found every wall scrawled with the hammer and sickle and with the acronyms of the revolutionary parties. He got a lecture from a hotel manager for trying to tip a lift boy. The barbers' shops had signs 'solemnly explaining that barbers were no longer slaves', and posters recommended the same metamorphosis to prostitutes. Revolutionary posters, 'flaming from the walls [..] made the few remaining adverts look like daubs of mud'. Loudspeakers in the Ramblas blared revolutionary music. Apart from an elderly lady with a poodle, the middle class seemed to have vanished. Everyone in the streets wore rough clothes or blue overalls 'or some variant of the militia uniform' (Orwell: 3–5).

Orwell was exhilarated by the sight of a city that had succumbed to a workers' revolution. For the victims and bystanders, however, the revolution evoked successively terror and boredom. Joan Pujol García - the future master spy - was frightened not only by the armed mobs of amnestied convicts who supplemented the authentic revolutionaries but also by the atmosphere of suspicion spread by denunciations between neighbours. It was a time of secret score-settling unparalleled since the days of the Inquisition. The renowned surgeon, Josep Trueta, who saved thousands of Republican lives during the battles of the Civil War, almost fell to 'revolutionary justice' in its earliest days, rescued from an anarchist kangaroo court by a squadron of armed socialist street fighters. Catalanists - whom the revolutionaries almost invariably classified as bourgeois - had particular reason to fear the triumphant workers' culture, which spoke in the same foreign tongue as Primo and Franco. The anarchist Durruti threatened to shoot the President of the Generalitat if he turned up for anti-fascist militia committee meetings (Pujol García: 36; Fraser: 148).

The committees soon out-chattered the guns and fear gave way to milder forms of disenchantment. When false papers enabled him to come out of hiding, Joan Pujol was obliged to 'hang around attending endless meetings of the poultry-farmers' union'. The revolution was 'made', after the barricades, in individual work places where, usually, local CNT chapels took over the management in defiance of the union leadership, the republican and Catalan governments and most of the political parties. The economic success of the experiment lasted only as long as pre-war stocks. In 1937, Pujol and his companions-in-arms had to desert to the Nationalists in order to get a square meal (Pujol García: 41).

The initial success of the revolution in Barcelona, and the relative security of the city's position, remote from the front, made it the cockpit of the self-indulgent squabbles of the parties that formed the Republican side. The local political situation was of more concern to the native Barcelonese than the progress of the war; only intending fugitives like Pujol or uncomprehending idealists like Orwell were fretting for the front. The conditions were ideal for ideological in-fighting: the fervour induced by war, without any immediate apprehension of defeat; the presence of large numbers of mutually hostile gangs of gunmen; a deteriorating material and economic position which equipped the contenders with fuel for mutual accusations. The hatreds of anarchists and communists, Trotskyists and Stalinists were arcane and tribal, hardly understood by outsiders. Orwell's naive question to his fellow left-Marxists who disapprovingly pointed out members of the socialist militia was, 'Aren't we all Socialists?' This was like asking 'Aren't we all Christians?' at the massacre of St Bartholomew. Creeds have their theologies and no conflicts of heresy and orthodoxy have ever been so embittered as those of the left in modern times. The doctrinal differences were complicated by a contest for power between the collectives, the Catalan government and the government of the Republic. At the same time, the half-baked nature of the revolution of July 1936 raised a fundamental problem of strategy which divided the revolutionary parties and unions from the rest: whether the revolution should be prosecuted without compromise, regardless of the feelings of the bourgeois allies of the left and in defiance of the potential allies of the Republic among the western democracies; or whether it should be arrested or reversed in the interests of 'winning the war'. Apologists of the revolutionaries have always insisted that the revolutionary line was justifiable as a means to victory as well as an end in itself, but the anarchist outburst - 'as if the war has any meaning unless we can make the revolution at the same time' (Fraser: 379) - reveals a real difference of priorities. In these circumstances it is less surprising that internecine violence should have broken out among the Republicans in Barcelona than that it should have been delayed for so long.

The events of the bloodletting of the Barcelonese left are well known. On 3 May 1937 police units attempted to wrest the telephone exchange from the control of an anarcho-syndicalist collective. This may not have been intended to provoke a general confrontation. For several months, government-controlled units had been gradually replacing the popular militias in strategic positions, always with acrimony but usually without violence. The government policy was twofold: by rolling back the revolution they hoped to make the Republican cause more internationally acceptable; and by strengthening central authority at the expense of the uncontrollables they hoped to make the war effort more efficient. But the issue became a catalyst for the enmities of the communists and anarchists and their anti-Stalinist allies. The militia defending the telephone exchange resisted the police. Five days of generalized fighting claimed 500 dead. Orwell, unwillingly caught up in the shooting, was amazed at how the people of Barcelona, with the city's long history of civil commotion behind them, accepted the violence as 'a natural calamity' which generated a topography of its own, and patterns of participation and evasion which the locals knew and lived with: 'people take their places almost as in a fire-drill'. Most people were indifferent. 'Such a pity', said Orwell's bootmaker, 'and so bad for business' (Orwell: 199). The defeat of the anarchists was also a defeat for the Catalanist cause, which had seemed marginal to the conflict. The city was occupied on 7 May by a well-armed force of paramilitary guards loyal to the government of the Republic, which was now dedicated to centralizing power, ostensibly in the interests of the war effort. Barcelona was thoroughly demoralized for the duration of the war; the alienated minorities no longer felt the Republican cause worth fighting for. After the days of May, communist strategy seemed to come straight out of a bunker, with as much energy - more perhaps - expended on the proscription of Trotskyists and the subordination of anarchists as on the prosecution of the war. Barcelona's self-proclaimed role as a European city was fulfilled when she became a theatre of pan-European conflict and a sacrifice for the international priorities of foreign powers.

The infighting would have been unthinkable had Barcelona been near the front line, where optimism was enforced and camaraderie contagious. Now that the damage wrought by remoteness from the front was done, the war struck the city with devastating force. In March 1938, an Italian bombing campaign frayed nerves and clogged the hospitals day and night for three days. The motive of these raids seems to have been experimental: the Italians wanted to test the morale of a great city under a merciless bombardment, and perhaps to try out new high-explosive bombs. Franco's own ponderous strategy gave the city a respite almost until the end of the year. His final offensive was launched two days before Christmas. The Republican resistance dissolved more from desertion than from the blows of the enemy. The right-wing Catalanist Tomàs Roig Llop took part in an unopposed and apparently unobserved walkout by 400 new conscripts. Those compromised by loyalty to the Republic thought rather of escape than resistance (Fraser: 481).

Orwell had realized, after some time in the city, that the working-class uniforms which impressed him so much on arrival were worn, in many cases, as a disguise. Tomàs Roig Llop, for instance, found it useful to change headgear when he travelled between anarchist and left-Marxist headquarters, for one group considered a bare head evasive, while the other thought a cap was treasonable. Boiler suits and loose collars were forms of disguise most of the middle class was happy to discard. There was never much of a 'fifth column' in Barcelona, but when Franco's troops marched in on 26 January 1939, a collaborationist bourgeoisie was waiting in the woodwork. The Francoist slogan, however - 'Spain Has Arrived' - could hardly be greeted with any enthusiasm by Catalanists. At best, they could praise the triumph of a lesser evil. The celebrations in the streets were caused, in most cases, perhaps, by one or both of two forms of reliefs: joy that the war was over, 'not that one side or the other had won'; and thankfulness again to be able to receive the sacraments of the church without fear. During the revolutionary supremacy, priests could only be sheltered in secret; when Joana Alier's daughter was baptised in 1937, there was no chrism for the anointing: the priest returned with some a year later (Fraser: 446).

'Spain has arrived'

The Franco troops were only the spearhead; in the next 40 years, 'Spain' arrived in a more durable and insidious form, when hundreds of thousands of immigrants poured into the city to swell its official population to 1¾ million by 1981, and over 3 million in the metropolitan area. Catalanism, repressed by Primo, superannuated by the Civil War and crushed by Franco, might have been buried under this avalanche.

Yet, when Franco died in 1975, and the President of the Catalan government-in-exile returned to the balcony of the Generalitat, he was acclaimed by natives and Spaniards alike. The words with which he triggered the cheers were an unconscious rebuke to 'Spain Has Arrived': 'Ja sóc aquí!', he cried: 'Here I am at last!' Since then, the Barcelonese working class has voted consistently for Catalan autonomy and broadly Catalanist cultural policies. There are differences of degree and of priorities between the programmes of the Socialist party and the Catalanists proper; but it remains true that in Barcelona's recent past a Spanish-speaking proletariat has been extraordinarily amenable to the sensibilities of a Catalan-speaking bourgeoisie. From the centre of Barcelona to the working-class suburbs there are cultural differences but little real antagonism.

In 1982, a survey revealed some of the immigrants' reasons for respecting Catalan identity. The most eloquent respondent was an immigrant worker who professed to consider himself 'Catalan, although I am an Andalusian. It is here that I have developed the ability to sell my labour; here I have learned the little culture I possess and have created my home. This is my land. This is how I think of it, although my inner self is full of other tendencies' (Solé: 116; Balfour: 193). The majority view, however, was the product of less highly developed sensibilities. Most respondents favoured Catalan autonomy out of weariness with the rigid centralism of the Franco dictatorship, not out of Catalanist fellow feeling. In the working-class districts today, the atmosphere and speech remain Andalusian, not Catalan. In the relatively central district of Sants, cases have been observed of immigrants who have been 'absorbed' - that is, who have mastered correct Catalan, in ten or twelve years (Esteva Fabregat: 41–68); but in the outer suburbs and townships, the context essential for this sort of 'absorption' cannot be found. Here, there is no evidence that a Catalan sense of identity has made any significant conquests among immigrants of the first generation; and Catalanization of their children has to proceed delicately and by degrees if they are not to be alienated. The alliance of workers and Catalanists, which was a product of the Franco era, has survived, but uncemented, since the dictator's death.

The economics of immigration are illustrated by an interview recorded by Sebastian Balfour with an immigrant from Badajoz, who sold his house at home in 1950 for 7,000 pesetas, paid off his debts and bought a cave in Sabadell for 3,000 (Balfour: 8). Accommodated in caves or shacks or squalid blocks, the workers were exploited with longer hours and lower real incomes than in any other industrialized zone of Western Europe; but the regime's policies of guaranteed work ensured that they were better off at home and gradually began to enjoy the comforts of consumerism and the economic benefits of a spectacular economic leap forward in the sixties. The traditionally combative masses of Barcelona no longer existed. The new hydra had drawn fangs. Political strikes were rare, even in the early seventies when anti-Francoist protest was at its boldest. The union elections of 1975 revealed a non-political majority among unionized workers (Balfour: 214–15). Instead of being goaded by repression into the arms of the communists, they had drifted, from boredom and *embourgeoisement*, into entente with Catalanism.

'The city of prodigies'

Hercules, the legendary founder of Barcelona, makes a suitable role model for a city whose history has strangely paralleled his mythical career. Both have been poised between the love of Pleasure and Toil, with a strong inclination towards the latter, tempered by a good deal of dalliance with the former. Both were called on to perform prodigious feats, the most conspicuous difference being, perhaps, that Barcelona's Herculean tasks have been accomplished under Sisyphean burdens. Hemmed in by mountains on the landward side, restricted to seaward by unserviceable currents, Barcelona became the capital of a territorial state without conquering an inch of territory, and the heart of a maritime empire without possessing a decent natural harbour. When the empire was lost and the state dismantled, she became an industrial power, despite her dearth of natural resources. All her labours were responses to difficulties or disasters: her first boom followed al-Mansur's raid. Her seaborne empire was acquired to gain previously thwarted access to Mediterranean trade. Her challenge to Joan II occurred almost at the nadir of her late medieval decline. The construction of her artificial port began when her trade had collapsed, and was sustained through two centuries of more or less chronic adversity. She tackled successively the Habsburgs and

Bourbons in times of mixed fortune and went on fighting when her cause seemed hopeless. The foundations of her manufacturing prosperity were laid when she was a conquered and occupied victim of a protracted era of war and defeat. Her industrial take-off in the mid-nineteenth century happened amid civil disorders that, in any other city, would have made long-term investment unthinkable. The struggle against Napoleon produced the first inklings of the modern Catalanist tradition. The tumults and bombardments of 1842–1843 were followed by the flowering of the Renaixença. The bloodshed of 1854 was followed by the building of the Eixample. In the same period, the challenge of the steamship age was met by the construction of new artificial ports. The spirit shown by the merchants who had begun the first port in the fifteenth century was renewed in the manufacturers of the nineteenth who created a metallurgical industry out of nothing. After 1909 the song of Maragall's 'Oda Nova' and the spires of Gaudí's Sagrada Família rose in defiance of the flames of the Tragic Week. The extinction of Catalan institutions in 1924 did nothing to interrupt a brilliant era in the arts or a dynamic period of growth for the city. After the double disaster of the Civil War - the revolution in 1936, the last 'Castilian' conquest in 1939 - growth was renewed at a faster rate than ever.

Today, Barcelona is a 'city of prodigies'- the glittering, even gaudy, marvels of modern arts with which the city is studded. Modern god-makers, her poets and artists, have begun work on an apotheosis to rival that of Hercules; the PR men of the 1992 Olympiad, who will bring Olympus to Montjuïc, have stepped in with their meretricious help. Yet despite the admirable resilience with which the Barcelonese, for more than a thousand years, have made an adventure of every adversity and wrung an achievement from every disaster, none of the city's historic ambitions has been fulfilled.

There are few 'second cities' in the world to rival her, by any standard of judgement; but to be the best of the second is a frustrating fate and within Spain, in recent years, Madrid has drawn far ahead, especially in the one field - 'high' culture or 'the arts' - in which Barcelona has hitherto always excelled. The government of Catalonia has returned to Barcelona since the restoration of Catalan autonomy in 1978; but Catalan statehood is still truncated and, though the Catalans have abundantly proven their ineradicable durability as a distinct ethnicity, the precise nature of Catalonia's future as a political entity, within Spain and within Europe, remains a matter of debate. The period of mass immigration, which threatened to swamp Barcelona's Catalan identity, may be at an end, with the menace apparently contained, but the marginal parts of the Catalan world - in Valencia, the Balearic Islands and southern France - have regional interests, cultural identities and political directions of their own and seem determined, for the foreseeable future, to resist Barcelonese aspirations to any sort of pan-Catalan capitality. Meanwhile, the 'Europeanization' of Spain - or rather, the accumulation of evidence of Spain's fully European identity - has deprived the Barcelonese of one of their favourite roles, as the most 'European' of Iberian cities. The year of the Olympiad will also bring the inauguration of the single European market, for which Barcelona's history of prosperity under protectionism may seem a poor preparation; but to judge from Barcelona's record, a new 'era of difficulties' in the offing only betokens a new era of triumphs ahead. Today, when Barcelona is the heart of the biggest conurbation on the western Mediterranean seaboard, the essential character detected by a visiting Castilian humanist in the small and struggling city of 500 years ago can be seen to be amply confirmed: 'Oh, God of grace, I now behold a city, securely placed, very plenteous in the midst of a poor land. And I see her citizens, triumphant despite their dearth of natural resources, and her people possessed of all worldly prosperity, thanks to their own efforts alone' (Palencia: 41).

Works cited

Actividad contemporánea, iii (1933), no. 11 (Barcelona: GATEPAC). http://hemerotecadigital.bne.es/issue.vm?id=0004015428&search=&lang=es [accessed 29 March 2017].

Balfour, Sebastian (1989). *Dictatorship, Workers and the City* (Oxford: Clarendon).

Balmes, Jaume (1948–1950). *Obras completas, V* (Madrid: Biblioteca de Autores Cristianos).

Berwick, Duque de (1931–1933). *Catálogo histórico y bibliográfico de la Exposición Internacional de Barcelona*, 2 vols (Madrid: n.p.).

Bohigas, Oriol (1963). *Barcelona entre el Pla Cerdà i el barraquisme* (Barcelona: Edicions 62).

Capmany, Antoni de (1961–1963). *Memorias históricas del comercio, marina y artes de la antigua ciudad de Barcelona*, ii (Barcelona: Cámara Oficial de Comercio y Navegación de Barcelona).

Castro, Américo (1954). *La realidad histórica de España* (México: Porrúa).

¡*Cu-Cut!* (1909, 21 January): 41. (Barcelona: ARCA). http://mdc2.cbuc.cat/cdm/compoundobject/collection/cucut/id/7019/rec/355 [accessed 30 March 2017].

Duran i Sanpere, Agustí (1973). *Barcelona i la seva història* (Barcelona: Curial).

Esteva Fabregat, Claudi (1975). 'Les relacions interètniques: el cas de Barcelona', *Perspectiva Social*, 5: 41–68.

Fraser, Ronald (1988). *Blood of Spain* (Harmondsworth, UK: Allen Lane).

Gómez Martínez, José Luis (1975). *Américo Castro y el origen de los españoles* (Madrid: Gredos).

Jardí, Enric (1972). *Història de Els Quatre Gats* (Barcelona: Aedos).

Mackay, David (1985). *Modern Architecture in Barcelona* (Sheffield, UK: Anglo-Catalan Society).

Mendoza, Cristina, and Eduardo Mendoza (1989). *Barcelona modernista* (Barcelona: Planeta).

Orwell, George (1938). *Homage to Catalonia* (London: Secker and Warburg).

Palencia, Alfonso de (1874) [1459]. '*Tratado de la perfección del triunfo militar*', in Antonio María Fabié (ed.), *Dos tratados de Alfonso de Palencia* (Madrid: Durán).

Ponz, Antonio (1788). *Viage de España* (Madrid: Joaquín Ibarra), xiv.

Primo de Rivera, Miguel (1923). *La Vanguardia*, 14 September: 3. http://hemeroteca.lavanguardia.com/preview/1923/09/14/pagina-3/33278432/pdf.html [accessed 30 March 2017].

— (1929). 'Comentos económicos y politicos', *La Vanguardia*, 9 October: 7. http://hemeroteca.lavanguardia.com/preview/1929/10/09/pagina-7/33229598/pdf.html [accessed 29 March 2017].

Pujol García, Joan (1985). *Garbo* (London: Weidenfeld and Nicolson).

Sánchez-Albornoz, Claudio (1956). *España: un enigma histórico*, 2 vols (Buenos Aires: Editorial Sudamericana).

Solé, Carlota (1982). *Los inmigrantes en la sociedad y la cultura catalanas* (Barcelona: Península).

CHAPTER FIVE

A fragile country*

Colm Tóibín

I was on the steps of the Cathedral in the early evening, the hour before twilight one day during the last week of April, when I saw the first swifts diving and darting across the sky. I watched how they suddenly seemed frenetic and out of control, and then how they glided calmly for a while over the Hotel Colon and the Via Laietana.

I remembered seeing them for the first time during the April of 1977 when it was still unclear how things would work out here, when everybody held their breath, united in wanting autonomy for Catalonia. It must have been the feast of Sant Jordi, and there were crowds of people in the Plaça de Sant Jaume. The stone plaque announcing that the Civil War was over and the 'red army' had been defeated by Franco was still on the wall of the Town Hall. I remember someone saying that it would be easy now to take it down or deface it, since the square was so full.

They called out for sweet liberty that day, a few months before they broke into factions and political parties. The same day the first brave swifts came back to the city.

---

* Colm Tóibín, 'A Fragile Country', in *Homage to Barcelona* (London: Picador, 2002), pp. 199–211. © Colm Tóibín, 2002.

Eleven years later, that week in April 1988 was a good lesson for me, in case I had forgotten, that everything was still political here, that politics was the mould in which everything was shaped: from art to religion, from football to a visit by the King of Spain.

He was scheduled to come to Barcelona on 23 April, the eve of the feast of Sant Jordi, the patron saint of Catalonia whose killing of the dragon was depicted on tapestries, stained glass windows and paintings all over Catalonia. His visit was to celebrate the Millennium of Catalonia at a function in the Palau de la Generalitat. No one believed much in the historical veracity of the Millennium, and it was perhaps no coincidence that within five weeks Jordi Pujol, President of the Generalitat, and his Government would seek a third term in office, which they would win.

There were posters all over the city protesting against the visit. Some depicted Pujol, a small man at the best of times, sitting on the king's knee. These were put up by La Crida, an extreme nationalist group; La Crida also broke into the Palau de la Generalitat and took down the Spanish flag, returning it with great ceremony the following day. They announced that they would disrupt the king's speech with fireworks from a nearby rooftop. That same day two men from Terra Lliure, a small Catalan terrorist army, were found with explosives in a car outside the city.

The following morning there were security men everywhere. Montserrat Caballé, the reigning queen of culture in Catalonia, was to sing; there would be medieval music; there would be speeches. It was a tense morning. Pujol later told journalists that when the drums began for the medieval music he thought it was a bomb. He and a historian spoke in both Catalan and Spanish, Pujol extolling the greatness that was Catalonia, the historian outlining its independent spirit in the tenth century. When the king began to speak the fireworks started.

It was like gunfire, or the sound of a small bomb, and it seemed close at hand, dead close. The sound shook the building. Everyone ignored it, pretended it was not happening, looked straight ahead. Everyone knew that it was the sound of fireworks, parodying another sound which these streets had known so well just 50 years before. It came at intervals, like a taunt, seeming to say: look what we could do with you if we wanted.

It didn't stop until the rooftop on Passeig del Crèdit was identified and the culprits arrested. By that time the king had begun to speak in Catalan talking about the 'art and the industry' of the Catalan people; he referred to the language, which Franco had banned, as 'the live expression of a great culture'; he referred to the Catalans' sense of solidity, their closeness to Europe. He seemed pleased with his Catalan subjects, and happy to use their language, even though his accent was heavy and foreign.

Later there was champagne and smoked salmon in the patio of the orange trees in the middle of the Palace. The day was becoming warm as the king moved from group to group, escorted by Pujol. All around the peculiar grammar and morphology of the Catalan language filled the air, as its ruling class talked to each other. Those clipped, harsh sounds, that intense seriousness, that pride in modernity and progress. The king smiled and grinned, a gamey, amused look on his face. Artists and significant figures in the society had been invited, as well as politicians, but no trade unionists. Pujol's party was dedicated to representing bourgeois values, conservative forces. This was the day for showing strength and establishing stability. The king was on their side.

The following day was the feast day of Sant Jordi and one of the anti-king demonstrations on the Rambla had a large photograph of the king in his former incarnation as Franco's heir, wearing a military uniform marching alongside the old dictator. *Fora el Rei Borbó*, their posters said, meaning 'out with the Bourbon king'. They also had a life-size model of Jordi Pujol with various anti-Spanish slogans around his neck. The Trotskyites, the Green Alternative, the Gay Liberation Movement all had stalls. Boys who wanted to raise money for fireworks at a forthcoming football match also had a stall.

But the main point of the day was not to protest, but to celebrate love and culture. It was the day of the book and the rose, the day when every male gave his girlfriend or wife or live-in companion a rose and got a book in return, or vice versa. The city was one big bookshop; the publishers, both Catalan and Spanish, had new titles launched. All the roses had little Catalan flags attached. The newspapers had published special literary supplements. By the afternoon there were stalls on both sides of the Rambla from the Plaça de Catalunya down to the port, all of them selling books, some specialising in political books, children's books, picture books, new books, novels in Catalan, new Spanish novels. Authors were in great demand for signing sessions at the various stalls.

Everybody seemed to take the day seriously; boys walked in the streets on the way to meet their loved ones with roses in their hands. A rich-looking old man had a large art book under his arm, while his wife walked beside him with an opulent rose. There were two streams of people moving up and down the Rambla perusing all the new books. You couldn't move. I sat for a while outside the Bar del Pi in the Plaça del Pi and watched three boys and three girls in their early twenties who had neither rose nor book between them. Eventually, the three boys went off and came back with roses. They kissed the girls formally and then handed them the roses. It was a serious occasion. The girls then went to the Rambla to buy books; all of the books they bought, when unwrapped, turned out to be about sex, including a book in Catalan on how to make love to a woman, as well as a new pornographic novel in Spanish. No one giggled or laughed about the books. They passed them from one to the other, showing each other significant passages.

All over the city that day the Catalan flag, the four red bars on a yellow background, had been put out on the balconies to make clear that this was a specifically Catalan occasion. They danced *sardanes*, the national dance, that afternoon, in front of the Boqueria market on the Rambla. Salvador Dalí did a special drawing, his first in five years, for the Sant Jordi edition of the Catalan-language newspaper *Avui*. The other Catalan-language newspaper ran a survey which showed that 40 per cent of Catalans supported complete independence from Spain.

A few days later it was the feast of the Virgin of Montserrat, the patron of Catalonia. Vast numbers left the city in cars and buses on the morning of the feast, 27 April, to visit Montserrat, one of Catalonia's sacred places. It has been a place of pilgrimage since the twelfth century when the famous Black Virgin was carved, but the significance of Montserrat is not simply religious; it stands as a beacon outside the city, the very soul of Catalonia. Over the last 50 years, through the work of its liberal abbots, it had become something of a symbol of hope and freedom for Catalans. Jordi Pujol's party had its first meeting there in 1973 and Miró was among those who marched there as a protest against the Franco regime in 1970.

It was a misty morning as we set off for Montserrat from the Plaça Universitat; the windows of the bus were steamed up with condensation. The other passengers were middle-aged; I was the youngest person on the bus. Everyone spoke to me in Catalan. These, my fellow passengers, were very different from the Catalans at the reception for the king who had oozed power and money and satisfaction. They were different, too, from the crowds on the Rambla buying books on the feast of Sant Jordi, who were younger and emphatically post-Franco in their clothes and manners and opinions. These people were the conservative, lower-middle class Catalans, the bedrock of Pujol's support, who had office jobs, owned small shops, who kept the faith, both Catholic and Catalan. Montserrat, for them, was Mecca, although, like good Catalans, they remained discreet and reserved about this as about all else.

The mountain comes as a shock when you first see it from the road, its rise is so sheer, the rock so white and smooth, the shape so conical. It looks artificial, as though someone had built it. The bus began the slow ascent, hampered by all the other traffic making its way up the mountain in time for Mass.

The buildings around the church are functional and straightforward; the whole place looked grey and uninviting that morning as the mist turned to a light rain; this meant that the cable cars, which went further up towards the summit, weren't working. We crowded into the church where, by now, there was standing room only. The Mass was in Catalan and everyone knew the responses. People listened attentively to the sermon which declared that the Catalan identity and the Christian faith were synonymous, and emphasized the importance of religion in the life of Catalonia. It was a nationalist sermon for an audience well used to the transforming of even religion into another facet of the self which Catalonia was in the process of remaking.

The Black Virgin was behind the main altar; a queue began of those who wanted to kiss her hand. She would not be paraded down the mountain, as the Spaniards did with their Virgins, she would be left in her place, stately and sedate. As the rain softened back to mist, the crowd got ready to dance *sardanes* in front of the church, celebrating once more their sense of nationhood on the feast day of their patroness.

I started to walk down the corkscrew road which wound around the mountain. The day was clearing now although the sky was still watery and grey. I stopped for lunch some way down the mountain, at the Hotel Colonia Puig, which stood as a monument to the past: the huge rooms dated from the 1920s and 1930s, all untouched, just as the people in the church and on the bus seemed to belong to a time which had gone.

As I walked further down the mountain I noticed a woman in a field picking flowers, and later I met a man who asked me in Spanish if I had seen a middle-aged woman. When I told him where he would find her, he asked me where I was going; I said I was going to Barcelona, but I wasn't sure how. He told me he would pick me up in his car when he was going down, once he had found his wife.

They both spoke Spanish and were from Madrid. They were retired now, they said, and had come especially for the feast of Montserrat. But they didn't want to stay any longer: they didn't like what they saw. The mountain was beautiful and they had enjoyed the journey. The problem was the language: they couldn't understand a word of the Mass, nor a word of the sermon. And they were in their own country, they emphasized. And to make matters worse, the wife had tried to buy some holy pictures with prayers printed on them but they only had them in Catalan, and she left without buying anything. She shook her head and sighed. Imagine, she said, imagine.

Was everything like that now? – they asked me. It was, I said. There was a television station in Catalan, several radio stations, two daily newspapers, signs in shops; in Barcelona, I said, the street names were in Catalan only. The husband said that he was first in Barcelona in 1939 and it was a great city. I wondered what he was doing there in 1939. He didn't know things were as bad as this now. He had never imagined, he said.

What do you Catalans want? – the wife asked me. Why do you want to have everything in Catalan? The husband turned to her and said he didn't think the passenger was Catalan. But the wife was sure, until I told her I was Irish. My Spanish was clearly that of a foreigner but she had assumed that my accent was merely part of the new order in Catalonia, which she and her husband found so puzzling and offensive. She stopped for a moment and then went on. She didn't understand, she said, why they couldn't use Catalan just among themselves; surely for big occasions, like the feast day of Montserrat, they could use Spanish, which was the language everyone understood. They said nothing more and for a second I felt as powerless and upset as they were, sensing their hardness and hostility.

We remained silent until we discovered that they had taken a wrong turn. They were going back to Madrid and planned to drop me at a train station, but they had gone too far. They were desperately apologetic and genuinely concerned as to how I would get back to the city. We parted then, using the Spanish language which they knew and loved so well, and I found myself at the entrance to the toll road to Barcelona, where I was picked up by one of the first cars which came.

The driver was alone, in his early forties and Catalan. When I told him where I had been, he looked at me as though I was mad. There was rock music on the car stereo, he was wearing trendy clothes; he had put Montserrat and all it stood for way behind him as we drove fast towards the city. He had bought a bar, he told me, in one of the posh suburbs of the city in the late 1970s. He had seen a gap in the market. The Catalan kids were a new generation, they wouldn't go to old-fashioned bars or loud, vulgar discos: they needed places which were modern and cool, which were subtle mixtures of old and new. He designed this bar, spent a lot of money on it, and it worked. Once Franco died, he said, Barcelona changed, everyone's habits changed, the market changed. The young people were different now.

So different, he said, that everyone picked up his idea, new places opened all over the city. He saw another gap in the market, he sold his bar (it still did great business, he said, and told me I should go there some time) and he began to design and make trendy furniture for bars. He was doing well and employed a lot of people. Barcelona was changing every day. You had to keep up with the changes. He was enjoying talking like this, and I was enjoying listening to him, as he went on, with confidence and innocence, seeing the arrival of democracy and the death of the old dictator in terms of gaps in the market, new ways to go in there and make a killing.

It was that week in April when chance encounters with Catalan businessmen seemed to take on political nuances and reverberations. It was also the week when a huge exhibition of recent work by Antoni Tàpies went on show in the two medieval buildings on the Plaça del Rei: the Sala Tinell and the Church of Santa Àgata. The exhibition, entitled *Tàpies els anys 80*, was sponsored by the Ajuntament, the Town Hall, which had also produced a sumptuous 274-page full-colour catalogue.

Tàpies' name also stands for something other than art: for the spirit of resistance to Franco and Fascism in the 1960s and 1970s. His paintings, however abstract and philosophical in their origins, often had a directly political message. His actions, as well, have frequently been overtly political, such as his part in the occupation of the Capuchin Convent at Sarrià in 1966 for which he was arrested and fined, his involvement in the march of protest to Montserrat in 1970, and his involvement after 1975 in the campaign for amnesty and democracy.

'Tàpies' Catalan identity', one of the essays in the catalogue reads, 'has been viewed as a constant in his career, which gave unity and continuity to his art ... Many motifs appearing in the work of Tàpies have been recognized as references to his Catalan roots, but his Catalan identity has also been explained on a deeper technical and formal level. The significance of craftsmanship in his work, especially his profound knowledge of the materials he employs, has been associated with Catalonia's traditional craftsmanship. Ultimately, Tàpies' intellectual attitude towards mysticism, the esoteric and the magical has been explained through his Catalan identity'. The catalogue was produced in Catalan with translations at the back in small print into Spanish and English, but at the exhibition the titles were in Catalan only.

He is a diffident man, Tàpies. At the press reception on the day of the opening, he shrugged a lot, kept his distance, answered questions in a bemused and self-deprecating tone. At one stage he slipped away and stood on his own while others who organized the exhibition answered questions. The work in the two big halls was a retreat from the public Antoni Tàpies back into the private artist. The paintings were big, big enough for the large Gothic space they had come to fill in the great square of Tàpies native city.

In an interview in the catalogue he had said that 'there was a time when the Franco regime was at its height, that I believed that certain clearer political messages could contribute to a general revulsion for the regime. These messages have not reappeared for some years now'. Politics had freed him then from having to paint about politics; now he was free to be playful and obscure, if he so wished. Franco was thirteen years dead now, and this was his legacy; that an artist would no longer need to protest, he could look inwards.

The fashionable people came that night to the big opening. Tàpies now looked slightly frightened but stayed on, even after the Mayor of

Barcelona had left. Tàpies was watching everyone, his hair tousled and untidy, looking owl-like, mildly sceptical. 'The artist', he had written, 'has always been something of a solitary bird, a perturbing spirit that constantly rocks the boat [..] he will continue to be so even under socialism'.

The fashionable people were wearing designer clothes, designer shoes, designer glasses. They were moving slowly, elegantly and carefully from painting to painting. They found nothing strange about the work, there was no beckoning over of a friend to come and look at this extraordinary object on the wall in which the artist has stuck two halves of a broken chair to a canvas; they were equal to this work, the use of old foam, old doors, old book covers, the use of glue, newspaper, numbers, squiggles, daubs and crosses. If you didn't know the city, you would wonder where they could possibly be from: they couldn't be Spanish, there were too many blond people and people with fair skin. They had to be from somewhere which valued design and modernity, Milan perhaps, except that several faces were too swarthy, too earthy, and there was a prudence in their watchfulness and their self-consciousness. Two girls arrived wearing skin-tight leggings; no one ogled them or stared at them. The sexual tension was carefully controlled and was not based on the macho ideal. Some of the conversations were deeply animated, people listened carefully, curled their lips, gesticulated with their arms, shrugged, touched each other, no one spoke in Spanish. This gathering was quintessential Catalan chic, as though everything - the paintings, the occasion, the building, the clothes - had always been thus. This was a gathering of those who had not simply recovered from Franco, or forgotten about him, this was a gathering of those who had shrugged him off.

It was the last week in April, and I was beginning to imagine that life in the city was one long set of symbolic occasions from which morals could be drawn about the state of the national psyche, in which politics sucked in everything that happened and spewed it back out again in the colours of the Catalan flag. It was like Ireland. But here, like nowhere else, the game of soccer meant everything. Barça, the richest football club in the world, was the most potent symbol of the city's greatness and of Catalonia's destiny. It was more powerful than the Liceu, the Sagrada Família or Montserrat because its fortunes could change, its team could lose, it could undermine the city and the country. And when it won, then the whole of Catalonia, its great traditions, its glorious future, would win as well, would shine like a light.

I remembered a Saturday in the early summer of 1981 when I had come to the city, left my bags in a hotel, bought no newspapers and contacted nobody, simply gone for a walk and ended up by chance at the first showing in a cinema in Barcelona of Fellini's *La Dolce Vita* (1960), which Franco had banned. The film had dated, but it was still worth seeing after all these years. When I came outside, after that mild encounter with heat and sex, it was as though the city was on fire. I walked over towards the Rambla, where the cars were blocked on both sides of the street, with their klaxons honking over and over the eleven-note rhythm of victory. In a frenzy of zest and celebration young fellows were attacking each car, hitting the car on the roof, beating the windows with their fists, and the people inside were laughing, and the driver was honking the horn. And then that car would be let go, and they would attend to the next one, standing in front of it to make sure that it couldn't go by until it got the treatment. A few of the cars were driven by people who, like myself, were unaware of what was happening, who looked frightened and tried to speed up and get past without any trouble, but these too were detained and then released, the driver by this time in a rage.

Barcelona had won the cup. And not just that, but Barcelona had beaten Madrid in the Camp Nou, Barcelona's own football ground. The top of the Rambla was full of people cheering and shouting, waving Catalan flags, wearing them around their shoulders. Some cars were circling the city, the passengers shouting out victory slogans, waving flags and proclaiming themselves the victors. Beating Madrid was a special pleasure.

Young Catalans brought bottles of cheap champagne and poured it over themselves and their companions, and then went back to stopping the cars. Not once over the next two hours was there any violence in the city, none of the cars was damaged. It was pure, unconfined joy, going on and on into the night.

Seven years later the atmosphere surrounding the Barça and the Camp Nou was darker. There were internal dissensions in the club, difficulties between players and management. Some blamed the players, others blamed the club's President Nuñez. The games at the

Camp Nou were no longer packed, the crowds weren't coming. Below the press box were the men who ran soccer in the city, the owners of the club. You couldn't avoid seeing them, in their sombre suits or blue blazers and slacks, they stood out against the crowd. Some people said that things would never be right until Nuñez left; other commentators wrote that football was merely a sport, the Camp Nou merely a football field, the Barça were merely eleven players, and, until the Catalans realized this and stopped using the Barça as a symbol, things would never be right. Everyone had a view on what should be done with the Barça.

In the last week of April, the players issued a statement of no confidence in Nuñez. They had won the King's Cup in Madrid, which had resulted in mild celebrations on the Rambla. But they were badly down in the League, which they now had no chance of winning and they were playing Madrid in the last round on the last day of April, and even if they won it would mean nothing. Some people said that the players should concentrate on the game.

The nearest Barcelona got to soccer hooliganism came from a small bunch at the front of the Camp Nou in standing room only, who cheered and whistled and banged a drum, threw cheap fireworks and bangers when the going was good. Tonight, when they moved too close to the field, or threw petards which let off coloured smoke, the police came after them, but it was a game; what was serious was the level of insult they roared up at Nuñez. He sat there surrounded by his henchmen, as they pointed their finger at him all through the game, as though it was he who had lost the matches, as though he was a politician, as though he ran the country.

And so he did, someone told me, he did run the country. The club was as important as the government. You had to understand that.

On the last day of April in the week when the first swifts appeared in the sky over the city, I watched the football, watched our team winning as night came down, but it wasn't football, it was another piece of pageantry, the vast parade which a fragile country was making of its sacred symbols.

PART II
City and society

CHAPTER SIX

Barcelona and modernity*

Brad Epps

For Joana Crespi, who taught me Catalan, introduced me to the streets of Barcelona, and invited me to my first dry Martini at Can Boadas; *in memoriam*

Great Enchantress; Rose of Fire; Manchester of Spain; Paris of the South; City of Bombs; City of Marvels; City of Architects; Olympic Village; design capital; gastronomic centre; soccer powerhouse; tourist mecca; cultural forum; international hot spot: modern Barcelona has been, and continues to be, many things to many people. For Rubén Darío, it was a place of cosmopolitan refinement, home to the only modernist 'brotherhood' in all of Spain (254). For Jean Genet, it was a place of exquisitely abject desire populated by beggars, thieves, queers, and whores (18). For designer Javier Mariscal, it is a place of bars and sky and waves, as his famous poster from 1979 attests: *Bar cel ona*. If Darío yearned for a select fraternity of sophisticated artists,

---

* This is an abridged and slightly altered version, approved by the author, Brad Epps, of 'Introduction: Barcelona and Modernity', *Catalan Review: International Journal of Catalan Culture* 18.1–2 (2004): 13–28. © Brad Epps.

and Genet for a sordid congregation of divine outlaws, Mariscal, who later created the happy Olympic mascot Cobi, has had his ear pressed to the profitable pulse of the culture industry. Broken down and built back up, *Bar cel ona* can be marketed and consumed – happily, giddily, drunkenly – as a place of perfect postmodern pomp where more culturally motivated visitors can sip a beer in the Quatre Gats (a beer house–café made famous by Picasso) and buy trinkets that commemorate the effective desacralization of the Sagrada Família (Antoni Gaudí's great unfinished expiatory temple) and where more raucously motivated visitors can fry themselves on newly sanded beaches and vomit their cold northern repression onto steamy summer streets.

The capital of Catalonia, a nation (*malgré* the Partido Popular) without a state (*malgré* Esquerra Republicana), Barcelona is a metropolis in which sangria, Mexican sombreros and tapas, Dior, Gucci and Armani, Starbucks and McDonalds, Deutsche Bank and ING, coexist – such a gentle, deceptive word – alongside such international successes as Miró, Gaudí, and Tàpies and such national specialities, some of them quaintly seasonal, as *panellets* and *pa amb tomàquet*, *calçots* and *caganers*, sardines and *sardanas*. In its vacillations between the material and symbolic manifestations of global capital and local pride, Barcelona is far from unique; and yet, as with so many other places, its movers and shakers strive to present it as unique, as marvellous and enchanting, as far removed from the industrial grime and class turmoil of times gone by. Even Manchester, which, like London, Leeds and Birmingham, led Engels to speak of the city in general as 'a strange thing' marked by 'barbarous indifference, hard egotism ... and nameless misery' (68, 69), even Manchester, after all, has tried to refashion itself.

Even though unicity can serve as a powerfully general lure (everyone, everything, every place is unique) or, more simply, even though Barcelona can be like so many other cities, it has in fact been remarkably adept at refashioning itself, so much so that it would come as little surprise if Manchester dreamt of becoming the Barcelona of Britain – were cities, in contrast to people, able to dream, desire, think or do anything at all. Refashioning, as a modification of what is á la mode, is here apposite, for it is in modernity, indeed as modernity, at least as Baudelaire so masterfully styled it, that fashion comes to the fore in the play of beauty, which is no longer simply and solely the stuff of eternal truths and invariable forms but also, and quite vertiginously, the fluff of the moment, the 'relative, circumstantial element' (3) that passes.[1] Double and contradictory as Baudelaire conceives it, beauty is modern, *particularly so* when it flits fleetingly away, when it outstrips or falls short of the permanence and staid stability of classical beauty (which has its own modernities). 'This transitory, fugitive element, whose metamorphoses are so rapid, must on no account be despised or dispensed with', Baudelaire asserts, because '[b]y neglecting it, you cannot fail to tumble into the abyss of an abstract and interminable beauty, like that of the first woman before the fall of man' (13). It is curious, no doubt, that security from an abyssal fall can best be purchased (ah, that is the word) by giving oneself over and unto that which runs away, which ever so concretely comes to an end: *sic transit gloria mundi.*

The glories of the world pass, so much fleeting beauty, so many vain fashions that leave in their wake the desire for more. The point is not idle. Internationally renowned art critic Robert Hughes opens his bestselling book on Barcelona (published just in time for the 1992 Olympics) by invoking the Devil's temptation of Christ that gives the Tibidabo mountain that overlooks the city its name. Firmly entrenched in the values of secular exchange, Hughes intones: 'Jesus refused the offer; the modern visitor need not' (1992: 3). What Hughes, an outsider, points to is, mutatis mutandis, what many an insider has pointed to: namely, the wealth of the city's commercial and cultural offerings, its art and industry, its openness, as port, to the business of the world. Long before the late twentieth-century secularism of Hughes, none other than Jacint Verdaguer, the most distinguished poet of the Catalan Renaixença, sings in his ode 'A Barcelona' the busy bounty of the sea: 'La mar, un dia esclava del teu poder, te crida, / com dos portells obrint-te Suez i Panamà: / quiscun ab tota una Índia rienta te convida, amb l'Àssia, les Amèriques, la terra i l'Occeà [*sic*]' (Verdaguer: 33). First presented in the Jocs Florals of 1883, Verdaguer's ode links

---

1 Of course, the 'relative, circumstantial element' (Baudelaire: 3) that passes can leave, in its passing, an impression, more or less enduring (depending on the circumstances and the thinking subject, to be sure), of something that does not quite pass: the sketch, the dress, the bibelot, and so on.

the city's prosperity and its genius – 'aqueixa estrella que et guia' – to the respectful maintenance of the Catholic faith: 'un poble que creu no pot morir' and, more resoundingly, 'Qui enfonsa o alça els pobles és Déu, que els ha creat' (33). With all of its spiritual sincerity, the ode, already ripe for patriotic propaganda, was promptly converted into municipal publicity: City Hall, under mayor Francesc Rius i Taulet's direction, had 100,000 copies printed in order to, as Verdaguer himself notes, 'repartir-la profusament i en particular fer-la conèixer als nois de les escoles públiques' (191, n. 1).

What exactly the schoolchildren learned from Verdaguer's poem, no less than what exactly the politicians and the poet wanted them to learn, may be a matter of speculation (a word richly resonant in the context of Barcelona's urban expansion), but along with the values of *patria*, *fides*, and *amor* championed in the Jocs Florals, trade, profit, and power were surely, if somewhat more subtly, at stake. Barcelona, even at its most devout, had its figurative eyes placed on other places, part and parcel of what Marx understood – critically, needless to say – as the drive to a world market. The Suez and the Panama canals that Verdaguer so proudly cites in relation to Barcelona's maritime prowess are, after all, not merely marvels of technology but monuments to imperialism. Now, while there was nothing new about the mixture of God and gold, what was new was the speed and efficiency with which things, thoughts, and people could move and, more specifically, with which Catalonia, long hindered by centralist forces beyond it, could regain a prominent place in the world.

Newness is the operative word here, linked, in its conceptual sweep, to modernity and its often frenetic, fleeting (re)fashionings. Ildefons Cerdà, engineer of Barcelona's Eixample, the rationally planned mid-nineteenth-century expansion to which Verdaguer alludes in his poem, justified his plan by identifying a break in history: a new age, a new city, a 'nueva civilización que se levanta joven, vigorosa y prepotente, montada en el vapor y armada de la electricidad' (Cerdà: 15). The new civilization that Cerdà esteemed was not, as he well knew, without problems: behind and below the proliferation of worldly goods and services, of enhanced communication and transportation, there still festered an old order of poverty, sickness, inequality, and injustice. Much maligned as Cerdà has been (modernist architect and Catalanist politician Josep Puig i Cadafalch called Cerdà's plan 'una malura geomètrica' (154); others have been even less kind), his inspiration was not just technological (steam movement) but also utopian socialist (human movement), and his aim was, as he expressly notes in his *Teoría general de la urbanización* (1967 [1867]), to realize a city that would be to the benefit of each and every individual, that is to say, a city for everyone.[2] Revolted by the terrible conditions of the growing working class, and by the potential for revolt of a more physically violent sort, he argued for a city of hygienic, humanitarian, evenly distributed spaces and services in which class differences would be greatly assuaged if not overcome. He was not alone. Josep Anselm Clavé, also influenced by utopian socialist thought, sought to harmonize society by way of music, creating choral societies for workers, the celebrated Cors de Clavé. Interestingly, the first chapter of Dolors Monserdà's Catholic feminist novel *La fabricanta* (1904) opens with a visit to a performance of Clavé's choir in the Jardins de l'Euterpe, 'en l'espai dels terrenys que avui ocupen, a l'esquerra del passeig de Gràcia, les cases situades entre els carrers de València i de Mallorca' (Monserdà: 39), and ends with a stroll down a dark, deserted, and still rural Passeig de Gràcia.[3] The bucolic feel of the thoroughfare that connected the old walled city of Barcelona to the town of Gràcia and that became a central avenue of the Eixample had acquired a nostalgic lustre by the time Monserdà dared to do what other women might have only dreamt of doing: write and publish fiction.

For if speculation in real estate laid waste to the gardens and open spaces that had been part of Cerdà's original plan; if the opulent buildings with their scintillating façades that are today a major tourist

---

2 Cerdà writes of 'las necesidades que han producido y siguen produciendo y acrecentando en la humanidad siempre activa, los últimos descubrimientos y adelantos que no pertenecen como los de otros tiempos a una sola clase o a un reducido número de privilegiados, que nadie puede monopolizar, que están al alcance de todos y de cada uno de los individuos, aun del mas [*sic*] desgraciado' (12).

3 Monserdà writes that, 'la baixada a la ciutat pel desert i fosc passeig de Gràcia, ja que la migrada llum dels fanals, en lloc de reflectir-se com avui en les parets de les cases, lliscant pel dessobre de la llarga filera de pedrissos i rosers que s'aixecaven a banda i banda de la via, anava a perdre's per entre les tenebres d'immensos camps de conreu' (50).

draw were often mounted – as progressive Catalanist Valentí Almirall deplored[4] – with ill-gotten colonial gains; and if the individual, as in Narcís Oller's 'El transplantat', could end up crossing 'entre mils i mils persones com ombra indiferent' (*Contes*: 41), the city nonetheless provided opportunities for collectivization and experimentation among women, workers, artists, homosexuals, freethinkers, Republicans, avantguardists, revolutionaries, and others. Size matters, and if greater numbers translate into greater possibilities for friction, exploitation, and insecurity, they also translate into greater possibilities for freedom. 'Contra tots els prejudicis romàntics resulta que el ciutadà d'una metròpoli és, en tots els ordres, més lliure que el d'una masia del Montseny. La suma d'opinions, tota sola, té una força que no poden desconèixer ni els temperaments més típicament autocràtics' (109): so wrote Carles Soldevila in 1925, who also extolled the 'gust de servar l'incògnit a través de la multitud desconeguda' (112). Soldevila, at least in his capacity as flâneur and urban chronicler, is arguably one of Baudelaire's closest heirs in Barcelona, and it thus is hardly surprising that he was a supporter of Josep Planes, whom another great chronicler of Barcelona, Josep Maria de Sagarra, hailed as a pioneer of investigative and – as Planes himself apparently preferred – 'decorative' journalism (Planes, 2001: 25). Planes, like Sebastià Gasch and others, demonstrated a fascination with the night life that came to flourish in the city after the advent of electricity, staged most spectacularly in the World's Fair of 1929 though present, in much more modest form, since the World's Fair of 1888.

This is the twenty-four hour city of the burgeoning entertainment industry, with cinema, the circus, popular theatre, cabarets, music halls, bars, jazz clubs, sporting events, and even venues for bullfights and flamenco at once expanding and altering the cast of metropolitan characters beyond the conservative shopkeepers (Santiago Rusiñol's emblematic Senyor Esteve), imposing industrialists, restless workers,

---

4 The passage from Almirall is worth reproducing: '[c]uando se recorren las calles, anchas y largas, aún a medio edificar, de la Barcelona nueva, se pueden apreciar fastuosas y elegantes construcciones. Pues bien, de cada diez de esas casas sólo habrá una cuyo propietario se haya enriquecido en el país por medio del comercio laborioso o de la industria. Los nababs, llegados de América, y algunos arribistas de la Bolsa, son dueños de la mayoría o, mejor dicho, de la casi totalidad de tan suntuosos edificios' (176).

disaffected aesthetes, and brooding revolutionaries, to encompass the underworld of gangsters, flimflam men, cancan girls, pimps, and prostitutes. In many respects, a good deal of the social topography of today's city is in place by the early twentieth century, with Pedralbes, Sarrià, and the Eixample at a far remove, economically and symbolically speaking, from the Raval or Barri 'Xino'. Despite the 'espectacle de barreja i confraternitat' (Oller, 1979: 34), despite the rubbing together of people that could result in polished refinement (Soldevila: 108), the city, like perhaps all cities, remained divided by class, its 'rubbing together' of people at times a source of considerable, even violent, irritation and conflict.

The avant-garde poet Joan Salvat-Papasseit, writing in 1919, provides a 'map' of Barcelona in which the splendour and misery of the city is given graphic, almost telegraphic, form. In 'Plànol', the vertical force of a limited number of verbal signs exceeds the more conventional horizontal force of syntax: from the first or, more precisely, top line of 'MONT AVENTÍ' (with its Roman resonance) down through 'decadència', 'esglésies', 'xalets', 'aristocracia', 'vici', and 'ironia en el crim', to 'surburbis' (in the sense of beneath or below the urban, the lower depths), 'rameres pobres', 'hospital' (in the sense of a place for the sick and dying poor), 'la galera', 'honradesa', and 'fam', Salvat charts a viciously hierarchal order in which 'El sol ho encén tot / – Però no ho consum' (58–59). Given the textual and extratextual circumstances, the sun that ignites everything without consuming it suggests less a peaceful enlightenment than an enlightened struggle, a brilliant conflagration fuelled by class consciousness and artistic innovation. Baptized during the time that Santiago Salvador – responsible for a bloody attack on the Liceu in 1893 – was tried and executed along with other anarchists (a coincidence that the poet mythified), Salvat construed himself as 'l'incendiari de mots d'adolescent' (67) and was a key figure in the introduction and dissemination of what Hughes, in another work, has called the shock of the new: a more contentious and nonconformist version of the newness that Cerdà and others understood as the motor of progress, order, and general wellbeing. The difference is significant, for modernity, as that which is just now passing, as (re)fashioning and newness, is far from being a unified phenomenon; in fact, if Baudelaire presents modernity as part of a dual conception of beauty, it is a part that has parts of its own.

Many people have observed that Barcelona is really at least three cities (Ciutat Vella, the Eixample, and a periphery that extends up and down the coast), but modernity is multiple as well. Although any attempt at periodization is questionable, even hubristic, it is nonetheless possible to speak of four *overlapping* modernities: one, marked by the triumph of bourgeois liberalism, that runs from the rise of industrialism, the demolition of the city walls, and Cerdà's planned expansion to the Universal Exposition of 1888 and beyond; another, marked by the growing contestation of bourgeois hegemony, that runs from the first bouts of Anarchist direct action or terrorism (depending on one's perspective) in the 1890s through the popular uprising against the mobilization of troops to Morocco in 1909 known as the 'Setmana Tràgica' or 'Setmana Gloriosa' (again, depending on one's perspective) and the revolutionary movements of the Civil War to the triumph of Franco; a third, under Franco, marked by a technocratic capitalism hostile to civil liberties and democratic process and largely oblivious or indifferent to historical and environmental preservation; and a fourth, generally called postmodern, in which neoliberal global capitalism grapples with environmentalism, historical memory, and the rights of citizens and neighbours. Multiple as modernity is, it has become a commonplace (perhaps because it is true) to say that in the Iberian peninsula modernity was forged in Barcelona first, and it is common, if not yet a commonplace, to present this as a triumph rather than a problem, as if modernity's ties to ever more efficient and devastating ways to kill and destroy did not, could not, cast a shadow on the plethora of lushly decorative objects and sensuous services – statues by Llimona and Miró, buildings by Domènech i Montaner and Bofill, vases by Dionís Renart, jewels by the Masriera family, arias by Montserrat Caballé, and cuisine by Ferran Adrià – that most people associate with pleasure.

Although the lure of pleasure may be ageless (as some might say), the popularization and commodification of the lure of pleasure, its fractured democratic expansion and worldwide massification, finds it most tantalizing materialization in the World's Fairs that begin in the mid-nineteenth century. This, at any rate, is Walter Benjamin's assessment, one that has proved compelling to students and scholars of the city. For Benjamin, '[t]he framework of the entertainment industry ha[d] not yet been formed' (152) until the World's Fair. What the Fairs inaugurate is a sumptuous feast of merchandise spread out before the avid eyes of new consumers (yet another avatar of the new) or, more accurately, *potential* new consumers. The *promesse de bonheur* that Baudelaire ascribes to Stendhal (Stendhal's exact phrasing is slightly different) is here a promise of material wellbeing. As I have elsewhere noted, the Fairs or Expositions become, as Flaubert puts it in his *Dictionnaire des idées reçues* (1911–1913), a 'sujet de délire du XIXe siècle' (351) and, as Benjamin puts it, 'sites of pilgrimages to the commodity fetish' (151).[5] The delirium of the nineteenth century, which seems to intensify as time passes, might just be that of ever-expanding commodification and, as Benjamin adds, entertainment, by which people 'submit to being manipulated while enjoying their alienation from themselves and others' (152). Manipulation is a relative term (normally implying an agent, a manipulator), for in many respects the 1888 World's Fair helps to haul control back into the hands of Catalans and to raise awareness, as it were, of the singularity of Catalonia, the first part of Spain to host an event more commonly the province of national than regional capitals.

Bluntly put, the 1888 Exposition served as spectacular proof of the transformation of the city from a militarized fortress controlled from Madrid into a monumental market open to the world. The Fair takes place, after all, on the grounds of the much-reviled Ciutadella that owed its punitive existence to the Bourbon victory in the War of Spanish Succession. Josep Yxart, bewitched by the riches before him, fancied the city in which they were displayed as 'algo continental y no peninsular, con sus negras chimeneas de suburbio inglés, con sus *restaurants* y sus librerías de bulevar parisiense, con sus jarcias y velas sobre un mar de puerto italiano' (165). While Yxart found in the Fair proof of the difference between Catalonia and the rest of Spain (and similarities between Catalonia and other European nations), others, including famed realist writer Narcís Oller, capitalized on the difference, finding in it fodder for their Catalanism.[6] If commodity

---

5 See Epps, 'Modern Spaces: Building Barcelona' (2001), from which I extract this and the following sentence.
6 As Oller writes in his *Memòries:* 'Tot aquell traüt, tota aquella febre de treball mai vista aquí, tot aquell esforç titànic que donava tan brava mostra de les nostres ocultes energies i de la nostra set de progrés, encenien la meva

fetishism is what Benjamin most thickly associates with the Expositions, nationalism is also at play, but a nationalism that comes to the fore in an international – though by no means internationalist – frame. The national implications of the international expositions are well known: under the guise of liberal trade (along with militarism, the mainstay of colonialism), Western nations jockeyed for position. Seduced and invigorated by the prospects of modernization and economic success, many Catalans came to imagine Catalonia, and not just Spain, as a nation among nations, and to do so more realistically than they had for a long time before.

Perhaps not surprisingly, the Catalan capital, not able to marshal military support of its own, came to rely not just on industrial production but also on art and design. In the words of Cristina and Eduardo Mendoza: 'la Exposición fue el trampolín del Modernismo y el Modernismo se convirtió a partir de ese momento en la marca de fábrica de Barcelona' (74). The trademark endures, not in the construction of yet more modernist buildings but in their preservation, rehabilitation, expansion (as in the Palau de la Música Catalana), and promotion, as well as in the very 'experience' of the city. The Ruta Modernista, an itinerary for pedestrians and tour buses alike, directs the otherwise errant flâneur to what 'really matters', subjecting the contingencies of the street to a masterful, artful rationale. Rational, aesthetic-minded mastery may well be a phrase more suited to *Noucentisme* than *Modernisme*, inasmuch as *Noucentisme* promoted a well-ordered city arbitrated by a group of select intellectuals, a city of civility in the face of contingency, of tranquillity amid the hustle and bustle, and of classical Mediterranean features at home with modernity. The select intellectuals included the linguist Pompeu Fabra, the politician Enric Prat de la Riba, the poet Josep Carner, and, most importantly, writer and critic Eugeni d'Ors, whose celebration of urbanity assumed a culturally imperial – and imperialist – form.

Reality, however, would prove more imperious than any hierarchically ordered imperialist plan, more restive than any putatively harmonious synthesis of classicism and modernity, and, for that matter, more destructive than any avant-garde paean to destruction. War,

---

imaginació, el meu catalanisme, la fe posada en aquest poble, l'esperança en dies millors' (Oller 1962: 105).

exile, dictatorship, poverty, injustice, hunger (given narrative form in such works as Carmen Laforet's *Nada* [1945] and Mercè Rodoreda's *La plaça del Diamant* [1962]), and mass migrations left their marks too, putting the brakes on the dreams expressed by Jaume Bofill (better known by his poetic pseudonym, Guerau de Liost) that Barcelona, as capital of Catalonia, should become an amplified temple or Acropolis – '[t]ota Capital és l'espandiment d'una acròpolis' (1) – and a summation and generalization of refinement and tolerance (3).

If the post-war period was characterized by tolerance of a more repressive sort and by refinement of a decidedly more delimited sort, it would also come to be characterized, as the years of hunger gave way to the profitability of Spanish difference, by the reinvigoration of a mode of life and of production intensely bound up in global capitalism. Eugeni d'Ors in a *glosa* from 1906 (and hence long before both the Civil War and its aftermath) praised London for being, as he put it, 'una gran Ciutat, plena, activa, *normal*, històrica i constantment renovellada alhora' (25; emphasis in the original). Little did d'Ors realize that an active, historical, and constantly renewed city, a *normal* city, in most of Europe at least, would by the end of the twentieth century become a tourist city.

The power of tourism, which had had a profound and problematic impact on the city of Barcelona, entails, as has been intimated above, a certain seduction, something that has not gone unnoticed by filmmakers, among others. Though the city figures significantly as a site of seduction in such films as Antonioni's *Professione: reporter / The Passenger* (1975) and Almodóvar's *Todo sobre mi madre* (1999), two examples by Catalan directors will here have to suffice: Marta Balletbò-Coll's *Costa Brava* (1995) and Ventura's Pons' *Food of Love* (2002) both present homosexual, transnational couples whose tales of friendship, love, and sex are played out against the glittering backdrop of modernist architecture – more ironically presented in Balletbò-Coll's case, more lovingly in Pons' case. They are also inflected by an Olympian or rather post-Olympian perspective (again, more ironically in one than in the other), which helped fuel investment and revitalize the city and its modernist legacy after decades of Francoist repression.

The Olympian perspective was subsequently endorsed by the Royal Institute of British Architects, which in 1999 granted its prestigious prize for the first time in its history to a city rather than to an architect or team of architects – another much-touted triumph of the municipal government. Although Barcelona's Arc de Triomf dates from the 1888 Exposition, the triumphant rhetoric of the Olympics also harks back to the 1929 Exposition, which, though held under less than optimal conditions (the Primo de Rivera dictatorship), spurred the urbanization of Montjuïc. Infamous as the site of a military fortress and political executions, Montjuïc became with the 1929 Exposition a site for drop-jawed awe and leisure, as visitors strolled through the proto-theme park known as El Poble Espanyol, watched the show of water and electric lights at the Plaça d'Espanya, and visited what would become – with the passing of time and the transformation of taste – one of the most celebrated structures of any Exposition ever: Mies van der Rohe's sleek, simple, and 'revolutionary' German Pavilion, which has become an almost obligatory reference in any history of modern architecture. So important did the legacy of the international style of modern architecture prove to be that the German Pavilion was reconstructed in 1986 under a Socialist government already gearing up for the Olympics (interestingly Barcelona had lost to Berlin a bid for what would become the notorious 1936 Olympics). And though it is no match for the Sagrada Família, the Palau de la Música Catalana, or the Museu Picasso in terms of popularity, the reconstructed German Pavilion has its place too on the tourist maps.

The repeated refashioning and constant newness (the oxymoron is deliberate) by which modernity passes are such that structures made of otherwise permanent materials – the steel, glass, marble, and travertine of the German Pavilion, for instance – are cast in an impermanent mode.[7] So cast, they are susceptible to the recuperation that goes, still now, by the name of postmodernism. Out of fashion, discarded and set aside, these structures, like so much else, can become, with time, invested with a renewed appeal, an additional value: that of history. For history is also caught in the web of commodity fetishism, served up,

---

7 The impermanence of potentially more permanent structures antedates the 1929 Exposition significantly. In the 1888 Exposition, the Gran Hotel Internacional by Lluís Domènech i Montaner, one of the greatest of modernist architects working in Catalonia, was built with the intention of being demolished – as indeed it was – shortly after the close of the event. Clearly, insofar as World's Fairs are concerned, the concept of built-in obsolescence has a particularly extensive history.

over and anew, in retrospectives, reconstructions, and rehabilitations that endow the remains of the demolished walls of the city, or the foundations of earlier buildings in the Mercat del Born, or the façades of many a gutted house, with a value that, behind or beneath the gleam of permanence, is both buffeted and buttressed by the forces of the market. True, under Franco, when history had become for many a nightmare too unbearable to retain and for others a luxury too costly to preserve, a great deal of the city, and particularly whatever did not meet the dictates of the official story, was scrapped, abandoned, or redone in a harder, colder, more efficient guise. In more local terms, this is the era of mayor José María de Porcioles, under whose rule an often unruly post-war turn to mass housing projects and automobile-driven sprawl took place, overwhelming, in the process, both a beleaguered Modernist model and a beleaguered *Noucentista* counter-model.

During nearly 40 years of dictatorship, such matters as citizen's rights, aesthetics, and the environment were severely compromised, even ignored. And yet, as Hughes and others have noted, the situation was certainly not limited to Barcelona, for the sprawl, massification, and automotive disregard for pedestrians affected cities under both liberal democratic and state-run communist regimes as well. Many recent projects – such as the creation of public parks and squares in peripheral neighbourhoods, or the establishment of pedestrian zones in more centrally located neighbourhoods, or the construction of highways that facilitate rapid transportation among long unconnected neighbourhoods (highways that are often underground or tree-lined to boot) – have attempted to correct the deficiencies of the past and to promote a more comfortable, pleasing, and civic-minded city without sacrificing efficiency and productivity.

Urban sprawl and the attempts to correct it are symptomatic of substantive changes in the conceptualization and constitution of cities in a global age. Immigration, first from the Catalan countryside, then from other parts of Spain (most notably Andalusia and Murcia), and most recently from Latin America, the Maghreb, Eastern Europe, Asia, and Sub-Saharan Africa, has profoundly altered the city – altered it, even as it has (re)made it. Barcelona, like any large city, is large not because of the rabbit-like fertility and steel-like health of its inhabitants (who nonetheless enjoy one of the highest rates of longevity in the world), but because of immigration. Whatever challenges immigration entails, the city would be a much more homogeneous and stagnant place, a much duller and drier place, let alone a much smaller and more provincial place, without the presence deep inside it of people from outside it. While challenges of racial intolerance, integration, segregation, cultural clash, and disenfranchisement can be found in any number of cities throughout the world, one of the challenges that complicates the already complex phenomenon of immigration and that obtains with special force in Barcelona (as a 'bilingual' city) bears on the Catalan language, its present and future in an era of increasing globalization in which only a few languages are deemed 'reasonable' for international communication.

Long suppressed by the central government as contrary to a unity rationalized as essential to both tradition and modernity alike, Catalan acquired a political charge in virtually all areas of expression, including popular music. Joan Manuel Serrat, one of the leading members of the Nova Cançó movement of the 1960s (which vindicated freedom of expression in the Catalan language), was forced to withdraw from the 1968 Eurovision music contest because he refused to sing the otherwise anodyne 'La, la, la' in Castilian, that is to say, Spanish. Instructive as the scandal of the Eurovision contest may be, a brief excursion into fiction may more effectively convey what is here at play: in Maria Barbal's *Pedra de tartera* (1985) and *Mel i metzines* (1990), the protagonists recall being confused and constrained, as children, by the institutionalized weight of Castilian in the educational system of their native Catalonia. In a rigidly dictated educational system, modernization and progress, they learn, are taught to be all but unthinkable in Catalan: to get ahead in Spain is to move away from any language other than Castilian. Tellingly, and among all the imbalances, many of the Castilian-speaking immigrants whose adventures Barbal recounts in *Carrer Bolívia* (1999) believe that progress also takes a specific linguistic form: for them, Catalan. Controversy regarding the status of Catalan and the stakes of progress in a democratically constituted regime continues to this day, most obviously in relation to the revisions to the Estatut d'Autonomia de Catalunya of 1979, and, more intensely, the question of national sovereignty. Progress, clearly enough, has been voiced in a number of contrasting, conflicting, far from equitable ways.

One of the least equitable manifestations of progress is what is

Barcelona and modernity 159

politely known as urban renewal and less politely known as gentrification. Josep Maria Benet i Jornet, in his play *Olors* (2000), and José Luís Guerín, in his film *En construcción* (2001), offer critical takes on the transformation of the Raval, an area that is increasingly home to Pakistani, Moroccan, and other immigrants, but which has historically been home to some of the poorest denizens of the metropolis. In Benet's play, Maria, the protagonist, ridicules the utopian aspirations of contemporary 'creative' architects and lambasts the erasure of the memory of the poor: 'No hi quedarà res que recordi la manera de viure dels que van fer la ciutat dels pobres. Pobres, què he dit! Quin horror de paraula! Quina paraula més ridícula! Hem de parlar de pobres a la meravellosa Barcelona d'avui?' (Benet: 70). Even as she invokes the poor, Maria finds the very word – 'poor' – absurdly out of place in contemporary Barcelona, where politically backed urban planners and architects, armed with (the rhetoric of) good intentions, leave some of the poorest parts of the city without 'un racó per guardar la memòria' (69–70). To be sure, many architects, urban planners, and architectural scholars have themselves made similar criticisms, not just of the transformation of the Raval and other parts of the old city but also, and even more intensely, of the mammoth urban projects associated with the Fòrum 2004, a much-hyped, would-be follow-up to the Olympics, located in a post-industrial section of the city beside the River Besòs. The Fòrum, which was publicized under the banner of diversity, sustainability, and peace, but which relied on huge sums of money from multinational corporations and was not 'free and open' to the public, motivated thousands to protest against what they saw as the hypocrisy of its claims.[8] According to the critics of the Fòrum, Barcelona was once again being converted, perhaps even more than ever, into a shopping centre in which the poor and disenfranchised, those without papers or work, or without any real job security, found themselves effectively cast as the least inviting subjects of the so-called Barcelona model, a model of urban renewal and refashioning that has

---

8 See Borja and Muxí's *L'espai públic*, which contains critical contributions on the Rambla del Raval (Carles Ribas and Joan Subirats), the Maremàgnum (Muxí), the Plaça dels Àngels (Isabel Bachs), and other areas. For highly critical readings of the Fòrum, see Horta's *L'espai clos* (2004) and the Unió Temporal d'Escribes' *Ba®celona, marca registrada* (2004).

generated such buzz, activity, and money in the late twentieth and early twenty-first century.

While it is true, as Oriol Nel·lo notes, that statistical data indicate that urban growth since the 1990s has been accompanied in the greater Barcelona area by 'una certa disminució de les desigualtats en la distribució de la renda, tant des del punt de vista territorial com de l'estrictament social' (127), it is also true, as Nel·lo goes on to note, that serious problems remain. When I first wrote this piece, in 2003, urban unrest in France had again resurfaced and had again laid bare the failure of a system that, captivated by the ideology of universalism, had assiduously avoided any substantive recognition of the complex intersections of economic disenfranchisement – that is to say, systemic, structural poverty – and ethnic, racial, and national difference. The unrest, visible in Britain, Belgium, Holland, Germany and elsewhere, left many in Catalonia wondering if the same could happen there. Some, all too many, wax nostalgic for supposedly simpler, more homogeneous times when a Barcelonan was a Barcelonan, a Catalan a Catalan (and, no doubt, a Spaniard a Spaniard); others, among them writer Juan Goytisolo, recognize that globalization may well be irreversible and that among its many undeniable problems, including its 'naturalization' of neoliberal violence, it contains the promise for a more pluralistic and promiscuous society, for more diverse conceptions of who a Barcelonan is, who a Catalan is. It is in this spirit that Goytisolo advocates: 'una Barcelona de tagalos y negros, capaces de recitar de memoria, con inefable acento, la Oda patriótica de Maragall' (149). To my eyes, the eyes of an admittedly privileged outsider who no longer feels quite outside, Goytisolo's image, utopian as it may be, may also – with time, intelligence, and a concerted effort – prove to be the proverbial real thing. Then again, in the light of more recent developments, throughout Europe, in which the realities of immigration, refuge and asylum are increasingly met with nativism, xenophobia and reinforced marginalization and exploitation, Goytisolo's utopianism, conjured out of the recognition if not the experience of so much pain, misery and violence, may be little more than a dazzling, dumbfounding enticement, one that Maragall, in the very Ode which Goytisolo invokes, had already recognized: Barcelona, 'la gran encisera!'.

Works cited

Almirall, Valentí (1983). *España tal como es* (Barcelona: Anthropos).
Barbal, Maria (1992). *Pedra de tartera* (Barcelona: La Magrana).
— (1999). *Carrer Bolívia* (Barcelona: Ediciòns 62).
— (2001). *Mel i metzines* (Barcelona: La Magrana).
Baudelaire, Charles (1964). *The Painter of Modern Life and Other Essays*. Trans. Jonathan Mayne (Greenwich, CT: Phaidon).
Benet i Jornet, Josep Maria (2000). *Olors* (Barcelona: Proa).
Benjamin, Walter (1986). 'Paris, Capital of the Nineteenth Century', in *Reflections: Essays, Aphorisms, Autobiographical Writings*. Trans. Edmund Jephcott (New York: Schocken), 146–62.
Bofill, Jaume (1915). 'Ciutadania integral'. *La Revista* 1.3 (10 July): 1–3.
Borja, Jordi, and Zaida Muxí (2001). *L'espai public: Ciutat i ciutadania* (Barcelona: Diputació de Barcelona).
Cerdà, Ildefonso (1967 [1867]). *Teoría general de la urbanización* (Barcelona: Instituto de Estudios Fiscales).
Darío, Rubén (1987). *España contemporánea*. Ed. Antonio Vilanova (Barcelona: Lumen).
D'Ors, Eugeni (1990). *Glosari* (Barcelona: Ediciòns 62).
Engels, Friedrich (1987). *The Condition of the Working Class in England* (London: Penguin).
Epps, Brad (2001). 'Modern Spaces: Building Barcelona', in Joan Ramon Resina (ed.), *Iberian Cities* (New York: Routledge), 148–97.
Flaubert, Gustave (1966). *Bouvard et Pécuchet; Dictionnaire des idées reçues* (Paris: Garnier-Flammarion).
Gasch, Sebastià (1997). *Barcelona de nit* (Barcelona: Parsifal).
Genet, Jean (1949). *Journal du voleur* (Paris: Gallimard).
Goytisolo, Juan (1982). *Paisajes después de la batalla* (Barcelona: Montesinos).
Horta, Gerard (2004). *L'espai clos: Fòrum 2004: Notes d'una travessia pel no-res* (Barcelona: Ediciòns de 1984).
Hughes, Robert (1991). *The Shock of the New* (New York: Knopf).
— (1992). *Barcelona* (New York: Knopf).
Mendoza, Cristina, and Eduardo Mendoza (1989). *Barcelona modernista* (Barcelona: Planeta).
Monserdà, Dolors (1992). *La fabricanta* (Barcelona: Ediciòns de l'Eixample).
Nel·lo, Oriol (2001). *Ciutat de ciutats* (Barcelona: Empúries).
Oller, Narcís (1962). *Memòries literàries: Història dels meus llibres* (Barcelona: Aedos).
— (1979). *Contes* (Barcelona: Ediciòns 62).

Planes, Josep Maria (2001). *Nits de Barcelona*. Prologue by Josep Maria de Sagarra (Barcelona: Proa).

Puig i Cadafalch, Josep (2003). 'La Plaça de Catalunya'. *Escrits d'arquitectura, art i política*. Ed. Xavier Barral i Altet (Barcelona: Institut d'Estudis Catalans), 253–69.

Salvat-Papasseit, Joan (1992). *Antologia de poemes*. Ed. Enric Bou (Barcelona: Ariel).

Soldevila, Carles (2004). *Fulls de dietari: Una antologia* (Barcelona: Nova Biblioteca Selecta).

Unió Temporal d'Escribes [UTE] (2004). *Ba®celona, marca registrada: un model per desarmar* (Barcelona: Virus).

Verdaguer, Jacint (2002). *Pàtria*. Ed. Narcís Garolera (Barcelona: Edicions de 1984).

Yxart, Josep (1889). 'La Exposición Universal: Antecedentes', in *El año pasado: Letras y arte en Barcelona* (Barcelona: Librería Española de López), 163–71.

CHAPTER SEVEN

Football and identities in Catalonia*

Alejandro Quiroga

Catalonia is dying. They are killing her and we have to react.
(Joan Laporta, President of F.C. Barcelona)[1]

On 10 July 2010 hundreds of thousands took to the streets of Barcelona behind the slogan 'We are a nation'. The demonstration was supported by all Catalan parties with the exception of the conservative People's Party and the anti-Catalanist Ciutadans and was reported as the biggest in the history of Catalonia.[2] The protest was conceived as a response to the Spanish Constitutional Court, which had published a review of the region's revised statute of autonomy denying that Catalonia was a nation in its own right. The day after the demonstration, Spain won the Football World Cup for the first time.

---

* This is an abridged version approved by the author of a chapter in Alejandro Quiroga, *Football and National Identities in Spain. The Strange Death of Don Quixote* (London: Palgrave Macmillan UK, 2013): 128–54. © Alejandro Quiroga.
1 *El País*, 13 December 2009.
2 The number of demonstrators varies hugely depending on the sources. Barcelona police reckoned there were 1.1 million people. *El País* calculated 425,000 demonstrators (*El País*, 11 July 2010).

Thousands of Catalans celebrated the triumphs of the *selección española* in Barcelona. The streets of the Catalan capital were taken by a tide of young supporters in red T-shirts waving Spanish constitutional flags and proudly chanting 'I am Spanish, Spanish, Spanish'.[3]

These two patriotic displays in the same city in the space of 24 hours are good indicators of the plurality of national identities in Catalonia. In the Principality the exhibitions of Catalan and Spanish identities in public is fairly common and not always antagonistic. In fact, most people hold dual identities and find feeling both Catalan and Spanish unproblematic. Yet, despite this high level of dual patriotism and multiple loyalties, Catalonia is also a territory of nationalist confrontation. Over a century, Catalan and Spanish nationalisms have competed for political and cultural hegemony in the Principality and football has been an important device in the creation and promotion of identities and narratives in this prolonged conflict. Fútbol Club (F.C.) Barcelona was associated with bourgeois Catalan regionalists from the beginning of the twentieth century, whereas its local arch-rivals, Real Club Deportivo (R.C.D.) Español, found support among many in the Barcelona pro-Spanish middle and working classes. F.C. Barcelona's public support for the 1918 Lliga Regionalista campaign in favour of Catalan political autonomy; the club's clashes with the dictatorship of Primo de Rivera; and the institution's backing of the 1932 Catalan Statute of Autonomy consolidated the Catalanist representation of 'Barça' as the symbol of Catalonia. In the last years of the Franco regime, F.C. Barcelona regained its association with Catalan identity and its role as an advocate of Catalan nationalism/regionalism. In the famous words of the left-wing intellectual Manuel Vázquez Montalbán, the club represented 'the unarmed army of Catalonia' (quoted in González Calleja: 157[4]). Nevertheless, Barça also performed a role of social integrator of Spanish immigrants. These newcomers used the club to assimilate themselves into Catalan society, but did not necessarily embrace Catalan nationalism. In contrast, the cliché about R.C.D. Español was that it was the team of

---

3 *La Vanguardia*, 12 July 2010; *Mundo Deportivo*, 12 July 2010. The Barcelona police reported 75,000 gathered in the Avenida María Cristina to watch the final on a gigantic screen.

4 Unless otherwise stated, all translations are by the author.

immigrants who were unable or unwilling to integrate into Catalan society (Colomé: 174).

Dual patriotism, fights for cultural and political hegemony and the use of football as an instrument to transmit national identities have remained central in Catalan society since the death of Francisco Franco in November 1975. In the following pages I analyse the role of F.C. Barcelona as the alternative national team of Catalonia; the recreation of Catalonia's national football team; and the dialectic between Catalan and Spanish national narratives via soccer reporting.

The transition to democracy in Catalonia (1975–1980)

The death of General Franco increased the role that F.C. Barcelona played as a conduit of Catalanism and democratization. In 1976, the club occupied a leading position in the Congrés de Cultura Catalana, an association that gathered over 1,500 agencies of different sectors of Catalan society in defence of the promotion of the vernacular language and the restitution of autonomous regional governments. Barça president Agustí Montal publicly proposed the democratization of Spanish football and sent his general secretary, Joan Granados, to France in order to give Josep Tarradellas, the president of the Generalitat – the Catalan government – in exile, a membership card of F.C. Barcelona. The club also facilitated the organization of the Catalan national team's first match after the death of the dictator.[5] The game was played on 9 June 1976 at the Camp Nou between the Soviet Union and a Catalan team made up of Barça and R.C.D. Español players. The Catalan squad featured Catalan and non-Catalan players (the Dutch footballers Johan Cruyff and Johan Neeskens played in the home team) but the symbolic connotation of the event was unmissable.[6] Members of the public showed Catalan flags and banners demanding political freedoms. Before the match, the Barcelona Municipal Band played the Soviet anthem followed by the 'Cant de la Senyera', a song with Catalanist overtones that had acted as a de facto substitute for the banned Catalan national hymn 'Els Segadors'. The dictatorship's authorities at the box did not

5 *Avui*, 27 May 1976.
6 *Mundo Deportivo*, 10 June 1976.

appreciate the choice of music and the police forced the municipal band to play the Spanish national anthem, which was subsequently booed by some members of the public. After the match, Joan Garandos, general secretary of F.C. Barcelona, was sent to the local police station and later fined 100,000 pesetas (Santacana: 243–45).

Economic penalties did little to prevent the political association of Barça with Catalanism. On 20 February 1977, hundreds of Barça and Athletic de Bilbao supporters paraded onto the Camp Nou pitch with *senyeras* [Catalan flags] and *ikurriñas* [Basque flags] before a league match.[7] On 13 April 1977, the club's general assembly passed a resolution declaring that 'Catalonia was prepared to live free and in harmony with other peoples of the Spanish state forever, under equal conditions in a real democracy' (quoted in Santacana: 310). In the assembly, the president's intervention insisted on representing F.C. Barcelona as a 'Catalan institution par excellence' and demanded a statute of autonomy for Catalonia following the club's political tradition: 'Let me publicly declare that F.C. Barcelona is in favour of the statute for our people [...] like the Barcelona supporters were in 1932. Up with Barça. Up with Catalonia' (quoted in Santacana: 310). Agustí Montal also increased his contacts with Josep Tarradellas throughout 1977. On 11 September 1977, a million people marched through the streets of Barcelona demanding 'freedom, amnesty and a statute of autonomy', an impressive demonstration that led the Spanish prime minister, Adolfo Suárez, to create a provisional Generalitat and to allow the return of the Catalan government in exile. Josep Tarradellas returned to Barcelona on 23 October 1977 and visited the Camp Nou the following week. Before the Barça v. Las Palmas match, a group of children with big boards formed the sentence 'Welcome home, President' in front of a huge *senyera* displayed in the middle of the pitch.[8] The Catalan anthem, 'Els Segadors', was played over the Camp Nou loudspeakers and the public waved thousands of *senyeras*, while Montal honoured Tarradellas with the club's gold medal. The ceremony presented an entwined representation of F.C. Barcelona and Catalonia at both symbolic and discursive levels. 'My dear president: Barça and you are one and the same, you both personify the best

7 *La Vanguardia*, 22 February 1977.
8 *La Vanguardia*, 1 November 1977.

virtues of our people', Montal told Tarradellas (quoted in Santacana: 252). 'Our club is great because it always remained loyal to Catalonia', replied the president of the Generalitat (quoted in Santacana: 252–53).

Far from diminishing its political connotations, football increased its role as a device to channel identities in Catalonia. Like other Spanish regions, Catalonia witnessed a sharp increase in the practice of sports during the years of the transition. In the case of the metropolitan area of Barcelona the growth was intensified by the actions of a widespread network of neighbour associations which fostered sports at grass-roots level (Abadía i Naudí 2010: 51). Moreover, the election of democratic town halls in 1979 paved the way for a close collaboration between local football clubs and local governments in a more horizontal manner, thus increasing the political overtones of sport at different municipalities (Abadía i Naudí 2011: 382). The Catalan media was transformed too. In September 1976, Radio Barcelona began to broadcast football games in Catalan. Joaquim Maria Puyal, the radio commentator, soon became a celebrity in Catalonia (Pérez de Rozas and Relaño). Equally important for the creation of a media space in the vernacular were the ever-increasing numbers of programmes that Spanish radio television (TVE) broadcast in Catalan during the transition to democracy, which by 1977 included daily news and sports programmes.[9]

Whatever the compatibility of Barça's Catalan and Spanish identities in the media, the truth of the matter is that the celebrations of the 1979 European Cup (the Cup Winners' Cup) turned into a massive political demonstration demanding a statute of autonomy for Catalonia. After Barça's victory, hundreds of thousands took to the streets of towns and cities all over Catalonia. In Barcelona, the revellers chanted the traditional 'Up with Barça and up with Catalonia', together with the newly invented 'We already have the cup, now we want the statute'.[10] Josep Tarradellas knew how to seize the political opportunity and decided to join the party from Saint Jordi Palace, the home of the provisional Catalan government. In a somewhat theatrical mise en scène, the veteran politician came out onto the palace's main balcony carrying a Catalan flag as thousands of Barça supporters sang 'Els Segadors'.

---

9 In 1978 TVE in Catalonia broadcast 68 hours per month in Catalan. By 1980 the number of hours had reached 83 (TVE Catalunya).
10 *La Vanguardia*, 17 May 1979.

Tarradellas then reiterated the union between football and politics: 'We already have the cup. Barça won it for Catalonia and our flag'.[11] The following day, a million people gave Barça players a heroes' welcome in the streets of the Catalan capital.[12] Upon arrival from Switzerland, the footballers first visited the Mercè Basilica to offer the title to the female patron of Barcelona, the Madonna de la Mercè, and then moved to Saint Jordi Palace. From the same balcony that Josep Tarradelas had used the previous evening, the socialist mayor of Barcelona, Narcís Serra, stated that when 'Barça won titles outside Spain it was like the city of Barcelona had triumphed too' and remarked that this victory in the Cup Winners' Cup had arrived the very same year Spain had a real democratic system.[13] Serra, who had been elected two months earlier in the first democratic municipal elections since the Second Republic, thus linked democracy and himself to F.C. Barcelona's successful destiny. In turn, Josep Tarradellas insisted on portraying Barça as an 'example of tenacity' that all Catalans should follow to achieve a new statute of autonomy.[14] The players later went to Camp Nou where they showed the trophy to the fans, as the latter sang 'Els Segadors' and a group of dancers performed *sardanas* on the pitch.

The issue of national identities was also present in Barça's local rival, R.C.D. Español during the transition years. In late 1976, Juan Vilá Reyes, president of Español, proposed to change the club's name to R.C.D. Cataluña, in an attempt to shake its anti-Catalanist image. Vilá Reyes justified his proposal by arguing that Español needed to be more ingrained in Catalan society.[15] The implications here were that the name 'Español' was a burden in a society that was rapidly Catalanizing and that the association with Catalonia would gain the club more popular backing. However, few Español supporters found the rationale acceptable and some right-wing Spanish nationalist sectors of the club's fan base demanded that Vilá apologise publicly from the centre of the pitch at Sarriá stadium for proposing the name change.[16]

11 *La Vanguardia*, 17 May 1979.
12 *La Vanguardia*, 18 May 1979.
13 *El Mundo Deportivo*, 18 May 1979.
14 *Avui*, 18 May 1979.
15 *El País*, 18 January 1977.
16 *El País*, 18 January 1977.

Notwithstanding the failure of Vilá's Catalanist turn, some Español supporters began to carry *senyeras* to Sarriá, showing that they found no contradiction between Catalan symbols and the pro-Spanish image of the club. On occasions, this symbolic overlapping led to peculiar situations, such as the waving of Catalan flags to celebrate Real Madrid goals when announced on Sarriá's screens.[17]

The different national and regional identities displayed at Barça and Español were somehow a reflection of the national plurality in Catalonia in the transition years. Surveys confirmed this variety of identities at the time. In 1979, 35 per cent of Catalans identified themselves as Spanish only, or more Spanish than Catalan; 25 per cent tended to characterize themselves as Catalan only, or more Catalan than Spanish; while 33 per cent felt equally Spanish and Catalan (Martínez Herrera: 435). Ballot boxes also substantiated the plurality of Catalans' identities in a complex and changing political arena. The Partit dels Socialistes de Catalunya (PSC) (the Catalan branch of the Spanish Socialist Workers' Party, the PSOE), was the most voted-for party in Catalonia in the 1977 and 1979 elections to the Spanish Parliament. However, in the 1980 regional elections, the right-wing Catalanist coalition Convergence and Union (CiU) pipped other parties to the post. The results of the 1980 Catalan elections led Jordi Pujol, the historic leader of the conservative Catalan nationalists, to replace Josep Tarradellas as president of the Generalitat and inaugurated over two decades of right-wing Catalanist hegemony in regional politics.

The Pujol era (1980–2003)

The formation and development of the Catalan Autonomous Community transformed and accelerated the process of nation-building in Catalonia. The CiU government used regional institutions at its disposal to transmit an alternative national identity to those of Spain. From the start of the 1980s, regional television channels, radio stations, schools and cultural institutions funded by the Generalitat were used to create an official imagined national community among Catalans (Flynn: 711). Socially, this institutionalization of Catalanism

17 *Avui*, 13 March 1979.

provided new employment opportunities for cultural elites and resulted in the emergence of a form of clientelism promoted by CiU (Dowling: 111). Discursively, the Generalitat popularized the triad Pujol–CiU–Catalonia, which equated any criticism of the Catalan president, or his coalition, with an attack on Catalonia itself. Additionally, the Generalitat developed a populist dimension when it claimed that Catalans were economically exploited by the Spanish government, an idea that resonated strongly with the wider public (Dowling: 111–12). This concept of the 'financial plunder' of Catalonia became prevalent because it reaffirmed one of the main myths of the Catalan nationalist narrative, namely the idea that Catalonia was superior, more modern and richer vis-à-vis Madrid/Castile/Spain and, at the same time, the victim of that very backward, poor and tyrannical partner.

The Corporació Catalana de Ràdio i Televisió (CCRT; the Catalan Corporation of Radio and Television) became a key device for the transmission of the official Catalanist narrative. Controlled by CiU since its inception in 1983, the corporation included an increasing number of TV channels and radio stations, seeking to create a Catalan media space capable of structuring the Catalan nation in the public's mind (Moragas; Gifreu and Corominas). To this end, Catalan public television fostered not only the Catalan language as a distinctive national trait but also a number of myths, traditions and references considered intrinsically Catalan in all sorts of self-produced programmes, from children's shows to TV series (Peris Blanes; Castelló). Likewise, TV news played a crucial role in the construction of the Catalan nation as they focused on reporting conflicts between the Spanish government and the Generalitat over competencies and budgets (Farré et al.: 88–89). These reports tended to present the confrontation as an unbalanced fight between the 'Spanish state', hence avoiding the characterization of Spain as a nation, and the Catalan nation, represented by CiU. The news emphasis on conflict also helped to maintain in the Catalan public's imagination the regional nationalist narrative that presented the central–regional governments' disputes over competencies in the 1980s and 1990s as just another episode in the perennial historical struggle between Catalonia and Madrid/Castile/Spain.

Football reporting was also an effective means of projecting the regional nationalist discourse onto Catalan society. It was no coincidence that the initial test programme broadcast live by the Generalitat-run

TV3 (the first channel 100 per cent in Catalan) was an F.C. Barcelona game played on 11 September 1983, Catalonia's national day (García Altadill: 98). In 1989, the Federation of Spanish Regional Televisions bought the rights of the First Division matches, which allowed TV3 to show a good number of Barça games over the following two decades. TV3 also broadcast the matches of the Catalan national team in the 1990s. Following the aforementioned 1976 game against the Soviet Union, the Catalan squad played no games until 1990, when a team made of Barça and Español footballers played against C.E. Sabadell to support the victims of an ETA attack. From 1997 onwards, the Catalan national team began to play friendly matches against national squads on a yearly basis as a way to claim official status for Catalonia in international competitions. The demand for Catalan national teams competing internationally came from the Generalitat, in what some scholars have interpreted as a populist strategy designed to divert attention from CiU's collaboration with the People's Party both in the Spanish and the Catalan parliaments (Dowling: 116). After all, from 1995 CiU governed in Catalonia thanks to the support of the Partido Popular (PP) and from 1996 the PP governed in Spain thanks to the support of CiU.

For all its support from the regional government and its widespread impact, the Catalanist narrative was not fully hegemonic in 1980s and 1990s Catalonia. Other Catalan and Spanish media reproduced alternative discourses to the official one in the Principality. State-wide TV channels and radio stations had altogether more viewers and listeners than the regional government-funded media in Catalonia. In the press, alternatives to the Catalanist narrative varied from the Madrid-based right-wing media, which tended to consider Spain a nation and Catalonia an autonomous community, to the liberal *El País* and the Barcelona-based *La Vanguardia* and *El Periódico de Catalunya* that were more ambiguous but showed different levels of compatibility between Spanish and Catalan identities. These media referred to Barça as both a Catalan and a Spanish club, endowing the club with a sort of dual identity.[18] This duality was also present in the Barcelona 92 Olympics, where Catalan and Spanish anthems, flags and discourses

---

18 For example, *La Vanguardia*, 13 May 1982, 21 May 1992; *El País*, 10 May 1989; *ABC*, 11 May 1989, 21 May 1992; *El Mundo Anuario 1993*: 401; *El Mundo Deportivo*, 21 May 1992; *Marca*, 20 May 1994.

were combined throughout. The Madrid-based media highlighted that the image of Barcelona, Catalonia and Spain improved all over the world, but the ultimate emphasis was on celebrating the organizational and sporting success of the Spanish nation.[19] An editorial in *El País* explained that the synthesis of symbols, ensigns and anthems was the proof of Spaniards' effective acceptance of the plurality of identities in the country and 'particularly, of the Catalan cultural and linguistic reality'.[20] The acceptance of plurality was presented as the reflection of a sort of existential merger between the Spanish and the Catalan nation: 'It is not only that Catalonia is a part of Spain, but that Spain is also part of Catalonia'.[21] Somewhat less sophisticated but surely having a wider impact was the Spanish public television discourse stressing the idea that the Olympics were a 'total success' for Spain.[22] Again, hierarchies were clear, Barcelona and Catalonia were considered an important part of the success story, yet they appeared subordinate to the Spanish nation.

F.C. Barcelona's rivalry with Real Madrid remained central in the articulation of the 1980s and 1990s Catalanist discourse. The team of the Spanish capital performed the role of the 'national other' of Barça and featured prominently in the Catalan nationalist press. Alongside an ill-defined 'Madrid press', Real Madrid were often equated with Spanish nationalism, accused of harbouring anti-Catalan sentiments and orchestrating conspiracies against F.C. Barcelona, and hence, the argument went, against Catalonia.[23] In fact, anthropological studies have shown that the games between Barça and Real Madrid acted as a metaphor of a 'cold war' that pitted Castile/Spain against Catalonia (Duch, 10–20). The Real Madrid v. Barça matches were (and still are) performed as theatrical battles on the pitch and narrated with a martial rhetoric in the media (Relaño; Naranjo de Arcos). Barça supporters experienced the rituals and symbolic universe associated with the

---

19 *El Mundo Anuario 1993*: 402, 406; *Anuario El País 1993*: 110.
20 *El País*, 9 August 1992.
21 *El País*, 9 August 1992.
22 For instance, *Telediario* 1, 9 August 1992 (Archivo RTVE, Tape 041CP30, Signature IV8AI027); and *Telediario* 2, 9 August 1992 (Archivo RTVE, Tape 041CP30, Signature IV8AI027).
23 For instance, *Avui*, 5 May 1994; 10 May 1994; 18 May 1994; 24 May 1994; 28 May 1994; 12 June 1994.

team as a sort of 'civic religion' that reached its spiritual climax in the bellicose confrontations with their arch-rivals (Duch: 179–264). In the 1980s and 1990s, Manuel Vázquez Montalbán's definition of Barça as the un-armed army of Catalonia still resonated strongly among Barça supporters. Notwithstanding the 'Catalanization' of R.C.D. Español in the 1990s – the club translated its anthem into Catalan, declared Catalan its main language, and changed its name to 'Espanyol' in 1995 – it was F.C. Barcelona that remained associated with Catalanism (Duch: 176; Crolley: 307).

Barça's international victories turned into manifestations of Catalanism too. The 1982, 1989, and 1997 Cup Winners' Cups and the 1992 European Cup titles were celebrated in the streets of all Catalan provincial capitals, although the number of fans never reached those of the 1979 Cup Winners' Cup revelries, a trophy won before Catalonia had a statute of autonomy.[24] The celebration at Barcelona usually followed a set pattern that included a bus parade from the airport to the Basilica of la Mercè; then the pageant went to the Palace of the Generalitat (the historic building that houses the government offices) at Plaça Sant Jaume, where the players, the mayor of Barcelona and Jordi Pujol, as president of Catalonia, displayed the trophy from a balcony to the fans. The show ended at the Camp Nou, where supporters congregated to see the cup displayed in the middle of the pitch. Alongside the institutional 'Catalanization' of the celebration that had the Palace of the Generalitat as a central stage, on some occasions Catalan Barça players added a regional nationalist twist to the party. The Barça midfielder Pep Guardiola was a case in point during the celebrations of the 1992 European Cup. With a *senyera* around his neck, he showed the trophy to the fans from the Generalitat Palace and shouted in Catalan: 'Citizens of Catalonia, you have the Cup here now'.[25] The cry was an unmistakable reference to the famous words of Josep Tarradellas on his return to Barcelona in 1977 following almost

---

24 On 18 May 1979, *Avui* reckoned there were a million and a half people on the streets of Barcelona and 90,000 at the Camp Nou in 1979. The same newspaper gave figures of 20,000 supporters at the Camp Nou in 1992. *Avui*, 22 May 1992. *La Vanguardia*, 22 May 1992, calculated there were around 20,000 people to welcome Barça at Plaça Sant Jaume.
25 *Avui*, 22 May 1992.

40 years of exile when he declared to the masses: 'Citizens of Catalonia, I am here now'.[26]

The road to independence (2003–2014)?

The year 2003 inaugurated a new era for F.C. Barcelona and Catalonia. On 15 June 2003, the lawyer Joan Laporta won the elections to the presidency of F.C. Barcelona. The victory of Laporta, a figure well known for his political past in a small secessionist party, meant the arrival of a young team of directors at the Camp Nou. Five months later, regional elections resulted in the creation of a coalition government led by the Catalan Socialist Pasqual Maragall. Together with the Catalan Socialists, the Partit dels Socialistes de Catalunya (PSC), the pro-independence party Republican Left of Catalonia, the Esquerra Republicana de Catalunya (ERC), and the eco-socialists of Iniciativa per Catalunya Verds (ICV), the Catalonia Green Initiative, entered the new three-party government, the *tripartit*. For the first time since the reestablishment of regional elections in 1980, CiU did not control the Generalitat.

Joan Laporta reached the presidency of Barça thanks to the support of ERC and some right-wing Catalanists, who preferred the young lawyer over the CiU's main choice, the so-called 'establishment candidate' Lluís Bassat.[27] Laporta did not disappoint his backers and developed a strong Catalanist discourse associated with Barça. He paralleled Barça with Catalonia and reproduced the two main pillars of the Catalanist narrative, namely the idea that the Catalan nation was the victim of a long-term injustice perpetrated by Spain/Castile/Madrid, and the self-representation of the Principality as a democratic and modern oasis in the desert of a backward state. Thus Laporta insisted on depicting Barça as a club that has always been democratic and Catalanist, a historical sweeping generalization that has nevertheless been uncritically accepted by some scholars.[28]

---

26 *La Vanguardia*, 24 October 1977.
27 *Público*, 20 September 2009.
28 For Laporta see *El País*, 13 December 2009. For the scholars, see, for example, the comments of the historian Josep Maria Solé i Sabaté in *La Vanguardia*, 25

At times Laporta's idealization of F.C. Barcelona resembled sentences taken from the script of Mel Gibson's 1995 film *Braveheart*: 'Barça embodies the epic that guides the freedom of oppressed peoples', he declared in an interview.[29] By contrast, the enemy remained familiar. Real Madrid and its alleged penchant for centralist policies, the attacks of the Madrid right-wing press and the sheer stupidity and greed of Spaniards, unflatteringly described by Barça's treasurer Xavier Sala i Martín as 'surly' thieves of Catalan money, were some of the components of the demonization of the 'other'.[30] The effects of the combined actions of this conglomerate 'other' were also recognizable as part of the Catalanist discourse. According to Laporta, Catalonia was suffocated by Spain, and the Principality could not progress due to the unbearable and humiliating burden that the Spanish state meant for the country.[31] In the dramatic words of Barça's president at the end of 2009, 'Catalonia is dying. They are killing her and we have to react'.[32]

Alongside the strong Catalanist discourse adopted by the Barça directors, Laporta embarked upon a programme 'to re-catalanize' F.C. Barcelona. This meant incorporating the Catalan flag on the back of the team's shirts; removing the Spanish flag from La Masia (the club's training academy); hosting the Correllengua (a meeting of different associations for the defence of the Catalan language); displaying a banner at the Camp Nou in support of the 2006 statute of autonomy; publicly backing the broadcasting of TV3 in the Autonomous Community of Valencia; acting as the speaker of a number of Catalanist associations; and proposing that new Barcelona signings should take Catalan classes.[33]

October 2009. He declared that 'Barça have always been the industrial, modern, democratic Catalan alternative to the Spanish status quo'. David Goldblatt, most intriguingly, writes about 'Barcelona's socios and directors' being 'among the many petitioning the Madrid government for Catalan independence in the early 1920s'. However, there is no historical record of such petition (Goldblatt: 211).
29 *El Mundo*, 4 July 2010.
30 *Público*, 20 September 2009; *Marca*, 11 November 2009, 2 December 2009.
31 *Marca*, 12 November 2009.
32 *El País*, 13 December 2009.
33 *El País*, 27 September 2009; *Público*, 20 September 2009; *El Mundo*, 27 November 2009. Duch (2005), *Futbol*, 156.

Joan Laporta's successor, Sandro Rosell, fostered a strong internationalization process of F. C. Barcelona. As soon as he took over, Rosell reached an agreement with Qatar Sport Investment, a company linked to the Qatari government. In the past, Rosell himself had done businesses with Qatari companies and the new deal involved incorporating Qatar Foundation, first, and Qatar Airlines, later, on the F.C. Barcelona shirts. In 2011, the Qatari publicity replaced UNICEF's and Barça ended up being sponsored by a dictatorship with an appalling human rights record. The club's board of directors defended the decision as the only way to secure the money to keep Lionel Messi at F.C Barcelona.[34]

The fact that Barça arguably became one of the best football clubs in the world and Lionel Messi the number one player on the planet also contributed to turn F.C. Barcelona into a successful global brand. The global dimension of the club did not seem to contradict Barça's Catalanist identity. After all, the club had a long internationalist tradition and stressing the universal nature of F.C. Barcelona was a way to tiptoe over the club's Spanish identity, as the triad Barça–Catalonia–World omitted Spain. However, the arrival of Sandro Rosell – a more moderate figure than Laporta – to the presidency of Barça in July 2010 rang alarm bells in some Catalanist quarters. Jordi Badia, Laporta's former director of communications, warned that Barça was immersed under Rosell in a 'process of slow, if not irreversible, de-nationalization', due to the internationalization of the club that has transformed F.C. Barcelona into a sort of global franchise (Badia 2012b). The implication was that only a constant catalanization of the club a la Laporta could counterbalance the effects of Barça's internationalization.

Success and very sophisticated football under the management of Pep Guardiola were also behind the transformation of Barça into Spain's favourite team. In 2003, support for Barça in Spain was 20 points below Real Madrid. By 2007 the difference had dropped to 7 points.[35] In the autumn of 2011, opinion polls showed that Barça had the support of 44 per cent of football fans, while Real Madrid was the

---

34 *El País*, 18 November 2013.
35 32.8 per cent supported Real Madrid and 25.7 per cent supported Barça (Centro de Investigaciones Sociológicas: 11).

first choice for 37 per cent of the survey's respondents. According to *AS*, the Madrid sport daily that commissioned the 2011 survey, Barça's international victories, the high number of *selección* footballers playing for the Catalan club, the arrogant behaviour of Cristiano Ronaldo and José Mourinho, and the fact that Rosell had stopped the 'over-catalanization of the Laporta era' were the main factors which contributed to Barcelona's ousting of Real Madrid as the country's first choice.[36]

Catalan society has gradually but importantly changed in the last decade. The socialist governments of Pasqual Maragall (2003–2006) and José Montilla (2006–2010) implemented more progressive but similarly Catalanist policies to those of CiU. By the beginning of the twenty-first century, the leader of the PSC, Maragall, decided to catalanize the party's political project even further, in an attempt to place himself in a position to defeat CiU at the polls. The socialists' choice was testimony to the profound 'Catalanization' of society wrought under two decades of CiU governments (Dowling: 115–16). When Maragall won the 2003 regional elections, the PSC had a strong Catalanist agenda and so did the PSC governing coalition partners – the eco-socialists of ICV and the secessionist republicans of ERC. Soon, the tripartite government called for a reform of the 1979 Statute of Autonomy, a proposal that found support with CiU. In 2006, first the Catalan Parliament, later, the Spanish Cortes, and last the Catalan people, voted in favour of a new Statute of Autonomy that increased the level of self-government and declared Catalonia a nation in its own right (see Generalitat de Catalunya).

Additionally, the campaign for the Catalan national teams soon entered high politics. In 2004, the PSOE and the PSC backed an ERC and CiU bill in the Spanish parliament promoting the participation of regional teams in international competitions.[37] The bill was, however, merely symbolic, as it did not contemplate the participation of the autonomous communities' teams in those sports where Spanish national squads were already registered. Three years later, an amendment of the Sport Law seeking to grant the right of Catalonia and the Basque Country to partake in international competitions was defeated in the Cortes by the votes of the PSOE and the PP. During the debate on the

36 *AS*, 10 October 2011.
37 *El Mundo*, 2 June 2004.

amendment, ERC *diputat*, or MP, Joan Puig and the Basque Partido Nacionalista Vasco (PNV) MP Aitor Esteban displayed Catalan and Basque national shirts at the tribune, while PP MP Francisco Antonio González reacted by showing a kit of *la Roja*, Spain's national football team.[38] Two months after the 'battle of the shirts' in the parliament, Josep-Lluís Carod Rovira, Vice Prime Minister of Catalonia, Miren Azkarate, Minister of Culture of the Basque government and Ánxela Bugallo, Minister of Culture of the Galician government, signed the so-called Declaration of San Mamés.[39] This petition again requested the right of the autonomic teams to take part in international contests and was presented at Athletic de Bilbao's stadium before a friendly between the Basque and Catalan national teams.

Alongside the Catalan *selecció*, the Spanish national team has generated an important debate regarding football and national identities in Catalonia. In the first years of the 2000s, most of the best-selling newspapers of the Principality, including *La Vanguardia*, *El Periódico*, *El Mundo Deportivo* and, to a lesser extent, *Sport*, defended the compatibility of Catalan and Spanish identities and supported the *selección española*.[40] As in the 1980s and 1990s, these newspapers especially focused on the role of Barça players in the Spanish national when reporting on *la Roja*, yet the celebrations of Spanish triumphs did not significantly differ from other non-Catalan media. Victory at the 2008 European championship did not alter the narrative of Spanish–Catalan compatible identities. On the contrary, these newspapers highlighted the key role that Catalans played in the *selección* of Luis Aragonés, which meant a sort of 'catalanization' of the Spanish national team.[41] Against those Catalanists who declared that they wanted anyone but Spain to win, the director of *La Vanguardia*, José Antich, rhetorically asked: 'In Catalonia, is it possible not to wish the victory of a team with the Catalans Puyol, Xavi, Iniesta (sic), Cesc and Capdevila'.[42] The 2010 World Cup and the Euro 2012 did nothing but increase the process

38 *ABC*, 18 September 2007.
39 *El País*, 30 December 2007.
40 *El Periódico de Catalunya*, 15 June 2006; 19 June 2006; 27 June 2006. For the coverage of the *selección* by *El Mundo Deportivo* and *Sport*, see González-Ramallal. For *La Vanguardia*, see León Solís: 77.
41 *La Vanguardia*, 28 June 2008; 30 June 2008; *Mundo Deportivo*, 28 June 2008.
42 *La Vanguardia*, 27 June 2008.

of 'catalanization' of the Spanish national team, as Vicente del Bosque included a majority of Barça players in his first-choice squad and the *selección* shared the style and flow of Pep Guardiola's team.

The Catalanist-leaning media were surprised by the popular displays of Spanish pride associated with the *selección* in Catalonia. Following Spain's victory in Euro 2008, *Avui* reported that thousands of Catalans with Spanish flags revelled on the Rambles and Canaletes – precisely the areas where Barça fans traditionally celebrate their triumphs. The Catalanist diary explained that popular support was due to the 'solid base of Catalan footballers' playing for *la Roja*.[43] Commentators at Catalunya Ràdio also underlined F.C. Barcelona's contribution to Spain's success.[44] They occasionally complained because this said contribution was not sufficiently acknowledged in Madrid, but recognized that, from 2008 onwards, the *selección* had left behind the *furia* to play a highly sophisticated and modern football, Barça's football.[45] Yet the sophistication and modernization of Spain necessarily had its limits in the Catalanist narrative. When discussing the emergence of a new *espanyolisme* (Spanish nationalism) associated with sporting victories and a restored international reputation in the realms of culture and cuisine, *Avui* noted the phenomenon, but dismissed it stating that, for all her efforts, the image of Spain remained linked to paella, bullfighting, and flamenco.[46] By emphasizing the persistence of old clichés, the newspaper presented Spain's newly acquired sophistication and modernity as superficial traits that could not conceal the real, long-lasting nature of the country. In doing so, the Catalanist discourse denied the national 'other' the possibility of changing. Understandably, Catalan nationalists could not accept that Spain had become a fully fledged modern and sophisticated nation, for that would seriously undermine their very representation of Catalonia as modern and progressive vis-à-vis Spain.

43 *Avui*, 30 June 2008.
44 'El matí de Catalunya Ràdio: Tertúlia d'esports'. Catalunya Ràdio, 30 June 2008; 'Catalunya vespre esports'. Catalunya Ràdio, 12 July 2010; 'El club de la mitjanit: 2a hora'. Catalunya Ràdio, 1 July 2012.
45 'El matí de Catalunya Ràdio: Tertúlia d'esports'. Catalunya Ràdio, 30 June 2008; 'El club de la mitjanit: 2a hora'. Catalunya Ràdio, 29 May 2011; 'El club de la mitjanit: 2a hora'. Catalunya Ràdio, 1 July 2012. The same argument in *Avui*, 26 June 2008.
46 *Avui*, 5 October 2009.

On 1 July 2012, Spain defeated Italy 4–0 to become European Champion for the third time. Minutes after the final whistle, thousands of Catalans celebrated the Spanish victory in the streets. That very night radio commentators on Catalunya Ràdio pointed out the peculiar historical situation of having Catalan players making a huge contribution to the *selección española*, at a moment when opinion polls showed the highest ever levels of popular support for an independent Catalonia.[47] The situation was even more paradoxical if we take into consideration TV ratings of the *selección española* matches. The Euro 2012 final reached an audience of 75 per cent in Catalonia, a share that demonstrates that the Spanish national team was hugely popular in the Principality.[48] Street parties, a profuse display of Spanish emblems, patriotic chants and balconies adorned with Spanish and Catalan flags added to the idea that many Catalans strongly identified with the *selección*. How can we explain the simultaneous growing support for independence and the popularity of the *selección* in Catalonia?

The question does not have an easy answer. The percentage of Catalans that would vote in favour of an independent Catalonia in a referendum rocketed from 13 per cent in 2006 to 51 per cent in 2012, a rise that research has associated with the economic crisis but also to the spread of a Catalanist identity that sees Spain as an oppressive entity (Muñoz and Tormos).[49] The old tenet that Spain exploited Catalonia found a wide audience at a time when the economy of the autonomous community was in tatters. The fact that the CiU government of Artur Mas (2010–2012) was responsible for the implementation of the vast majority of the austerity measures that led to record unemployment and growing social inequality did not seem to carry a big weight for those who thought that Spain was ultimately to blame for the crisis in Catalonia. The 2010 ruling of the Constitutional Court striking out key parts of the 2006 statute and the PP government's opposition to the creation of a Catalan inland revenue also contributed to the emergence of a new generation of secessionists (Muñoz and Tormos: 6–7, 28–30).

---

47 'El club de la mitjanit: 2a hora'. Catalunya Ràdio, 1 July 2012.
48 The Euro 2012 final reached ratings of 75 per cent in Catalonia. *La Vanguardia*, 7 July 2012.
49 The 2012 data in Centre d'Estudis d'Opinió de 2012.

The popularity of *la Roja* has to be understood within this context of fluent, multiple identities in Catalonia. Some analysts have pointed out that the 'catalanization' of the *selección* was crucial for marketing the Spanish national team in Catalonia (Badia 2012a). Although there is some truth in the observation that the high number of Catalans in the team and the *selección*'s Barça-like style of play were important, the popular support showed in Catalonia for *la Roja* should not be read as the exclusive by-product of the Catalanization of the team. Clearly, the process of Catalanization made the *selección* more acceptable to some Catalans with misgivings about what Spain still represented in Catalanist imagery. Yet the popularity of the squad in Catalonia has to be interpreted against the background of a symbolic universe and a national narrative that has promoted identification with Spain over the years (Juncà: 317–18). The Spanish media, the Spanish governments, and the *selección española* all contributed to create a mental frame of national identification with Spain at different levels. Dual identities are possible because this Spanish frame of national identification is not perceived as incompatible with a complementary frame of national/regional identification with Catalonia. Hence, long-term held dual identities facilitated the unproblematic identification of many Catalans with the Spanish squad in 2008, 2010, and 2012. Support for the *selección* fitted well into the predetermined mental frame of Catalans who felt attached to Spain.

It is difficult to measure to what extent this narrative is entrenched in Catalan society. Research has showed that there is a sharp contrast between the discourse of the Catalan establishment and the way Catalan citizens feel in the realm of identities. By and large, Catalans are more fluent in their multiple identities, more generous when asked about solidarity with other Spanish autonomous communities, and more willing to keep the current constitutional system than the discourse of most of Catalan political parties and media indicates (Martínez-Herrera and Miley).[50] Nonetheless, it is also undeniable that, in recent times, support for an independent Catalan state has rapidly grown out of grass-root movements that have incorporated into their discourse the narrative of the Catalanist political and media elites. Following a massive pro-independence demonstration on 11

---

50 See also the results of the Metroscopia survey in *El País*, 6 October 2012.

September 2012, the President of the Generalitat, Artur Mas, decided to call for new regional elections that would in effect serve as a plebiscite on Catalonia's future in Spain. Mas's plan was to obtain an absolute majority in the regional parliament and lead the formation of an independent Catalan state. However, things did not work out as expected. CiU won the November 2012 elections but lost a dozen MPs at the Catalan Parliament. The results led Mas to seek support from ERC, the separatist Catalan Republicans. In December 2012, CiU and ERC signed an agreement that included the pledge for a referendum of independence by 2014 and the promotion of Catalan national teams in international sporting competitions.[51] On 9 November 2014, the consultation was held. Despite the referendum being declared illegal by the Spanish government, 2,250,000 people turned out to vote – 80 per cent of them for independence.

A hypothetical secession poses a number of questions difficult to answer. Would an independent Catalonia be part of the EU? Could Spain veto the entry of Catalonia into the EU? And, in footballing terms, would F.C. Barcelona play in the Spanish league? Would Barça have to compete in a Catalan league? If so, would Espanyol follow suit? Would Barça lose its Catalanist connotations should a Catalan national football *selecció* compete in international tournaments? Could Catalan players play for *la Roja* should they wish to? One can only speculate about an independent Catalan state and its sporting repercussions, but it seems more than likely that football will remain a conduit to elaborate, transmit and recreate Spanish and Catalan identities in Catalonia.

Works cited

Abadía i Naudí, Sixte (2010). 'El movimiento asociativo vecinal', in Xavier Pujadas (ed.), *La metamorfosis del deporte. Investigaciones sociales y culturales del fenómeno deportivo contemporáneo* (Barcelona: UOC).
— (2011). 'Deporte, ciudadanía y libertad. La transición en España y el deporte, 1975–1982', in Xavier Pujadas (ed.), *Atletas y ciudadanos. Historia social del deporte en España, 1870–2010* (Madrid: Alianza).

---

51 *El País*, 21 December 2012.

Badia, Jordi (2012a). 'La causa del fútbol'. *El País*, 8 July 2012.
— (2012b). 'Barça is not Catalonia'. *El País*, 11 September: 46.
Castelló, Enric (2007). 'The Production of Television Fiction and Nation Building. The Catalan Case'. *European Journal of Communication* 22 (1): 49–68.
Centre d'Estudis d'Opinió (2012). 'Baròmetre d'Opinió Política (BOP). 2a onada 2012 – REO 694'. (Barcelona: CEO). http://www.ceo.gencat.cat/ceop/AppJava/pages/home/fitxaEstudi.html?colId=4128&lastTitle=Bar%F2metre+d%27Opini%F3+Pol%EDtica+%28BOP%29.+2a+onada+2012 [accessed 28 December 2012].
Centro de Investigaciones Sociológicas (2007). *Estudio n. 2.705. Barómetro de mayo* (Madrid: CIS): 11.
Colomé, Gabriel (1999). 'Conflictos e identidades en Cataluña', in Santiago Segurola (ed.), *Fútbol y pasiones políticas* (Madrid: Debate), 169–74.
Crolley, Liz (1999). 'Football and Fandom in Spain', in Barry Jordan and Rikki Morgan-Tomasunas (eds), *Contemporary Spanish Cultural Studies* (London, Arnold), 304–12.
Dowling, Andrew (2005). 'Catalonia and the new Catalanism', in Sebastian Balfour (ed.), *The Politics of Contemporary Spain* (London: Routledge).
Duch, Jordi Salvador (2005). *Futbol, metáfora d'una guerra freda: estudi antropològic del Barça* (Barcelona: Proa).
Generalitat de Catalunya (2006). 'Estatut d'autonomia de Catalunya'. http://web.gencat.cat/ca/generalitat/estatut/estatut2006/ [accessed 13 January 2013].
Farré i Coma, Jordi, Enric Saperas, Josep Esplug Trenc, and Andreu Casero-Ripollés (2003). 'La identidad de España entre el Estado autonómico y la Unión Europea', in Víctor Francisco Sampedro (ed.), *La pantalla de las identidades* (Barcelona: Icaria), 81–102.
Flynn, Mary K. (2001). 'Constructed identities and Iberia'. *Ethnic and Racial Studies* 24/5: 703–18.
García Altadill, Elisabet (1996). 'La televisió', in Daniel E. Jones (ed.), *Esport i mitjans de comunicació a Catalunya* (Barcelona: Centre d'Investigació de la Comunicació), 85–111.
Gifreu, Josep, and Maria Corominas (1991). *Construir l'espai català de comunicació* (Barcelona: Centre d'Investigació de la Comunicació).
Goldblatt, David (2006). *The Ball is Round. A Global History of Soccer* (London: Viking).
González Calleja, Eduardo (2006). '"Bon cop de falç". Mitos e imaginarios bélicos de la cultura del catalanismo'. *Historia y Política* 14: 703–18.
González-Ramallal, Manuel Eduardo (2008). 'La identidad contada: la

información deportiva en torno a la selección española de fútbol', *Universitas Humanística* 66: 220–38.

Juncà, Albert (2010). 'Esport i identitat nacional a Catalunya. Anàlisi de sis esdeveniments esportius a la premsa d'informació general de Catalunya (2006–2009)', PhD Dissertation (Barcelona: Universitat de Barcelona).

León Solís, Fernando (2003). *Negotiating Spain and Catalonia* (Bristol: Intellect).

Martínez Herrera, Enric (2002). 'From Nation-building to Building Identification with Political Communities: Consequences to Political Decentralization in Spain, Catalonia, the Basque Country and Galicia, 1978–2001'. *European Journal of Political Research* 41: 421–53.

Martínez-Herrera, Enric, and Thomas J. Miley (2010). 'The Constitution and the Politics of National Identities in Spain'. *Nations and Nationalism* 16(1): 6–30.

Moragas, Miquel de (1988). *Espais de comunicació: experiències i perspectives a Catalunya* (Barcelona: Edicions 62).

Muñoz, Jordi and Raül Tormos (2012). 'Identitat o càlculs instrumentals? Anàlisi dels factors explicatius del suport a la independència'. *Papers de Treball* (Barcelona: Centre d'Estudis d'Opinió).

Naranjo de Arcos, Alicia (2011). 'Tratamiento de la información deportiva en la prensa. La crónica como género prevalente. El caso de los encuentros entre Real Madrid y F.C. Barcelona', PhD. Dissertation (Malaga: Universidad de Málaga).

Pérez de Rozas, Emilio, and Alfredo Relaño (1982). 'Barça, Barça, Barça'. *El País Semanal*, 10 October.

Peris Blanes, Álvar (2011). 'La nación española en la tele-realidad: símbolos, cultura y territorio', in Ismael Saz and Ferran Archilés (eds.), *Estudios sobre nacionalismo y nación en la España contemporánea* (Zaragoza: Prensas Universitarias de Zaragoza), 203–43.

Quiroga, Alejandro (2013). *Football and National Identities in Spain. The Strange Death of Don Quixote* (London: Palgrave Macmillan UK).

Relaño, Alfredo (2012). *Nacidos para incordiarse: un siglo de agravios entre el Madrid y el Barça* (Madrid: Martínez Roca).

Santacana Torres, Carles (2006). *El Barça y el franquismo. Crónica de unos años decisivos (1968–1978)* (Madrid: Apóstrofe).

TVE Catalunya (2008), 'Història de TVE a Catalunya', 2a part. *Rtve.es*, 19 November. http://www.rtve.es/television/20081119/2-part-historia-tve-catalunya/196116.shtml [accessed 29 March 2017].

CHAPTER EIGHT

The family and the city: Power and the creation of cultural imagery*

Gary Wray McDonogh

Beyond its value as an economic and social institution, the Catalan family has also been the basis for cultural imagery. As a metaphor for Catalan society the family became the cornerstone of cultural legitimization and domination by the upper class. As Bourdieu has noted, 'The dominant factions, whose power is based on economic and political capital, seek to impose the legitimacy of their domination whether through their own symbolic production or through the intermediary of conservative ideologists' (80).[1] In other work I have examined the cultural presentation of the family in terms of political and economic strategies that positioned the Catalan polity between local class conflicts and state politics (McDonogh). Here the family will be analysed with regard to specifically urbanistic themes, including the control, and even the construction, of modern Barcelona.

The family was a key symbol in the political strategies of the Catalan

---

* This is an abridged version approved by the author of a chapter in Gary McDonogh (1986), 'The family and the city: Power and creation of cultural imagery' in *Good Families of Barcelona: A Social History of Power in the Industrial Era* (1986). © 1986 by Princeton University Press. Reprinted with permission.
1 Unless otherwise indicated, all translations are by the author.

bourgeoisie of the late nineteenth and early twentieth centuries, through which they sought to establish and unify a national movement. It was both an emotive image and an ambiguous one. In contrasting Catalonia and the rest of Spain the Catalan Civil Code was a symbol of unity, of a distinctive socioeconomic heritage, and of the right to political hegemony. At the same time, when challenged by internal conflicts, the elite and its ideologues interpreted the family in terms of hierarchy, authority, and order. It was the complexity of the image that made it uniquely valuable to one elite in its epoch and to a particular embodiment of Catalan nationalism.

Within everyday interaction in the Catalan capital, however, family was evoked as the basis for a new understanding of the changing social order. In this regard it became an element in an elite sociology of classes and rights. To understand this cultural manipulation of the family, it is necessary to analyse more complex representations of urban society and their impact upon urban planning and urban life.

This chapter focuses on two institutions that embodied an elite 'sociology' of industrial society: the Cementiri Vell (Old Cemetery) and the Gran Teatre del Liceu (the Barcelona Opera House). Both were built in the nineteenth century under the aegis of the emergent elite. Both have been dynamic constructions whose physical structure and interpretation have been sensitive to shifting power relations. Both continue to stand in modern Barcelona as historical monuments to class differentiation and the cohesion of the 'Good Families'. Thus, these edifices are keys to past and present world views of the power groups that dominated Catalan industrial society.

The cemetery, however, is a walled and ordered world. When it was built, it lay outside the physical limits of the city. Today it has been marginalized from the social life of modern Barcelona. Yet it may be situated within a succession of burial sites and patterns in Barcelona that reflect changing ideas about family and city. Furthermore, the isolation of the graveyard gave it a special integrity as a laboratory for urbanistic planning. Necropolitan patterns do not simply reflect metropolitan development: the Cementiri Vell actually modelled the architectonics of a later Barcelona as envisaged within the ideology of the industrial–financial elite.

The Liceu stands on the Rambles, the main artery of central Barcelona. It is central to the social and cultural life, even the mythology, of all Catalonia. For Barcelona this theatre is the paragon of loci in which power groups interact for social, economic, *and* cultural ends. The building in which this interaction occurs – housing the theatre and an exclusive social club – derives its basic form from international usage of the opera as a prestige marker. At the same time it has entered the heritage of every member of the elite through family and life cycles. As in the cemetery, class membership and boundaries are clearly demarcated. In contrast to the former, however, the interaction of *living* Barcelonians at the opera has also made it an arena in which boundaries are crossed by acts of violence that spring from social and economic inequality.

The theatre of the city

In his introduction to Loewenberg's standard *Annals of Opera*, Edward Dent situates opera as a cultural product within its social milieu,

> beginning with what we might call academic opera in Florence, produced before a small audience of excessively cultivated people. And because the only people in that period who were in a position to become excessively cultivated were princes and cardinals and courtiers attendant upon them, opera struck root as an eminently aristocratic and court entertainment, becoming gradually more sumptuous and spectacular as the seventeenth century progressed. In spite of simultaneous currents in different directions, what we might call 'dynastic' opera survived indeed right up to the end of the eighteenth century, even after the French Revolution had begun to change the face of European society. (Dent: xxvii)

While everyone dies and faces the prospect of some burial/disposal, opera has consistently been defined within Western culture as a domain of High Culture and of wealthy, learned, and powerful patrons. Beyond this distinction, though, there are similarities in its development to the pattern already illustrated for elite representation in cemeteries, even after the genre was established as a commercial form.

In seventeenth-century Venice the opera house was as familial as the pantheon; commercial houses 'were known by the names of noble families which erected and supported them' (Dent: xviii). By the next century the opera house became a public work, under the aegis of new forms of domination rather than a single patron. Thus, the Teatro San Carlo in Naples became 'not only in size but also in position a symbol of the new state' (Robinson: 8). San Carlo represented the social and political order of the Neapolitan monarchy for which it was constructed in 1737. It was built adjacent to the palace and was dominated by the presence of the king, whose central box was flanked by the stalls of the nobility. This social pattern was so fixed that no aristocrat could even relinquish his box without express royal approval. The king was also arbiter of behaviour for the theatre: 'No person other than the king or his official deputy [..] could order an encore' (Robinson: 111).

In the nineteenth century the opera found patrons in new elites. These drew upon the history of opera houses, while modifying these associations to accommodate social differences. Such modifications were often minimalized. Thus in 1849, when the new rich of New York were rebuffed in their attempts to enter Knickerbocker society at the Academy of Music, they decided to build an alternative institution. In designing the Metropolitan Opera patrons and architects turned to European aristocratic models:

> To invoke such non-American influence was, of course, absurd: the nineteenth-century European houses were built to suit the hierarchy that supported them. Imperial boxes, and others arranged at reasonable distances from the throne, were appropriate enough in theaters that endured through the bounty of one class. It could be contended that the Vanderbilts and Morgans regarded themselves in somewhat the same light, but it is apparent that only the display appealed to them, not the attendant responsibilities. (Kolodin: 51)

In the later 1800s, however, the opera became the nexus for the synthesis of old and new elites. Both its symbolic value and its social patterns facilitated exchange in business, courtship, and politics. In Paris, Vienna, and Barcelona, aristocracy and bourgeoisie coalesced in the halls and boxes of the theatre.

In the changing social climate of the twentieth century opera has tended to gradually follow the fading of older elites before the bureaucrats and managers of new state formations. London's Covent Garden was built in 1858 with three full tiers of boxes for the nobility in addition to the Central Royal Box. After World War I this number was nearly halved to 57 boxes, mainly concentrated in a single Grand Tier. Since World War II further social change has been evidenced in the conversion of boxes to ordinary seats and stalls. Only 22 boxes remain, huddled around the Royal Box (Rosenthal: 118–19).

Obviously, the sheer visual and acoustic properties of the opera house limit democratization: there is always potential for the representation of stratification, even if only on the basis of the ticket market. If a royal hierarchy is absent, other leadership may substitute. Yet these uses are in reaction to, more than as a continuation of, the national and international traditions within which the Barcelona opera house took on meaning as an arena for the expression of – and contestation to – class divisions and elite coherence.

Three themes from this general overview are particularly important to the examination of the Liceu. All coincide with the analysis of the cemetery, while elaborating upon distinct aspects of social and cultural life. First, the opera house was constructed under the tutelage of a power group to which it gave special prominence. As a corollary the opera also has embodied the succession of elite groups through time, either in structural changes in a single building or in the competition between theatres. The opera has also served as a locus for the coalescence of competing elites.

Second, the opera house is a microcosm of society as a whole. That is, as in the cemetery the hierarchical position of the elite was meaningful in relation to other classes. Again, as in the cemetery, class differentiation extended to the expression of fundamental social units and values: the family, property, and social cohesion.

Finally, the opera has been a scene of social drama. As a key symbol of power and privilege within Western society it is also the focus of dispute within class conflicts. As will be evident in Barcelona, this drama could become violent even off the stage.

These themes to some extent presuppose another significant point: namely, that communication among international elites which led to a universalization of symbols of power in the nineteenth century. Opera houses implied prestige as much to the entrepreneurs of a rubber capital in Brazil and the newly enriched miners of the American West as to bankers and industrialists in European capitals. As in the cemetery or in the values of gentlemanliness the formation of the Good Families of Barcelona rested on both adaptations of Catalan traditions of status and the adoption of foreign prestige paradigms. The Liceu has been, historically, a place where internationalized claims have meshed with local elite formation – and with counter-events from other classes.

The Liceu and the rise of opera in Barcelona

The upper-class memoirist Joaquín María de Nadal Ferrer distilled the image of the Liceu that was constantly reiterated in my conversations with contemporary Barcelonians:

> The Liceu that I knew in my childhood was not a theatre – it was an institution. Even today, when many of its characteristics have disappeared, one goes to the Liceu with a spirit different from that with which one attends any other theatre: one goes there as someone fulfilling a ritual. (Nadal Ferrer, 1952: 103–04)

Nadal's introduction of the term *ritual* is particularly apt. Although secular by comparison to the cemetery, the Liceu gradually has come to enshrine widely accepted symbols and behaviours through which membership in the ruling class and the conflict between urban classes are both re-enacted. Even so, the Liceu is only one representation within a history of spectacle and celebration in Barcelona (Fàbregas Surroca; Amelang). The use of theatrical spectacles in aristocratic consciousness is a telling prelude to the emergence of a new nineteenth-century elite.

Opera antedated the Liceu in Barcelona. Early representations took place in private noble homes, using aristocratic amateurs as well as professional singers (Curet: 60). In 1587 the Teatre de la Santa Creu (Theatre of the Holy Cross) was established by a royal privilege granted to the Hospital of the Holy Cross. This theatre survived wars, invasions, and fires to become the chosen theatre of the eighteenth-century elite. Urban nobles patronized its reconstruction after a fire in the late 1700s, and families transmitted their boxes from father to son through generations. The old urban power structure, including the canons of the hospital and various aldermen, also supported the Santa Creu (Alier: 11–88).

The Liceu was founded in 1837 as a money-raising project for a company of national militia. After using an expropriated convent for its first performances, the group made plans for a permanent building on the Rambles. The building was begun in 1844 and finished in 1847. This triennium also witnessed such economic milestones as the foundation of the Bank of Barcelona (1844), the Barcelona Savings and Loan (1844), and the giant textile firm La España Industrial (1845).

Like these institutions, the Liceu was founded as a joint-stock corporation – drawing on much the same membership as the other ventures. Manuel Girona Agrafel was a key figure in the construction of the building. Others had more aristocratic connections. Joaquín de Gispert Angli, first president of the Society, was a Noble of the Principality (like the stratum who founded the Savings and Loan). His family was also linked by marriage to the industrialist–banker José María Serra. Manuel Gibert Sans, the third key figure in the theatre's construction, was a former military man who devoted his wealth to the improvement of Barcelona. His house, in fact, became a symbol of the new bourgeois city.

In order to finance the construction, boxes were sold rather than rented. The cheapest ticket price was one-third of a peseta. Ownership of a box ran as high as 15,000 pesetas in addition to a yearly service fee (Capmany: 82). While the cheap tickets permitted a wide audience, power rested only with the box *owners*. Until the late twentieth century they formed a commission that leased responsibilities each season to an impresario. Since the death of Franco this system has given way to partial control and financing by the Generalitat de Catalunya, further exemplifying the decline of the Good Families and the role of government in replacing their power and patronage.

In 1847 the addition of the Círculo del Liceo amplified the interactional dimensions of the opera house. The Círculo has been an extremely important and elegant male social club that became a ready meeting place for urban leaders. It is physically incorporated into the opera house: in the present building there is an entrance from the street and from the *planta noble*, the main or 'noble' floor on which the boxes of the upper class are concentrated. Its hours and functions have been more diverse: beyond the short opera and ballet season the club hosts elite meetings to discuss politics, business, and social matters. Furthermore, it is a specially defined space. While the lower classes were expected to observe the display of the boxes, the club was separated as a class prerogative. Its membership also encompasses only the males of the primary families of the city. Women are allowed to enter as guests but not as members. The box, as an extension of the household, is the female domain for social networking and knowledge. The Círculo, by contrast, becomes a more sociable extension of the male office. Yet both club and box are parts of the Liceu as institution.

By mid-century the Liceu was in active competition with the Santa Creu. A theatrical interpretation of this conflict was recorded by the Catalan playwright Serafí Pitarra. Pitarra saw the competition as one of classes as much as theatres. In his play the partisans of the Santa Creu are introduced as 'bald, ancient, and bewigged': stereotypes of a declining aristocracy bound by eighteenth-century fashions. The Liceists are 'young, elegant, and rich', even though a Cruzado reviles them as 'mere manufacturers' (Soler Hubert and Carreras; see Fabregas Surroca: 103).

Competition was not the only difficulty of the Liceu. The building was destroyed by fire in 1861. Yet a new edifice was financed and built within a year. The rapidity of this process manifests the importance that opera had assumed within the social life of the city. Meanwhile, the decline of the Santa Creu became more apparent. Those eighteenth-century families who could afford a box there also attended the Liceu. The Santa Creu, renamed the Teatre Principal, did produce the Catalan premier of Wagner in 1883. But it, too, was hard hit by a late-nineteenth-century fire. Unlike the Liceu, it has never regained its status and now functions as a cinema and entertainment centre.

Other amusements also competed for elite patronage. The Hippodrome was memorialized in satirical couplets about elite families. Other members of elite families regularly attended zarzuelas, as well as more popular theatrical performances.

There were also individual statements of class and imagery. The

Teatre dels Camps Elisis, for example, was built as a commercial opera house in the new and fashionable Eixample. The patrician banker Evaristo Arnús Ferrer converted it into the Teatre Líric, which he patronized almost like a family opera house. After his death the 1,600-seat theatre proved economically burdensome, and it was torn down in 1902. The Liceu flourished.

In the twentieth century the career of the Liceu has been susceptible to the political and economic fluctuations of its patrons. Many informants recalled a Golden Age in the early decades of the century, including the Primo de Rivera dictatorship. This ended with the social reforms of the Second Republic and with expropriation during the Civil War, when the Liceu was rebaptized the 'National Theatre of Catalonia'. In the 1940s and 1950s efforts were made to revive the Liceu. The Francoist bureaucracy and military joined the Catalan upper bourgeoisie. A magazine, *Liceo*, was even founded to carry musical and social news.

Changes continued with the end of the Franco regime and the increasing collapse of the older factory elite. In 1978, for example, a news magazine ran the headline 'Is the Liceu Dying?' (*Destino* 9–15, March 1978: 20–24). In an interview the theatre's manager blamed the crisis on anachronistic structures: 'It lives with those of one hundred years ago, when the current situation is very different' (Moya-Angeler: 21). Both anachronisms and decline are facets of the same problem: the Liceu as an institution is a product and reproducer of a historically particular elite formation and has followed the trajectory of this elite. Recognition by the Generalitat de Catalunya of the theatre as part of the cultural and historical patrimony of Catalonia has led to support in exchange for control. Political leaders of the socialist and nationalist parties mingle with the older aristocracy there – and programmes are printed in both Catalan and Castilian.

Like the cemetery, the Liceu has had a rich and changing participation in the cultural meanings of the elite in Barcelona and an even greater participation in day-to-day social interaction. The 'meanings' of the Liceu, however, must be elucidated by reference to architectural design, social interpretation, and elite usage as a marker of upper-class life cycles and cohesion.

The structure and meaning of the Liceu

The Liceu is built in a horseshoe design common to many opera houses. Its 3,500 seats fill an orchestra level overhung by five balconies. Three of the balconies, as well as the orchestral floor, have boxes as well as individual seats. The top two tiers contain only individual seats.

The differentiation of balconies is reinforced by other features of ornament and access. Only the lower four floors can be reached from the main entrance. A triumphal marble staircase leads from the lobby to the *planta noble*, or *principal* (second) floor. There it divides into smaller and less decorated staircases to the third and fourth floors. The topmost balconies, from whose cheaper seats the opera itself may be invisible, are entered through an undistinguished entrance on a side street. Today an elevator takes patrons directly to these seats, without any possible connection to the lower balconies.

The *planta noble* was designed with special care to emphasize its high prestige. In addition to the focal ceremonial staircase it has a large salon for conversation and the entrance to the bar and dining rooms of the Círculo del Liceu. It shares with other floors a wide passageway that girds the seating area, onto which the boxes open. This is the scene of a constant promenade between the acts; the passageway is 5 metres wide to accommodate considerable movement.

The floors with boxes have another special feature: the anterooms. Doors open from the passage onto an elegant room that holds four to six people, a private space between the corridor and the seats. The box is semi-public, enclosed by walls roughly 1 metre in height. It has seats and benches on each side, with a raised seat at the back. Boxes on the main floor hold six to ten guests.

This distinction between floors permeated nineteenth-century architecture in Barcelona. The second floor of the palaces of the Rambla de Catalunya or the Passeig de Gràcia was the desirable floor for residence, indicated by a separate and formal entrance staircase, larger and ornamented bay windows or balconies, and more spacious rooms. The ground floor would hold businesses, a concierge, and space for carriages. Upper floors repeated the pattern of the *planta noble* with decreasing ornamentation and size. In some palaces these were allocated to the children of the owners who occupied the *planta noble*. The topmost floors, containing servants' quarters, were cramped and dark, with small windows or none at all. Only in the construction boom after the 1950s has the penthouse emerged as a new symbol of social prestige. The six floors of the opera house, however, were distinguished by more than design features. The seats of best visibility were also those of highest prestige: the *planta noble* and, to a somewhat lesser extent, the orchestra and third floor. The fourth and fifth floors (third and fourth balconies) were less valued. Boxes were owned by less important families, by *peñas* (groups of friends), or by younger couples whose parents held boxes on lower floors. Individual seats were also owned by modest families. The uppermost balconies have been associated with those of limited resources, who might otherwise not hear any opera: students, artisans, and workers. One Catalan author interpreted these levels of meaning by contrast to another non-elite institution:

> Although conceived and constructed by the wealthy and aristocratic, it has never been a theater of class. Every social category fits: in the orchestra, second, and third floor, the *aristocracy*, on the fourth and fifth floors, the *mesocracy*, and on the sixth and seventh, the *democracy*... the confusion and mingling of all these classes took place in the celebration of the splendid dances of Carnival. (Puig Alfonso: 25–26)

While the Liceu juxtaposed classes, it did so within a controlled differentiation. It was a theatre of one class in active distinction from others. The opposite of this was Carnival, a traditional festival of disguise and critique of social roles. Even within the Liceu, Carnival was an image of the world in reverse. Thus its mingling was in direct opposition to the clear demarcation of categories in the Liceu itself. While there was a nineteenth-century custom of Carnival balls in the theatre, this was increasingly frowned upon, for the elite Carnival was limited to private and single-class parties. Under Franco the Barcelona Carnival was completely banned as a threat to public order. Under the new Generalitat it has been revived as part of Catalonia's national public heritage.

In the Liceu social groups existed in relationship to each other rather than in isolation. The upper floors were linked to the lower by their observation of the social activities below. Those in the aristocracy displayed not only to other families of the elite but to a popular audience above. The contrasting yet interwoven perspectives can be regained from two authors born at the turn of the century in different social backgrounds. Josep Pla attended the Liceu as a poor student in the *galliner* ('chicken roost': a nickname for the uppermost balconies) and later recorded his impressions:

> The spectacle of the Liceu on a good night is magnificent when viewed from the top floor [..] the view is literally fabulous – an ocean of bourgeoisie, dripping with jewels and diamonds. What a spectacle, by God! On the fifth floor... a group of people carefully positioned, with the faces of train mechanics... In addition, there were the music fanatics, with or without score in hand, for whom nothing but the music of the drama was important. These fans had an Olympian disdain for the bourgeois sea below them. (Pla: 40)

Meanwhile, Joaquín María de Nadal Ferrer described the thoughts of a member of the aristocracy looking upward – or at least conscious of those looking down:

> The public of the Liceu was formed by all classes, but not all went for the same reason. If they were not all friends, at least all were acquainted [..] the inhabitants of boxes and choice seats knew the preferences of the denizens of the upper floors, and those were aware of the engagements and the loves that were important on the principal floors. They knew perfectly well that X had broken with Y, or who had made the dresses of Mrs Z or Countess A, and what the emerald of this or that woman would cost [..] the most humble seamstress of the *galliner* could have named without error the owners of the boxes on the principal floor, and even those of many individual seats. (Nadal Ferrer 1950: 133–34)

These two commentators suggest the dialogue within which the social meaning of the Liceu took shape. Nadal, the elitist, imputes a music-hall ambience to the social dramas of the Liceu, with benign interest on the part of those above. Pla's memories are more charged with a hostility that Nadal could not impute to the upper floors, for that hostility had already scarred the security of the elite within its ordered domain. Neither account of itself expressed the complete perception of the Liceu. Instead, they illustrate the clash of the generally hegemonic expression of the elite with the less than complete acquiescence of those over whom this control was to be exercised.

To speak of elite appropriation of the Liceu it is necessary to go beyond the static framework of urban society embodied in the edifice. For the elite, by contrast to other groups, the Liceu was a fundamental locus of social and cultural identity. This is apparent in the way in which the theatre enshrined the concept of family and ownership, in its use in the upper-class life cycle, and in its value for the integration of the upper class as a whole.

Boxes in the Liceu are property. Families are identified with the boxes that they have owned for generations. At least one family displays the original bill of sale from 1844 in the anteroom of its box. In the testament of Juan Güel the box is specifically included in the distribution of resources as going to his son and primary heir.

Since the box has a capacity of ten to twelve an extended sense of family or network can be cultivated for any performance; distant relatives and others can be accommodated on the second and third performance of the opera. On the other hand, since this is not an expandable or divisible resource, the box, like the family pantheon, tends to follow the main male line. Other lines may buy new boxes. Middle-class owners, by contrast, might have only a pair of tickets or a single seat.

Because of this confluence of family, box, and status, lack of a box raises serious questions. Retirement from the Liceu is a withdrawal from assertions of prestige and from connections of friendship and potential marriage. In economic crises of the twentieth century some older families with declining revenues sold their rights, relinquishing this display. Their private protestations of disinterest did not always coincide with public evaluation of their actions.

For those who have owned boxes over generations the 'theatre became a complement of family life and an extension of the house. Its boxes enjoyed a certain privilege of extraterritoriality: people went to them without leaving their home' (Nadal Ferrer 1952: 105). Nowhere was this connection more evident than in the elaborate etiquette that surrounded rites of passage. This began in earliest childhood:

> The juridical condition of the boxes as private property had repercussions on the audience. Children invaded them on Saturday with governesses and retainers, and even wetnurses. Is there anything more extraordinary than a wetnurse at the opera? (Nadal Ferrer 1952: 105)

The transition to adulthood was also marked at the opera house, especially for women. As late as the 1950s women made their social debut by appearing in formal dress at an evening performance. This was followed by visits and courtship, according to the strict rules already discussed. One woman who made her debut in the 1920s noted that male visitors were only permitted to pay their respects to her in the public box, in the presence of her parents and chaperone (as well as in view of the rest of the group). Only after her 1929 marriage did she receive guests in the privacy of the anteroom. Nonetheless, the Liceu was central to both the contacts and the flow of information that made marriage the foundation of social cohesion.

Death was also ritualized in the Liceu. Any family who lost a member was expected to close its box and cancel its social calendar for the season. The failure of one family to do so was memorialized in a turn-of-the-century satirical couplet: 'En memoria de un ser querido / Los Fabra han venido' [In memory of a loved one / The Fabras have come].

Finally, the Liceu was a meeting ground for the cohesion of the elite as a group. Well-placed individuals at the Liceu's apogee had rights to several boxes according to their different roles. One woman recalled that her father had a family box on the second floor that was owned by his parents, a box on the third floor with his wife and children, and a third floor tontine of male friends. Boxes on the upper floors were also rumoured to be used for mistresses or assignations. This information is difficult to verify but emphasizes the subtle decrease in status in the middle to upper floors.

Elite spectators circulate during the evening. Between the acts males talk in the passageways or visit the ladies in their boxes. More extensive discussions take place in the Círculo, over drinks or a meal. Conversation includes the exchange of social, political, and business information as well as musical criticism. Before the Civil War non-musical displays of solidarity were even more frequent, including political rallies and social events.

The Liceu was familiar in another sense, in the comfort of constant interactions. In 1985 an octogenarian described to me the theatre in her youth: 'It was like a get-together (*reunión*) of the families of Barcelona. It was not Fulano goes one day and some other stranger the next. Instead, you looked around and asked "Who isn't here today?"'.

In all these characteristics the Liceu is a living cognate of the stratificational projections and usages of the cemetery. But the opera house was never outside the city in a spatial, ritual, or social sense. Hence it has been less an urbanistic projection than an arena for urban social confrontation.

Social drama at the Liceu

On the opening night of the 1976 season spectators leaving the Liceu were confronted by protestors who reportedly pelted them with fruit or vandalized their cars. This was also reported for the next season. Such occurrences were seized upon by those who wished to withdraw for other reasons, including economic difficulties. They insisted that the Liceu was dead, that 'no one goes any more'. These rumours were also used to criticize the destabilization of the post-Franco era. It was not, however, the first time that class violence had erupted at the opera.

The Catalan folklorist Joan Amades cites an anecdote about the fire that destroyed the first Liceu:

> It is said that the associates were people of position who felt disdain and lack of consideration for the common people to such an extent that, in building the theatre [..] they were deeply concerned that those who sat in the upper floors could not descend to the orchestra or lower floors where the builders had their seats or boxes. Because of this, the first theater had no communication between upper and lower floors. If someone in the house wanted to go from a higher floor to a lower, or vice

versa, he had to exit to the street. Popular opinion said that the blaze had been set by theater workers or members of the lower class who met the disdain of the owners with fire. (Amades: 72)

Amades gives no context or reference for this story. While it may be suggestive of the class tensions of mid-nineteenth century Barcelona, it may also have been influenced by the more decisive action that followed at the end of the century. On the opening night of the 1893 season, during the first intermission of *William Tell*, two bombs were thrown from the top floor of the theatre into the seats below. One exploded on the first floor between rows thirteen and fourteen. Twenty people were killed.

The turn of the century was a period of extremely violent class confrontation in Barcelona. In retrospect, the Liceu incident fits into a dialectic of terrorism and repression between owners and workers that included the bombing of the Corpus Christi procession of 1896, the Tragic Week and its aftermath in 1909, and the pistol gangs that roamed the streets following World War I. Yet the reaction of the upper class both in its repression and in its transformation of the Liceu bombing in historical consciousness provides important insights into their sense of order and control.

The bombing of the Liceu was an excuse for a widespread crackdown on anarchists and dissidents. Over four hundred were arrested and seven executed. The bomber himself, Santiago Salvador Franch, was arrested in February and executed in July. Later historians have suggested that since he had no previous background as a militant this action might have been a personal reaction to the execution of the anarchist Pallas. The elite judgment, even 50 years later, is more sweeping: 'His intent was to destroy society' (Bertrán: 217).

The Liceu bombing has tended to eclipse later and more destructive confrontations, like the Tragic Week, in elite historical consciousness. It is commemorated by a relief on Barcelona's Temple of the Holy Family and has also been enshrined in popular novels, such as Ignacio Agustí's *Mariona Rebull*, which was serialized on Spanish television in 1976 and 1977. Agustí's depiction, widely known among elite families during my stay in Barcelona, focuses on the mythic carnage of the upper class rather than on the actual events that transpired:

> From one of the front boxes they carried a young girl, screaming like a demon, trailing blood on the rug – as the last drops of her life escaped. On the main staircase men and women sat, their faces glazed by pain and shock, shirt fronts and collars disarrayed, the most intimate flesh revealed as tragedy overcame shame... He was horrified and turned away in the other direction, but the macabre display continued. That was Jacinto Miralles, who said that he never went anywhere. And this, Carolina Millet, who had played Schumann on the day of her debut. (Agusti: 196–97)

Agustí uses the bombing as a climactic intervention to eliminate the heroine and her lover, struck down behind the closed door of the anteroom of a box. His account is clearly fictionalized: casualties were limited to middle-class or foreign patrons in the orchestra seats. Yet Agustí was appealing more to the *consciousness* of the event among elite families than to the facts. While contemporary members of the Good Families dismissed Agustí's exaggeration, the tale of the Liceu bombing – and a more genealogical link through 'someone' in the family who was there that night – was a common feature of interviews.

Once again, Nadal summarizes the impact of the Liceu bombing on elite historical memory:

> A long time passed before the seats and boxes recovered their life, and a group of orchestra seats remained deserted forever, as a silent memorial to that great catastrophe. People involuntarily raised their eyes to the roof as if they feared to discover the same criminal act from another hand, repeating the tragic gesture, sowing that seed of death in the midst of life. (Nadal Ferrer 1952: 111)

Why did this event, this one bombing among so many incidents of its epoch, take on such a mythic power in the historical consciousness of the Good Families of Barcelona? The answer lies in the ideological meaning of the Liceu as a projection of the social order of Catalonia and the stability of control that the new elite sought to hold in that society. The bombing of the Liceu was a direct challenge to the 'Good Families'' image of power and society, on its presentation of its own identity. By attacking within the Liceu, the confrontation assumed even greater meaning – and left greater uncertainty. As Nadal notes, even brutal repression could not restore the integrity of that model of the city and its classes that the Liceu and the cemetery had been built to display.

The further comments of a bourgeois writer who actually attended the Liceu that night may further illuminate the depths of connection of the Liceu, the social order, and the family. Joan Maragall added the subtitle 'returning home from the Liceu' to his poem 'Paternal'. In it he mixes images of chaos with a sinister vision of the family as nexus of violence:

> Furious, the hatred explodes across the land
> The contorted heads rain blood,
> and one must go to the *fetes*
> With heart well-fortified, as if to war.
> ...
> Watching the child who suckles – the mother
> sighs, the father wrinkles his brow.
> But the innocent infant,
> Who, satisfied, leaves the empty breast
> looks at him, – looks at her,
> and laughs, barbarously. (Maragall: 47)

In the workplace and the voting booth this same bourgeoisie sought to use the family as a metaphor by which to control the proletariat as if children. The sanctity of the family was further ritualized in the Liceu. Hence, any attack on the social order of the Liceu betrayed a lie at the heart of not only the symbol but also the family as the ideological projection of the whole class.

Conclusions

Both the Liceu and the Cementiri Vell share an ideological model of social structure, class cohesion, and control. The necropolis reveals the urbanistic mentality of the nineteenth-century elite in a way that the city of Barcelona itself and its documents can do no longer. The opera house has been more actively intertwined with urban life. Thus, it has been the subject of more visible challenges to the elite image of an ideal society.

In both of these social projections the family is a central motif. It is the basic unit of the well-ordered society. Tombs and theatre seats delineate the boundaries of households, while patterning the interaction among them. Rights to tomb and loge are established in familial succession. Both become an extension of the house, a cultural manipulation of the structure that was so effectively used in the economic and social life of the emergent elite.

Yet in both of these models the symbolism of the family has been subsumed by the projection of an ordered inequality among classes. Hence, elite models abandon the uniform traditional values of the family evident in political rhetoric to condone differences in rights of property, size of the household, and continuity through time. Was there no contradiction in imagery?

In fact, this variation in the use of the family as metaphor tends to reaffirm a point made in the earlier analysis. The family has obviously been important to the Barcelona upper class for its practical values in economic and social life, for its historical associations, and for its deep emotive appeal. Yet other images might have met the same conditions or have been adapted to the ends of the group in different ways. The special value of the family as metaphor also lay in its multiplicity of meanings and the consequent ambiguity or indeterminacy it allowed in cultural projections. In political rhetoric the family was emphasized in its dual capacities as unifying and hierarchical. In modelling the ideal urban society it was depicted as fundamental to membership in that society but fundamentally differentiated according to the segmentation of rights and privileges within that society. Ambiguity rather than contradiction was the key to the value and usage of the family as a cultural image to legitimize the elite's claim to domination.

Addenda

Looking back on the ethnohistorical fieldwork that underpinned *Good Families* (McDonogh) from the distance of four decades of continued fieldwork in Barcelona and other cities is itself an experience of history, power, and change in the city. Working among Barcelonians of powerful families and other positions, as informants, colleagues, critics and friends, allowed me to analyse cultural strategies and fields that had continued to evolve through the Franco era but faced more convulsive changes during the 1970s transition. Looking at different, albeit convergent, processes of elite formation and reproduction over two centuries highlighted intersecting scales important in this work – where the trajectory (and narrative) of individual success and failure became part of the dynamics of family and network over time, that might or might not converge with cycles of industrial and financial growth (and recession) or the changing values of land, capital or knowledge. All of these remained uniquely embedded in and embodied by the development of Barcelona as a city in the nineteenth and twentieth century, perhaps in no way more so than in the physical monuments whose meanings were teased apart in this chapter: the opera house at the centre of the city and the cemeteries on the periphery of the city, iconic places that staged the cohesion and claims of an elite on a local and global stage, if not an eternal one.

Yet changes were under way. The 1970s protests in front of the Liceu formed currents of democratic manifestations and counterclaims of urban power, as did the burgeoning media from newspapers to satirical reviews to television that discussed and even created newly visible elites. Even these changes seem antiquated in the twenty-first century, where digital media, instantaneous social connections and manipulations of information and flow have layered new forms of visibility and invisibility into urban societies and threaded them across continents and global elites. In retrospect, these changes reveal how much Barcelona's financial–industrial elites were shaped by their mediation – visibilities in places, in companies, in newspapers, in humour and protests – even as they used the media of their eras.

The built forms of their city were themselves media in flux. Palaces were already becoming museums (or hotels), fortresses becoming parks or tourist attractions, and private elite spaces becoming public institutions, while new building altered the city. These changes in physical presence and meaning, in fact, comment on changing patterns of power, but like the palimpsest of the city itself, old meanings fade yet are never quite completely erased.

In contemporary Barcelona, monuments and institutions created by this financial–industrial elite perdure and are popular destinations for tourists or sites of civic events. Yet they now participate in a newer fabric of the city dominated by new elites and by public expenditure and control. New monumental constructions speak to Barcelona as a global hub around the construction of the 1992 Olympics, the 2004 Forum, tourism and conventions, from the ever-growing airport to the continual revisions of the Port Vell and the seafront, without enshrining names of wealthy donors or families in a global spotlight. Global corporate logos – from McDonald's to FNAC to more local chains of global presence like Mango and Zara – dominate streetscapes shaped by transnational commerce rather than manifestations of local memory or status.

Indeed, the changes of the two central institutions of this essay speak to the continuing evolution of power, connection and visibility in Barcelona as a Catalan, Spanish, European and global city. By the 1980s, when *Good Families* appeared, new discussions of cost, quality and accessibility of opera performances at the Liceu brought public stakeholders into a new consortium for development. A cataclysmic fire in 1994 that gutted the theatre, however, forced its fundamental transformation; the Liceu was only rebuilt as a public institution, where centurial families and shareholders in the society transferred ownership to a new foundation that now takes responsibility for the space and performances. Attention focused on the stage rather than the balconies, where global tourists and connoisseurs replaced the tightly knit display of earlier times. This, after all, had already been the story of other major opera houses like the Met in New York; as in the past, power and display in Barcelona followed global as well as local patterns.

Meanwhile, urban cemeteries, which were juxtaposed to the Liceu in the original monograph, have also changed even if we might expect these monuments, like the Cementiri Vell, consecrated by centuries of construction and entombment, to be more permanent. Revisiting this space in 2012, though, I saw evidence of families who continued to use tombs and pantheons they had established centuries before, although most modern burials in the city take place at newer and more distant locations. Nonetheless, it was also clear that some early pantheons had reached such a state of neglect, of disappearance, that they had been reclaimed by the municipal management and were available for purchase for new owners. Meanwhile, the 'Protestant' section that embodied the limits of citizenship in the nineteenth century had been made illegal by laws against discrimination in the twentieth century; walls and graves had been moved and the whole reincorporated as a new burial space into the wider cemetery. At the same time, projects raging from tour maps to performances of Zorrillo's *Don Juan Tenorio* incorporated this cemetery as a global space into a necro-tourism with global resonance.

Does this mean that families of wealth and power have disappeared? Or even that old families and their institutions, however concrete, only pass 'into history' as relics of altered meaning amid new flows and power-holders of capital, decision-making and connection? The image of the palimpsest reminds us that urban change is never complete. When asked to talk about my elite research to new graduate students in Barcelona in 2012–2013, for example, I spoke not only of the need for continued historical research (including spatial features), and ongoing connective research to link elites to changing structures of economic, social and political power, but also of an awareness of mediated visibility and invisibility that remains fundamental to the city. A digital gossip report from *panorama.laverdad.es*, on a Pronovias fashion show in a 42nd-story attic of the Hotel des Arts evoked a world that could certainly have been understood in the nineteenth century Liceu:

> Tamara Falcó and Cynthia Rossi showed themselves to be, in spite of very different styles, worthy daughters of their mothers, the former celebrity sweethearts Isabel Preysler and Carmen Martínez Bordíu. The bouquet was completed by Carla Goyanes, daughter of Cary Lapique and Carlos Goyanes, Eugenia Ortiz Domecq, daughter of Sandra Domecq and Bertín (Ortiz) Osborne, Olivia and Cristina de Borbón, daughters of Beatriz de Borbón, Vega Royo Villanova, sister of Carla, Princess of Panagyuriste, María León, Mercedes Bohórquez, Teresa Astolfi, Inés Domecq, Alejandra Raventós (one of the heiresses of the Codorníu empire), Cósima Güell, descendent of Gaudí's patron, y Judith Andic, heiress of Mango stores, the only one who, without a resounding surname has a father who appears in the Forbes 500. Which shows us money is changeable. (Furundarena)

'All that is solid melts into air', Marx and Engels warned us in the *Communist Manifesto* at one time of crisis. Marshall Berman recalled the statement in his book written during another crisis of modernism in the 1970s. Yet as solids – even buildings – melt, the lives and models of cities like Barcelona, their divisions and debates, endure and remain processes of interest for academic study and civic reflection, especially in a case so rich as Barcelona.

Works cited

Agustí, Ignacio (1969). *Mariona Rebull. El viudo Rius: novelas* (Barcelona: Planeta).
Alier, Roger (1979). *Conèixer Catalunya: L'òpera* (Barcelona: Dopesa).
Amades, Joan (1947). *Auca dels edificis notables de Barcelona* (Tàrrega: F. Camps Calmet).
Amelang, James S. (1986). *Honored Citizens of Barcelona: Patrician Culture and Class Relations, 1490–1714* (Princeton, NJ: Princeton UP).
Bertrán, José Marcos (1931). *El Gran Teatro del Liceo. 1837–1930* (Barcelona: Instituto Gráfico Oliva de Vilanova).
Bourdieu, Pierre (1979). *La Distinction: critique du jugement sociale* (Paris: Minuit).
Capmany, Maria Aurèlia (1943). *El Café del Liceo, 1837–1937: El teatro y sus bailes de máscaras* (Barcelona: Dalmau).
Curet, Francesc (1935). *Teatres particulars a Barcelona en el segle XVIIIè* (Barcelona: Institució de Teatre).
Dent, Edward J. (1978). 'Introduction', in Alfred Loewenberg (ed.), *Annals of Opera 1597–1940. Compiled from the Original Sources by Alfred Loewenberg* (London: John Calder).
Fàbregas Surroca, Xavier (1975). *Les formes de diversió en la societat catalana romàntica* (Barcelona: Curial).
Furundarena, Arantza (2004). 'Noche de Niñas Bien'. *Panorama/La Verdad*.es, 27 June. http://servicios.laverdad.es/panorama/corazongente270604.htm [accessed 20 March 2017].
'Is the Liceu Dying?' (1978). *Destino* 9–15, March: 20–24).
Kolodin, Irving (1968). *The Metropolitan Opera 1883–1966: A Candid History* (New York: Knopf).
Maragall, Joan (1929). *Obres completes*, I (Barcelona: Sala Parés).
McDonogh, Gary Wray (1986). *Good Families of Barcelona: A Social History*

of Power in the Industrial Era (Princeton, NJ: Princeton University Press).

Moya-Angeler, J. (1978). 'La saga de los Muntadas-Prim. ¿Quién es quién en la familia?'. *Destino* 2, 106: 13–15.

Nadal Ferrer, Joaquín María de (1950). 'La proyección social del teatro del Liceo', in A. Artís (ed.), *Primer centenario de la sociedad del Gran Teatro del Liceo* (Barcelona: n.p.), 133–35.

— (1952). *Memòries d'un estudiant barceloní* (Barcelona: Dalmau).

Pla, Josep (1956). *Obres completes* (Barcelona: Editorial Selecta).

Puig Alfonso, Francisco (1943). *Recuerdos de un setentón* (Barcelona: Dalmau).

Robinson, Michael F. (1972). *Naples and Neapolitan Opera* (Oxford: Clarendon Press).

Rosenthal, Harold (1958). *Two centuries of Opera at Covent Garden* (London: Putnam).

Soler Hubert, F. (Serafí Pitarra) and Enric Carreras (1855). *Liceistas y Cruzados* (Barcelona: Antoni López. Llibreria Espanyola).

CHAPTER NINE

Memory and the city in Barcelona's cemeteries

Elisa Martí-López

Cemeteries constitute the most important urban site of memory and commemoration in modern society.[1] In the nineteenth century the emotional focus of death moved from the dying to the survivors. Death was constructed as the *death of the other*, that is, around a new intolerance of separation and, consequently, around the suffering and distress felt by survivors (Ariès: 65–66). This new relationship between the living and the dead is based also on the peculiar fear of death felt in modern societies. As William Hazlitt explained in 1930, the modern fear of death is the fear 'of no longer mattering in the world of affairs and, projecting back, of never having mattered at all' (qtd. in Laqueur: 29). What is disturbing for the modern individual, what makes the thought or sight of death so unbearable, is 'death as being forgotten': 'Memory is its antidote, and the cemetery made possible an undreamed of elaboration of personal commemoration and contemplation' (Laqueur: 29–30). Modern – now historical – cemeteries came about, thus, as a remedy to the particular modern fear of death: oblivion. Fear of being

---

1 In this essay I focus my discussion on cemeteries as private sites for commemoration. I do not engage the cemeteries as privileged grounds for the patriotism of nations and states, or as sites of political activity and other social practices.

forgotten and mourning are thus the basis for the extensive culture of death that characterized the nineteenth century. New cemeteries, funeral processions and memento mori objects were important sites for both private and public memory and commemoration and, as such, privileged sites for the construction of individual and collective identities. It is no surprising that they figure prominently in nineteenth-century culture and its literary and artistic imaginations.

The dominant nineteenth-century medical discourse on burial grounds considered cemeteries sites of the viral destructiveness of life. The constitution of cemeteries as counter-image of this hygienic discourse – that is, into a fundamental site for the construction of both individual and collective identities through commemoration – reconciled the inhabitants of the city with the new *extramuros* burial sites. The cemetery as *lieu de mémoire* gave the hygienic discourse on cemeteries the social and emotional meaning it lacked and made the new urban spaces of death readable. As Pedro Felipe Monlau, an eminent Catalan doctor whose work contributed decisively to the modernization of medicine in Spain in the nineteenth century, wrote in 1871:

> Por último, en este siglo han prevalecido las leyes higiénicas: los cementerios han sido alejados de las ciudades; no se cometen en ellos los escándalos de otras épocas: las sepulturas van recibiendo un carácter monumental; y en las bellísimas necrópolis de Pisa, de Nápoles, de París, etc., a favor de consoladoras ilusiones, parece que se haya conseguido familiarizar la vida con la muerte. (Monlau: 110)

> [Lastly, in this century hygienic laws prevailed: cemeteries were distanced from cities; the scandals of other eras are not committed in them: tombs are given a monumental nature; and in the beautiful cemeteries of Pisa, Naples, Paris, etc., in order to promote consoling illusions, it appears that they succeeded in familiarizing life and death.]²

The tomb as monument transformed the cemeteries into one of the 'principal loci, material or immaterial, in which memory had

---

2 Unless otherwise stated, all translations are by the author.

become embodied and which, through the actions of men or the work of centuries, remained their most specific representations and most dazzling symbols' (Nora: xviii). As *lieux de mémoire* Barcelona's cemeteries exemplify wonderfully that 'the community's idea of itself in history cannot be disentangled from the ways it represents death' (Goodwin and Bronfen: 15). The question is, however: What kind of space of memory is the cemetery?

How is memory constructed in cemeteries? Whose memory?

As depositories of social relations and belief systems, cemeteries are at once the locus and the instrument of power. As such, they were sites of contention between different social institutions and groups: cemeteries were 'a terrain where Church, State, and family had to negotiate carefully in order to protect what they considered to be crucial moral and economic interests' (Kselman: 10). As contested sites of power – as contested as the cities that created them – cemeteries are 'critical symbolic adjuncts to the city' (Heathcote: 12). They are, thus, intimately related to the particular historical experience of the city that creates them and, as such, must be discussed in local terms.

The existing link between a *general* problematic of memory and the *particular* thematic of 'places' – mentioned by Pierre Nora when discussing *lieux de mémoire* – is, in my view, the principle of inclusions and exclusions that constitutes most, if not all, memorial sites. Thomas Kselman points out that '[o]f all the changes involving cemeteries in the nineteenth century none reflects so dramatically new attitudes toward the dead as the right of everyone to be buried in his or her own grave' (183). It is precisely this 'right' to individual sepulture, to a privately owned tomb, or rather the lack of this 'right', that constitutes, in my view, the existing link between memory and place in cemeteries. In other words: property – memory siding with property. Modern cemeteries fulfilled the bourgeois desire for a 'dignified' – hygienic and private – burial site. More importantly, they effected the transformation of the hygienic and private tomb into a site of civic memory and commemoration. In Barcelona's cemeteries, religion separated but did not exclude. Cemeteries, all Catholic, had attached *recintes* [burial grounds] for other religions which had a significant demographic presence in the city. El recinte dels protestants for non-Catholic Christians opened in the 1830s next to the Cementiri de Poblenou; the 1883 Cementiri de Montjuïc had both a burial ground for non-Catholic Christians and a civil – non consecrated – section known as the Cementiri Lliure; the Cementiri jueu opened in 1931 in the Cementiri de les Corts; and the Cementiri de Collserola, inaugurated in 1972, included specific burial grounds for Jews and Muslims.[3]

The radical exclusion effected in and by modern cemeteries corresponds to the class exclusion articulated by the property-based liberalism of the nineteenth century; that is: a man of property, a vote and, I would add, a tomb, Epitaphs, mausoleums, artistic works, designs for burial sites, cemetery regulations and other polices are instruments of memory in so far as they are the displaced forms of property. It is relevant to remember here that modern cemeteries entered the commodity circulation of goods and its speculative creation of value: both cemeteries and tombs could now be bought and sold for a profit. Memory as property organizes the symbolization of social relations and the strategies of legitimation and distinction effected in and by cemeteries. Barcelona's cemeteries are a case in point and, as such, can be read as an 'archive', that is, as sites where private and public property records are kept.

It is, thus, not a coincidence that at the precise time when the city's bourgeoisie had consolidated its industrial revolution and the colonial scope of its commerce – the Banco de Barcelona was created in 1844 and in 1854 the demolition of Barcelona's medieval walls was initiated to make room for the construction of the new bourgeois city, Ildefons Cerdà's Eixample – the only cemetery for the city, the Cementeri de Poblenou, was the site of one of two highly symbolic urban initiatives carried out by Barcelona's bourgeoisie: the construction of a new funerary enclosure exclusively for mausoleums. The Recinte dels panteons, the new enclosure where the city's new wealthy classes would be buried (Figure 9.1), and the 1848 construction of the new opera house, the Liceu, were the new social spaces where the bourgeoisie displayed its new power and ambition. Real walls were falling down and symbolic ones were

---

[3] With the exception of the Second Republic (1931–1939), cemeteries were officially Catholic from their creation at the beginning of the nineteenth century until the restoration of democracy in 1978.

Memory and the city in Barcelona's cemeteries 213

Figure 9.1 A mausoleum in the Recinte dels panteons,
Cementiri de Poblenou

Cementiris de Barcelona, S.A.

being built up in the city by the new cultural, economic and political assertiveness of a new hegemonic class – the Catalan bourgeoisie. Those same years put an end to the city's revolutionary period.[4]

In the last decades of the nineteenth century, the number of people who could afford individual/family tombs in cemeteries and, thus, claim a place in the collective space of memory, grew substantially – as did voting rights for men.[5] The fact remains, however, that throughout the nineteenth century, the liberal notion of citizenship – based on property – failed to comply with the bourgeois hygiene principle for cemeteries: 'La regla higiénica es que *cada cadáver ha de tener su hoya especial*' (Monlau: 132; emphasis added) [The hygiene rule is that each cadaver must have its own individual grave]. Most sectors of the working classes and the urban proletariat, that is, most inhabitants of the city, were buried in common, unmarked graves – pits – in an enclosure next to but outside the cemetery's proper space of commemoration (Figure 9.2). Thus, they were excluded from one of the most important sites of memory created by the new bourgeois city, their memory socially erased by the new space of death: as Louis-Vicent Thomas reminds us, 'le pouvoir s'exprime par le discours' (1978: 175) [Power is expressed through discourse]. The dominant class, as Louis-Vicent Thomas explains, creates and manages its image; the dominated class, on the other hand, does not have the right to produce its image: the memory of the underclass is often subject to destruction or appropriation and, thus, to the extortion of knowledge.[6]

The communal grave was still extensively used in Barcelona during the post-war period and up to the late 1970s, when everyone was guaranteed by law an individual tomb for only two years (the approximate time needed for the body's putrefaction). The economic crisis that began in 2007 has recently increased substantially this type of burial. Edwin Heathcote was right: the cemetery is 'like a text: a book in stone narrating the turbulent and revolutionary history of the city' (26).

---

4 The social unrest known as *bullangues* had ended by the mid-1840s.
5 Universal male suffrage was established definitively in Spain in 1890.
6 'Car l'intérêt de la classe dominante est de gérer l'image qu'elle se fait de soi (P. Bourdieu); la classe dominée, a fortiori les marginaux, n'ont pas le droit a produire. C'est en vertu de ce même principe qu'on procède, en certains situations, à la destruction ou à l'appropriation de la mémoire de l'autre, à l'extorsion du savoir' (Thomas 1978: 181).

Figure 9.2 Commemorative monument for the deceased buried in the communal grave at the Cementiri de Poblenou in 1862
Cementiris de Barcelona, S.A.

Recently, some private initiatives ('friends' of cemeteries) or public ones such as those promoted by the Association of Significant Cemeteries in Europe are trying, with different degrees of success, to bring to the attention of locals and tourists the historical and artistic heritage found in cemeteries organizing guided tours, lectures, and other events. Some of these initiatives tend overwhelmingly to ignore the deep relationship between memory and property that is at the basis of historical cemeteries and to uncritically repeat what Michel Foucault referred to as the 'voice of the archive', that is, the material – and ideological – traces left behind by a particular historical period and culture, the historical a priori of the period: its order and its ideology. In these initiatives, cemeteries are turned into – reduced to – a kind of National Pantheon, that is, into an open gallery for the biography and commemoration of 'important' – 'significant' – people in the discourse of a nation. These tours include, as one might expect, war heroes, politicians, successful entrepreneurs and artists, and even revolutionaries – very few, if any, women, or individuals from the lower classes. Pierre Nora, discussing *lieux de mémoire* in France, noted 'the hidden connection between all true memorials –monuments to the dead, as in the Panthéon – and objects as seemingly different as museums, commemorations, archives, heraldic devices or emblems' (xix). The tours often ignore the intimate dependence of memory on diverse degrees of property and authority, that is, power, and thus repeat uncritically the act of remembrance of a few, and the oblivion of the many that constituted cemeteries. The most important challenge cemeteries pose as *lieux de mémoire* in the nineteenth century is precisely how to deconstruct the oblivion cemeteries effected over the memory of most inhabitants of the city. In David Robinson's wonderful reflection, cemeteries are like libraries; quiet, catalogued and annotated (104). The problem is that all these records that constitute the places of the dead, because they are based on property, are in their complex contradictions and avoidances, to paraphrase Ken Worpole's words, often very hard to read (104).

Cemeteries: Public representations and private lives

Funerary monuments are the result of the confluence of the modern fear of death – oblivion –, the unprecedented opportunities for permanent and private burial offered by new urban cemeteries, and the reliance of liberal politics on public representations of private life. Tombs, tombstones, epitaphs, and mausoleums are all substitutions for an absence – the deceased loved one – and substitutions for what they hide: the corpse and its corruption. As such, they are displaced representations of the departed individual, or, more precisely, ways of building and conveying the life meaning – and social significance – of the departed. Louis-Vicent Thomas has written about the 'corpse as pretext' (1980: 57). In this respect, sepultures built in the new cemeteries fully restored what Erwin Panofsky identified as the 'retrospective funerary monument', that is, their dedication to the memory of the social relevance of the departed and his family (24).

These commemorative – retrospective – representations are not normally prepared by the deceased in advance of their passing, but instead by the family or, in the case of public personalities, by social and national institutions. They thus represent the family's, or the national community's, sense of the meaning of the life of the departed, not the departed's sense of self. The third-person style of epitaphs – 'In Memoriam of', 'Here lies' – always points to something else: it refers to the living, who try to make some sense of the lives of the deceased.[7]

---

[7] 'Mais de toutes façons, qu'il soit minutieusement d'ecrit ou simplement évoqué, le cadavre n'est jamais pris pour lui-même; tant pour l'écrivain que pour tout un chacun, le cadavre est bien l'outre-signifiant; le discours sur le cadavre renvoie à autre chose, il est tourné vers le vivants qui tenent désespérément d'y trouver le sens de leur vie' (Thomas 1980 58).

Moreover, in an increasingly changing world cemeteries provided the space for the permanent and patriarchal home for the family. They allowed for 'an expression of family solidarity', and became 'symbols of identity and continuity' (Kselman: 188, 191). The lists of names of the deceased on gravestones – accompanied later on by photographs – proclaim the family's triumph over death: its definitive reunification. 'Família' followed by the patriarchal last name, and words and expressions such as 'Reunited', articulate the bourgeois notion of the tomb as 'the enduring metaphor for the final family home' (Worpole: 11):

Epitaph in the Cementiri del Poblenou (c. 1830–1840)

Aquí reposando están
Dos esposos, hija y nieta
Aguardando en paz completa
A cuantos en pos vendrán:
Mudos son, clamando van,
Y su voz escucharás
Piadoso que aquí estás
Suplicando al Redentor
Que salve al Revendedor
Y familia de Cuyás

Here lie
Husband and wife, daughter and granddaughter
Waiting in complete peace
all those who will join them later
They are silent, they are crying out,
And their voices you
Merciful, who are here,
Will hear pleading the Redemptor
To save the Shopkeeper
And the Cuyás family

(*Colección de los Epitafios más notables que existen en el Cementerio General de Barcelona*, 1842: 10)

The visit to the tomb – the journey to the extramural cemetery – became the most important memorial rite for families in the nineteenth century. The street layout and landscaping in many modern cemeteries correspond to the Romantic ideas of life as a struggle for self-discovery and death as final rest: the cemetery roads were to effect 'a narrative journey through the buildings and through a series of experiences, moods and ages' (Heathcote: 14). The visit to the tomb of a loved one or a public figure guides this journey: 'a journey through the landscape which could relate a story – a walk through real and mythical time and a return to a lost age' (Heathcote: 25). Romantic literature such as Nicasio Álvarez de Cienfuegos's popular long poem *La escuela del sepulcro* (published in 1816) helped to give form and meaning to this new funerary and memorial ritual, to find 'consolation and moral illumination [...] from remembered attachments', and to reflect 'the intense feelings that were supposed to accompany the visit to the tomb' (Kselman: 214–15). Families visited the cemetery all year long, but on 2 November – the day following All Saint's Day – the inhabitants of the city would visit the cemeteries as a collective expression of remembrance. By the mid-nineteenth-century this religious festivity, as well as the custom of leaving flowers at the tomb, had become a social rite. In this respect, it is interesting to note that in cemeteries – as in department stores, where interior (private) and exterior (public) space collapse – women could appear respectably in public. Cemeteries did, thus, contribute to the remapping of the spacialization of sexual difference in the modern city.

Epitaphs were at the centre of the cemetery as stage for the self-dramatization of life and death during the Romantic period. Narrative authority in epitaphs belonged to families and they made sure the narratives on tombs reflected the image the family wanted to project to society, the story that would represent them. Epitaphs are, thus, often narratives where identities are represented as coherent, often, also as goal-oriented, in opposition to implied – or real – images of destructive fragmentation: they substitute for the corpse and, just as importantly, make up for any social and familial conflict, violence, disorder, or guilt. As Roland Barthes reminded us, 'narrative authority is an assertion of property rights: the text "belongs" to the speaker' (48). Epitaphs make patterns of meaning from isolated details, revealing gestures or episodes: 'The fragment, like the tomb poignantly represents a lost whole [...]. The task of the epitaph [...] is to condense a life or a body

Figure 9.3 Cementiri de Poblenou. 'Paz a los muertos'
Arxiu Històric de la Ciutat de Barcelona

of knowledge into a single sentence' (Heathcote: 19). These 'fragments' articulate diverse desires of being and reflect the recently triumphant civic virtues of a laissez-faire and liberal society.

Romantic epitaphs full of passion and rhetoric were common in Barcelona's oldest modern burial ground, the Cementiri de Poblenou:

> Doña Maria de las Nieves Tresángels y Espona, consorte de
> D. Pedro Nolasco Tresángels, murió el día 13 de febrero de
> 1838, en la edad de 29 años

> Mrs. Maria de las Nieves Tresángels y Espona, wife of
> D. Pedro Nolasco Tresángels, died on 13 February 1838
> She was 29 years old

(*Colección de los Epitafios...*: 15)

> Aquí yace una hermosura
> Que fué, y la muerte arrancó
> De un esposo, a quien amó
> Con lealtad y ternura:
> En la mayor desventura
> Y en estado el mas lastimoso
> Sumergió a su fiel esposo...
> Perder la que tanto amaba
> Y en la que siempre encontraba
> Amor, consuelo y reposo!!

> Here lies a beauty
> Who was, and death tore her away
> From her husband, whom she loved
> with loyalty and tenderness:
> In the greatest unhappiness
> And in the most pitiful state
> It sunk her loyal husband...
> To lose she whom he loved so much
> And in whom he always found
> Love, consolation, repose!

(*Colección de los Epitafios...*: 39)

Memory and the city in Barcelona's cemeteries 221

Figure 9.4 Cementiri de Poblenou
Cementiris de Barcelona, S.A.

Epitaphs (Figure 9.4) – or sculptural representations – with striking biographical narratives of male professional pride, economic achievements and financial success, were, however, the model to follow. This type of epitaph was very popular in all of Barcelona's modern burial grounds. Cemeteries ended up being the intended stage for the achievements of the bourgeois entrepreneur (Figure 9.5).

> Don Erasmo de Gonima y Pasarell Son of honest but poor parents born in Moyà the 4th of August, 1746 his intelligence, rectitude, and entrepreneurial genius made him successful in the textile industry, quickly increased his wealth and general appreciation, all of which earned him a title of nobility for him and his descendants; as well as other privileges and honors that his Majesty bestowed on him. These circumstances did not diminish his hard-working nature. This is why in his old age, noble and wealthy he passed away the 30th of April, 1821 at the age of seventy five victim of the explosion of a boiler
>
> HIS GRANDSON DON ERASMO DE JANER Y DE GONIMA DEDICATES TO HIM THIS BRIEF MEMORIAL

Figure 9.5 Sepulture of the Família Patxot (1858). *Cementiri de Poblenou*
Cementiris de Barcelona, S.A.

In the case of women, epitaphs and funerary monuments overwhelmingly reproduced the nineteenth-century feminine ideal of 'the angel in the house', that is, the nurturing traits of women as wives and mothers:

El amor conjugal dedica esta lápida a la memoria de
Dª Francisca Ragull y Guell, que murió a los 21 de febrero de
1838 de edad de 35 años

Matrimonial love dedicates this tombstone to the memory of
Mrs Francisca Ragull y Guell, who died on February 21, 1838
She was 35 years old

Aquí debajo de esta fría losa
Yace de las esposas el modelo:

> Yace la bella, cuya faz hermosa
> Cubrió la muerte con oscuro velo:
> La madre tierna, ardiente y cariñosa,
> Virtuosa y fiel consorte vedla hielo.
> Ay! Espiró... Encierra este ataud
> Madre, esposa, bella, fe y virtud.

> Here under this cold slab
> Lies she who was a model of wives:
> Lies the beautiful one, whose lovely face
> death covered with a dark veil:
> The tender mother, passionate and affectionate,
> Virtuous and loyal wife see her ice cold.
> Ah! She passed away... This coffin locks away
> Mother, wife, beauty, faith and virtue
> (*Colección de los Epitafios...*: 9)

Barcelona's Cementiri de Poblenou, however, provides, in some extraordinary instances, striking epitaphs that express the bare truth of female fecundity: its relation to productivity and the economy of the family. In this case, the epitaph becomes unapologetically an accounting book:

> Nicho de Francisco Pujol y Marcé
> Aquí descansa el cadaver
> de su madre Maria Pujol y Marcé viuda,
> natural de Olot:
> falleció en 3 de abril de 1830
> de edad de 82 años
> 7 meses y 19 días, habiendo dejado
> de su único matrimonio

Vivos	Muertos
5 hijos	8 hijos
42 nietos	32 nietos
46 bisnietos	43 bisnietos
93	83

> Total 176

Sepulture of Francisco Pujol y Marcé
Here lies the corpse
of his widow mother Maria Pujol y Marcé
born in Olot:
she passed away the 3rd of April, 1830
at the age of 82 years
7 months and 19 days, leaving in this world,
from her only marriage

	Alive	Dead
	5 children	8 children
	42 grandchildren	32 grandchildren
	46 great grandchildren	43 great grandchildren
	93	83

Total 176

In another exceptional epitaph found also in the Cementiri de Poblenou, Woman's particular hardship in a patriarchal society is emotionally acknowledged:

A la memoria de Mª de la Concepción
Marrugat,
que murió de edad 2 años y 11 meses
Mueres hoy, naciste ayer
Prepárate a la partida:
Al acabar de nacer
¿Tuviste miedo á la vida
Por temor a ser mujer?

In memory of Mª de la Concepción
Marrugat,
who died at the age of 2 years and 11 months
You die today, you were born yesterday
Prepare yourself for the departure:
Just when you were born
Were you afraid of life
because you feared being a woman?

(*Colección de los Epitafios...*: 85)

All of these epitaphs, these biographical and familial narratives made up of isolated – selected – details became a kind of 'milestone': 'a marker colonizing a space and identifying the deceased's part in historical and territorial terms' (Heathcote: 19).

After 1836, the plural enactment of memorial practices found in epitaphs caught the attention and displeasure of the 'guardians' of the *law of the place* in Barcelona (Certeau: 117; emphasis added), La Junta del Cementerio, which sought to censure epitaphs and other memorial practices that did not support the 'required decorum':

> [D]esde la instalación de la Junta en 1836 se ha puesto un coto a los disparates que afeaban algunas de las inscripciones, porque sujetándose estas a previo examen y aprobación de personas inteligentes, si no puede lograrse siempre el que se aparten e la ordinaria rutina, se evitan cuando menos en lo posible las faltas de corrección y lenguaje que se observan en las anteriores. Y aún debe añadirse en obsequio de la verdad que, desde aquella época, introduciendo y aumentando el buen gusto en la calidad y ornato de las lápidas sepulcrales (con destierro de las de azulejos que tan perjudiciales eran), se nota igualmente una mejora en la composición de los epitafios, de manera que pertenecen a la última época la mayor parte de los que componen esta colección. (*Colección de Epitafios…*: 6–7)

> [Since its constitution in 1836, the Board has put a stop to the absurdities that ruin some inscriptions, because under previous revision and approval by intelligent people, most of the improper form and language observed in existing ones can be prevented, even though it is not always possible to keep them from common vulgarity. And to be honest, we should add that, since then, having introduced and increased the refinement in the quality and ornament of the tombstones (with the banishment of the tiles that were so harmful), an improvement in the composition of epitaphs can be noted, so most of the epitaphs collected here belong to this recent period.]

The need to prevent 'disparates' [absurdities] reappeared in 1854 when the Junta del Cementerio required the assistance of the Academia de

Buenas Letras 'para el verdadero hermoseo bajo todos los conceptos del establecimiento' [for the true beautification in all aspects of the establishment] (Pi i Arimón: 585). But as the prohibition of the use of the Catalan language in the cemetery clearly indicates, the purported 'embellishment' of the new burial ground, the 'seriedad' [seriousness] and 'cultura' [culture] expected and required in the cemetery (Pi i Arimón: 586), was intended to control –censor – those identities, and class and national allegiances, that did not fit into the ideological and cultural design of the new liberal Spanish state: 'De esta manera se han proscrito del Sagrado recinto las inscripciones defectuosas o ridículas que no una intención torcida, sino más bien la ignorancia obrando a sus anchuras, fijaba en la cobertura de los nichos' [In this way, the ridiculous and defective inscriptions, consequences not of a twisted intention but rather of unrestrained ignorance, that were used on the covering of niches, have been banned from the Sacred ground] (Pi i Arimón: 585–86). Indeed, cemeteries were 'a point of contention between groups that sought to control the ways in which people identified through their tombs' (Kselman: 182).

Epitaphs in Catalan were common before 1836. In 1838, shortly after the Junta del Cementerio initiated its campaign to 'improve' and 'embellish' epitaphs, 'Un amante de la lengua catalana' [One who loves the Catalan language] denounced in the newspaper *El Guardia Nacional* that the use of Catalan in the cemetery had been banned. He had sent the text of the epitaph he meant for his family tomb to Joan Cortada, a member of the Academia de Buenas Letras, asking him for advice, and Cortada had replied to him that, even though he saw no problem with it, the Junta del Cementerio would tell him to remove it because it was written in Catalan: 'per sa part no hi tenia inconvenient, pero que me exposava a que la Junta del cementiri m'obligui a treure'l' [He himself had no objection, but I was taking the chance that the Board of the cemetery would make me take it out] (24 October 1838). On 26 October Joan Cortada confirmed in the same newspaper the Junta's decision to ban any epitaphs in Catalan, as well as his opposition to this measure:

> que lo dia 26 del corrent rebí un ofici de la Junta del cementiri en que en substancia me dihuen que la nostra llengua no es d'ús públic, que no está autoritzada per la lley y que los epitafis catalans no son

de fácil inteligencia per los forasters, per lo cual me encarregavan á mi i altres companys d'Academia que no permetessem tals inscripcions. (El Guardia Nacional, 26 October 1838)

[that on the 26th of the current month I received a notification from the Cemetery Board in which essentially they tell me that our language is not for public use, that is not authorized by the law, and that epitaphs in Catalan cannot be easily understood by foreigners, therefore they put me and my colleagues in the Academia in charge of not allowing such inscriptions.]

As soon as the cemetery became a consolidated and essential memorial and commemorative site for the city, the Catalan language and the diversity of social speech became issues of contention and the direct recipient of the state's censorship: 'proper maintenance of the place', de Certeau reminds us, 'eliminates these criminal tricks' (89).[8]

By 1871, when Pedro Felip Monlau discussed cemeteries in his *Elementos de higiene pública*, most of the current – modern – memorial customs had been established. The insistence on the need to regulate – censure – memorial practices effected by individuals and groups had not, however, diminished:

Autorícense cualesquiera monumentos, pero sin faltar al decoro y al gusto especial que corresponde a un campo de reposo para los restos mortales de los fieles... Autorícense igualmente las coronas y las flores, las luces en determinados días, y los retratos o fotografías, etc. Cuélguense en buen hora la cruz..., la inmarcesible *siempreviva* amarilla (*helichrysum orientale*, de Gaertner), gracioso símbolo de la immortalidad, elegido por el instinto, siempre certero, de los pueblos. (Monlau: 134)

[Authorize all monuments, but without going against decorum and the special taste that is appropriate for a burial ground where

---

8 The only Catalan epitaph permitted in the cemetery was one thought to be by the popular writer Josep Robrenyo (who died in 1838). It is a humoristic epitaph, a satirical indictment – not entirely surprising – of the new dominant medical discourse on life and death, of the new tyranny of doctors. The epitaph can still be seen at the cemetery, to the right of the chapel (Perímeter, níche num 3719).

the mortal remains of the faithful are put to rest... Authorize also wreaths and flowers, lights on certain days, and portraits and photographs, etc. Put up crosses..., yellow everlasting plants, gracious symbol of immortality, chosen by the always accurate instinct of the people.]

Epitaphs continued to generate specific comment and 'la gramática y la retórica, con la ortografía y el buen gusto' were still the instruments used by the authorities to impose its own discourse on death, socially acceptable forms of bereavement – 'el dolor legítimo y el sentimiento melancólico' (Monlau: 134) [legitimate pain and melancholic feeling], and identity: 'Ninguna inscripción sepulcral debiera autorizarse sin la previa revisión de una persona o de alguna Corporación entendida' [No sepulchral inscription should be authorized without prior review by one person or appropriate Institution]. It is interesting to note here that at the peak of the cemetery's popularity as a memorial site, Monlau's recommendation of exemplary epitaphs highlights the foundational modern fear of the cemetery as an infectious site. The 'excellent' epitaphs mentioned by Monlau do not commemorate the lives of the two physicians, but rather 'el pensamiento higiénico que entrañan' [the implied hygienic concern], that is, the fear created by the danger supposedly posed to society by corpses and, thus, the need to banish them from the city and enclose them within the new walled cemeteries: Simon Pierre's epitaph expresses his desire to be buried 'outside' to prevent his corpse from 'harming' anybody; and Philipus Verheyen's reveals his determination to be buried in the *extramuros* cemetery in order to prevent the profanation of the church by 'infectious and damaging exhalations' (Monlau: 135).

The epitaph as central memorial practice in modern cemeteries ended with the Romantic period, giving way to brief funerary inscriptions – containing the name of the family, the names of the deceased, and an affectionate message or religious expression. Photographs were added to the gravestones when they became popular and affordable. More recently, biographical – and familial – narratives have found their way back into tombs by means of the small objects associated with the deceased that are left on the narrow shelves of niches.

From the 1870s up to the Great War, cemetery roads and hillside terraces consolidated and expanded the bourgeoisie's move to turn the

Figure 9.6 Family tomb in the Cementiri de Montjuïc
Cementiris de Barcelona, S.A.

cemetery into an amphitheatre for the exhibition of its wealth and power.

Tombs, as social representations of the family (Figure 9.6) and prime real estate for burial plots – the best sections of the cemetery were reserved for the affluent classes – transformed the spiritual narrative journeys, particularly the feast of All Souls, into a form of social spectacle for the upper classes.

The extraordinary family mausoleums built in Barcelona's cemeteries (Figure 9.7) – sites to be visited and subjects of reviews in newspapers such as *El diario de Barcelona* in the days prior to All Saints' Day – show the bourgeoisie's deep reliance on commemoration to create its public image. Narcís Oller captures ironically this new strategy of social legitimation by the Catalan bourgeoisie in his 1890–1892 novel, *La Febre d'or*. After having laid to rest his mother-in-law in a simple niche-like sepulture, the protagonist, Gil Foix, – a nouveau riche whose newly acquired wealth has its origin in speculation, comes to

230 City and society

Figure 9.7 Cementiri de Poblenou
Arxiu Històric de la Ciutat de Barcelona

the sudden realization that wealth requires the spectacle of a family mausoleum. He must have a mausoleum:

> Per fi un pensament nou l'assaltà: 'un home ric com ell havia de tenir panteó; un panteó gran, ben alt, que es veiés de lluny'. I no eixí del cementiri sense haver triat el punt on el faria fer. (Oller, I: 298)

> [Finally, a sudden thought struck him: 'a rich man like him had to have a mausoleum; a large mausoleum, very tall, so it could be seen from afar'. And he did not leave the cemetery until he had chosen the spot where it would be built.]

Thus, as spaces of social visibility and cultural legitimation, mausoleums and other funerary monuments were not unlike the salon in the bourgeois household: 'the area in which intimacy is staged for the benefit of others, the place where, unlike the private rooms in the back

Figure 9.8 'Resurrection', a 1920 sculpture by Enric Clarasó adorning the sepulchre of Jaume Brutau in the *Cementiri de Montjuïc*
Cementiris de Barcelona, S.A.

of the house, the bourgeois compose a symbolic equivalent of their subjectivity' (Resina 1994–1995: 48).

With the triumph of *Modernisme* – Catalan art nouveau – the female body also came to represent in cemeteries the collapse of interior (private) and exterior (public) spaces. Voluptuous female bodies at different stages of nakedness, the personification of eroticism and its intimate ties to death, were then used by the most daring Catalan bourgeois families to publicly display their modern aesthetic tastes (Figure 9.8).[9]

Most families, however, sought the social and cultural legitimation of their newly acquired wealth and power through a more conservative public image: through their identification – appropriation – of the artistic achievements of past societies and their elites. Thus, they made extensive use of past styles – Egyptian, Greco-Roman, Romanesque, Gothic (Figure 9.9) – in their family mausoleums. As Joan Ramon Resina has said, the appropriation of the artistic styles associated with past elites served 'the bourgeois dream of full enfranchisement from the past. [..] Reducing the past to the status of ornament... [the bourgeoisie's achievements] stood for history conquered' (2008: 51). David Robinson has pointed out the intimate relationship between funerary monuments and civic values, and the 'inverse proportion' existing between 'the strength of personal expression realized in memorial sculpture' and 'the strength of religious feeling': 'it was in the secular cemeteries that sculptural expressiveness developed to new heights' (21). As narratives of life meaning and public representations of the family, mausoleums built by the Catalan bourgeoisie seem, however, to point to a different fruitful combination. Most of the extraordinary funerary monuments built by the Catalan bourgeoisie are the result of the need to commemorate its social and economic achievements by means of the appropriation of the artistic styles of past societies and a similarly strong desire to convey its religious feelings. In fact, the framing of its historical achievements by religious convictions in funerary monuments is at the base of the strategies of legitimization effected by the Catalan bourgeoisie in cemeteries. The retrospective funerary monument – the memory of the social relevance

---

9 'Là où triomphe l'image de la mort doit triompher aussi l'élément exorcisant qu'est la sensualité génératrice de vie' (Chabot: 26).

Memory and the city in Barcelona's cemeteries 233

Figure 9.9 Mausoleum (1894) of the Riva family. Architect: Antoni M. Gallisà. Sculptor: Eusebi Arnau. Cementiri de Montjuïc
Cementiris de Barcelona, S.A.

Figure 9.10 Mausoleum of José Olano Iriondo, 1896. Architect: Claudi Duran i Ventura. Sculptor: Eusebi Arnau. Cementiri de Montjuïc
Cementiris de Barcelona, S.A.

of the departed (and the family) – finds, then, its full actualization in the 'prospective funerary monument', that is, in the evocation of the vision of the hereafter and the idea of personal apotheosis (Panofsky: 24) –hence the popularity of Romanesque and Gothic styles in Catalan mausoleums and cemeteries.

The deep connection between religion and public image in Catalan society from the mid-nineteenth century to 1918 is exemplified by the representation of an Orsini bomb – symbol of the city's working-class political violence around 1900 – at a mausoleum in the Cementiri de Montjuïc. In 1893 the Liceu was the object of an anarchist attack: three Orsini bombs were thrown into the orchestra seats, killing 20 people from among Barcelona's most powerful members. In the 1896 mausoleum of José Olano Iriondo (Figure 9.10) an Orsini bomb is reproduced on a column capital, where the beautiful combination of leaves and flowers common to all the capitals of the mausoleum is abandoned for a sort of nightmarish profusion of leaves and two claw-like forms emerging at each side of the bomb. This capital is located next to a half skeleton, a reminder of death.

The representation of the Orsini bomb in a mausoleum whose central image is Christ's resurrection and apotheosis reveals not only the intimate relationship between these two emblematic urban sites of modern Barcelona – its cemeteries and its opera house – but also its common function as a showcase for the bourgeoisie's anxieties, fears, aspirations, and ambitions. Moreover, it shows the bourgeoisie's deep reliance on the complementarity of the prospective language of redemption and the retrospective commemoration in funerary monuments in their efforts to create a public image that would legitimate its newly acquired, and threatened, power. In Barcelona's cemeteries, the social violence that accompanied industrialization and the consolidation of a Catalan bourgeoisie is transformed through art into a manifestation of high historical achievements, and these historical 'conquests' are transfigured through religion into spiritual rewards and divine blessings.[10] Thus, Barcelona's modern cemeteries not only effected the violence of oblivion upon large groups of urban working classes by excluding them from the city's main space of commemoration but they also articulated the political and moral values that legitimated depriving them of the right to property and to their own image.

The modern desertion of cemeteries

The Great War's unprecedented large number of dead, which put a definitive end to modernity by blowing up the bourgeois illusion of moral progress by way of technological advancements, marked the withdrawal of funds from the cemetery and the end of the cemetery as a stage for social visibility. In this context, the particular tension between the de-familiarization of death – its strangeness to modern man and woman – memory, and oblivion, played out by and in

---

10 At the Rosary Chapel in the Sagrada família (the new cathedral whose construction began in 1882), an anarchist worker is reproduced receiving an Orsini bomb from a dragon-like form symbolizing evil.

cemeteries in the nineteenth century, gave way to a new and radical separation between city and its burial grounds that changed definitively the cemetery as *lieu de mémoire*. Since the mid-twentieth century, the loneliness that threatened the modern cemetery from its creation (its expulsion – and the walls that separate them – from the city) has rapidly evolved into desertion. Indeed, desertion constitutes the postmodern attitude towards the city's cemeteries, and this new loneliness has eroded one of the spatial practices of commemoration that 'secretly structure[d] the determining conditions of social life' in the modern city (Certeau: 96).

In the Jardí americà (American Garden), a popular spot in the 1972 Cementiri de Collserola, the city does not commemorate, but rather forgets, and this oblivion has very little to do with the natural passing of time.

Responding to the increasing demand for cremation and the disposal of ashes, the American Garden reveals the later stages of the radical vanishing of the body and that of representational and memorial practices effected in post-modern burial grounds. There the ashes –those ineradicable traces of the corpse and its putrefaction– are covered by a small plaque, flat on the ground, that marks the location of the ashes. This small plaque indicates just the name and the dates of birth and death. Radically different from the biographical notes or emotional expressions in epitaphs, the ostentatious mausoleums, or the accumulation of personal objects often found in the narrow recesses of niches, this burial ground reminds us of an administrative record. The inscription bears the aspects of individual identity – name and dates – as official records would do in a bureaucratic notebook. Around the discreet plaques, we find the only concession to representation: an Elysian field, whose artificial (human-made) nature is hidden under a pretence of naturalness. It is a representation that denies itself – its cultural referent, by proclaiming the self-evident truth (and meaning) of nature, and that of man in it. In the American Garden nature is postulated as the only meaningful referent, hiding its origin in culture and, thus, its contentious meaning. The pretended natural beauty of nature suggests the conformity, the harmonious and rightful, place of man in the world. It substitutes for the individual identity – its historicity – and erases all traces of human struggle and conflict. It ignores also the special place the symbolization of death has in

Memory and the city in Barcelona's cemeteries

Figure 9.11 El Jardí americà, Cementiri de Collserola
Cementiris de Barcelona, S.A.

our search for meaning. It eliminates all notions of the cemetery as (contentious) memorial site for the city, or rather, not all, since the mark of property and, thus, of exclusion, persists.

If we were to visit the cemetery on any given day, we would still see the occasional family member, often a widow or parent who visits the tomb of a loved one; the periodical cleaning of family tombs (mostly by old women); the spectacular sepultures recently built by gypsies; the diverse appropriation of the harshest places of death in the cemetery – the niches – by love, pain and nostalgia; or the devotion to different *santets* (unofficial 'saints' canonized by popular devotion) by anonymous citizens who for a brief moment revive the old belief in the interaction between the living and the dead, asserting briefly a 'local authority' – that of superstition – against the 'proper' law of the place (Certeau: 106). And in Barcelona, as in many other cities, an important number of people visit the cemetery on 2 November, the day following All Souls Day (substantially fewer, if the festivity happens to fall at the weekend). But more than these microbe-like practices of appropriation of the cemetery, ordinary people act out a disappropriation of death and its most important proper place: the cemetery. Modern cemeteries, still *lieux de mémoire* – recipients of fragmented individual and collective memories – are increasingly becoming mere aestheticized spots for the anonymous and communal dissemination of the remains of the deceased with no room for memories: after the dissemination of the ashes, the family of the deceased does not intend to return. Constant, persistent, neglect in cemeteries is the sign of this collective desertion, a neglect and abandonment threatening cemeteries from their Enlightened beginnings. It would seem, then, that the cemetery's identification with the depository of the city's waste and, consequently, its exile from the city, in the end has defeated the cemetery as *lieu de mémoire*. Pedro Felip Monlau had already imagined in 1871 the increasingly larger numbers of people who nowadays opt to disperse the ashes of loved ones in unmarked natural – or apparently natural – sites:'¿quién sabe si ... las inhumaciones esparcidas, espaciadas, *diseminadas*, serán los *cementerios del porvenir?*' (121; emphasis added).

The deep connection between body, memory, and space that characterized the modern urban experience is progressively and decidedly disappearing. What remains is to ask how these new social practices are transforming our notions of individual and collective identity, and the processes involved in the creation of public images.

Works cited

Álvarez de Cienfuegos, Nicasio (1816). 'La escuela del sepulcro', in Álvarez de Cienfuegos, *Obras poéticas*, I (Madrid: Imprenta real), 175–88.

Ariès, Philippe (1974). *Western Attitudes Toward Death: From the Middle Ages to the Present* (Baltimore, MD: The Johns Hopkins University Press).

Barthes, Roland (1970). *S/Z* (Paris: Seuil).

Certeau, Michel de (1988). *The Practice of Everyday Life* (Berkeley, CA: University of California Press).

Chabot, André (1989). *Érotique du cimetière* (Paris: Henry Veyrier).

Colección de los Epitafios más notables que existen en el Cementerio General de Barcelona (1842). (Barcelona: A. Brusi).

Goodwin, Sarah, and Elisabeth Bronfen (1993). 'Introduction', in Sarah Goodwin and Elisabeth Bronfen (eds), *Death and Representation* (Baltimore, MD, and London: The Johns Hopkins University Press), 3–25.

El Guardia Nacional (1838). Barcelona. 24 and 26 October.

Heathcote, Edwin (1999). *Monument Builders: Modern Architecture and Death* (Chichester, UK: Academy Editions).

Kselman, Thomas A. (1993). *Death and the Afterlife in Modern France* (Princeton, N.J.: Princeton University Press).

Laqueur, Thomas (2002). 'The Places of the Dead in Modernity', in Colin Jones and Dror Wahrman (eds), *The Age of Cultural Revolutions: Britain and France, 1750–1820.* (Berkeley: The University of California Press), 17–32.

Monlau, Pedro Felipe (1871). *Elementos de higiene pública* (Madrid: Moya y Plaza).

Nora, Pierre (2001). *Rethinking France. Les Lieux de mémoire* (Chicago/London: The University of Chicago Press).

Oller, Narcís (1993). *La Febre d'or* (Barcelona: Edicions 62).

Panofsky, Erwin (1964). *Tomb Sculpture: Four Lectures on its Changing Aspects from Ancient Egypt to Bernini* (New York: Harry N. Abrams).

Pi i Arimón, Andrés A. (1854). *Barcelona antigua y moderna* (Barcelona: Tomás Gorchs).

Resina, Joan Ramon (1994–1995). 'The Sublimation of Wealth and the Consciousness of Modernism in Narcís Oller's *La Febre d'or*'. *JHR* 3: 259–75.

— (2008). *Barcelona's Vocation of Modernity* (Stanford, CA: Stanford University Press).

Robinson, David (1996). *Beautiful Death: Art of the Cemetery* (New York: Penguin Studio).

Thomas, Louis-Vincent (1978). *Mort et Pouvoir* (Paris: Petit Bibliothèque Payot).

— (1980). *Le Cadavre. De la biologie a l'anthropologie* (Bruxelles: Éditions Complexe).

Worpole, Ken (2003). *Last Landscapes: The Architecture of the Cemetery in the West* (London: Reaktion).

PART III
Art, architecture, and the city

CHAPTER TEN

Picasso among his fellows at 4 Gats: Beyond *Modernisme*?*

Jordi Falgàs

The international renown of the tavern called 4 Gats (4 Cats) on Carrer Montsió in Barcelona is due mostly to the fact that Pablo Picasso had his first solo show there, in February of 1900. Biographers and scholars have stressed the importance of this show because it was then that the young painter's work left behind the academicism of his formative years and began to show remarkable maturity and individuality. The fact that Picasso burst upon the scene in a tavern, in this tavern, is worth noting, because 4 Gats became the place where three things came into contact or, perhaps, rubbed against one another, and served to catapult Picasso to fame. First of all, as we will see, 4 Gats was intergenerational, in the sense that two generations of artists met there. 4 Gats was also an interdisciplinary space, where painters interacted with sculptors, illustrators, architects, musicians, and, especially, writers of various genres. And, finally, 4 Gats was the place where travellers met on their way to and from Paris, then the capital of Western culture. Pere Romeu's bar was a failure as a business, but for a few years, from its opening in June of 1897 until it closed in

---

* This article is a revised version of 'Picasso's Fellows at the Tavern: Beyond Modernisme?', 2006 (Falgàs). © Jordi Falgàs.

July of 1903, 4 Gats actually managed to emulate the mythical cafes of Montmartre that were its inspiration. For Picasso, as Eduard Vallès has written, 'it was a place for meeting the intelligentsia of the time [..] and it foreshadowed, on a small scale, the modernity that he would later encounter in the French capital' (2015a: 78; my translation).

The Catalans who knew first-hand the milieu of the Parisian cabarets patronized by important Impressionist and Post-Impressionist painters such as Manet, Degas, Renoir and Toulouse-Lautrec were the artists Ramon Casas, Santiago Rusiñol and Enric Clarasó, and the critic Miquel Utrillo. Together and separately, they had spent time in Montmartre, and with their exhibitions and activities in Barcelona during the nineties, they became ambassadors of the latest trends in art and magnets for the young artists of Barcelona. Just like their French predecessors, the Catalans became firm proponents of *plein air* painting and rejected altogether religious, historic and other subject matters favoured by the Academy. From Paris they brought along the myth of bohemian life, together with a predilection for urban topics that portrayed the new scenarios of the urban middle class. From the music hall to the bourgeois interior, from the boulevard the hippodrome, it was all about modern life. As in most major European cities, modernity in Barcelona transformed all the arts – the visual arts as well as architecture, literature, and applied arts – and coincided with a profound social and urban transformation of the city itself. It was never an organized movement and therefore it was called art nouveau, as well as many other names, throughout Europe. In Barcelona it became known as *Modernisme*, and painters such as Casas and Rusiñol and architects such as Gaudí and Domènech i Montaner were the *modernistes*. It is not surprising, then, that Casas was one of the founding members of Pere Romeu's tavern, for which he designed posters and promoted the homonymous magazine, after the example of the Swiss painter and illustrator Steinlen at Le Chat Noir, and Toulouse-Lautrec at the Moulin Rouge (Figure 10.1).

For the younger artists who frequented 4 Gats, Casas and Rusiñol were masters to be copied, though they were soon to become models to be left behind. Like them, the new batch of artists and writers wanted to break with the academic fustiness and conservatism that dominated the taste of the emerging social class, the urban industrial bourgeoisie. In fact, Picasso and his Catalan friends were 15 to 20 years

Figure 10.1 Ramon Casas, *4 Gats* (1900),
colour lithograph on paper, 58.2 × 34.4 cm
Museu Nacional d'Art de Catalunya, Barcelona

younger, and they were not long in suspecting that the bohemianism represented by Casas and Rusiñol – both offspring of the industrial bourgeoisie – was superficial and inauthentic. Instead, they focused directly on the current events taking place in the Parisian art life so as to avoid the obsolescence that they saw in the work of the recognized veterans. To see what Casas and Rusiñol had in common with the younger generation of painters around the turn of the century, and at the same time to appreciate the strides taken by the latter, we can compare a painting by Casas such as *Aux aguets* or a drawing by Rusiñol such as *After the War, The Sad Home* (figures 10.2 and 10.3) with works by Picasso such as *The Artist's Sister, Lola* (Cleveland Museum of Art) and *The Street Violinist* (Museu Picasso, Barcelona), both dated c. 1899. Picasso dedicated himself as seriously to portraiture and caricature as did Casas, and he was attracted to popular and marginal figures, or themes such as sickness and death, like Rusiñol. Picasso painted and caricatured Casas and Rusiñol, together and separately, on numerous occasions. But the heightened vigour of his strokes and brushwork reveal a different intensity, a desire that these visual elements should have a significance of their own, a significance that would express the intention of the artist as well as constitute an image.

Picasso's relationship with Rusiñol, which has been characterized by Vallès (2010: 336) as a process of 'systematic absortion', went from admiration and acceptance of his postulates and practices – in the sense that Rusiñol represented all that was associated in Barcelona with art and the modern artist – to caricature and satire. With respect to Casas, Picasso's challenge turned into his first show, a display of more than a hundred charcoal portraits at 4 Gats, in clear competition with the 132 shown by Casas in the Sala Parés the previous October. Their rivalry, in any case, was always friendly, as shown by the portrait Casas made of Picasso when they coincided at the Universal Exposition in Paris in 1900 (Figure 10.4), and the fact that Picasso was always welcome at the tavern where Casas was considered the house artist. Moreover, Picasso had another show at 4 Gats in July of that year, he did illustrations for the menu, for an advertising diptych, a poster announcing the special of the day (Hunt Museum, Limerick, Ireland), a drawing for another advertisement in which he and some of his friends appear around a table, a portrait of Corina Jáuregui, Romeu's wife (Musée d'Art Moderne de Céret), and a

Picasso among his fellows at 4 Gats 247

Figure 10.2 Ramon Casas, *Aux aguets* (*c*.1891),
oil on canvas, 58 × 47.5 cm
Fundació Institut Amatller d'Art Hispànic, Barcelona

Figure 10.3 Santiago Rusiñol, *After the War. The Sad Home* (c.1898), conté crayon, ink, pastel, and colour pencil on paper, 42.8 × 34.6 cm Museu Nacional d'Art de Catalunya, Barcelona.

Figure 10.4 Ramon Casas, *Portrait of Pablo Picasso* (1900), charcoal and pastel on paper, 69 × 44.5 cm
Museu Nacional d'Art de Catalunya, Barcelona

Figure 10.5 Ramon Casas, *Portrait of Ramon Pichot* (c.1897–1899), charcoal, pastel, gouache, and ink on paper, 62.9 × 29.8 cm
Museu Nacional d'Art de Catalunya, Barcelona

drawing of his son Perico for a 1903 Christmas card. In addition, at the request of Utrillo, Picasso lent a group of works on paper to Sala Parés, to be shown at the same time as an exhibition of works by Casas in May and June of 1901.

Who were Picasso's young fellow travellers, most of them unjustly forgotten or unknown, and how was he influenced by his contact with them in the setting of 4 Gats? Ramon Pichot was the oldest of the group of painters known as the Colla de Safrà (the Saffron Gang), which also included Isidre Nonell, Ricard Canals, Joaquim Mir, Juli Vallmitjana and Adrià Gual. Pichot was also one of the youngest of the group considered to be the first generation of *modernista* painters to come of age in the shadow of Casas and Rusiñol (Figure 10.5). In 1895 he had a show with Casas at Sala Parés; in 1897 he was part of the tavern's inaugural exhibition; and early in 1898 he travelled with Rusiñol to Granada. There he was able to share experiences and techniques and, above all, to imitate Rusiñol's artistic exploitation of a popular theme: the exoticism of Spanish female stereotypes such as *manolas*, *chulas*, flamenco dancers, and gypsy girls from the neighborhood of El Albaicín. Pichot titled his paintings of Granada *España vieja* (Old Spain) and showed them first in Madrid and then at 4 Gats, in February of 1899, at the time of Picasso's return to Barcelona after his crucial first stay in Horta de Sant Joan. They became close friends, and their friendship would continue, in Paris and in Barcelona, until Pichot's death in 1925. They were admirers of Steinlen's illustrations in various French publications, and during the 4 Gats years both of them published drawings in newspapers, books and magazines in a style clearly influenced by his. In 1898, for example, Pichot illustrated *Fulls de la vida* (Pages of Life), a collection of short narratives by Rusiñol. The following year, for his show at the tavern, *Quatre Gats* magazine put his drawing *De l'Albaicín* on the cover and, inside, the critic Miquel Utrillo (3) explained that he had been 'Casas's favourite disciple' and that his 'second guide' was Rusiñol.

Art historians have repeatedly ignored the fact that Pichot's work was shown in Gallery VII of the Salon d'Automne of 1905, alongside that of Matisse, Marquet, Vlaminck, Rosen, Manguin, Camoin, Girieud, and Derain – the gallery that critic Louis Vauxcelles (1905) called the gallery of the 'fauves', the wild beasts, in the famous chronicle of *Gil*

Blas that gave name to Fauvism. Pichot was never a Fauvist; in fact, he never went beyond Post-Impressionism. But his presence in the Salon along with other artists of the 4 Gats group such as Nonell and Torent – whose work was hung in other galleries – shows that Barcelona was exporting young painters who were welcomed by the Parisian avant-garde.

All of the young Catalan and Spanish artists who showed their work in Paris had to paint many *chulas, manolas*, bullfighters and other Iberian stereotypes to please the French public. But there is another common denominator in the works created by the 4 Gats circle: a strong desire to portray the life of the urban working class, the marginalized victims of poverty, the dispossessed. This is the thread running through Picasso's work in his last years in Barcelona and his first in Paris, between 1902 and 1904, known as his Blue Period. Along with Picasso, Xavier Gosé, Carles Casagemas, Pablo Gargallo, Isidre Nonell, Ricard Opisso, Juli Vallmitjana, Ricard Canals and *Els Negres* (The Blacks, because of their use of charcoal to draw dark urban scenes), Manuel Ainaud, Joaquim Biosca and Martí Gimeno, and the sculptor Enric Casanovas, among others, frequented 4 Gats and showed their work there. Francesc Fontbona (2006: 54–60) called them *postmodernistes* because they wanted this subject matter and their visual treatment of it to go beyond the formal and symbolic limits of the *modernista* painting being done in Barcelona. Not all of them succeeded.

Casagemas has become part of the narrative of art history because he was one of Picasso's best friends during this period, because of the tragic circumstances of his suicide in Paris in February 1901, and the effect that such loss had upon his friend. It has also been claimed that Casagemas deserves attention by himself regardless of his relationship with Picasso. *A Couple* (Figure 10.6) is probably one of the works on paper he exhibited at 4 Gats from 26 March to 10 April 1900 (Vallès 2014: 245–48). Like the rest of his friends, and despite the small number of his works that survive, it is obvious that Casagemas was also interested in outcasts, urban decay, brothels, sinister landscapes, and street scenes that capture social class contrast. Picasso was already emerging as a powerful voice, though it appears that theirs was an exchange of ideas, or a shared domain of experimentation, not only between him and Casagemas, but with their friends at 4 Gats as well.

Figure 10.6 Carles Casagemas, *A Couple* (c.1899), ink and coloured crayon on paper, 21.5 × 14.5 cm
Artur Ramon Collection, Barcelona

254 Art, architecture, and the city

Figure 10.7 Isidre Nonell, *At the Boqueria's Meat Stands* (1894), conté crayon and charcoal on paper, 28.9 × 21.5 cm
Museu Nacional d'Art de Catalunya, Barcelona

A good example is Isidre Nonell's sketch *At the Boqueria's Meat Stands* (Figure 10.7). Casagenas seems to have taken Nonell's series of 'Tipos populares' and, further removed himself from the subjects, caricaturing them. This approach – half sketch, half caricature – can be seen in other drawings by Casagemas, as well as by Picasso. From Picasso, who sketched many caricatures at this time, he borrowed a tendency to draw thick black outlines and enclose them within a thick black frame.

Xavier Gosé is possibly the best example of his generation's withdrawal from social engagement, despite an early start that seemed to point in the opposite direction. In 1895 his work was already featured in the satirical *L'Esquella de la torratxa*, followed by illustrations in *Barcelona cómica* in 1897, and *La saeta*, *El gato negro*, and *Madrid cómico* in 1898. The following year he illustrated the covers of issues 6 and 9 of the magazine *Quatre Gats* and had a successful solo exhibition at the tavern (25 April–10 May). The first cover, published on 16 March, was a drawing closely related to *Meditation* (Figure 10.8). It was titled *Throwing the Tackle* and was part of a series devoted to the urban working class: farmers, fishermen, and fishing activity on the beach (Figure 10.9).

Employed or unemployed, Gosé's subjects at the time all have an air of displacement, showing that Barcelona's sudden industrialization and growth had pushed them to the fringes of society. The second cover, *Cloudy*, was an illustration for Frederic Pujulà i Vallès's short story of the same title published in that issue. All these works show Gosé's talented draftsmanship and powerful realism, characterized by a confident line and a slight distortion of volumes that would soon be featured in French and German magazines such as *Le Rire*, *Simplicissimus*, *Jugend*, and *L'Assiette au Beurre*. Nevertheless, he would soon turn his back on that subject matter, and after his arrival in Paris in 1900 he devoted himself almost exclusively to portraying and enjoying the Belle Époque, until his return to Barcelona at the outbreak of World War I.

4 Gats was not only a meeting place for artists; many writers – or at least aspiring writers – also went there. Picasso's portraits and caricatures show that there were many young literati among his friends, and it is no exaggeration to say that much of his humanistic and literary education came from the conversations and readings he shared with his friends at the tavern. For Vallès (2015b: 43–87),

Figure 10.8 Xavier Gosé, *Meditation* (1900),
graphite and Conté crayon on paper, 25 × 25 cm
Museu d'Art Jaume Morera, Lleida
donation from Maria Teresa Barrio (Llobet widow), 1985

who has studied these relationships, four names stand out. First, the cultured and multifaceted Miquel Utrillo, who was well acquainted with fin de siècle Paris, and was one of the prime movers of the artistic activity of 4 Gats. In June of 1901, coinciding with the show of works by Casas and Picasso that he organized at Sala Parés, he published the first major review of the young painter's work in the magazine *Pèl & Ploma*. For the same issue, Utrillo also wrote a complimentary article about Ramon Pichot. Picasso himself had just left for Paris with Jaume

Figure 10.9 Xavier Gosé, *Throwing the Tackle*, cover for *Quatre Gats: publicació artística–literària*, no. 6 (16 March 1899) (Barcelona), magazine, 30.5 × 25.4 cm.
Universitat de Barcelona, CRAI, Biblioteca de Lletres

Andreu Bonsoms to prepare his first solo show at Ambroise Vollard's gallery, which opened on 24 June.

The dean of the Catalan intellectuals that Picasso met at 4 Gats was Pompeu Gener, known as 'Peyo' or 'Peius'. At the beginning of the century he had already worked in Barcelona and Paris as a journalist, critic, playwright, essayist of progressive and Catalanist ideas, and translator of Nietzsche. According to Xavier Vall, at the turn of the century Gener was above all an importer and proponent of the new European political, philosophical, literary, and artistic tendencies of the time (185). He was known for his characteristic slouch hat, which he is wearing in Picasso's portrait of him (Museu Picasso).

Juli Vallmitjana, who was also painted by Picasso (Metropolitan), was a member of the above-mentioned Colla del Safrà. During the 4 Gats period, he left painting to become a successful novelist and playwright. His first literary works can be considered literary parallels of Picasso and Nonell's paintings in the first years of the century: sympathetic descriptions of low life, marginalization and gypsy culture in Barcelona. As Miquel-Àngel Codes has explained, much of his early fiction can be considered autobiographical, as it contains descriptions not only of that world but also of the relationship of artists to it and their motivations (65–77). The case of Frederic Pujulà, also painted by Picasso (Metropolitan) is equally fascinating. Pujulà was a journalist, and during the 4 Gats years he published his first stories and plays. Later he would become the first Catalan author of science fiction, and the foremost proponent of Esperanto in Catalonia.

Rafael Nogueras is usually associated with a group from El Rovell de l'Ou, another old tavern on Carrer Hospital, where a different circle of artists and intellectuals met during the same years as the Carrer Montsió group. Nogueras was then an aspiring writer who contributed to *La Talaia Catalana*, *La Catalunya Artística*, and *Joventut*. He must also have been a regular at the *tertúlies* in 4 Gats because he appears in a Picasso painting depicting the tavern's interior (private collection) and a few drawings. He is also the subject of a portrait by Pablo Gargallo (Figure 10.10), who never formally exhibited his works at 4 Gats, but is believed to have frequented Pere Romeu's place. Fontbona (2004: 66) describes Gargallo's portrait of Nogueras as very intense, a large work on paper almost entirely covered by charcoal shadows out of which emerges a captivating gaze. The young apprentice sculptor

Figure 10.10 Pablo Gargallo, *En Nogueras* (1900),
charcoal and pastel on Ingres paper, 49.9 × 47.5 cm
Museo Pablo Gargallo, Ayuntamiento de Zaragoza

exhibited a fine sketching technique and accomplished the same penetrating effect as his friend Picasso did in his charcoal self-portrait of the same year (Museu Picasso).

Soon after Picasso and Casagemas arrived in Paris in October 1900, they settled in Montmartre, at 49 rue Gabrielle, in the studio vacated by Isidre Nonell. Frustrated by his uneven success in the French capital, Nonell went back home and against all odds devoted

260 Art, architecture, and the city

Figure 10.11 Isidre Nonell, *Consuelo* (1901),
oil on canvas, 131 × 90 cm
Museu de Montserrat. Donation from Josep Sala i Ardiz

his work almost exclusively to the subject of gypsy women. *Consuelo* (Figure 10.11), exemplifies this radical change and forecasts his series of canvases of 1903–1905. This work reveals Nonell's initial glance at the subject: the bent figure turning her back on us, the rough strokes, the play of dark and light, the large and almost flat areas of colour, and his reduced palette.

All the unique and highly expressive features that would become his own are present here. Nonell's works run parallel to several of Picasso's works from 1901 and 1902, such as *Saint-Lazare Woman by Moonlight* (Detroit Institute of Arts), his two *Crouching Woman* (Art Gallery of Ontario, Toronto, and Musée Picasso, Paris), *Absinthe Drinker* (Kunstmuseum Bern), and *Two Women at a Bar* (Hiroshima Museum of Art). Picasso's series of prostitutes begun in Paris was further developed in Barcelona on his return to the city in January, when Nonell's scandalous show at the Sala Parés was still open. Unaware of Nonell's earliest work, many scholars have repeatedly argued in favour of Picasso's influence on him, even though Nonell was nine years older and had started to develop his personal depiction of the dispossessed as early as 1894. Nonell's influence on Picasso has also been argued (Escala). So rather than discuss who was first or who influenced whom, I prefer to speak of convergence. The confluence of the two artists is no surprise, since they had known each other for years, had both returned disillusioned from Paris, and were then working not far from one other and spending many leisure hours at 4 Gats, El Rovell de l'Ou and El Guayaba. They also shared the rejection of critics and collectors. Moreover, as we have seen, the portrayal of poverty and utter desolation was at the core of the 4 Gats circle.

Though a wide range of anecdotal rural and urban lower class scenes had for some time been accepted in academic circles as subjects worthy of attention (that is, certain works by the Sitges school, the Olot school, or Casas's *The Garroting*, 1894, and Mir's *The Cathedral of the Poor*, 1898), we have seen how some of the younger artists of 4 Gats not only tried to make political statements in terms of subject matter but also attempted to experiment with the formal qualities of their work. Unlike their elders, they were no longer supported by bourgeois patrons and found work only as magazine illustrators, most often for the political and satirical press, where more thematic and formal freedom was allowed than in their academic training. Yet even if their attention had shifted towards social marginalization, their statements were often ambiguous, and – as Lubar has noted – this generation's 'failure to articulate a clear social message' ultimately turned into either generalized symbolic representations or a 'mixture of condescension and revulsion' (98–99). Lluís Bonnín, Sebastià Junyent, Ricard Opisso, Francesc Sardà, Joaquim Biosca and Evelí Torent are only a few of several other young artists who had some relationship to 4 Gats. Most of them had not yet attained independence and their bourgeois and Catholic background was still a barrier to any truly groundbreaking group initiative. Barcelona, after all, was not Paris. The Catalan capital did not provide the network of galleries, salons, dealers, critics, publications and, above all, clients who were flocking to the French capital in search of the latest avant-garde. Picasso and, later on, Miró, González, Dalí, and many others did not have a chance to find any success for their radical proposals in Barcelona. For those who stayed there was no other alternative but to eventually tame their social critique in accordance with the dominant conservative taste and religious beliefs, so their art was tolerated as long as it did not attack bourgeois morality. Poverty was accepted and even favoured as a subject matter in art as long as it was confined within the social order maintained by the ruling class. For a few artists, then, 4 Gats was certainly a springboard, but for many others it was nothing more than a playground.

Works cited

Codes Luna, Miquel-Àngel (2008). 'Fermí vs Juli Vallmitjana: breu noticia sobre les incursions de l'escriptor en el camp de l'art'. *Butlletí de la Reial Acadèmia de Belles Arts de Sant Jordi* 22: 65–78.

Escala, Glòria (2015). 'La influència d'Isidre Nonell en el jove Picasso'. *Locus Amoenus* 13, 169–85.

Falgàs (2006). 'Picasso's Fellows at the Tavern: Beyond Modernisme?', in William H. Robinson, Jordi Falgàs and Carmen Belen Lord (eds), *Barcelona and Modernity: Picasso, Gaudí, Miró, Dalí*. Exhibition catalogue. (Cleveland, OH: Cleveland Museum of Art/Yale University Press), 96–103.

Fontbona, Francesc (2004). 'Gargallo y Cataluña', in Kosme de Barañano et al. (eds), *Pablo Gargallo* (Valencia: Institut Valencià d'Art Modern).

— (2006). 'The Second Generation of Modernista Painters', in William H. Robinson, Jordi Falgàs and Carmen Belen Lord (eds), *Barcelona and Modernity: Picasso, Gaudí, Miró, Dalí* (Cleveland, OH: Cleveland Museum of Art/Yale University Press).

Lubar, Robert (1997). 'Barcelona Blues', in Marilyn McCully (ed.), *Picasso: The Early Years, 1892–1906* (Washington D.C.: National Gallery of Art), 87–101.

Utrillo, Miquel (1899). 'En Ramon Pichot'. *Quatre Gats* 3, 23 February.

Vall, Xavier (2012). *Pompeu Gener i el nacionalisme regeneracionista (1887–1906): la intel·lectualitat, la nació i el poder a Catalunya*, PhD dissertation (Barcelona: Universitat Autònoma de Barcelona).

Vallès, Eduard (2010). 'The Rusiñol Paradigm. From Curiosity to Homage', in Eduard Vallès et al. (eds), *Picasso* versus *Rusiñol* (Barcelona: Ajuntament de Barcelona), 334–38.

— (2014). 'Casagemas Exhibits at Els Quatre Gats', in Eduard Vallès, *Carles Casagemas. L'artista sota el mite* (Barcelona: Museu Nacional d'Art de Catalunya).

— (ed.) (2015a). *Picasso: obra catalana.* 2 vols. (Barcelona: Enciclopèdia Catalana).

— (2015b). 'Picasso i el món literari català 1897–1904', in *Picasso: obra catalana*, II (Barcelona: Enciclopèdia Catalana).

Vauxcelles, Louis (1905). 'Le Salon d'Automne'. *Gil Blas*, 17 October.

CHAPTER ELEVEN

Gaudí:
Poet of stone, artistic hedgehog*

Marià Marín i Torné

New research has revealed a pioneering Gaudí who was well ahead of his time, the creator of innovative work processes in addition to the architectural forms that we all now know. The architect has left us a legacy that can be applied to a range of disciplines. The Diocesan Museum of Barcelona houses the book of condolence from the death of Gaudí. It is a considerable tome, documentary evidence of the architect's renown and the resonance of his presence. In it we find the names of political and cultural personages along with countless unidentified individuals. Of these individuals, who represent the majority – proof of how Gaudí was loved by the people – one name in particular caught my attention. It was nobody. What I mean is that this person was no authority, no one well known. Struck by the tragedy and aware of what the loss meant, this person expressed his grief and admiration on a sheet of paper. The text is beautifully written, measured in tone and rather long. The author must have given it careful consideration, because there are no second thoughts or erasures, and the text ends with a brilliant analogy: 'If Verdaguer

---

* An earlier version of this article was published in *Barcelona Metròpolis Mediterrània*, 93 (September 2014). © Marià Marín i Torné.

was the architect of literature, Gaudí was the poet of architecture'. Full of determination, the man must have gone to the chapel with his own paper, only to find that there was an official book of condolence. So he attached his text with pins, on the very page opposite the signatures of major figures in politics, art and society. The book is exhibited with this page open.[1]

The magnitude and power of the collective grief expressed in writing is impressive. For the authors of the countless letters, telegrams and press articles, a saint, genius and patriot had died – the architect of God and the universe, the Dante of architecture. So clear, so resounding and so shared. But the fate of Gaudí quickly fell into a prolonged period of neglect and even contempt. Paradoxically, almost three-quarters of a century later, he would become one of the most original icons of Barcelona and in the history of art.

From the time of his death in 1926 up to today Gaudí has been the subject of much debate: a debate that has often been more ideological and political than artistic in nature,[2] while the majority of the original avant-garde – as well as the second and third generation – have been overtly fascinated by him. That is the way it was and has been from Walter Gropius and Le Corbusier,[3] to Miró and Perejaume, crossing over elective antipodes such as Tàpies and Dalí at the other end of the spectrum, who defended the 'organic, terrifying and edible forms, sacred in essence' (Dalí: 69–76, n.3–4). A curious case: in 1927, Herman G. Scheffauer, a journalist from *The New York Times Magazine*, said that Barcelona was 'the most fantastic city in the world' thanks to the innovative and creative nature of the new art in Catalonia, the leading exponent of which was Gaudí, creator of the Sagrada Família, 'a stupendous building' representing 'a harking back to the Gothic', with 'forms from the animal and vegetable worlds' and 'smooth spires designed in corkscrew form' that 'ape the long, slender, tapering lines of the Rhine wine bottle' (Scheffauer).

---

1 This book of condolences is exhibited at Museu Diocesà de Barcelona. For more information, see the exhibition catalogue, *Gaudí, l'home i la seva obra* (Gaudí Exhibition Centre 2002).
2 For more information about Gaudí's thinking see Pujols 1927.
3 For more information, see Le Corbusier (Joaquim Gomis) and Joan Prats Valles 1967; see also http://fondationlecorbusier.fr [accessed 6 April 2017).

More apparent paradoxes: despite the ups and downs, Gaudí's works have always enjoyed popular appeal, which has considered the forms its own until the economic cannibalization of tourism took them, in a process of a public expropriation for public use. A continuously accelerating process of reducing Gaudí to an economic asset, more related to 'Gaudimania', to the contribution of merchandizing and tourism to GDP than to culture and civic use. L'Hospital de Sant Pau and Parc Güell are recent examples, along with the loss of the expiatory and charitable meaning of the Sagrada Família. It is a topic worthy of debate.

The many and protracted comings and goings, the losses and claims, have resulted in the creation of permanent islands of effort dedicated to the salvation, research and preservation of Gaudí's legacy, although they have always been surrounded by storms of controversy:

1) The continuity of the work on the fabric of the building and the desire to complete the Sagrada Família. Always resistant to attacks from numerous insults and smear campaigns, thanks to the moral authority bestowed on the building by the importance invested in it by its supporters, figures such as Ràfols, Matamala, Jujol, Martinell, Puig Boada, Bonet Garí, and others etc.).[4]

2) The few individuals such as the art and architecture historians, Joan Garrut and Joan Bassegoda, who, often from the sidelines, saved and studied pieces, works and documentation, and strove to preserve Gaudí's interpretative stone words. These individuals worked very often in contact with the research and efforts of the international avant-garde (from Frei Otto to Collins). Meanwhile, in Catalonia the topic lay dormant. Special mention should, however, be given to the humble yet persistent work of the Amics de Gaudí [Friends of Gaudí].

3) A series of intellectuals who, while not moving in the same circles as the followers of Gaudí recognized his value and

---

4 The main texts of these figures are listed in the Bibliography. The Jujol archive can be accessed at http://webfacil.tinet.org/arxiujujol/148620.

fought against scandalous vacuity. This group includes Juan Eduardo Cirlot, with his innovative, prophetic and spirited vision.[5]

4) And, especially, an anonymous collective of supporters who have safeguarded both Gaudí's memory and the material and documentary evidence that, upon being rediscovered, have revolutionized the understanding of the genius. I would like to make special mention of the people at Colònia Güell as well as Gaudí's employees and collaborators, who Manuel Medarde has come to know, study and love. An archaeologist and engineer, master of the scientific research method, Medarde has managed to combine the direct study of Gaudí's works – a multidisciplinary project undertaken without preconceptions – with the study of sources and documents, while also applying anthropological fieldwork methods to those who knew and worked with the master. This research method has led him to recover hundreds of pieces and items, and most notably 5,800 unpublished documents written by Gaudí himself.[6]

The results of this now erupting research are so alluring that we can (re)write an authentic and well-documented story about Gaudí, reaffirming some things, clarifying others and providing contradictions where necessary. Along with a return to original documentary sources (an original manuscript by Gaudí from Reus written between 1876 and 1879 – preserved at Museu Comarcal de Reus, Ràfols 1999, Matamala 2001, Puig Boada 2011, among others), the new knowledge forces us to directly re-examine his works from fresh perspectives and position Gaudí in his rightful place from an academic perspective. The first step: publish. The second: display. The third: fill inexplicable gaps such as the lack of academic chairs in the study of Gaudí.

But there is more. We have uncovered aspects of Gaudí that came as a surprise. The research, in an unexpected twist, has become a seed and a driver for present innovation. We have discovered a Gaudí

---

5 Cirlot (1950) and Dalí were pioneers in re-establishing the importance of Gaudí.
6 Visit the websites of The Gaudí Research Institute and the Gaudí World Congress, listed in the Bibliography.

who was pioneering, well ahead of his time, creator of innovative work processes, in addition to the new architectural forms that we all now know. A creator-cum-inventor-cum-innovator who, beyond his identity as an architect, and based on his matchless style, brings us a legacy that can be applied to many disciplines today, from ergonomic design to business management.

... Gaudí is complex, very complex

Gaudí meandered between architecture and social action, wending his way through all areas and paths of art, science and management. Through chemistry, 3D and high-resolution photography, lighting and chromatics for practical and symbolic purposes. Through the worlds of film, social cooperatives, education, feminism, Christianity and anarchism. Through the corporate and business worlds, where he broke ground by taking the first steps in co-working, co-design, networking and just-in-time production. Through health and safety at work. Through mastery of craft and the incorporation of design. Through ceramics and woodwork. Through inventions of whatever he needed and wanted and through the admiration for Edison as a model and guide. Through ecology as an idea and foundation, through energy efficiency as a desire and a necessity, and through naturalism, recycling and sustainability. Through something as modern as engineering as a necessary partner for architecture, through constructive physics, geometry, calculus and modelling before plans. Through gastronomy, health and sport in the functions of the architect's practice. Through music and the acoustics of objects and spaces. Through liturgy and social use in architectural design. Through urban planning and landscaping. Through R&D&I as a work method....

Gaudí was all of these; he concerned himself with every detail, studying and working with ad hoc teams, creating a masterful combination of fixed and flexible teams that were always interdisciplinary. He applied everything that was appropriate or necessary to his work, and if it did not exist he invented it, whether it was an object, material, technique, or method. With Gaudí, everything is united and makes sense: there is no room for improvisation or futility. Work and thought, human and technical functionality are the warps and wefts that, if taken away, leave you without a garment and with a fistful of senseless threads.

It is like a puzzle whose pieces are seemingly incomprehensible and isolated, some surplus. The key that gives us the overall, clear and defined picture is the method that Gaudí created. Therein lies the inventive genius of the master and the only way to understand his style, which during his time was said to be so strange and original that it was incomprehensible. The Japanese sculptor Etsuro Sotoo told me years ago that 'Gaudí's contribution was so immense that it could not be understood during his time. Maybe in the twenty-first century....'[7]

'The wind destroys them and they are never spoken of again'

The phrase Gaudí used to compare oak trees – endowed with strength gained over many years – with reeds – which grow fast but are extremely fragile – aptly expresses the artist's thinking and spirituality.[8] used to compare oak trees – endowed with strength gained over many years – with reeds – which grow fast but are extremely fragile – aptly expresses the artist's thinking and spirituality. One of the most obvious yet fascinating gaps regarding in our understanding of Gaudí is the lack of a precise mapping of his imaginary world; his physical, intellectual, cultural, social and spiritual universe as it relates to his personality and his creativity. In *The Hedgehog and the Fox*, Isaiah Berlin (1953) said that interest in an artist does not lie so much in the formal analysis of his work as in identifying how ideas, attitudes, conceptions, interests, ideals. and value systems are assigned. This is, hence, the perspective that corresponds to Gaudí.

Gaudí's revolutionary and creative power arises from a historically controversial triad: he was a great artist (i.e., highly personal); he was radical (completely free, on the sidelines of fashion and the

---

7 Interview with Etsuro Sotoo, *Gaudí, l'home i la seva obra* (2002).
8 For the thought and works of Gaudí see Puig Boada 1981; Martinell 1969; Matamala 2001. Puig, Martinell and Matamala were collaborators and disciples of Gaudí, direct witnesses.

avant-garde, despite setting precedents in some respects), and there was a fundamental spiritual component to his being.

'The wind destroys them and they are never spoken of again'.[9] This phrase in which Gaudí compared the strength of oak trees – endowed with strength gained over many years – and reeds – which grow fast but are extremely fragile – aptly expresses the artist's thought and spirituality, as if we were talking about a new Pascal. Gaudí was thus aware of the importance of his life and work. He was a hedgehog, according to the division of human characters between hedgehogs and foxes made by Berlin (1953). That is why he is called– recalling another distinguished hedgehog – the 'Dante of architecture'.

Gaudí created bonds of identification between art, society, nature, beauty, and God. In his words, he was not a mutilated man because he did not let any of his potential go to waste (body, intelligence, and transcendental sense), and this inner strength brought out his creative genius and ideas about social justice, the working class, culture, nationalism, poverty, people, friends.

An analytical spirit capable of synthesis, the result of having observed and studied nature; technical mastery; prodigious use of his imagination and original creativity; spirituality as a driver – these are some Gaudí-esque features that are associated with today's popular ideas: for the Swiss-German philosopher, Karl Jaspers, as earlier for the Russian painter Wassily Kandinsky, artistic practice is the ability to see the absolute in finite, material forms, from a perspective of authenticity. Hence Gaudí's *return to the origins* to be original. Hence 'the tree that I see from my workshop is my master'.[10] Hence looking to nature to find forms and structures, materials and meaning. To quote Plato, Beauty is the splendour of Truth. As such, nature – God's work – is perfect and beautiful. Art is understood as personal collaboration with creation; everything is symbolic in the material sense. This is why Gaudí's work requires contemplation, reflection and study. This is why he was devoted to the Sagrada Família: of 48 years of work, he dedicated 44 years to it, 12 exclusively. His 'personal mission', in the words of Josep M. Tarragona (2016).

---

9 Puig Boada, Isidre (1981). *El pensament de Gaudí.*
10 Puig Boada, Isidre (1981). *El pensament de Gaudí.*

The fascination of the avant-garde

Frederic Mompou, a Catalan composer known for his metallic chord and 'silent music', said to those who were in vogue that maybe his music was to be popular when theirs was no longer in fashion. Mompou was a self-made avant-garde artist, like Gaudí, with whom he shares parallels worthy of further examination.

There are some paradoxical relationships between some avant-garde artists and Gaudí. On the one hand, they find him innovative, brilliant and with practically boundless creative ability. On the other hand, they see him as being too tied to tradition, their craft, nature, and religion. Le Corbusier admired Gaudí's concept of space and material aesthetics (Le Corbusier and Prats Vallés 1967). Joan Miró paid tribute to his telluric creativity.[11] Salvador Dalí, more caustic, recovered him for the history of art. Walter Gropius, Mies van der Rohe, and Frank Lloyd Wright all sensed his genius. In the social and spiritual sense of art, he was on a par with his contemporaries Kandinsky, Malevich, and Van Gogh, and preceded American abstract expressionists, such as Rothko, in the search for the absolute.

Gaudí was ahead of his time when he theorized about the use and meaning of straight lines and curves, before Kandinsky and the Bauhaus. He was also advanced in the strict field of modernism: Casa Vicens was finished in 1888, while Hôtel Tassel by the Belgian Victor Horta, considered to be the first modernist house, was finished in 1893. Picasso maintained his silence or reacted aggressively, perhaps because Gaudí was the only artist he could not surpass, as it is rumoured he confessed to Miró, or because Gaudí's *trencadís* [broken tile] technique preceded cubism....

---

11 Miró created *Sèrie Gaudí* (2002), 21 etchings (Fundació Joan Miró, Barcelona). Miró says about Gaudí: 'Thinking on Gaudí, who maketh a stone in a field of stars with a chrysanthemum in the middle'. Quoted by Fundació Joan Miró on the occasion of the temporary exhibition Joan Miró. *Homenatge a Gaudí* (2002). See https://www.fmirobcn.org/ca/exposicions/113/joan-miro-homenatge-a-gaudi

Figure 11.1 The four columns which support the ceiling of the crypt of the Colònia Güell and symbolize the four evangelists are made with basalt pieces from Castellfollit de la Roca combined with lead. Gaudí always used local materials or materials from nearby areas, which is now a popular concept. The crypt was the first construction to make use of parabolic structure resistance
© Pere Virgili (2014)

The foundations of a new architecture

Nothing new is created without research, taking risks and teamwork. Gaudí knew this and became the manager of his artistic project. His attitude was identical to that of great physicists such as Albert Einstein, Max Planck, and Peter Higgs.

Recent research on the work of Gaudí can be summarized in four points. The first indicates that Gaudí's aim was to create a new kind of architecture (Figure 11.1); this is what made him original and revolutionary, and is the reason that after a hundred years it serves as a source of inspiration for today's architecture and engineering. Second, the research establishes that what he had learned was of no use to him: he had to invent everything from methods and processes to equipment. His

274   Art, architecture, and the city

workshop was a laboratory where innovation and inventions were born. Third, he could not achieve his goals by himself; he needed a team, an interdisciplinary focus, and thus came up with the modern idea of managing mixed teams. The fourth point is that the research concludes that the investment and creative partner who made his work physically possible was his friend the Catalan entrepreneur Eusebi Güell.

Nothing new is created without research, taking risks, and teamwork. Gaudí knew this and became the manager of his project. 'Should we call you a genius or a madman?' asked the president of the tribunal at the School of Architecture to a young Gaudí, who said: 'There is no reason not to try something new just because no one has tried it before'.[12] The same idea and the same attitude as Einstein, Planck and Higgs. Let us have a look at some of his main contributions.

Father of light structures

Gaudí introduced the constructive use of twisted ruled surfaces (paraboloid, hyperboloid, hyperbolic paraboloid, conoid, ellipsoid and helical). Never used before, they enabled the building of structures and interiors that were larger, higher and more open, without external or additional supports, which makes them lighter,[13] more functional and symbolic. In addition, these surfaces provide greater mechanical stability, require less material and can be built faster. Hence, Gaudí is considered the father of buildings based on lightweight structures, typical of sports halls, conference halls, train stations and any buildings designed to accommodate large numbers of people.

Gaudí created functional forms based on geometry ('I calculate everything, I'm a geometer', he said (Puig Boada, 1981)); such as inclined and double-twist columns and intersecting combinations that are both functional and decorative. Structure, form and function merge. Geometric ratios describe and parameterize these structures: Jordi Bonet, chief architect of Sagrada Família for many years, said 'If

---

12 These words are attributed to Elies Rogent, at that time director of Provincial School of Architecture in Barcelona.
13 Frei Otto, German architect and structural engineer, was a pioneer in seeing the importance of this aspect in Gaudí's works. See also Jordi Bonet 2001a.

you carefully examine the trajectory of the ideas and geometry and structural forms Gaudí used, you almost undoubtedly reach the same solutions that Gaudí had already determined, or the ones he surely would have come up with' (Bonet 2001b: 70). Starting with curves, Gaudí moved towards rationalism and contemporary architecture, where he found the reasoning that led him to solutions.

Gaudí's innovations included: previously unheard of construction processes and materials, such as devising safer and more efficient scaffolding systems that were easy to assemble, used less material and were recyclable, as the planks made of different kinds of wood were reused for the construction of doors, frames, etc; building a structure starting with the façade or without load-bearing walls, anticipating modular and diaphanous architecture; the invention of *trencadís*,[14] an ingenious technique for covering curved walls: durable, washable, made from recycled materials, serving as both decoration and covering: ceramic and glass pointillism transferred to exterior walls. All of these techniques were contributions to the new architecture.

Gaudí shared the spirit of his modernist colleagues in the use of new techniques and materials such as reinforced concrete, ironwork, and electricity. He took them a step further thanks to his creative research and to the application of new ruled surfaces, in a fusion of structure, beauty, and functionality, in an aesthetic line that would later be defended by Le Corbusier. He thus became a pioneer of expressionism, brutalism and architecture that is organic, efficient, and makes use of recyclable materials.[15]

Work method

Gaudí's work method is what today we would call 'co-working' and 'co-design'. In other words, working in multidisciplinary teams, based on research and innovation, in terms of systems as well as structures,

---

14 For more on *trencadís* at Park Güell, see Kent 1992 and Kent and Prindle 1996.
15 The church of Colònia Güell is built with 70 per cent recycled materials. See Manuel Medarde in *L'església de la Colònia Güell...* (Gaudí Exhibition Centre 2008).

Figure 11.2 Model to scale 1:25 of the church of the Colonia Güell, which Gaudí never finished, produced by the Chair of the History of Construction and Architectural Heritage of Innsbruck University
© Pere Virgili (2014)

materials, and ways of working, with a clear commitment to science. For its time, this was something extraordinary (Figure 11.2).

Gaudí rejected improvisation outright, calling himself a 'meticulous bugger'. Simultaneously architect, artist, and manager, he took on the planning, building, and business aspects of his work. The proof: thousands of documents from Gaudí that outline both the cost and planning of the work. The example: almost half a century before the Japanese invented 'just-in-time' inventory strategy and it was taught in business schools, Gaudí applied this technique to the management of orders, warehouse stock and building processes, with the aim of achieving efficiency in the work and financial effectiveness. Everything was well planned and documented.

Gaudí's method made it possible to invent the required technology, tools, and materials, if they did not already exist, just as companies committed to R&D&I do nowadays. And when something already exists, it gets reused. Examples include:

1) The polyfunicular model as a system to represent and calculate the force loads of a building in a structural way, to scale and in three dimensions, before plans are drafted, as do many of

Gaudí: Poet of stone, artistic hedgehog   277

Figure 11.3 Inverted polifunicular model – based on ropes or chains – in the church of the Colonia Güell, a system for calculating forces which inaugurated the Gaudian architectural revolution

© Vicens Vilarrubias (c.1898)

today's architectural firms (Figure 11.3). It was a precursor to Autocad. This application combined with high-resolution photos obtained by manipulating the chemical formula of the flash; when implemented in a viewer it rendered a three-dimensional image and enabled, for example, the urban impact of a building to be seen before it was built.

At Moscow Polytechnic, they explain that it is difficult to understand that Gaudí, using only models,[16] was able to perform the same calculations that are done using supercomputers today. Moreover,

---

16 Leonid Demjanov of the Faculty of Architecture at Moscow University, 'The Model of Strings to the Architecture of Stone, Brick and Stone Structures in the Church of Colònia Güell' (address to 2nd Gaudí World Congress, Barcelona, 2016).

Arnold Walz studied Gaudí when developing 3D geometry processes for architectural design.[17]

2) The invention of trichromy. Combining data from astronomical observations, annual sunshine amounts and optical physics, Gaudí obtained natural light with multiple shades by layering three glass plates treated with primary colours. He covered the glass with stencils that left some areas open and others protected, and poured on liquid hydrofluoric acid, which diminished the tone of the colour in open areas, until he reached the desired degree. The bell shape of the windows made it possible to capture the desired amount of light. He thus achieved the effects of colour, luminosity, and reverberation that he wanted for each place and each time of the day. For Gaudí, light and colour were key elements in giving architecture a symbolic value of life and beauty.

3) Recycling. Gaudí spent when spending was called for and saved when saving was required. He used a chair leg to replace a broken handle, while also ordering light bulbs to be sent from the United States and Kern precision compasses from Switzerland. He was an amazing teacher of recycling, a radical precursor of Arte Povera. He recycled whenever there was an operational, practical, and, furthermore, artistic reason for reuse (Figure 11.4). Thus, he collected refuse from tile makers and foundries for the ductile, light and thermal walls of the Colònia Güell church; wood from loom crates and steel bands from cotton bales from a nearby factory – an authentic local product, with near-zero transport costs – to make benches that were beautiful and mechanically ultra-resistant, both owing to their materials and because the lower section was parabolic (perhaps the first place where this form was tried). Very economical at the time, today one of Gaudí's benches is valued at €370,000 at auction.

---

17 See Tomlow 1989. Arnold Walz worked with the Graefe team (with Jan Molema, Jos Tomlow, and others). Walz has worked with architects like Norman Forster, Frei Otto, etc.

Figure 11.4 The crypt of the Colònia Güell under construction in the year 1910. The architect invented a cheap, efficient and easy-to-assemble scaffolding system, based on the recycling of materials.

© Vicens Vilarrubias (1910)

Collaborators and apprentices

Gaudí had no disciples, but he did have colleagues and apprentices (Ferrer and Gómez Serrano 2002). That is why he did not create a school. He worked with a team to invent, not to copy. He wanted the best of each trade for each job.

Work was collaborative and Gaudí repeated that it was necessary to listen and ask those who knew the most, starting with the mason and carpenter at each site. He must have been history's first co-architect. 'If I have an idea', he said, 'Jujol [architect, designer and artist Josep Maria Jujol] or Cudós [artist Tomás Cudós] will be able to find the right colour' (Flores 1982). If you look at Park Güell, you'll only find one signature, and it is not that of Gaudí.

Beyond. If you had to invent a way to get coloured light from sunshine – and stained glass artist Louis Comfort Tiffany had failed here – you would have to find specialists from outside the building trade – physicists, astronomers, opticians, chemists, musicians, dynamiters – and work on it scientifically. To our knowledge, Gaudí is the first to have used/created a laboratory for testing materials, which he did at the Industrial University of Catalonia.

280 Art, architecture, and the city

Figure 11.5 Sketch – drawing and painting on photography – by Gaudí for the initial studies for the design of the church of the Colònia Güell (*c*.1910). Public domain

Each material – such as each of the 47 types of wood we have identified at Colònia Güell – was studied and chosen based on ductility, resistance, functionality, use, beauty, and position (Figure 11.5).

Purpose, mission, and context

Gaudí's intended objective was to make a rational kind of art, at the service of the people (which is why he said that to create a work, first comes love and then technique), an art, therefore, that is both functional and imbued with life, full of colour and movement, inspired by solutions, shapes, and colours drawn from nature, that is perfect and from which the values of beauty, humanization, efficiency, ergonomics, usability, and recycling derive.

Two curious examples: a seat tailored to the buttocks of a woman who sat on soft plaster to create the mould, and the design of the box where a cord runs through four cylinders to make a rattle turn, which he made thinking of a left-handed bell ringer. What could be more ergonomic?

Symbolism and beauty were his mission:[18] to create works that achieve the ideal of beauty, defined as the radiance of the truth. Hence the use of local materials, the widespread use of recycled materials and even refuse, the integration with or reference to nature (the crypt in the forest or tree columns), the human scale/the scale of the environment (the height of the Sagrada Família, below the highest point of Montjuïc); and symbology (in the classical, historical or popular tradition). The most beautiful example is perhaps represented by the leaning basalt columns in the crypt at Colònia Güell. Pere Viñas, the apprentice, confessed to Gaudí: 'I don't like them. They are rough, cracked and I don't understand them'.[19] Gaudí was pleased by the interest and explained the structural function of the leaning column – like someone who leans on a cane – and read him a passage from Exodus where Moses asks God not to curse the stone by working it to make him a temple. We would not know all this, or we would engage in speculation, if Manuel Medarde had not done anthropological research and found Gaudí's workers and their descendants, uncovering a hidden treasure: the diary of one of his apprentices, explaining in detail the daily life of the master, how he thought, worked and why he did what he did. Exciting.

Gaudí's art integrated, in an absolute manner, tradition, the current trend and inventiveness of the avant-garde, Catalan national consciousness, social concern, and religious yearning. A case that summarizes this is the use of the flat brick vault. In this feature, inherited from popular tradition, Gaudí saw extraordinary functional

---

18 Armand Puig has studied the symbolism in Gaudí with the architects of Sagrada Família: see Bonet and Puig 2012.
19 The diary by Viñas cannot be made public without permission of his heirs. Manuel Medarde, as depositary, can publish some fragments, as quoted here, with their permission.

possibilities (larger spaces, daylight openings, etc.) in combination with the ruled surfaces he invented. Artists are individuals who can take what is around them and turn it into something new. From the New York architecture of Guastavino to Otto's Olympiastadion in Munich and Candela's Sports Palace in Mexico, right up to Isozaki's modern Convention Centre in Qatar, the ruled surfaces, with trees and in the Catalan tradition, are traceable, identifiable, and obvious. Isozaki believes that Gaudí's embrace of the modern broke the formal limits of known architecture.[20]

Barcelona and Gaudi: City and artist rethink

The Barcelona at the turn of the century was thriving with art. It went through its largest urban expansion in its history, and artists, therefore, had a lot to say. It was a city of opportunities, of experiments, of bohemian environments and circles, like the legendary modernist tavern Els Quatre Gats, where the artist encouraged a very young Picasso to go to Paris (Palau 1966), despite everything, it was the real capital of industry and art. But Gaudí, who in his younger years had exhibited in the French capital,[21] decided, sure of himself and of his creation, to remain in the city of Barcelona, anticipating that people would come from around the world to see what he and his team were doing. This prophetic decision about his success as an artist in his own city was, at the time, a very risky decision, especially when Gaudí decided to settle his design and creative lab in a significantly suburban place such as an industrial colony, from which he would forge the bases and reasons for his prophetic vision. The periphery was a place that should also be designed as a place of dignity and balanced opportunities.

Proof of the prophetic vision of Gaudí and his attachment to Barcelona, lies, for example, in Le Corbusier's visit to the city: artists told him that he should see Gaudí's work; he came to admire it to the point of starting a study tour of Gaudí works and their sources, from Barcelona to Palma

---

20 This sentence was quoted by Toshiaki Tangue, director of Arata Isozaki y Asociados España, at the 1st Gaudí World Congress, Barcelona 2014.
21 In Paris Gaudí was discovered by his future patron, Eusebi Güell.

de Mallorca. These studies were included by the Swiss architect in his notebooks. The relevance of Le Corbusier was such that the republican Catalan government would commission from him a project for the expansion of Barcelona – which was never executed.

But the relationship of Gaudí with Barcelona goes beyond the simple fact of his having carried out the bulk of his work there. At the Pedrera, for example, he designed a parking space for cars in the basement (one of the first in the city), foreseeing the increase of traffic in a city in expansion. The most symbolic example, since its conception, is the Temple of the Sagrada Família, which Gaudí himself said would become a symbol of the city, a harp resonating in its heart, and guide those arriving by sea.[22]

Other aspects of Gaudí's conception of a new city in expansion was the idea of building a self-sufficient garden city within the city, both isolated and connected with it as a real and symbolic model of alternative ways of living. This was the Parc Güell. The project failed: it was felt by bourgeois and workers alike that they did not want to get away from the bustle of the city centre. They wanted to see and to be seen and, therefore, rejected the idea of colonizing the mountain to join it to the rest of the city as a sustainable and fully integrated 'nature town'.

Gaudí also had an impact on the old city, taking into account the historical legacy. Gaudí acted as a consultant for fellow modernist architects on questions such as how the design of the new city affects the remodelling, transfer, preservation, and restoration of historical heritage, especially in the old centre of the city, the Gothic Quarter. Paradigmatic examples of this are Gaudí's input into the restoration of Santa Maria del Mar or the intimate relationship he had with the cathedral as a place of reflection.

Gaudí planned each project as a unique one, but thought in terms of the city and how new buildings would interact with their surroundings. Thus, to recall the example mentioned earlier, the parking at the Pedrera, is a perfect example of incorporating modern design elements while including at the same time new elements, such as the increase in automobile traffic flow. The street where he built the Pedrera was a

---

22 The area of the Temple, called Camp de l'Arpa (Harp Field), was recently annexed to Barcelona.

main artery that connected the city with the surrounding towns that had been annexed to the capital, but at the same time, lay beside the new city's main boulevard. Gaudí added the value of public representation, converting the buildings into icons of both new architecture and of the new city through ideological and religious symbols full of meaning.

Casa Batlló is an example of a house that was renovated after an anarchist attack on a businessman, showing the bloody social conflict that existed. On the other hand, Bellesguard appears as an example of myth and history rediscovered by a country in full social, cultural and political revival.[23] Gaudí also made into stone some Renaixença [literary revival movement] symbols. An example worth mentioning is his use of writer Jacint Verdaguer's epic poem *L'Atlàntida*[24] Verdaguer was a good friend of Gaudí; they imagined – symbolically – a country, and built – physically – a city, so that both became symbolic reconstructions. In the Güell Pavilions we notice a brilliant example of transfers to architecture from Verdaguer's poetry. The level of identification between the two artists and their work on the global projects of city and country (re)construction was such that they became celebrities in their own right. When Gaudí died, somebody wrote in the book of condolences that Gaudí was the poet of stone and Verdaguer the architect of the word.

The importance of Gaudí in Barcelona has been the main reason why so many international conferences have been organized in recent years to study his work. The congresses organized by The Gaudí Research Institute in collaboration with the University of Barcelona have attracted the collaboration of great personalities like Arata Isozaki, Rainer Graefe, Arnold Walz, Manuel Medarde, Jan Molema, Etsuro Sotoo, Tokukoshi Torii, Leonid Demyanov, Arnau Puig and Ferran Adrià. They offer an exciting challenge: to make Barcelona not only a tourist attraction but also a hub of architectural knowledge and contemporary applications.

The following sections highlight some extraordinary and little-known examples of multidisciplinary creativity by Gaudí that are the result of new research.

23 Manuel Medarde Sagrera and Esteban Galindo López, 'Bellesguard, twenty centuries of history' (communication at 2nd Gaudí World Congres, Barcelona, 2016).
24 See Torrents 2006; Marià Marín in *Gaudí, l'home i la seva obra* (Gaudí Exhibition Centre 2002).

A place for research

All of Gaudí's research was done in the Colònia Güell workshop and, later, in the Sagrada Família workshop. A real laboratory mimicking Edison's Black Maria studio. A wonderful place where Güell said he was delighted with everything Gaudí did regardless of what he did, how long it took or the cost. The dream of every artist. The Colònia was, in Gaudí words, the place for research and innovation, for trying out everything you could imagine: 'Without having carried out the tests I did at the Colònia, I would have never dared to apply [my innovations] to the Sagrada Família'. There he engineered the bulk of his revolutionary innovations, from design to constructed reality: the polyfunicular model; the leaning pillar that follows the direction of thrust; the tree structure; the wall surface folded in parabolic shapes...

Colònia Güell is also atypical, a triple model of artistic, architectural, and scientific revolution and technical–industrial innovation, social and cultural revolution (education expert Xavier Melgarejo once told me: 'I was seeking a model of educational success in Finland, and in the end I've had it right here all along, and for the past 100 years').

The goals were always, first of all, practical and social. At the Sagrada Família: because the *client* was not in a hurry, the first thing that was built was the school for the workers' children, that humble building made of bricks that outlined the conoids that amazed Le Corbusier. At the Colònia: the factory, houses, school, the cultural centre – everything that was essential – came first. And after Gaudí had made houses for men, he designed the house of God, the work that would open the door to new architecture, built when he was in no hurry and under no pressure and could be the consummate artist (Figure 11.6).

Bear this in mind: the revolution in the history of architecture, which began with this *avant la lettre* calculator that is the polyfunicular model[25] was built with a never-before-seen team: a mason, a teenage apprentice and an engineer. This was conceived as being helpful in discovering how to do calculations that had never been done

---

25 The breaking news on Gaudí's studio and his model can be seen in the 2nd Gaudí World Congress: Rainer Graefe presented 'The projects held by The Gaudí Research Institute and Presentation of Unpublished Images of Gaudí's Workshop in Colònia Güell', by Manuel Medarde, Pere Jordi Figuerola i Maria Marín.

286   Art, architecture, and the city

Figure 11.6 A corridor which goes through the entire lower part of the crypt of the Colònia Güell, built in the shape of a hyperbolic paraboloid which Gaudí created as a resonance box for the organ and which also contributes to the climatization of the building.

© Pere Virgili (2014)

before (the architect–engineer team is common today, but we have no evidence of it before Gaudí); the other person would be an effective apprentice and, because of his age, a polite troublemaker who will ask about what is so new and strange when nobody else would dare to do so. And the mason because he holds in his hands all the construction traditions that work well, due to the passing on of experience.

Health, hygiene, and safety

I was not very surprised that those most interested in the findings of the research were business people and professionals even more than historians and architects. They asked me to give a talk. When I finished, a man approached me and asked if I knew who he was and what he did. I said no. 'I work in the area of ISO quality and hygiene certificates at work, and you've just said that Gaudí did the same job as me!' Yes, Gaudí established safety, quality and hygiene standards when they were not accorded great importance. And he was harsh if standards were not met.

A few examples: Gaudí made the women working in the Colònia textile mill work sitting down, not standing up, to prevent spinal column injuries. He also had them wear hairnets to keep their hair from getting caught in the machines, a common workplace accident. In construction, Gaudí watered the ground to avoid having people breathe in dust, scheduled breaks to eat and made washing and personal hygiene mandatory. He offered advice on walking and exposure to sunlight, and diet, and instruction on hydrotherapy treatments from the Bavarian priest, the Abbot Sebastian Kneipp; and he encouraged workers to play sport (thus, one of the facilities at the Colònia was... a football pitch).

Air, water, light, colour, sound

It is relatively easy for an architect to endow a building with natural light. It was even easier for him, as he applied the ruled surfaces. Now, how can life and movement be given to a building which, by definition, is static and heavy? Gaudí recreated nature because nature is movement, the expression of life. He achieved it through a combination of materials and their irregularities, through the orientation of the building, curved shapes, the optical treatment of colour and natural integration, and so on; his buildings become changeable, and sometimes volatile, to erase the constructive limits when light and colour change the shape of the spaces.

More constructive physics: through his choice of materials for the ventilation systems (such as those provided by false columns that are actually chimneys; due to a Venturi effect they suck in and refresh the air, forming a sort of natural air conditioning system at no energy cost) and drainage (pits, elevated floors, ventilation tunnels, water collection systems that were used for irrigation, etc.), Gaudí was able to regulate temperature variations and the level of humidity between indoors and outdoors (just imagine the savings on heating that *that* enabled). This combination of ventilation, drainage, natural lighting, and the choice of materials forms a real system of ecological sustainability and energy efficiency.

Thanks to the study of physics applied to construction, the use of natural forces complemented Edison's research on electricity when it was in the midst of commercial expansion. Examples that open up horizons: Gaudí designed a cinema, taking into account lighting and the transmission of sound and live music (none of Gaudí's buildings echo). In terms of acoustics and music, the most spectacular thing to point out is that the towers of the Sagrada Família are belfries with enormous tubular bells, shapes he had previously tested in miniature in a Wagner opera at the Liceu. And from the largest to the smallest: the rattle (wooden percussion wheel) at Colonia Güell is a marvel in choice of wood for producing sonic scales, while also being a symbol of the textile mill, as it mimics the sound of looms operating (Figure 11.7).

Business and social innovation

Artistic, technical and process innovation are inalienable assets of the Güell–Gaudí binomial. Güell, the patron–businessman, and Gaudí, the politician–creator, established a relationship of mutual influence. In other words, they created a genuine co-working situation that provided artistic challenges and business opportunities, as well as civic, national, social and worker engagement, based on innovation and design.

This unusual way of working, combining business, social needs, and innovation in order to create something radically new, did not become an artistic, political, or economic pillar, but instead remained on the sidelines in an industrial village that was a social model and unique for its design. Consider, then, creation and industry – in close proximity and interconnected – as complementary factors of growth.

Figure 11.7 Bars made with pieces repurposed from textile machinery from the Colònia Güell

© Pere Virgili (2014)

Who was Gaudí?

If it is extremely difficult to know ourselves completely, it is even more difficult to know somebody else, especially if a century separates us and if the information about the individual that has reached us is no more than a few declarations from those who knew him, so that we have to focus mainly on his works and what historians and critics have written. But that is always a risk.

Gaudí has been defined in many ways, including during his lifetime, but if we put all of the definitions together and list them as a series, there appears a curious fact, a connecting point that links them. Let us take a look: 'builder of dreams', 'inventor of forms', 'pioneer of avant-garde', 'architect of fantasy', 'poet of stones', 'urchin artist', 'architect of God or the universe'…. The connecting link between different definitions is the word 'imagination', that is, the act of being bold, like pioneers, like avant-gardeists.

After years of researching documents and observing his work to study what others, wiser than me, have said, and to contrast that with the memories, indescribable, and unforgettable, of Gaudí's disciples and friends, I think that imagination is the characteristic that defines him. And then, amazingly, I realize another curious fact, that Gaudí himself gave us a few hints. It was just after graduating as an architect when he reflected on a question posed by a professor presiding over the committee: 'Am I a genius or a fool?' It is a question of Shakespearean significance. After college, he had to make a decision on what he should start on, a vital decision on the direction of his task as an architect and as an artist. For the first time Gaudí dared to start off in an unheard way of freedom, engaging little by little in a struggle of courageous decisions throughout his life. Fools are those who, detached from reality, can see other imaginary worlds. Geniuses are those who imagine other worlds before anyone sees them. Was he a fool or a genius? Could he become the latter? His goal was to make a new kind of architecture, and to achieve it he had to invent almost everything, method, materials and techniques. He had to do what nobody had ever, I repeat ever, done before. The decision was firm: if nobody has tried it before does not mean there is no reason not to try it. He was not lacking ambition, right?

So Gaudí played hardball. Naturally, all this happened in and during a long process, but I want to point out that there was a key moment, a time zero, that of the first decision, the freedom of choice to have creative freedom. So Gaudí was not a builder, but an artist, a creator of forms and dreams, and of structures, methods and techniques, a pioneer who did not know where he would arrive (try and attempt – after his studies these were his three main verbs of choice) but who was guided by a higher ideal than building with bricks. He wanted to reach Beauty,[26] a beauty that to be true could only materialize as something rational and useful to people. A beauty that, found and obtained from Nature – origin of all things – Gaudí could transform into poetry made out of stone.

---

26 See Cussó 2011: 8–11. Cussó was a worker at Sagrada Família.

Works cited and bibliography

Books

Andruet, Mario, and Sciortino Bibiana (1995). *Gaudí y la geometría de las superficies regladas alabeadas* (Barcelona: Cátedra Gaudí).

Bassegoda Nonell, Joan (1989). *El gran Gaudí* (Sabadell: Ed. Ausa).

—, Joan (2011). *El senyor Gaudí. Recull d'assaigs i articles* (Barcelona: Claret).

Bergós, Joan (1954). *Antoni Gaudí: l'home i l'obra* (Barcelona: Ariel).

Berlin, Isaiah (1953). *The Hedgehog and the Fox: An Essay on Tolstoy's View of History* (London: Weidenfeld & Nicolson).

Bonet, Jordi (1999). *Temple Sagrada Família.* English version. (Barcelona: Escudo de Oro).

— (2001a). *Essential Gaudí* (Barcelona: Ed. Pòrtic).

— (2001b). *L'últim Gaudí: el modulat geomètric del Temple de la Sagrada Família* (Barcelona: Ed. Pòrtic).

Bonet, Jordi, and Puig, Armand (2012). *Arquitectura i símbol de la Sagrada Família* (Barcelona: Ed. Pòrtic).

Bonet, Jordi, Rigol, Joan and Giralt-Miracle, Daniel (2011). *La Basílica de la Sagrada Familia: El Templo Expiatorio de Gaudí desde sus orígenes hasta su dedicación* (Barcelona: Lunwerg).

Bonet, Lluís (2000). *La mort de Gaudí i el seu ressò en els diaris i revistes de l'època* (Barcelona: Claret).

Burry, Mark (1993). *Expiatory Church of the Sagrada Familia. Antoni Gaudí* (London: Phaidon).

Cirlot, Juan Eduardo (1950). *El arte de Gaudí* (Barcelona: Omega).

Collins, George R. (1973). *A Bibliography of Antoni Gaudí and the Catalan Movement: 1870–1930* (Charlottesville: The University Press of Virginia).

Crippa, Maria Antonietta and Gösse, Peter (2015). *Gaudí* (Berlín: Taschen).

Cussó, Jordi (2011). *Gaudí's Sagrada Familia: A Monument to Nature* (Lleida: Milenio).[27]

Dalí, Salvador (1933). *De la beauté terrifiante et comestible, de l'architecture modern'style* (Paris: France).

Descharnes, R.; Prevost, C. (1969). *La Vision artistique et religieuse de Gaudí* (Lausanne: Edita).

Faulí, Jordí (2012). *Sagrada Família: Opus Magnum de Gaudí* (Barcelona: Mediterrània).

---

[27] Editions of this work are published in Catalan, French and Spanish.

Faulí, Jordí (dir) (2014). *Les naus de la Sagrada Família: Els secrets arquitectònics d'una obra irrepetible* (Barcelona: Mediterrània).
Ferrer, David, and Gómez Serrano, Josep (2002). *Els arquitectes de Gaudí*, (Barcelona: Col·legi d'Arquitectes de Catalunya).
Flores, Carlos (1982). *Gaudí, Jujol y el Modernismo catalán* (Madrid: Aguilar).
Fundació Joan Miró (2002). *Homenatge a Gaudí* https://www.fmirobcn.org/ca/exposicions/113/joan-miro-homenatge-a-gaudi.
Gaudí Exhibition Centre (2002). *Gaudí, l'home i la seva obra. / Gaudí, the Man and his Work. / Gaudí, el hombre y su obra* (2002). Exhibition catalogue. (Barcelona: Museu Diocesà de Barcelona).
— (2008). *L'església de la Colònia Güell. El primer temple de Gaudí, la recuperació d'una obra mestra*. Exhibition catalogue. (Barcelona: Museu Diocesà de Barcelona).
Gaudí i Cornet, Antoni (1982). Curator: Marcià Codinachs). *Manuscritos, artículos, conversaciones y dibujos* (Murcia: Colegio Oficial de Aparejadores y Arquitectos Técnicos).
Giralt Miracle, Daniel (1999). *La Pedrera, arquitectura i història* (Barcelona: Caixa de Catalunya).
Gómez Serrano, Josep; Burry, Mark; Coll, Jordi (2008). *Sagrada Família s. XXI, Gaudí ara* (Barcelona: Edicions UPC).
González, José Luis, Casals, Albert (2002). *Gaudí y la razón constructiva* (Madrid: Akal, Col. Textos de Arquitectura).
Jujol, Arxiu. http://webfacil.tinet.org/arxiujujol/148620.
Kent, Conrad (1992). *Hacia la arquitectura de un paraíso: Park Güell* (Madrid: Herman Blume).
Kent, Conrad, and Prindle, Dennis (1996). *Park Guell* (New York: Princeton Architectural Press).
Le Corbusier (Joaquim Gomis) and Joan Prats Vallés (1967). *Gaudí* (Barcelona: Polígrafa).
Lloveras, Kim; Tanaka, Hiroya. (1991). *Gaudí y la Mesura* (Barcelona: Gaudí Club).
Maragall, Joan (1986). *El Temple de la Sagrada Família. Edició de tots els seus artices referents al Temple* (Barcelona: Patronat de la Junta Constructora del Temple Expiatori de la Sagrada Família).
Martinell Brunet, César (1951). *Gaudí i la Sagrada Família, comentada per ell mateix* (Barcelona: Aymà).
Martinell Brunet, César (1967) [1952]. *Gaudí. Su vida, su teoría, su obra* Barcelona: Col·legi d'Arquitectes de Catalunya i Balears).
— (1969). *Conversaciones con Gaudí* (Barcelona: Punto Fijo).

Matamala, Joan (2001). *Antoni Gaudí. Mi itinerario con el arquitecto* (Barcelona: Claret).

Mercador, Laura (2002). *Antoni Gaudí. Escritos y documentos* (Barcelona: El Acantilado).

Molema, Jan (2008). *Gaudí: The Construction of Dreams* (Rotterdam: Episode Publishers).

Palau i Fabre, Josep (1966). *Picasso a Catalunya* (Barcelona: Polígrafa. Col·lecció Biblioteca d'Art Hispànic).[28]

Puig, Armand (2011). *La Sagrada Familia según Gaudí: Comprender un símbolo* (Barcelona: El Aleph).

Puig Boada, Isidre (1929). *El Temple de la Sagrada Familia* (Barcelona: Barcino.

— (1979). *L'església de la Colònia Güell* (Barcelona: Lumen).

— (1981). *El pensament de Gaudí* (Barcelona: Col·legi d'Arquitectes de Catalunya).

—, (2011 [1952]). *El Temple de la Sagrada Familia*. Facsimile edition of 1952 Spanish version. (Barcelona: Omega).

Pujols, Francesc (1927). *La visió artística i religiosa d'en Gaudí* (Barcelona: Catalònia).

Ràfols Fontanals, Josep (1929). *Gaudí (1852–1926)* (Barcelona: Canosa.

— (1999) [1929]. *Gaudí (1852–1926)*. Facsimile ed. (Barcelona: Claret).

Rubió Bellver, Joan (1991). *Dificultades para lograr la síntesis arquitectónica* (Barcelona: Del Serbal).

Sert, Josep Lluís; Sweeney, James J. (1961). *Antoni Gaudí* (Buenos Aires: Infinito).

Scheffauer, Herman G. (1926). 'Barcelona build with a bold fantasy; Spanish city, quitting tradition, evolves new architectural forms glorifying commerce a new Barcelona is rising', *The New York Times* (New York, USA), http://query.nytimes.com/gst/abstract.html?res=9D07E2DF17 39E633A25752C2A9679D946795D6CF&legacy=true.

Tarragó, Salvador et al. (1991). *Antoni Gaudí*, in Rubió Bellver, Joan, *Dificultades para lograr la síntesis arquitectónica* (Barcelona: Del Serbal).

Tarragona, Josep Maria (2016). *Gaudí, el Arquitecto de la Sagrada Família. Biografía* (Barcelona: Torsimany Books).

Tomlow, Jos (1989). *Das Model. The Model. El Modelo*, Frei Otto (Stuttgart: Institut für leichte Flächentragwerke (IL). Universität Stuttgart).

Torii, Tokutoshi (1983). *El mundo enigmático de Gaudí* (Madrid: Instituto de España).

---

[28] Palau's book includes texts in German, English, Spanish, and French.

Torrents, Ricard (2006). *Art, poder i religió. La Sagrada Família en Verdaguer i en Gaudí* (Barcelona: Proa).

Magazines

El propagador de la devoción a San José (editions 1866–1947. Barcelona: Òrgan de l'Associació Espiritual de devots de Sant Josep, promotora del Temple de la Sagrada Família).
Templo. Temple (editions from 1948 to present. Barcelona: Junta Constructora del Temple de la Sagrada Família).

Original documents

Gaudí i Cornet, Antoni. *Manuscrit de Reus,* 1876–1879. Museu Comarcal de Reus.

Websites

Càtedra Antoni Gaudí, Universitat de Barcelona and The Gaudí Research Institute: http://www.ub.edu/web/ub/ca/menu_eines/noticies/2016/02/039.html#? [accessed 7 April 2017].
Càtedra Gaudí, Universitat Politècnica de Catalunya: https://catedragaudi.upc.edu/ca [accessed 7 April 2017].
The Gaudí Exhibition Center (Museu Diocesà Barcelona): http://www.gaudiexhibitioncenter.com [accessed 7 April 2017].
The Gaudí Research Institute: http://www.tgaudiri.org [accessed 7 April 2017].
Gaudí World Congress: http://www.gaudicongress.com/ca [accessed 11 April 2017].

CHAPTER TWELVE

El Poble Espanyol / El Pueblo Español (1929)*

Jordana Mendelson

> Expositions are arsenals where hardworking people build up their defensive arms...
>
> Seville has been Spain's mirror in Hispanic-America, and Barcelona the reflection of our European spirit.[1]
>
> *España en sus exposiciones: Barcelona–Sevilla 1929–1930* (1931)

In 1929 General Miguel Primo de Rivera, King Alfonso XIII, and Queen Victoria Eugenia opened two expositions in Spain: the Ibero-American Exposition in Seville and the International Exposition in Barcelona. The government promoted the expositions as triumphant demonstrations of Spain's place in the world community and Spain's entrance into the twentieth century. At the same time, the expositions were meant to bear witness to the nation's historical (and political)

---

* This is an abridged version approved by the author of a chapter in Jordana Mendelson, *Documenting Spain. Artists, Exhibition Culture, and the Modern Nation, 1929–1939* (University Park, PA: Penn State University Press, 2005), pp. 1–37. Reprinted with permission from Penn State University Press.
1 All translations into English are by the author unless otherwise indicated.

connections to both Latin America and Europe. In the case of the Barcelona Exposition, the dictatorship's dual goals of promoting modernity and tradition were mediated in part by Catalonia's own ambitions and position in relation to the rest of Spain and Europe. Barcelona, the capital city of Catalonia, had been the site of the 1888 International Exposition and was Spain's leading industrial port. The publicity for the Barcelona Exposition portrayed the city as the centre of a revitalized, unified, and technologically advanced modernism, as well as a postwar haven of peace and prosperity for the European nations that had suffered extreme losses during World War I. Barcelona was offered to the public as a dreamscape.

One of a series of widely published advertisements asked readers whether the exposition was 'Dream or Reality?' Once the exposition had been built, visitors were encouraged to view the monumental spectacle as a dream transformed into reality. A poster designed by Francesc d'Assís Galí and featured on the cover of the popular Catalan magazine *D'Ací i d'Allà* gave an image to these national aspirations by portraying Barcelona allegorically as a classically robed woman gracefully rising above the steel tubular forms of industry with a white dove of peace in her hand (Figure 12.1).

At the exposition, Carles Buïgas's syncopated illuminated fountains and projected light beams turned the exposition grounds into a spectacular fantasy of sight, sound, and movement that put technological ingenuity and entertainment on conspicuous display.

Despite these celebratory depictions of Spanish modernity, the national advances that the government claimed were evidence of its success were tempered by economic and political crises. Spain wrestled with long-standing problems of political violence that were compounded by the effects of the war with Morocco and the fallout from the 1929 Wall Street crash.[2] The government was controlling rumours of instability well before the Barcelona Exposition was inaugurated on 19 May 1929. A leaflet issued by the Spanish Travel Bureau in London in March 1929 reassured potential visitors that there was 'No Revolution in Spain': 'There is no disturbance in any part of the country, neither is any impending. The government is

---

2 On the effects of the Depression and the financial crash of 1929 on Spain, see Juan Hernández Andreu 1986.

Figure 12.1 Francesc d'Asís Galí, *D'Ací i d'Allà*, special number (December 1929): cover.

capable of maintaining order.... The British public is the victim of alarmist reports deliberately circulated [by] ... the revolutionary scum of Europe, who seek the failure of the Seville and Barcelona expositions as part of a manoeuvre calculated to help their own ends'.[3] The 'alarmist reports' were not unfounded. In the face of Primo's ambitions, the dictatorship was on the brink of collapse. As the anonymous author of 'La clausura de l'Exposició' [The Close of the Exposition] reminded readers in 1930, these expositions were organized in an effort to sustain the government by offering an image of prosperity, harmony, and modernity to international and national visitors in the hope that this illusion of grandeur would ward off the growing discontent and civil unrest that would ultimately outlast both the dictatorship and the monarchy.

Nowhere at the Barcelona Exposition were the stakes of Spanish and Catalan nationalism put into play more visibly than in the Pueblo Español (in Castilian) or the Poble Espanyol (in Catalan).[4] Measuring about 23,000 square metres, the Poble consists of 115 interconnected examples of Spanish vernacular and monumental architecture. It is the only construction of its kind built for an international exposition to still stand today (Greenhalgh 1988). The Poble is located prominently at the base of Montjuïc, a mountain overlooking the city that was converted from its original military use as a fortress and prison into an elaborate complex of gardens, gallery spaces, theatres, and pavilions. The Poble became one of the most visited and acclaimed sites at the exposition. Some went so far as to call it one of the exposition's three 'miracles'. Others upheld it as the symbol of the exposition's achievement: The Poble Espanyol outdid all previous typical town constructions at world's fairs – including the 1900 Ville de Paris and the 1908 Irish Village – in realism, cohesion, and national charm.[5] The history of the town's construction, the methods

---

3 Spanish Travel Bureau leaflet 'No Revolution in Spain', March 1929. Printed in England by A. Woods & Sons (Exposició Internacional de Barcelona de 1929. Z102: Varià, 158; Ajuntament de Barcelona, Arxiu Municipal Administratiu).

4 Throughout the text, I will refer to the complex as either the Poble Espanyol or the Spanish town.

5 Even before the Poble Espanyol was completed it was being compared to earlier reconstructed towns featured in international expositions, and it was praised for far surpassing its predecessors. See, for example, 'El Pueblo Español',

used by the architects to formulate its design, and the reception the town received after its inauguration indicate its central position in the government's objectives. The Poble was both an ideal dreamscape in which rituals of citizenship and nationality were performed, and an obvious construction in which the balance of harmony and fragmentation was constantly in danger of becoming undone. The use of photography in the town's creation and promotion is key to the ways in which it operated as both fact and fiction for visitors who attended the exposition. Photography provided the necessary foundation on which the architects were able to construct the realistic illusions on which the dictatorship initially depended to build a coherent vision of nationality. To understand the layers of political significance that the Poble Espanyol and the exposition in general held for politicians and the public in Barcelona and throughout Spain, we need to revisit the historical crises that marked Spanish (and Catalan) nationalism during the early twentieth century. Primo's relations with Catalonia began well before the opening of the 1929 Exposition. The planning for the exposition is marked by his presence in the political fortunes of the Catalan government.

Planning the Poble Espanyol

The design, construction, and reception of the Poble Espanyol should be interpreted in relation to the duality of the Barcelona Exposition as a product of both Catalan and Spanish nationalism. The press played a fundamental role in creating a debate around the Poble about origins and nostalgia that set up a fragile balance between national unity and disjuncture. Even before the exposition opened, authors had written competing narratives about the Poble's prehistory and the possible reasons for its popular appeal (Minguet and Vidal 1992: 688). In 1929,

---

Barcelona Atracción, no. 206 (August 1928): 230–31; and *Myself*, 'El què és el "poble típic espanyol"', *D'Ací i d'Allà*, 1929, December (Special Number): 47. Typical towns were a common attraction at World's Fairs after the 1873 Old Vienna, and included the Bruxelles Kermesse in 1897 at Brusselles, the Vieux Liège in 1905 at Liège, and the Le Quartier vielle Flandre in 1913 at Gand. See Schroeder-Gudehus and Rasmussen 1992; and Greenhalgh 1988: 82–111.

one writer explained the relationship between the Poble's uncertain authorship and the subsequent media frenzy caused by its construction: 'As complicated as it is to look into the origins of the Great War, so it is to clarify whose glory it was to have imagined this half-archaeological, half-picturesque reconstruction that has brought forth such enthusiasm and such a tremendous pile of photographs' (Domènech 1989). Behind this probing into the paternity of the Poble Espanyol resided a more fundamental debate over origins ('Myself' 1929: 43). Where did this Spanish town come from (in the broadest sense), and who was responsible for its history? For critics at the time, as the quotation above so vividly illustrates, at stake in any investigation into the origins of the Poble Espanyol was a terrain as thorny and muddied as 'the Great War'. In making the comparison with World War I, from which Europe was still recovering, the writer was no doubt acknowledging Spain's own recent battles, both foreign and domestic.[6]

At least two sets of authors drafted plans for construction of a typical Spanish town at the exposition. The first was Puig i Cadafalch, whose participation in the exposition's planning was virtually absent from press coverage about the Poble's history. In contrast, the second group of authors was widely referred to (and authenticated) in numerous articles during the late 1920s and early 1930s. This group of artists and architects was selected and approved by the International Exposition's Central Committee in Madrid. A comparison of the two plans suggests important differences in the ways in which architecture was used to convey ideas about nationality through public display. At the centre of both plans was what the writer of the above quotation described as 'a tremendous pile of photographs'. Photography had taken on a powerful role in twentieth-century Spain, especially in relation to the study of indigenous architecture and customs and, indeed, became the primary visual evidence used to establish regional differences within Spain's nationalist discourses.[7] By looking at the two plans, it is possible to

6 'La paternitat del Poble Espanyol', *Mirador* 31 (29 August 1929): 3.
7 Although Spain did not participate in World War I, it engaged in a war with Morocco that generated widespread discontent with the Spanish government, including massive strikes and riots. On the history of Spanish rule in Morocco and the crises that followed the war, see David S. Soolman 1968, and Sebastian Balfour 2002.

discern how *noucentista* ideas about photography were transformed under the dictatorship.

Puig i Cadafalch's proposal for the group of buildings, titled *Tipos de la vida española* or 'Types from Spanish Life' (a phrase that refers to both building types as well as more picturesque ideas about traditional folk and customs), appeared in his 1915 plan for the Exposición Universal de Industrias Eléctricas. In a 1987 study on the evolution of the Poble Espanyol, Josep Maria Rovira has detailed the architect's original design. While he acknowledges that Puig might have designed his version of the Poble Espanyol with previous international expositions in mind,[8] Rovira argues for a more historically and geographically specific reason: Puig's previous theoretical and architectural projects, Puig studied various aspects of Catalan architecture, from the Catalan rural manor house, or *masia*, to the region's artistic traditions. In his impulse to integrate countryside and city, to bring the vernacular traditions of Catalonia to bear on urban projects. Puig was drawing on *Noucentisme*'s lessons.[9] However, in his plan Puig limited the vernacular Spanish buildings to a marginal position within the exposition. As Rovira recounts, the seemingly disorganized array of the buildings, combined with their location outside the fairground's central axis, above and to the left of the National Palace, gave Puig's *Tipos de la vida española* a secondary status within the exposition's overall layout.

The Barcelona Exposition was first conceived as a showcase for electricity and industrial innovation, drawing on the promise of Catalonia to link the region's economic prospects to those of Europe and North America. With this clearly stated aim, it hardly seems odd that a representation of rural Spain would be planned for outside the main axis. Here rural Spain is a supplement, an addition that has no formal or meaningful influence on the rest of the exposition. But if we look at the array of buildings not as a carelessly arranged grouping of individuated structures but as a conscious montage of Puig's understanding of Spain's political and cultural profile, then another story emerges: the group of buildings represented a statement about

---

8 On the distinctions between the 'peripheral' nationalisms and Spanish nationalism, see Ucelay-Da Cal 1995: 32–39.
9 For a study of Spain's architectural contributions to previous world's fairs, see Bueno Fidel 1987.

regional autonomy and cultural differentiation. Rather than trying to forge unity out of difference, Puig drafted his examples of rural architecture as unique in their difference. The fact that no overall scheme tied the structures together might be read symbolically as a statement about the independence of Spain's regions over any unifying national programme.

After witnessing Primo's turn of policy and the liquidation of the Mancomunitat, Puig left for France in 1924 and continued his studies on the stylistic characteristics and origins of Romanesque art. His archaeological projects drew on two specific aspects of Catalan nationalism: the relationship between artistic style and ethnicity, and the study of cultural heritage through the humanities and the social sciences. One of the styles most highly regarded as a symbol of Catalan moral and aesthetic character was the Romanesque. Prat de la Riba wrote in *La nacionalitat catalana*, 'The unity of the artistic ideal of our nation was embodied in the simple and well-proportioned naturalism of Romanesque art, which is the art of our people' (Prat 1978: 91). For Prat as for Puig, the nation and the *pàtria* resided in its geography, traditions, and artistic manifestations. The laws and language that developed in close relationship to these customs provided the legal boundaries of that nation. With Primo's dictatorship, the centrist government in Madrid would operate with opposite political tenets, seeking to impose on Catalonia a vision of national hegemony that radiated from Madrid. Regional difference was emptied of its political force and turned into a mere spectacle at the service of the dictatorship's political agenda (Rovira 1987: 184).

The *Noucentista* archives

Before turning to the second set of architects and artists responsible for the Poble Espanyol, it is important to describe the role of photography within the ethnographic institutions that allied themselves with the theories of *Noucentisme* and the Mancomunitat's politics. In Puig's 1915 plan for the exposition, it is difficult at first to discern where photography might have played a part in his conception of typical Spanish buildings. The absence of photography's conspicuous presence may tell us something about the way photographs worked in relation to archives and architecture at this time. What connects photography to Puig's original plan is the importance of photography to *noucentista* archives, and Puig's involvement with popular architecture and Catalan traditions that were located in these same archives.

Many of the cultural institutions that emerged in Barcelona under the influence and support of the Mancomunitat integrated photography as one of the tools for documenting and studying different forms of Catalan life and art. The centrality of photography to the articulation of Catalan nationalism was voiced early on by Prat, who in his chapter titled 'The Feeling of *Pàtria*: The Personality of Catalunya' in *La nacionalitat catalana*, lauded the efforts of the generation of writers, artists, and folklorists influenced by Romanticism: 'From their songs and parchments, book folios, collections, and photographs, there emerged the essential affirmation of Catalonia's "being"' (Prat 1978: 42). Prat recognized the importance of photography in the nineteenth century, but he also qualified his praise for this generation of Renaixença writers by observing that 'the work [of *Catalanisme*] was incomplete' (1978: 42).

For Prat, these earlier collectors lacked the scientific procedures necessary to take the proof of Catalan unity one step further: to show not only that a specific Catalan culture existed but also that it was different from the rest of Spain. To do this, the most innovative and objective techniques of representation, in this case photography, would have to be combined with a comparative system of documentation. As early as 1909, Geroni Martorell, a public administrator in Barcelona's museums, brought these *noucentista* theories to bear on the photographic archive in his desire for a 'graphic inventory of Catalonia'. Reaffirming the equivalence of photography and civilization that was at the core of Prat's discourse, he wrote: 'Catalogues, archives of negatives and photographs, and national museums are the means civilized people make use of to inventory their artistic riches and make their history'.[10]

---

10 Geroni Martorell, 'L'Inventari Gràfic de Catalunya', *Butlletí del Centre Excursionista de Catalunya XIX* (Barcelona, March 1909): 51. Cited and translated into Castilian in Calvo 1994a: 25. In 1915 Martorell became director of the 'Servei de Conservació i Catalogació de Monuments' of the Diputació of Barcelona. He collaborated in the expansion of museums and the conservation of traditional Catalan art.

From about 1915 to 1923, three important ethnographic archives were initiated in Barcelona, bringing together documentary practices in an organized and institutionalized framework: the Arxiu d'Etnografia i Folklore de Catalunya (AEFC),[11] the Obra del Cançoner Popular de Catalunya,[12] and the Estudi de la Masia Catalana.[13] Although the focus of each archive varied, all relied on photography as the principal medium to record their subjects with the utmost clarity and objectivity. Scientific precision, one of the most effective agencies through which these archives sought to renovate the city's older traditions of folklore and excursionism, was thus accomplished by the introduction of photography (Calvo 1994a: 18). Initiated years before Primo's coup, all three archives became symbols of the encyclopedic efforts of the Mancomunitat's supporters to provide the cultural support necessary to accomplish the aforementioned objectives of Prat.

The AEFC developed the most comprehensive system of archival organization. As the first and most inclusive of the three archives, it became a model for the Obra del Cançoner Popular de Catalunya and the Estudi de la Masia Catalana. While the Obra del Cançoner Popular de Catalunya focused on popular songs and the Estudi de la Masia Catalana was dedicated to the Catalan rural manor house (the *masia*), the AEFC studied all aspects of the region's traditional culture and folklore, including architecture, labour, trade, and 'types', a popular way of describing a characteristic group through a generalized representation. In addition, because of the direct support that it received from

---

11 The principal source of the original photographs and notes located in the A.E.F.C.'s archive is Lluís Calvo i Calvo 1994c.

12 The archives of the Obra del Cançoner Popular de Catalunya are now held at the Abbey of Montserrat, and efforts are being made to publish the reports and administrative records from the project. For more on the project's history see Massot i Muntaner 1992.

13 The Estudi de la Masia Catalana is conserved today in the Centre Excursionista de Catalunya. For a history of the Estudi, see Josep Danés i Torras 1933 and José Maria Armengol y Viver 1934. Several other archives of Catalan folklore, customs, and geography emerged at the same time in Barcelona. Though they were not officially funded by the Mancomunitat, they participated in its impulse to create encyclopedic compendiums of Catalan history. They include the commercial archive Arxiu Mas, the still-functioning Arxiu Fotogràfic del Centre Excursionista de Catalunya, and the personal archive of the folklorist Joan Amades.

the Mancomunitat – the AEFC was funded first by the Mancomunitat and later by the Diputació de Barcelona – and because of its efforts to professionalize the discipline, the AEFC became an authoritative voice within the emerging fields of cultural anthropology and ethnography. Its director, Tomàs Carreras i Artau, along with his assistant, Josep Batista i Roca, set forth an ambitious plan for establishing methodological uniformity and a comparative system for organizing a vast array of visual and written documentation. The AEFC encouraged the creation of a Museu d'Etnografia de Catalunya, which, though interrupted for various reasons, had received the support of Puig and d'Ors (Calvo 1994b: 103). The scientific plans of the AEFC were welcomed within *Noucentisme*'s cultural programmes. Carreras i Artau published essays in such standard-bearers of *Noucentisme* as the magazine *Cataluña* and the anthology *Almanach dels noucentistes* (Calvo 1991: 86–89).

In 1922, the AEFC edited its *Manual per a recerques d'etnografia de Catalunya* (Manual for Catalan Ethnographic Research), which detailed every aspect of ethnographic investigation, from drafting questionnaires to organizing an archive. The device relied on most in the renovation and modernization of ethnography was the camera. Already on the third page the authors affirmed: 'It is of great importance and usefulness to complete every ethnographic investigation with photographs that serve to illustrate and clarify [the study]. After all, one photograph explains more than long descriptions' (Manual 1922: 3). In favouring the photograph over more subjective visual and written modes of description, the manual further marked its separation from the *Renaixença*'s Romanticism. For Carreras i Artau, the camera, 'easy to carry and manage', was a necessary tool 'in the baggage of every investigator during his ethnographic excursions' (Manual 1922: 33–34). His faith in photography came from years of experience within the University of Barcelona and from working with fellow folklorists, like Jaume Oliver Castañer, who had written to him in 1916, just one year after the AEFC was officially created: 'Folklore is, well, a complex science, not an art. For this reason, it is not necessary for a folklorist to be an artist or writer, but a psychologist and naturalist ... who is in greater need of a phonograph and a Kodak than of a brush and rhetoric'.[14]

---

14 Jaume Oliver Castañer, Letter to Tomàs Carreras i Artau, Barcelona, 24 December 1916, Arxiu A.E.F.C., cited in Calvo 1994b: 108.

The manual also recommended subjects to photograph and how best to compose the picture. In both cases, photography was used to present a classifiable impression of whatever the ethnographer was studying: 'Types and their customs should be *representative*'. The photographs of collective subjects were to treat 'traditional issues or moments in the life of the people' (Manual 1922: 64–65). Scale was accurately portrayed by including objects within the frame that measured the 'true dimensions of the photographed object' (Manual 1922: 34). Because ethnographic photographs had to be an exact copy of reality, the manual opposed posing or preparing scenes. The photographers exercised natural spontaneity with careful craftsmanship to integrate the everyday and the universal, the type and its context.

Carreras i Artau was an ethnographer who understood images. In addition to being an accomplished photographer in his own right, his visual literacy was trained by the way in which he and Batista i Roca constructed the AEFC's photographic archive. Images went through two stages of integration. First they were pasted onto cards, on which all relevant data about the image was recorded, then they were organized by subject. This primary archive of original photographs was complemented by collections of other kinds of photographic reproductions, including press clippings and postcards. These images, too, were attached to cards and annotated. All this material was then categorized, starting from Catalonia and broadening out to Spain, Europe, and the rest of the world, and that organizational model served both archival and ideological functions. The AEFC created a system of cross-referencing not only by subject and location but also by representational codes. This system of categorization, both geographic and thematic, embodied Prat's *imperialisme* and d'Ors's *arbitrarietat*. Carreras i Artau's descriptions often included comments on the accuracy or inaccuracy of the mass-produced image, as well as extended remarks about the costume, event, or region represented. The *Manual per a recerques d'etnografia de Catalunya* advised its readers: 'There are many photographs today that figure in private collections or in postcard collections, etc., and that contain facts of ethnographic interest. ... It is convenient to gather all these graphic documents together and complete them with detailed references and descriptions (Manual 1922: 3).

With the help of photography, ethnographers (and their archives) became monitors, even controllers, of a far-reaching Catalan patrimony.

The photographic archive helped establish a measure against which all other popular manifestations and claims to tradition could be measured. In short, photography helped these ethnographers invent a template for the past, and for the Catalan nation, that could be used to maintain notions of ethnicity and character.

In Barcelona, the methodology established by the AEFC for the use of photography in the study of ethnography continued to be reiterated by ethnographers well into the 1930s.[15] In 1928, just one year before the inauguration of the International Exposition, the folklorist Rossend Serra i Pagès published an article titled 'Photography, Folklore's Great Auxiliary' in the bulletin of a small hiking club.[16] There he reaffirmed two important points from the AEFC's manual: context and truth. Both were crucial to the *noucentista* notion of photography and the archive. The role of the photographic document was to offer a total picture, not a fragment: 'To take a photograph of a procession, is to have just another note, above all fragmentary; it is like seeing one moment out of a long movie. It is necessary to keep photographing all characteristic incidents from the first to the last: flags, attributes, images, popular participants ... and still more to capture [the procession] from a typical point of view, that gives an idea of the role that the people play in it' (Serra 1928: 59). Serra i Pagès stated unequivocally why photography was enlisted in a project that sought to demonstrate Catalan nationalism: 'To make a serious study, it is necessary to have the document that is [the most] faithful reproduction of the original'

---

15 The character of the folklorist became one of the many types of inhabitants in modern Catalonia portrayed in Carles Soldevila's novel of 1936, *Moment musical*. In the novel the main character, who is a financial baron in Barcelona, is approached by his brother-in-law, a folklorist who has spent all of his years living in rural Catalonia documenting its traditions and folklore. When he wants to publish the study he approaches the financial baron, who sees it as a liability. In the interim, his study *Folklore de Catalunya* is eventually published by the Institut d'Estudis Catalans, one of the most important cultural organizations established by the Lliga. Soldevila includes in his description of the folklorist a reflection on the desired objectivity and rigour of the new folklore studies established by archives like the A.E.F.C. Soldevila 1936: 20.

16 For more on the relationship between hiking clubs, nationalism, and Romanticism, see Prats 1988. For a study of the scientific aspects of the Catalan hiking clubs and 'excursionism' in the nineteenth century, see Martí Henneberg 1994.

(1928: 58). With such ideological weight placed on the document, there was no room for slippage between original and copy. The same model that was created to demonstrate Catalan nationalism as a historical and cultural fact through the institutionalization of the photographic archive was deployed in the fabrication of the Poble Espanyol to a far different effect.

Photography and performance at the Poble

The Poble Espanyol became the backdrop for a new set of postcards and press photographs in which visitors participated in the town's authentication. Instead of being presented with a photograph that already demonstrated the relationship between a subject and his or her architectural and national context, as had been done in the AEFC's archive, the visitors to the Poble Espanyol were encouraged to complete the ideological picture of Spain's architecture by taking the place of the original rural subject. A new relationship between Spain's rural architecture and its now urban inhabitants was established. This new group of consumer-driven photographs became just as important in validating the dictatorship's programme of modernization as its model had been in embodying that of the Mancomunitat.

The Poble Espanyol relied on the commercialization of culture to activate national identity. One example of how exchange mingled with folklore to set the terms of nationalism in circulation as a commodity was reported in a June 1929 issue of the exposition's *Diario Oficial*. As Félix Centeno placed his reader geographically within the Poble Espanyol, he exclaimed: 'There they are, at the intersections and in the picturesque little plazas, waiting for the visitor, a few beautiful girls: they wear the characteristic costumes of each region; they justify well, in the foreigner's eyes, the fame that our women have for being pretty and beautiful, charming and discrete. They offer a photograph. A "snap shot"'.[17] After discussing the tipping habits of the various clients of these female photographers, which established the women as engaged in both photography and commerce, Centeno

---

17 Félix Centeno, 'Una "foto" y un rato de palique', *Diario Oficial de la Exposición Internacional Barcelona 1929*, 15 (23 June 1929): n.p.

described each of the young women's physical characteristics and dress. A documentary film from the time recorded some of the female photographers at work and gives a sense for what Centeno might have seen as he came on them in the Poble Espanyol's main plaza. In his article, Centeno focused most of his attention on the young Catalan, Mercedes Vila. Commenting on her statuesque physique and classical proportions, he wrote: 'Those 72 kilos are conscientiously and artistically distributed, made in the memory of the Greek order. She is a blonde ... of fine gold'. More than an accurate description of the photographer herself, Centeno's rhetoric vividly recalls Eugeni d'Ors's 1911 novel on the virtues of Catalan womanhood, *La ben plantada* [The Well-Planted Woman]. In the novel, d'Ors and his male peers are intrigued by a young woman vacationing in a Catalan beach town: 'From where did this star come? From where did this cute girl come?' (Ors 1980: 19). As d'Ors answered that question for his readers, he established a canon of *noucentista* beauty. She was a homegrown beauty whose physical traits were just what the classically minded Catalan bourgeoisie were looking for: 'The chest... generous and totally Hellenic, would have been excessive in 1909; but it fits perfectly with the soft, leisurely, classic, very harmonious fashions of 1911' (1980: 21). The 'ben plantada' of the Poble Espanyol cheerfully breaks with d'Ors's Edenic vision of beauty. Mercedes is a camera-wielding career girl participating in the exponential production of photographic documents.[18] As she proudly announced to the reporter, 'I have taken more than 500 photographs'.

Along with this ad hoc production of photographic souvenirs came professionally marketed picture postcards, which were also reproduced in the press. As we know from recent studies on postcards, their production and distribution was integrally connected to modernization (see Staff 1966; Ripert and Frere 1983), imperialism (Prochaska 1991), and nationalism.[19] As noted earlier, postcards as well as original photographs were collected in archives of Catalan building types,

---

18 The Exposition committee was highly aware of the need to find educated women to attend to customers at the Poble Espanyol. 'Exposición de Barcelona, "El Arte en España"', LP25-16, Fons Lluís Plandiura, Arxiu Històric de la Ciutat, Barcelona.

19 For recent art historical work on postcards, see Mendelson 2001.

labour, and architecture. Postcard sellers like J. Esquirol formatted their images in a manner akin to the comparative methods used in scientific archives. These same postcards, especially Esquirol's photographs of types from La Escala, a beach town on the Catalan coast, were included in many of Barcelona's ethnographic archives. In these postcards and those depicting the newly constructed Poble Espanyol, repetition was capitalized on as both evidence and demonstration of a pre-existing truth.[20] By being able to purchase a postcard, visitors were encouraged to treat the Poble as they might have treated any other representation of national culture: as something whose origins were indisputable. The difference at the Poble was that, with the help of a team of female photographers, they could picture themselves within history (and an idealized pre-industrial town) and become part of it.

The postcards published to accompany the exposition represented the Poble Espanyol as uncontaminated by urban rush or temporal decay. The separation of the town from the rest of the city, and the exposition's celebration of modernity and technology, is reinforced through pictorial conventions. The photograph of the exterior walls and gate of the Poble, which were modelled after Ávila, was the first postcard in a series published and sold at the time of the exposition. The photographer used the fair's main thoroughfare as a dividing line. A group of women stand poised between the front edge of the postcard and the turnstile entrance, waiting to pass from the dangerous urban traffic to the town's quiet, 'provincial' setting. The Poble was an enviable space of relaxation and entertainment. It was the symbol of both a well-functioning exposition and a well-functioning nation. As Josep Pla, one of Catalonia's most prolific novelists of the first half of the twentieth century, explained just a few years later, 'In every country where politics functions in a stable and normal manner it is evident that a situation of equilibrium is produced between the spectacular

---

20 It has also been observed that the confluence of postcards and the hegemonic discourses of power and money occur precisely in settings like international expositions, where the exchange of goods and national identities is encouraged by mass display and publicity. In Naomi Schor's words, 'the coupling of the popularization of the picture postcard and these spectacular events [i.e. international exhibitions] confirms not only the postcard's democratic vocation but also its less attractive penchant for propaganda and nationalistic self-promotion' (Schor 1992: 213).

nervousness of the great centres of population and the solid and stable calm of life outside [the city]' (1931: 1). The Poble Espanyol embodied the government's dream that city and countryside would coexist as harmonious complements. The remaining postcards in this series represented empty vistas. In postcards of the main plaza and the Calle de los Caballeros, it is precisely the town's spatial openness that makes it ideal. When rephotographed during the town's opening, tourists filled the streets. In both cases, the Poble Espanyol is represented as outside the political dimensions of historical time; it is a vision of an idealized Spain that both ignores recent events and replaces them with the spectacle of the distant past or the immediate present.

John Gillis's observations on memory and identity in relation to national acts of commemoration clarify how the space of the Poble Espanyol and its representations involved the visitor/viewer directly in the act of remaking history: 'If the conflicts of the present seemed intractable, the past offered a screen on which desires for unity and continuity, that is, identity, could be projected' (1994: 9). That the city's troubled recent past was on the public's mind is evidenced by writers' comments both before and after the exposition's inauguration. One explained that the Poble Espanyol 'served to erase the memory of the recent past, so catastrophic'.[21] Through the intervention of the architects' plan and the photographers' postcards, the visitor/viewer was encouraged to manufacture and relive a dreamlike, phantasmatic childhood far away from political conflict. The Poble was constructed and perceived by many writers as a site of collective memory for the Spanish people. One commentator praised the town as an abstract notion of the past: 'This is the Pueblo Español, an evocation of the past of each and every one of us'.[22] Another bridged this general past to personal nostalgia: 'The national visitor encounters his corner, his little street, that reminds him of the beloved corner of Spain where he was born'.[23]

---

21 Editors, 'Balanç de l'any', *Mirador*, 49 (2 January 1930): 1.
22 Antonio de Carranza, 'Evocación en el Pueblo Español', *Diario Oficial de la Exposición Internacional Barcelona 1929*, 22 (11 August 1929): 24.
23 'Inauguración de "El Pueblo Español"', *Barcelona 1929–1930. Recuerdo de la Exposición. Anuario de la ciudad. Publicación oficial de la Sociedad de Atracción de Forasteros* (Barcelona, 1930), n.p.

312   Art, architecture, and the city

The architects' task was to offer the visitor a replica of a journey across Spain. Only through careful orchestration could the Poble Espanyol bring about such praise as 'In the Pueblo Español, turning a corner is like travelling many kilometres'.[24] So convincing was the montage that more than one writer affirmed, 'The sight could not be more exact'.[25] As a reproduction of the effect of travel, the town was successful. At a time when tourism in Spain was being promoted by the dictatorship through the establishment of a national tourist agency, the Patronato Nacional de Turismo, the town enabled visitors to get a glimpse of what the country offered them without any of the hassle that actual travel entailed. In addition to being able to follow their own trajectories through the town, visitors were encouraged to walk through a multiroom diorama behind the façades of the main plaza. Like their predecessors of the nineteenth century who used panoramas and dioramas to reconstitute the views and landscapes that became a blur when experienced by train, the architects of the Poble Espanyol relied on dioramas to recapture the customs, sites, and national myths that might have been lost to the contemporary motorist. Artificial travel, as promised to visitors to the Poble, also lacked the kinds of risks that the artists and architects involved with the Poble's design had experienced first hand. As the architects made their trips across Spain with cameras, another group of artists sketched typical aspects of the countryside and revisited places from Spain's legendary and literary corpus, from el *Cantar de mío Cid* to *Don Quijote*, which formed the basis for the diorama's illustrations. One of the artists, Olegario Junyent, wrote to Plandiura to explain his delay in sending back sketches: he had been in a near-fatal car crash while on his way to the Cathedral of Girona, to the north of Barcelona.

At least 48 'Views of Spain' were included as part of the programme of dioramas. Among the praise registered for the dioramas in the press,

---

24 Vicente Gribau, 'Retazos (Al modo de las greguerías de "Ramon")', *Diario Oficial de la Exposición Internacional Barcelona 1929* 25 (31 August 1929): 21. See also, 'Las maravillas del "Pueblo Español"', *Diario Oficial de la Exposición Internacional Barcelona 1929* 3 (5 May 1929): n.p.
25 Àngel Marsà, 'Geografía descriptiva del Certamen', *Diario Oficial de la Exposición Internacional Barcelona 1929* 43 (28 September 1929): n.p.

one reporter singled out their importance in completing the visitor's experience of Spain: 'The diorama relives for us the relationship between commerce and sea, industry and soil, and Spanish towns and cities. He who has walked around the Pueblo Español with the eyes of a tourist and stops in the diorama of the provinces and, after, enters more slowly in the diverse shops that exhibit a collection of samples from the industrial life of the regions, is a happy traveller. He has learned a lot about Spain, through his eyes' (España 1931: 35). As with the virtues of photography, here the diorama was presented as offering an unmediated visual experience. The selection of landscapes and subjects represented in the dioramas was promoted as a complete and accurate depiction of all of Spain. In focusing on the visual experience, the objectivity of photography rubbed off on the conventions of painting. Once contextualized within the Poble Espanyol, everything took on the veneer of reality. What were subjectively motivated choices now carried the weight of authoritative truths.

The entrance to the dioramas was installed in a highly visible part of the main plaza.[26] In nearly all the photographs taken of different activities organized in this part of the Poble Espanyol, one catches a glimpse of the large painted lettering announcing 'Dioramas', alongside which was painted a list of the different places represented. The architects' plan for the dioramas indicates at least six different viewing areas. One entrance brought the viewer into a space where he or she could then choose between the different dioramas. In many ways the space of the diorama was comparable to that of the Poble Espanyol. In both, it was the viewers' task to recombine different fragments of a larger picture and synthesize them in their minds. To activate the illusion of coherence, both depended on the viewer moving through an enclosed space, either that of the diorama or that of the reconstructed walls of Ávila. The different spaces played off each other, creating a self-sustaining experience of travel for the visitor in which

---

26 Already in 1926 plans for building diaromas in the centre of the town had appeared in the architects' drawings submitted to the Exhibition committee. 'Pliego de condiciones para las obras del Pueblo Español', 32C/Caja 9/Carpeta 45, Fons Francesc Folguera, Arxiu Històric del Col·legi d'Arquitectes de Catalunya. Utrillo made a number of trips during 1926 for the dioramas. See Caixa 5: Quadres d'Historia, Fons Lluís Plandiura, Arxiu Històric de la Ciutat, Barcelona.

one was encouraged to compare different reconstructed spaces with one another (and not to the actual experiences of travel that one might have encountered outside the Poble's walled precinct). It is interesting to note that Utrillo originally only wanted to build dioramas. The architect-photographers lobbied for construction of a replica town. By incorporating both forms of visual display, they set into motion a comparison between pictorial and architectural depictions of Spain's national characteristics that was reiterated in the press.

One of the most interesting commentaries written on the occasion of the exposition's inauguration was by geographer and folklorist Francisco Carreras y Candi. It is worth quoting at length because he touches on almost every aspect of the discourse that made of the Poble Espanyol a real town:

> Those who unconsciously possess good models of the past, without knowing what they have, in seeing them honoured in reproduction will possibly open their eyes and see.... Because, thank God, in the Pueblo Español, nothing is invented. Everything that was erected there still lives, here or over there, in our Peninsula. They went there to copy [the town] and transported it to the Barcelona Exposition, in exact reproduction, taking the necessary moulds.... As a work in reproduction, the Pueblo Español could not be improved' (Carreras y Candi 1929)

What would the ultimate proof of the Poble Espanyol's authenticity be for Carreras y Candi? According to his own admission, 'Its success will increase if one day we see, painted, in some art exhibition, "A corner of the Pueblo Español of Barcelona".' Reproductions authenticated other reproductions. There was no demand that this copy of rural Spain be compared with actual conditions or data. The only paradigm for judging the town's accuracy, according to Carreras y Candi, was if another artist believed in the illusion enough to paint it and submit it for competition. In the context of the propagandistic efforts of the dictatorship, Carreras y Candi defended a criterion for truth that depended only on the success of a copy's commercialization. He did not, however, wait for the Poble Espanyol to be painted in order to authenticate its commercial or ethnographic value. He paid his own homage to the Poble's veracity by including two images of the artificial town in his widely distributed multi-volume *Folklore y costumbres de España*, published from 1931 to 1934.

To naturalize what otherwise would have been considered impossible juxtapositions of different styles and geographic locations, the organizers imbued the Poble Espanyol with all the characteristics of a typical, functioning town, complete with imported performers and craftsmen from nearly all of Spain's regions. M. Aguilar (1929), writing in the widely distributed national magazine *La Ilustración Iberoamericana*, exclaimed to his readers: 'This is more than an Exhibition, it's a nation'. The presence of local products and festivals was an integral part of the typical towns constructed at world's fairs beginning in the late nineteenth century. In the case of the Poble Espanyol, the trading of difference was established between Spanish rural types and the nation's urban population and foreign visitors. Like the exotic towns at other world's fairs, here too difference was diffused and assimilated through a multiplicity of events and products. For the nationalist rhetoric of the dictatorship to succeed, the diversity of Spain's regions had to be fused together within a broader picture of entertaining pluralism.

Even before it was completed, plans had been submitted for introducing goods and services into the Poble Espanyol. Various entrepreneurs drafted lists of typical objects and foods that should be offered for sale. One of Barcelona's largest department stores, 'El Siglo', proposed dividing the types of goods to be offered among the different sections of the town according to region. In one report by the exposition's sales director, each product was explained in relation to its value for tourism and attraction. Throughout the town, ceramic, lace, and other handcrafted items were sold in region-specific shops, like the stalls and more permanent shops set up in the areas devoted to Zamora, Catalonia, Galicia, and Castile. Several cafés were opened in the town, among them was the Café del Pueblo Español, located in the main plaza. The original menu from the café features a drawing of a view from the terrace into the plaza; the Poble's cafés were also publicized in the exposition's official newspaper. The café offered typical Spanish fare like *horchata de chufa* from Valencia, sherry from Andalucía, and red wines from Rioja.

Along with the merchandising of regional difference, the organizers of the Poble Espanyol envisaged it from the outset as a place where festivals, tournaments, and typical dances could be performed. One organizer referred to the architects' reconstruction as the model for authenticity when he petitioned the exposition committee with a plan for the 'creation of regional environments through the reproduction of its customs, festivals, and typical characteristics, not carelessly simulated but following a criterion of the most careful realism, [already] begun with the reproduction of the buildings'.[27] The firm that proposed to orchestrate the folkloric festivals stressed that caution would be taken in selecting all the dancers and entertainers: all performers would respect, with the utmost attention to realism, each region's particular traditions.

Through the staging of hourly, weekly, and monthly events, the Poble Espanyol offered visitors the opportunity to renew his or her connection to folkloric traditions. A review of articles published in Barcelona's tourist magazine *Barcelona Atracción* suggests that there were few weeks at the Poble Espanyol that did not highlight a particular region. With the performance of region-specific events, the town's architects were able to evoke the memory of many traditions that had long disappeared from Spain's cities and towns. During the celebrations, visitors enacted the customs and manners of nearly every part of Spain. Even the typical dance of Catalonia, the *sardana*, which had been intermittently prohibited by Primo de Rivera, was performed at the Poble Espanyol. Contemporary writers considered these dances and festivals to be the key to the town's success, so much so that photographs of the celebrations were published in magazines throughout Spain. Valencia's *La Semana Gráfica*, for example, featured a multipage spread when the region was featured at the Poble.[28] Thus, even Spaniards who were unable to attend the International Exposition could participate vicariously as consumers of the folkloric festivities in print.

In describing the processes through which visitors came to identify with the Poble Espanyol as an operative space for the enactment of national ideals, I do not want to imply that the government's project to create a surrogate nation went unchallenged by architects, artists, visitors, critics, and foreign tourists. In fact, I suggest the opposite. In the newsreel mentioned earlier that was taken of the female photographers at the Poble, it is the smirk on the women's faces that most attracts my

---

27 LP25-13b, Fons Lluís Plandiura, Arxiu Històric de la Ciutat, Barcelona.
28 'La semana valenciana', *La Semana Gráfica* (19 October 1929): n.p.

attention. Knowing that they are being filmed, they pose while taking photographs of visitors. Behind the female photographers, the newsreel captures a performance of the *sardana*. Here, the Catalan national dance finds expression not in the first plane but in the background. I see in this newsreel a lesson about the potential heterogeneity that existed all along at the 1929 exposition. Despite Primo's desire to regulate the design and promotion of Barcelona's Poble Espanyol, one finds instances of the town's fragmentary illusions made visible to the public as an alternative mode of consumption. Sheets of Xavier Nogués's stamps of the Poble supplied repetition as a possible response to claims of authenticity. Similarly, the *Ilustración Iberoamericana* published a cutout of the town in April 1930; children could build (and unbuild) their own paper version of the Utebo Tower. The fact that the town had been designed out of a series of photographic records collected by the architects finds its moment of disclosure in a child's game. Rather than being a seamless illusion, these publicity materials reveal that the Poble Espanyol was a construction. Instead of the fable of unification, it may have been the possibility of difference that ultimately led to the town's great success and its unexpected survival into the present, long after the fall of Primo's dictatorship.

Works cited

Aguilar, M. (1929). 'La exposición milagrosa', *La Ilustración Iberoamericana*, 1 December: 44.
Armengol y Viver, José Maria (1934). 'La masia catalana', *Barcelona 1933: anuario de la ciudad* (Barcelona: Sociedad de Atracción de Forasteros), 177–81.
Arxiu d'Etnografia i Folklore de Catalunya (1922). *Manual per a recerques d'etnografia de Catalunya* (Barcelona, Universitat de Barcelona).
Balfour, Sebastian (2002). *Deadly Embrace: Morocco and the Road to the Spanish Civil War* (Oxford: Oxford University Press).
Bueno Fidel, María José (1987). Arquitectura y nacionalismo (pabellones españoles en las exposiciones universales del siglo XIX) (Málaga: Universidad de Málaga, Colegio de Arquitectos).
Calvo i Calvo, Lluís (1991). *El 'Arxiu d'Etnografia i Folklore de Catalunya' y la antropología catalana* (Barcelona: Consejo Superior de Investigaciones Científicas).

— (1994a). 'L'Arxiu d'Etnografia i Folklore de Catalunya', in *Temps d'ahir. Arxiu d'Etnografia i Folklore de Catalunya 1915–1930.* (Barcelona: Fundació 'la Caixa').

— (1994b). *Tomàs Carreras i Artau o el tremp de l'etnologia catalana.* (Bellpuig: Ajuntament de Bellpuig and Publicacions de l'Abadia de Montserrat).

— (1994c). *Catàleg de materials gràfics de l'Arxiu d'Etnografia i Folklore de Catalunya* (Barcelona: CSIC, Institució Milà i Fontanals, Generalitat de Catalunya, Centre de Promoció de la Cultura Popular i Tradicional Catalana).

Carreras y Candi, Francisco (1929). '1929 El "Pueblo Español" de la Exposición de Barcelona', *Barcelona y sus exposiciones 1888–1929, Las Noticias*), 19 May (Supplement).

Danés i Torras, Josep (1933). 'Estudi de la Masia Catalana', *Butlletí del Centre Excursionista de Catalunya*, XLIII, 458: 272–84.

Domènech i Polo, Joan (1989). 'El Pueblo Español', in *El Pueblo Español* (Barcelona: Lunwerg Editores): 39–41.

España en sus exposiciones: Barcelona–Sevilla 1929–1930. (1931) (Barcelona: n.p).

Gillis, John (1994). 'Memory and Identity: The History of a Relationship', in *Commemorations: The Politics of National Identity*, ed. John Gillis. (Princeton, N.J.: Princeton University Press).

Greenhalgh, Paul (1988). *Ephemeral Vistas: The Expositions universelles, Great Exhibitions and World's Fairs, 1851–1939* (Manchester, UK: Manchester University Press).

Hernández Andreu, Juan (1986). *España y la crisis de 1929* (Madrid: Espasa-Calpe).

'Inauguración de "El Pueblo Español' (1930). *Barcelona 1929–1930. Recuerdo de la Exposición. Anuario de la ciudad* (Barcelona: Sociedad de Atracción de Forasteros).

Martí Henneberg, Jordi (1994). *L'Excursionisme científic i la seva contribució a les ciències naturals i a la geografia* (Barcelona: Alta Fulla).

Massot i Muntaner, Josep (1992). 'Els nous camins de l'Obra del Cançoner Popular de Catalunya', *Catalunya Música. Revista Musical Catalana*, 98: 6–9.

Mendelson, Jordana ed. (2001). 'From Albums to the Academy: Postcards and Art History', *Visual Resources: An International Journal of Documentation*, 17 (Special Issue): 4.

Minguet Batllori, Joan, and Jaume Vidal i Oliveras (1992). 'The Avant-garde in Catalonia. Critical Chronology (1906–1939)', in *Las vanguardias*

en Cataluña 1906–1939. Trans. Anthony Keily. Exhibition catalogue. (Barcelona: Fundació Caixa de Catalunya).
'Myself' (1929). 'El què és el "poble típic espanyol"', *D'Ací i d'Allà*, December (Special number).
Ors, Eugeni d' (1980). *Eugeni d'Ors: La ben plantada/Gualba, La de mil veus*. Ed. Carme Arnau. (Barcelona: Edicions 62).
Pla, Josep (1931). 'Per el catalanisme de la pagesia: Plantejament de la qüestió', *La Veu de Catalunya*, 23 January: 1.
Prat de la Riba, Enric (1978) [1906]. *La nacionalitat catalana*. (Barcelona: Edicions 62/'la Caixa').
Prats, Llorenç (1988). *El mite de la tradició popular. Els orígens de l'interès per la cultura tradicional a la Catalunya del segle XIX* (Barcelona: Edicions 62).
Prochaska, David (1991). 'Fantasia of the *Photothèque*: French Postcard Views of Colonial Senegal', *African Arts* 24.4: 40–49.
Ripert, Aline, and Claude Frere (1983). *La Carte postale: son histoire, sa fonction sociale* (Paris: Editions du CNRS; Lyon: Presses Universitaires de Lyon).
Rovira, Josep M. (1987). *La arquitectura catalana de la modernidad* (Barcelona: Universitat Politècnica de Catalunya Edicions).
Schor, Naomi (1992) '*Cartes Postales*: Representing Paris 1900'. *Critical Inquiry* 18: 188–244.
Schroeder-Gudehus, Brigette, and Anne Rasmussen (1992). *Les Fastes du Progress. Le Guide des Expositions Universelles 1851–1992* (Paris: Flammarion).
Serra i Pagès, R[ossend] (1928). 'La fotografía, gran auxiliar del folklore'. '*Mai Enrera*' *Butlletí del Club Excursionista de Gràcia* 41, June.
Soldevila, Carles (1936). *Moment musical. Els anys tèrbols* (Barcelona: Llibreria Catalonia).
Soolman, David S. (1968). *Rebels in the Rif. Abd el Krim and the Rif Rebellion* (Stanford, CA: Stanford University Press).
Staff, Frank (1966). *The Picture Postcard and its Origins* (New York and Washington D.C.: Frederick A. Praeger).
Ucelay-Da Cal, Enric (1995). 'The Nationalisms of the Periphery: Culture and Politics in the Construction of National Identity', in Helen Graham and Jo Labanyi (eds), *Spanish Cultural Studies: An Introduction* (Oxford: Oxford University Press), 32–39.

PART IV
The Olympics and the city

CHAPTER THIRTEEN

Barcelona:
Urban identity 1992–2002*

Donald McNeill

Across the European continent cities are being transformed, reconfigured, reoriented, reimaged. Barcelona, a city that was long constrained by a Francoist straitjacket, now bears little resemblance to the gaudy guidebooks of the 1960s and 1970s with their lurid images of the Sagrada Família, their dusty statues of Columbus, the *golondrines* bravely navigating the working port. The city has been, in no particular order, catalanized, globalized, informationalized, gentrified, redesigned, and Europeanized. Its sounds and smells have changed; some streets have gone and others have arrived; high buildings have soared above the two-story housing in Hostafrancs and Poblenou. The Ciutat Vella (Old City) and the Barrio Chino (Chinatown) are, contrary to some opinion, as vital as ever. And all around, in virtual and territorial spaces, the city is being pulled open and stretched wide by fibreoptic cables, an ever-expanding airport, *rondes* (expressways) and a high-speed train network. The city is unbound, snaking beyond its

---

* Donald McNeill, 'Barcelona: Urban Identity 1992–2002', *Arizona Journal of Hispanic Cultural Studies*, Volume 6 (2002) – Special Section: Barcelona and the Projection of Catalonia, pp. 245–61. Reprinted with permission from *Arizona Journal of Hispanic Cultural Studies*. © Donald McNeill.

municipal limits into the valleys and along the north and south coast, and it is disembedded, feeding on the skill of its football team and the aesthetics of its architects, its icons projected globally by the media.

There have been dramatic changes, yet all taking place against an unusually stable backdrop of social democratic governance, where a centre-left coalition has been in power in the city council since 1979. In this chapter I want to explore how some of the diverse processes mentioned above might be related to issues of urban identity, and how interventions in the urban landscape are intimately political. I want to reflect on the city's emergence from dictatorship through the Olympic phase, where the urban left (in a range of guises) found itself having to rethink how its politics fitted the changing city and how the city, in turn, fitted the transformation of the political options of the centre-left. After briefly tracing the evolution of this relationship, I discuss the changing nature of the old town, the growing dogma of a technologically modernized city, the impact of deterritorialization on the city's icons, primarily its football club, and finally draw some comparisons between the 1992 Olympics and the city's next 'megaevent', planned for 2004.

Urban policy and the left

1979–2002

Perhaps the most striking aspect of the city's development since the re-establishment of democracy is its uninterrupted governance by a social democratic party, the Partit dels Socialistes de Catalunya (PSC). Here, under the mayoralties of Narcís Serra (1979–1982), Pasqual Maragall (1982–1997), and Joan Clos (1997– present), the city has followed a reasonably coherent and carefully rationalized urban policy, a situation which makes it unusual both within Spain and the wider European context. This also makes it an interesting laboratory in which to follow the possibilities of public sector-led planning and development.

Since 1979, it is clear that the Barcelona left has understood itself by looking through an urban lens and, moreover, that its self-identity has changed alongside its vision of the city. In the years of the transition, and the earliest days and months following the 1979 elections, many on the left hoped for a radical, strongly participatory, non-marketized urban policy. Yet the changing climate of politics in Spain and the world economy prevented such a direction. The PSC in Barcelona found itself facing the same dilemmas that the PSOE government faced in the early 1980s, when:

> in order to eventually give impetus to the European project of democratic socialism, Spain [had] first to catch up with the most developed member states; but the restructuring needed to obtain economic convergence [tended] to strengthen all those social and political forces which [were] less concerned with ideology and more with instituting market reforms. (Holman: 124)

Here, adapting Montaner's periodization of the city council's urban policy since 1979, we can identify four phases of political–urban development.

1979–1986

The 1979 municipal elections gave the left a huge majority, with Serra, then Maragall, confidently leading the city through a traumatic period of political instability. Under chief planner Oriol Bohigas, the city attracted attention internationally for its policy of small-scale, but avant-garde, interventions in public space, as well as for its shift away from destructive road and infrastructure policy. The changes were aided by a highly mobilized neighbourhood association movement, under the Federació d'Associacions de Veïns de Barcelona (FAVB), which constantly lobbied the council over the environmental problems or the absence of services that the Francoist councils had left as legacy.

1986–1992

This period was marked by increasing tensions between Jordi Pujol's CiU- controlled (Convergència i Unió) Generalitat and Pasqual Maragall's city council, controlled by the Partit dels Socialistes de Catalunya, which came to a peak with the awarding of the Olympics in 1986. Maragall's increasingly distinctive mayoralty developed into a fully fledged world view (*Maragallisme*) of how the city related to other institutions and places (including Catalonia, Spain and Europe). The city received substantial financial aid from the central government to prepare the infrastructure needed to host the Olympics in 1992, and realized major expressways (*rondes*), two new communications towers, Olympic stadia, and a comprehensive improvement of the built environment. An entire new district in Poblenou was masterplanned and constructed as the Olympic Village, subsequently turned into permanent, middle to high income residences. Other key ex-industrial zones known as 'New Downtown Areas' or *Àrees de Nova Centralitat*, including the office blocks at Carrer Tarragona next to the main railway station in Sants and new retail projects at Diagonal–Sarrià and Glòries, became the focus of the city's urban policy.

1992–1997

This period has been seen as one of crisis, coinciding with the cessation of the flow of public money after the Olympics and a generalized recession in the world economy. The city turned increasingly towards the private sector to secure partial funding for new cultural projects, such as the Museum of Contemporary Art (MACBA) designed by Richard Meier, which was part of a broader attempt to inject diverse economic activities into the Ciutat Vella. The period was marked by widespread job cuts, such as at the SEAT factory in Zona Franca, and demonstrated the city's dependence on wider trends in economic restructuring. As a consequence, the council pushed forward its 'Barcelona New Projects' portfolio of preparing major sites for development such as Sagrera, Diagonal–Mar, and Glòries. The projects were designed to balance and spread development within the municipal territory, and especially to decentralize the office market from the overstretched Eixample, yet they also provoked fears of increasing gentrification and loss of green space.

1997–2002

With Clos as mayor, the city began to show a far clearer opening towards foreign capital. For example, between 1992 and 2002, six large new multi-use shopping centres opened, all on ex-industrial land: L'Illa Diagonal (between Les Corts and Sarrià, 1993), Les Glòries

(1995), La Maquinista (in Sant Andreu, 2000), Diagonal Mar (adjacent to the site of the 2004 Forum, 2001), Maremàgnum (on the old town waterfront, 1995), and Heron City (in Sant Andreu, 2001) (Recio: 18–19). The impact of such a massive increase in retail floorspace has been the subject of some controversy: in the classic neo-Marxist analysis of land use that dominated debates in the 1970s, most of these sites are seen as speculative ventures divorced from the demands of the adjacent neighbourhoods. While the council has argued that the new shopping centres are required to *resist* the power of the peripheral centres (*hípers*), their effect on local business is clear inasmuch as they have facilitated the penetration of multinational retail chains such as Habitat, Carrefour, H&M, FNAC, McDonald's and a range of increasingly internationalized Spanish chains such as Zara, Mango, Cortefiel, Pans & Company. Furthermore, the cinema multiplexes attached to these sites are overwhelmingly in the hands of multinationals – Cinesa, Warner, Lusomundo and AMC account for four of the five sites, with only Glòries in the hands of a 'local' group, Balañà (Recio: 18–19). The city has undertaken major strategic planning projects to link into the high-speed train network, has expanded the airport, has witnessed the building of the World Trade Center at the mouth of the old port (albeit undertaken by the independent port authority), and has set its sights on the next major urban spectacle to follow in the tradition of the 1888 and 1929 World's Fairs and the Olympics: a 2004 Forum for World Cultures to be located in the eastern reaches of the city towards the Besòs river.

It is the fourth and most recent phase that will be the focus of the pages to follow. With the left's confidence nourished by strong showings in the 1999 Generalitat elections, and a landslide victory by Clos in the 1999 municipal elections, the PSC leadership has once again turned to placing Barcelona at the centre of Catalan development. This agenda – Clos declared himself against the idea of a directly elected metropolitan *superalcalde* – is tied into the anticipated post-Pujol landscape. While Maragall scored a pyrrhic victory (though a shattering defeat in reality) by outscoring Pujol in the Generalitat elections of 1999 (the vagaries of the voting system conspired to give CiU more seats in the regional parliament), there seems to be little doubt that the PSC has been enjoying a substantial degree of popularity among the electorate. Yet how the renewed popularity of the PSC has been affecting the city, its distinctive identity and its urban policy, has been controversial, and I now turn to some of the dynamics of the post-Olympic city.

The right to the (Old) City

> The old city would not be a problem if it were on the periphery. The awful thing about the district is that it is in the centre, next to the architectural jewels of the past. To make matters worse, several [civic] institutions are located here, among them the Palau de la Generalitat and the Ajuntament and the Liceu (Opera House). And, you just have to deal with it, the Mediterranean is here too, though how convenient it would be if it found itself among the tennis courts of La Bonanova or the mansions of Pedralbes. (Torres: 78[1])

Maruja Torres summed up the ambivalence felt by many of the city's upper middle class residents towards the Ciutat Vella: so much beauty and culture, yet so marginal, so unpredictable, so *other*. Aside from special days such as Sant Jordi or the Mercè, the Old City – and not just the Barrio Chino – has long been perceived as politically rebellious, bohemian, bacchanalian, and sexually immoral (Villar). Yet voices are being raised about the new direction of the Old City. Crowded by tourists, increasingly gentrified, its slightly cosy waterfront has raised fears that Barcelona is going the same way as many cities in the United States, in a process that Thomas Bender calls 'city lite':

> a place to visit, a place to shop; it is no more than a live-in theme park [..] this new urban recipe is insidious, for it pretends to offer what it is not. Such pseudo-city culture offers scenes of city life, not the city itself. The City Lite is safe, orderly, simplified. It demands little [..] and gives little. (Qouted in Soja: 247)

To what degree does the concept of 'city lite' resemble current debates surrounding the future of the Ciutat Vella? From my perspective, it

---

1 Unless otherwise stated, all translations are by the author.

differs in two ways. First, the linking of citizenship with centrality has been part of a discourse associated with Europe's urban renaissance, what Edward W. Soja describes as:

> a retrospective longing for the alleged spiritual glories of the 'democratic' Athenian polis, ancient Rome, the great Renaissance cities of Italy, the medieval Hanseatic league of cities and its famous motto, *Stadt Luft macht frei* (city air makes one free), and now, it would seem, the early modern metropolis. (248)

The emphasis on building a public and legible urban landscape is rife with such ideas – not for nothing was Maragall, adept at careful 'scheming', known as 'the Prince' by his political opponents. Furthermore, the city possesses a relatively healthy and active set of grassroots movements which closely examine the council's policies and the plans of developers. Second, the old town is under such demand from its citizenry, and citizens from around the world, that all sorts of conflicts have begun to emerge.

Lloretizando

> If someone were to ask you, dear friend, if the Rambla is *un paseo*, what would you say? If you asked me, I would answer without hesitation, no. What's more, I'd say, with the same seriousness, that it's not even *un lugar de paso* [...]. I understand strolling as a serious activity, that requires its rhythm, that leaves the mind free, open to every kind of suggestion, to dally at will and stop when one wishes to look at shops or other interesting things, still or moving. Don't forget that the stroller, even more after Walter Benjamin's theories, is not a superfluous being, but the most rounded representative of a city's tone [...]. Anyway, walking down the Rambla has turned into an exercise in syncopation, bearing some relation to the slalom or the obstacle course [...]. Here you can't walk, only stop [...] because more and more it seems like a theme park, formed by a string of absurd statues, inane acts, *trileros* [find-the-lady players] and attention-seekers that bring movement to a standstill [...]. The Rambla was once a popular *paseo* that joined the serious side of the city with its

uninhibited and seedy side. Its identity lost, its function annulled, now the Rambla is a non-place. (Espadaler)[2]

Anton Espadaler's opinion piece captures the reality of the Rambla in the summer. Swollen with crowds, the street is increasingly log-jammed, its old kiosk-inspired role as an informal ingestion of news replaced, or at least hindered, by an array of performance artists, the protrusion of metallic café chairs, caricaturists, and trinket stalls. That said, the street still retains many of its charms, not least at night. Yet its function as thoroughfare, deepened no doubt by the completion of the Rambla del Mar and Maremàgnum in the mid-1990s, has dissipated. As Quim Monzó noted in *La Vanguardia* in 2002, the verb *lloretizar*,[3] apparently coined by the cartoonist Nazario, aptly conveys the disreputable consequences of the city's reopening to the sea. Calling it the 'ground zero of tourism', Monzó complains that the streets of the Old City are now filled, even cluttered, with scorched bathers in flip-flops and swimming gear. Approvingly citing the decision of many southern French beach towns to introduce spot fines for inappropriate dress, he suggests that it may get so dark that the impossible has to be thought: decamping to Sant Cugat.

We can contrast Monzó's criticisms with Vázquez Montalbán's view of the Rambla of 1976 in *The Angst-Ridden Executive*:

> As night settled on the Rambla, Carvalho began to register the symptoms that marked the onset of the daily confrontation. The riot squad had begun moving into position, according to the prescribed rituals of the ongoing state of siege. Apolitical counter-cultural youth and young counter-cultural politicos maintained their customary distance from each other. At any moment a gang of ultra-right provocateurs might appear, and you would see the militants of this or that party disperse and head for their now legalized party offices [..]. Between the hours of eight and ten the prostitutes, the pimps, the gays and

---

2 *Pasear* means 'to stroll', while *un lugar de paso* means 'a place of passage', such as in a narrow road.

3 Lloret de Mar is the most notorious of the Costa Brava's mass tourist destinations, a Torremolinos of the North.

the crooks great and small would disappear off the streets so as not to find themselves caught up in a political battle that was not of their making. (Vázquez Montalbán 1990: 85)

Vázquez Montalbán's presentation of the Rambla (and Orwell made its former political–territorial significance famous internationally) holds up the street, and the behaviour of its crowds, as symptomatic of the political and social state of the city. During the transition, however, the Rambla became a somewhat traumatic red light, with not infrequent cases of drug-fuelled physical attacks and even murder serving to disconnect the old town from *la zona alta*.

Thinking about this disconnection, and its subsequent tourist-spurred rejuvenation, and how it is all tucked into the morphing of state and society, I was struck by Marshall Berman's account of the three phases of New York's Times Square. In phase 1 (1900–1945), the Square symbolizes American commercial vitality and show business; in phase 2 (the 1950s to the 1980s), the Square, indeed the island of Manhattan, is 'cut off' by virtue of federal highways; and finally, in phase 3:

> the Square's first signs are celebrating European sportswear and Asian software, and multinational media conglomerates – not just Disney and Time Warner, but Condé Nast, Bertelsmann, Reuters, and more – are taking over the real estate and harvesting huge city tax breaks and subsidies to create new forms of 'too much': more massive buildings and brighter light; more luxury shops than the Square has ever seen; more police, private as well as municipal; ever more people, happy to be out in public [...]. Mayor Rudolph Giuliani presides over the Square's fast-track commercial development [...]. 'Civility' is promoted with the manners of a nightclub bouncer, in vendettas against food vendors, newsstand operators, taxi drivers, artists selling their work on the streets, musicians trying to play in the subways, and many more. The city puts barriers up in the most crowded streets, making them harder than ever to walk in [...]. Explaining this policy, authorities proclaim that New York is afflicted with 'pedestrian glut'. Many people on the street think the city's real affliction is 'authority glut', but no one asks them. (Berman: 42–43)

Something similar happens with Barcelona, and particularly the Rambla. The Barcelona of the Civil War and the Republic gives way to the post-war edginess captured so well by Vázquez Montalbán (1990), and then, from the 1980s... phase 3? The logical extension of Monzó's and Espadaler's arguments is, perhaps, the Rambla as Business Improvement District, where wardens in *senyera*-themed waistcoats watchfully ease the passage of the flip-flops, check to see if the living statues are licensed, eject the pickpockets (driving them back down Sant Pau or into the Santa Caterina backstreets), introduce pedestrian traffic lights and make sure that the football jerseys that dangle from the streetsides are genuine. Still and all, what Monzó calls *el turismo basura* is surely still preferable to Disney's attack on Manhattan.

The right to the night

While the visit of Europe's leaders to Barcelona in 2002 did not generate the levels of conflict seen at Genoa the summer before, there was another issue simmering in the flats of La Ribera and steaming up the windows of the bars below: the right to the night. Mirroring similar instances in Madrid, the phenomenal popularity of the zone around the Born – far more than in the traditional territories of the Chino and Raval – has become a key electoral issue in the Ciutat Vella. As *La Vanguardia* reported:

> Eleven councils sanctioned in only two days. And there's more on the list.
> The Ciutat Vella district office has started an offensive against the terraces of bars and restaurants obliging the closure of nearly a dozen of them. Excessive noise, failure to observe closing time, excessive occupation of the outdoor space and insufficient smoke extraction systems are some of the reasons given by the district [...]. The refusal of a new license for the terrace of the bar El Rosal mobilized around a hundred people who, in solidarity with the owners, and defying administrative orders, took tables and chairs outside at night. ('Ciutat Vella ...')

The action taken by the authorities reflected a growing backlash from local residents against the nightly barrage of noise that echoed through the narrow streets of the old town, particularly around the Passeig del Born. While the nature of the protests were complex – many of the bars users were local, and many of the protestors were attracted to the area because of its vitality – it nonetheless opened up a range of debates over the political rights of city users, as opposed to residents.

On the other side of the Rambla, the issue is complicated by strong traditions of nocturnal revelry associated with the old town, particularly the Barrio Chino. As the Chino, associated with deep-rooted problems of criminality (Villar), went into decline in the 1980s, the city council undertook comprehensive demolition and rehousing programmes. The opening of the Rambla del Raval – a new tree-lined boulevard that replaced and cleansed the degraded zones of poverty and prostitution, not dissimilar in modernizing gusto from the opening of the Via Laietana in the early decades of the twentieth century – has been presented as a means of allowing 'daylight' into the cramped streets of the old Chino, with funding by the European Union (Von Heeren). The reference to light was continued in the competition for a new hotel and residential development on a key site in the new Rambla. Holding between 250 and 300 rooms, a 10-storey, 4-star building of translucent glass was hailed by the zone's master planner, Josep Acebillo, as 'a giant lamp [that] will become the focus for the Rambla del Raval', sitting with 5 blocks of rent-protected housing (Angulo). As a microcosm of the European Union's multicultural reality, the local community, including many Pakistanis, uses the arc lights and carefully paved surfaces to re-enact any number of floodlit test cricket matches.

TechnoBarcelona

It all comes together in the city. The new city-states are said to be emerging as the information and communication centres of global business. Their elite status is linked to the proliferation of satellite dishes and cable grids. And now they are entering the popular imagination as symbols of the new economic order and of the new lifeworld it is supposedly bringing into being. The information city, the virtual city: this, we are being told, is the city of the future. What will life be like in these new virtual environments? The ideologies of the technoculture tell us to look forward to tele-working and cyber-shopping, to the comforts of virtual community, and to the recreation of the Athenian agora by electronic means [..]. Why am I having difficulty in containing myself in the face of this confident virtual triumphalism? [..] Well, for a start, because there is nothing that is significantly revolutionary in this mission. It merely continues and perpetuates, by other means, the project of urban modernism, which has involved the progressive rationalisation and ordering of city cultures. (Robins: 47–49)

In seeing the informational city as continuing with the modernist project of comprehensive redevelopment and rationalization of urban space, can we draw any parallels with the ongoing replanning, rezoning, and redevelopment of the city under the Clos mayoralty? The genealogy of the thought of the PSC leadership cannot be understood without a consideration of the role of Manuel Castells in piloting the city as a means of embedding global flows within a comprehensible urban planning regime. But while Castells clearly distanced himself from the grassroots organizing of the late dictatorship, it is apparent that the new urban ideology of technoregeneration has clear parallels with efforts to accommodate the city's space to a globalized market. Here, Clos and Maragall have been proactively reshaping the city in its post-Olympic guise, particularly in the Poblenou 22@ project. In 2000, Clos was interviewed by Madueño and Gómez and had the following to say:

> Clos: The leading cities in the US [..] no longer depend on financial capital, but rather on capital in the form of knowledge [..]. We have this large area where we can apply this concept of the city of knowledge, i.e. Poblenou, where we have the opportunity to harmonise public use with the uses that require us to move towards this objective [..]; it's the same as what happened in New York, in Soho.
> Madueño and Gomez: You and Maragall seem rather obsessed with New York.
> Clos: Well, New York was a decaying city, one with severe safety problems, and every other kind of problem as well. But, by

chance, the multimedia and publishing industries moved in, and it has been on the road to recovery ever since [...]. We want the same sort of thing to happen here. Exactly the same. (Madueño and Gómez: 36)

From New York to Poblenou: the Catalan Manchester, with its old industrial landscapes, remains a powerful image within the Barcelona mental map. Yet what Clos describes is an ambitious plan to rezone much of the remaining industrial fabric of Poblenou for knowledge-based new economy functions. The project – running under the name '22@' – will, if realized, have a massive impact on the city's urban structure. The overall project is centred on two main areas, one between Glòries and the Olympic Village, the other to the east of Glòries and the north of the Diagonal. Approved in July 2000, the plan envisages over 4,500 new flats, green spaces, and, most importantly, over 4.5 million square metres destined for *punt.com* businesses. And yet some worry that the projected new economy businesses may fail to materialize, resulting in further rezoning of the area for flats sold on the free market (Andreu et al.: 12–13). Such, it may be recalled, was the case with the Olympic Village.

Accordingly, the 22@ project raises memories of a whole series of recurrent battles over Poblenou that stretch back to the era of Porcioles (the mayor of Barcelona from the late fifties to the early seventies). As Capel (11) has suggested, the current redevelopment of Diagonal Mar and Poblenou is but the latest stage of the Pla de la Ribera, the landmark victory by the neighbourhood associations in the early 1970s that was reprised – under the flag of the Olympics and led by the social democrats – with the building of Nova Icària (the Olympic Village). Here, the proximity to the city's beachfront and the coastal expressway has attracted high-spending investors in a gentrification process somewhat different from that which took place in the Ciutat Vella. In 1992, Vázquez Montalbán predicted this process as he surveyed the Olympic-driven redevelopment:

Where are the state-subsidized houses? [...]. Who has rationalised the market city? One cannot write down this inventory of suspicion and dissatisfaction without being consumed by a terrible fear of making a complete fool of oneself [...]. When the future Olympic Village ends up as a radial centre for the redevelopment of mile after mile of working-class housing, nobody will ask whether things might have been different. (Vázquez Montalbán 1992: 10–11)

In many of the cities of North America, and in many other parts of the world, we may be seeing the emergence of what Graham and Marvin (2001) have called a 'splintering urbanism', where metropolitan change is related to the increasing emphasis on access to information technology and the protection of elite lifestyles. Could it be, they ask, that we may see future urban landscapes as being made up of

> layers of premium network spaces, constructed for socio-economically affluent and corporate users, which are increasingly separated and partitioned from surrounding spaces of intensifying marginality – spaces where even basic connections with elsewhere, and basic rights to access spaces and networks, are increasingly problematic. In this understanding of contemporary urban change, dominant practices of urban design, network configuration, electronic access control, and police, security and institutional enforcement are increasingly seen to be working in parallel to support the sociotechnical partitioning of the metropolis and, indeed, societal fabric. (Graham and Mavin: 383)

Interestingly, the key challenge that Graham and Marvin see is something that Barcelona has been famed for coming close to achieving: the problem of constructing a metropolitan landscape from fragments.

One of the clearest rationalizations has been the council's new policy of giving permissions for new skyscrapers. The existing tall buildings that have exceeded the 100-metre mark in the city are as follows:

1.	Collserola Tower	Mast	288m	1992
2.	Hotel Arts	Hotel	154m	1992
3.	Mapfre Tower	Offices	154m	1992
4.	Montjuïc Tower	TV tower	136m	1992
5.	Sagrada Família	Cathedral	112m	
6.	Edificio Colón	Offices	110m	1970

(Source: www.skyscraper.com)

So aside from the twin towers built at the start of the Olympics, which were bedevilled with low occupancy rates on their completion, the city skyline is relatively low-rise compared with many of its comparator cities. Yet the beginning of the twenty-first century saw a wave of new buildings being given planning permission, six of which will exceed the 100 metre mark, with another handful coming in close to that altitude (Herranz: 22). Significantly, most will be designed by internationally renowned architects such as Richard Rogers, Ricard Bofill, and – most strikingly in terms of design – Jean Nouvel, whose 145-metre Torre Agbar, nicknamed, variously, in Castilian and in Catalan, 'el pepino', 'el vibrador', and 'el supositori', is already beginning to rise above Glòries housing Aigües de Barcelona. Despite the impact that such buildings will have both on the aesthetics of the skyline, and, more significantly, on the city's existing infrastructure, opposition to them has been sporadic.

It could be suggested that the PSC council may have acted to reconcile, as best it can, the redevelopment of the city within a post-industrial, Europeanized market and the social demands for new public spaces and affordable housing. Of course, the shift is not unique: other city councils, with equally strong left-wing traditions, have undergone a transition from municipal socialism to urban entrepreneurialism, as Quilley shows with reference to Manchester. The political desire to adopt a discourse of globalism and competitiveness is as apparent in Barcelona as in Tokyo or Toronto, with the global serving as an excuse to undertake drastic plans of urban restructuring. In many ways, however, the council *has* consulted local groups in an attempt to foster participative planning. Yet, as Capel argues,

> if all this has happened with a leftist council, run by social democrats and communists, we can only fear what will happen if the parties of the right (CiU and the Partido Popular (PP)) manage to win the mayoralty once the changing social composition of the city brings its logical political consequences. (11)

Disembedding the City

> Sport has an unrivalled capacity to capture the attention of huge numbers of people the world over and, no matter how exciting or glamorous an event is, the number of attending spectators is necessarily dwarfed by those vicariously present through the medium of television, radio and the press [..]. From title sequences to cut and paste montages of the week's events, television, in particular, can help set a particular tone that penetrates deep into the public's perception [..] [and has] also involved the increasing identification of cities as centres for the switching of images and symbols. (Whitelegg: 802–803)

Whitelegg's account of how Atlanta used the 1996 Olympics to project an image of the city to a global audience has certain parallels with what happened in Barcelona in 1992 – 'nervous boosters' worried about how the city competed with its competitors. With respect to Barcelona, the power of symbolic urban landscapes, projected in bite-sized packages to potential tourists, gave the Rambla and the buildings of Gaudí, particularly, an airing they had not previously enjoyed.

In many ways, such projections are part and parcel of the impact of globalization on the city, though perhaps it might be better specified as expressing a deterritorialized identity where sport and place (strongly associated ideas) are projected out of any physical, or even climatic, context. The year 1992 has often been discussed as a perfect example of the oversimplified, yet often-used, notion of a global–local interplay, where ethnic particularisms use the reach of global media or capital to project, or advertise, their 'difference' to the rest of the world. Thus, for instance, Josep Miquel Abad, who won admiration for his fierce negotiations over television rights, was described as embodying 'el "seny" global', the application of essentialized Catalan commonsense and stubbornness to a global media context (Álvaro).

Yet away from the Olympics, a similar, though more pervasive, process was under way, as 'el Barça' slipped its Camp Nou moorings and became ever more identifiable to a global audience, eager for top-range European club football. By 1998, FC Barcelona was among the three richest clubs in the world, alongside Manchester United and Real Madrid. Crucially, between 1978 and 1998, the share of the total revenue drawn from supporters and membership fees had dropped staggeringly, from 87 per cent to 35 per cent (Burns: 349). While in many ways the drop can be seen as a positive trend when compared with the astronomical prices charged to attend British football matches, it represented the dominance of television revenues and, in its train, the emergence of a class of footballing superstar unmatched even in the days of Maradona and Schuster. The business acumen of club president Josep Nuñez has perhaps replaced the highly politicized relationship with Catalan nationalism that had previously existed. The decline in the number of Catalan-born players, along with the concurrent rise in the number of Dutch and Brazilian imports, reflects the increasing internationalization of the football labour market. The Barça 2000 project, which seeks to redevelop a considerable portion of Les Corts into a theme park and leisure centre, may once have been tolerated for the good of the community, but many see in it a speculative development – at which Nuñez excels – akin to the controversial rezoning of Espanyol's Sarrià ground in the mid-1990s.

And so if one of the manifestations of *turismo basura* are the cheap replica shirts hanging in the Rambla, or the expensive replica shirts hanging in the club shop in Maremàgnum, and paraded around by pale-skinned Northern Europeans in flip-flops who clog up the centre gawping at banal statues, another is the homage to the city's other major icon: Antoni Gaudí. The year 2002 was declared the 'year of Gaudí', heralding the 150th anniversary of the architect's birth with a range of exhibitions, floodlighting projects, open days, and merchandise. Yet as Deyan Sudjic has argued:

> the truth is that the architect has been turned into a sacred monster, casting a darkening and ever kitscher shadow over the city he did so much to shape. The celebration of his memory has turned into an excuse for a deluge of junk that serves to diminish his reputation and stunt the imagination of his successors.

Sudjic draws parallels between the 'cult' of Gaudí and the similar rediscovery of Charles Rennie Mackintosh by the municipal authorities of Glasgow.

As Balibrea has noted, such initiatives are indicative of a qualitative change in the nature of how culture is perceived in the city. More pointedly, local government now sees culture as commodity or industry as much as aesthetic or symbol. The national agenda again comes into play, for Barcelona's regeneration was bound up in the post-Francoist restatement of regional identities:

> Within this propitious climate, Barcelona has been able to consolidate itself, politically and symbolically, as the capital of a Catalan nation without a state [...]. The conception of the Museu Nacional d'Art de Catalunya, the reconstruction and extension of the Liceu, the building of a Teatre Nacional de Catalunya, of a new Arxiu de la Corona d'Aragó, or the Auditori, have been implemented by the autonomous and/or local government as ideological instruments of a nineteenth-century style nationalism. (Balibrea: 196)

Other major institutes, such as the Centre for Contemporary Culture (CCCB) (the 'Beaubourg of Barcelona') and MACBA have contributed to the transformation of the Raval through their high-grade architectural spaces, but have simultaneously sought to provide very different urban-driven cultural programmes. Balibrea's unease – echoed, for example, by Guillamón – stems from the increasing intervention in the sphere of media and public opinion by the city government and associated authorities to construct a 'global' (in the sense of total) vision of the city. From publicity campaigns on billboards, leaflets and brochures to the co-opting of several key figures onto the city's underground graphic art scene, such efforts represent a return to a long-absent tradition of representing the city as a whole.[4] Such representational practices actively reinforce how the name of the city is understood and used, which may help foster a sense of citizenship: naming practices are, after all, a key aspect of identity construction (Amin and Thrift: 24–25). These practices, these opportunities to think of the city as 'whole', tend to be most frequently used in short-term, concentrated events, such as those of 1992 and 2004.

---

4 Balibrea draws on Albert García Espuche's 1995 exhibition 'Retrats de Barcelona', organized at the CCCB, which contains a fascinating trove of visual representations of the 'city' of Barcelona across several hundred years.

2004 and the Post-Olympic left

It's the 25th of July, and the Olympic Stadium is filled with 40,000 spectators listening to speeches by Pasqual Maragall and Jordi Pujol. Under the Olympic mascot Cobi's watchful eye, the Olympic flame is lit by an archer, and the spectators settle back to enjoy the kind of ceremony for which the Games have become famous. The year is 2002, not 1992, and while the invited medallists, volunteers, and families of children born during the Games are there to remember what was – by all accounts – a magical, almost utopian, fortnight for the city, the ceremony has a second purpose: the transition to the staging of the city's next world event: Fòrum de Les Cultures 2004, a UNESCO-supported festival with the theme of multicultural understanding.

The Forum's location was controversial, however. Here, where the Besòs flows into the sea, and where the Diagonal finally ends its cross-town journey from the leafy heights of Pedralbes, developers are already eyeing the opportunities to be gained from a waterfront location. Despite its location adjacent to the Sant Adrià power station, the area – one of the eight New Downtown Areas – already houses a large shopping centre and high-end residential apartments. As a result, while many saw the 1992 Games as being about more than just property development, there is doubt over the extent to which 2004 is just an excuse to open up more of the city to developers.

If the 1992 Games were mercifully free of much of the rancour surrounding most of the other events that the city has hosted, it has become abundantly clear that the Olympics have lost much of their 'nobility'. As Lenskyj has described in gory detail, Olympic events have tended to entail corruption in selecting the host city, wasteful and environmentally destructive sports facilities, and corporate dominance of sporting events. Of course, there was considerable scepticism raised by the neighbourhood associations and assorted critics over the direction of the city's urban policy in the run-up to the 1992 Games. It was argued that many of the developments merely repeated the efforts of the Francoist mayor Porcioles, albeit carried through with greater finesse and more attention to public goods (McNeill 1999: 114–33). Not least among the concerns was the protagonism of Juan Antonio Samaranch in the staging of the Barcelona Games.

After all, Samaranch was a prominent Francoist, speculative property developer, and target of the left during the transition. As president of the International Olympic Committee, Samaranch subsequently became embroiled in the worst crisis in the history of the organization of the Games. After emerging from the Salt Lake City bribes fiasco as the apparent saviour of the International Olympic Committee (IOC), Samaranch was honoured by the city in a cross-institutional gathering in 2002 and was invited by Joan Clos to assume an honorary role in the staging of the 2004 event – all of which raises questions about continuity (see Samaranch).

At any rate, the 2004 event – ostensibly set up to promote intercultural understanding – is in danger of becoming even more subordinate to private sector planning aims than the Olympics, with property development rendered anodyne by the 'intercultural' celebrations. As Balibrea argues:

> The use of terms such as dialogue, solidarity, human rights, civil society and sustainable development play a prominent role in defining a fashionable kind of progressive rhetoric which is in fact contradicted and refuted by the increasing inequalities that the facilitation of the project is generating in the city. (199)

As Capel ironically notes, the juxtaposition of the new districts and some of the most marginal (socially as well as territorially) corners of the city will make for some interesting interactions among Barcelonans:

> Only one of the projects seems to have been well thought out – the enormous shopping mall next to the Diagonal Mar's towers, right on the junction of the avenue with the Mediterranean, which can be the meeting place of the inhabitants of the working class districts of La Mina and the Southeast Besòs and the new inhabitants of the deluxe apartments [...]. That is if the Centre's guards [...] don't keep [the former] out as being undesirable. (11)

However the social mixing unfolds, it is clear that the 2004 project has shifted the centre of the city to the east. With the new skyscrapers at Glòries, the 22@ project, the Diagonal Mar developments, and

– not least – the high-speed train interchange at Sagrera (a long and highly politicized saga), Barcelona's eastern districts are now of growing strategic importance. This is a fact well recognized by Clos, and it awakens the political debate of the mid-1980s over the possible 'macrocephaly' of Barcelona within Catalonia, temporarily stalled by Pujol's abolition of the Metropolitan Corporation:

> There's a new frontier: the metropolitan area [...]. Where will La Fira grow? And the Ciudad Judicial? In l'Hospitalet. And the Forum 2004? In Sant Adrià. Our biggest projects are taking place outside our territory'. (Madueño and Aroca)

And as Barcelona changes shape, how are urban theorists to understand it?

Conclusion: Barcelona and urban theory

I have tried to chart briefly some of the themes and controversies that have dominated the post-Olympic transformation of Barcelona. But where does this leave our understanding of the city after 23 years of democratic governance in the broader context of urban studies? There are a number of issues fundamental to contemporary urban theory that I have only touched upon in this article, but these are issues that Barcelonophiles might wish to consider. First, the idea of erasure, the things of the city that are not there any more, be they buildings or experiences. This is a theme that has dominated the thinking of Vázquez Montalbán, for example, as he has dramatized the transformation of the Barrio Chino and Poblenou. Yet other writers have been exploring the same issues in different contexts (for example, Cobb on Paris; Klein on Los Angeles; Robb on Naples; and Spring on Glasgow). One might engage the sensory city as formulated by Amin and Thrift and think about noise and illumination (24–25). Or one might develop arguments made by Von Heeren regarding the apparent gentrification of the Old City.

Second, although I have mentioned splintering by way of Graham and Marvin, I have only hinted at the impact of the city's new extraterritoriality on its spatial logics, as it is Europeanized and encased in an ordering ideology of technoculture. How will the high-speed train, surviving *punt.com* culture, and skyscrapers affect the city's urban order? Third, how will the city be narrated in future years by its institutions, planners, and writers? Here, Guillamón offers numerous insights into how Barcelona is, just possibly, losing its cultural distinctiveness or identity. At the same time, however, it may be gaining new perspectives and imaginaries. One might also attend to how politicians script or embody the city (as Pasqual Maragall did and continues to do), or how the city engages with Catalonia as a whole. Fourth, how will the left cope with the increasing pressures of migration, economic restructuring, and Madrid-based neo-liberalism in its attempts to carve out a distinctive Barcelona model? Will the neighbourhood associations and the growing numbers of anti-globalization protestors in the city be able to mount a successful defence of the livable, cosmopolitan city? In many ways, even ten years after the Olympics, Barcelona is of growing relevance to urban theory.

Works cited

Álvaro, Francesc-Marc (2002). 'El "seny" global'. *La Vanguardia Digital.* 21 July. http://www.lavanguardia.es.

Amin, Ash, and Nigel Thrift (2002). *Cities: Reimagining the Urban* (Oxford: Polity).

Andreu, Marc, J. Gol, and A. Recio (2001). '22@, a cara o creu'. *La Veu del Carrer* 69: 12–13.

Angulo, Silvia (2002). 'El hotel del Raval tendrá forma elíptica y se iluminará de noche'. *La Vanguardia Digital.* 8 March. http://www.lavanguardia.es.

Balibrea, Mari Paz (2001). 'Urbanism, Culture and the Post-industrial City: Challenging the "Barcelona Model"'. *Journal of Spanish Cultural Studies* 2:2: 187–210.

Berman, Marshall (1999). 'Too Much is not Enough: Metamorphoses of Times Square', in Lynette Finch and Chris McConville (eds), *Gritty Cities: Images of the Urban* (Annandale, New South Wales: Pluto), 11–43.

Burns, Jimmy (1999). *Barça: A People's Passion* (London: Bloomsbury).

Capel, Horacio (2001). 'El Poblenou y la ciudad de los prodigios'. *La Veu del Carrer* 69: 11.

'Ciutat Vella cierra once terrazas en dos días por ruido y ocupación excesiva' (2002). *La Vanguardia.* 19 July.
Cobb, Richard (1995). *Paris and Elsewhere: Selected Writings* (London: John Murray).
Espadaler, Anton Maria (2002). '¿Es la Rambla un paseo?'. *La Vanguardia Digital.* 7 July. http://www.lavanguardia.es.
Graham, Stephen, and Simon Marvin (2001). *Splintering Urbanism: Networked Infrastructures, Technological Mobilities, and the Urban Condition* (London: Routledge).
Guillamón, Julià (2002). '¿Barcelona? No, Heron City'. *La Vanguardia Digital.* 10 July. http://www.lavanguardia.es.
Herranz, Elia (2001). 'A Barcelona li creixen els gratacels'. *La Veu del Carrer* 69: 22.
Holman, Otto (1996). *Integrating Southern Europe: EC Expansion and the Transnationalisation of Spain* (London: Routledge).
Klein, Norman M. (1997). *The History of Forgetting: Los Angeles and the Erasure of Memory* (London: Verso).
Lenskyj, Helen Jefferson (2000). *Inside the Olympic Industry: Power, Politics and Activism* (New York: SUNY Press).
Madueño, Eugeni, and Jaume V. Aroca (2002). 'Es la hora metropolitana, pero no defiendo un "superalcalde"'. Interview with Joan Clos. *La Vanguardia Digital.* 14 July. http://www.lavanguardia.es.
Madueño, Eugeni, and Josep Martí Gómez (2000). 'La entrevista: Joan Clos'. *Barcelona: Metròpolis Mediterrània* 44: 29–36.
McNeill, Donald (1999). *Urban Change and the European Left: Tales from the New Barcelona* (London: Routledge).
Montaner, Josep Maria (1999). 'Els models Barcelona', in Josep Maria Montaner et al., *Barcelona 1979/2004: del desenvolupament a la ciutat de qualitat* (Barcelona: Ajuntament de Barcelona), 24–26.
Monzó, Quim (2002). 'El turismo basura'. *La Vanguardia Digital.* 17 July. http://www.lavanguardia.es.
Quilley, Stephen (2000). 'Manchester First: From Municipal Socialism to the Entrepreneurial City'. *International Journal of Urban and Regional Research* 24: 601–15.
Recio, Albert (2002). 'Espais del capitalisme global'. *La Veu del Carrer* 72: 18–19.
Robb, Ian (1999). *Midnight in Sicily* (London: Vintage).
Robins, Kevin (1999). 'Foreclosing on the City? The Bad Idea of Virtual Urbanism', in John Downey and Jim McGuigan (eds), *Technocities* (London: Sage), 34–59.

'Samaranch: "Siempre estaré a disposición de Barcelona"' (2002). *La Vanguardia Digital.* 25 July. http://www.lavanguardia.es.

Skyscraper.com. http://www.skyscraper.com/english/worldmap/city/skyscrapers.html.

Soja, Edward. W. (2000). *Postmetropolis: Critical Studies of Cities and Regions* (Oxford: Blackwell).

Spring, Ian (1990). *Phantom Village: The Myth of the New Glasgow* (Edinburgh: Polygon).

Subirós, Pep (ed.) (n.d.), *El vol de la fletxa: Barcelona '92: Crónica de la Reinvenció de la Ciutat* (Barcelona: CCCB/Electra), 19–103.

Sudjic, Deyan (2002). 'There but for the Grace of Gaudí'. The *Observer.* 7 April. http://www.guardian.co.uk/archive.

Torres, Maruja (1988). 'Barcelona: Regreso a la ciudad de los prodigios'. *El País.* 13 March. Partly reproduced in Subirós n.d.: 19–103.

Vázquez Montalbán, Manuel (1990). *The Angst-Ridden Executive.* Trans. Ed Emery (London: Serpent's Tail).

—— (1992). *Barcelonas.* Trans. Andy Robinson (London: Verso).

Villar, Paco (1996). *Historia y leyenda del Barrio Chino (1900–1992): Crónica y documentos de los bajos fondos de Barcelona* (Barcelona: La Campana).

Von Heeren, Stefanie (2002). *La remodelación de Ciutat Vella: un análisis crítico del modelo Barcelona.* Trans. Arnim Schulz (Barcelona: Veïns en defensa de la Barcelona Vella).

Whitelegg, Drew (2000). 'Going for Gold: Atlanta's Bid for Fame'. *International Journal of Urban and Regional Research* 24: 801–17.

CHAPTER FOURTEEN

From the Olympic Torch to the Universal Forum of Cultures: The after-image of Barcelona's modernity*

Joan Ramon Resina

> Culture is just another name for propaganda.
>   Marc Fumaroli
>
> Sometimes an old, singular city, like Barcelona, by oversimplifying its identity, turns Generic. It becomes transparent, like a logo.   Rem Koolhaas

In the early 1930s, Élie Richard remarked of Catalans, 'This is a peasant race that is becoming conscious of modernity' (313). Richard was one of many French writers who visited Barcelona between the beginning of the century and the Civil War, but only he was able to capture the gist of the city's transformation in one sentence. Today, of course, we would not use the term *race* to designate ethnicity. Instead we would use the word *people*. Even so, the gap between the cultural reality that stared Richard in the face and the reality that

---

* This is an abridged version approved by the author of a chapter in Joan Ramon Resina, *Barcelona's Vocation of Modernity. Rise and Decline of an Urban Image* (Stanford: Stanford UP, 2008). © 2008 by the Board of Trustees of the Leland Stanford Jr. University. All rights reserved, Reprinted with permission of the publisher, Stanford University Press, sup.org.

meets the eye today is enormous. At that time, Barcelona was still a Catalan city bound to its hinterland by familial ties and by the steady flow of people, foodstuffs, and manufactured goods that sustained its growth through an osmotic relationship between the capital city and the territory. Today, Barcelona relates to Catalonia in an ambivalent, superficial way. Its primary connection is no longer kinship, history, or language, but the motorway and the weekend residence. At variance are many aspects of social and political life, to the point that it is justified to speak of a change of paradigm and not only of scale. I hesitate to call the new paradigm postmodern. My uneasiness with this term does not stem only from its proliferating connotations but above all from my suspicion that its usefulness for periodization is now exhausted, while the city's new historical cycle has just got under way. The implications of the 'post-' are particularly problematic in this case, because the present city does not activate all its historical resources but on the contrary seeks a rupture and a new beginning every so often, preferring short-lived illumination to the consciousness of what it experienced in the recent and not-so-recent past.

Some years ago I coined the term 'after-image' to designate temporally thick representations (Resina 2003). The term tries to account for the ghostly concurrence of phenomena originating in different temporal strata. This concurrence, which should not be mistaken for simultaneity, is counterintuitive only if one adheres to a linear conception of time in which events succeed each other seriatim, such that the arrival of one means inevitably the dismissal of another. But history does not work this way. A new social imaginary never completely replaces the old one. A memory of its origin in previous traditions lingers in the new value, making it difficult to establish the historical watershed with any certainty. But this continuity is often repressed and consigned to the social unconscious. Images have much to do with this process. Social images, which include images of the social, are belligerent; they contend with other images and occlude in order to make visible.

In the case of Barcelona, however, certain dates can be used as referents of an epochal shift, not least because they were originally conceived as such. Periodically, Barcelona stages rituals of self-display as a way of expediting urban renewal. Two Universal Expositions (1888 and 1929), two Olympic Games (1936 and 1992), a Catholic 'Eucharistic'

Congress (1952), and the recent Universal Forum of Cultures (2004) are defining moments for Barcelona's metropolitan consciousness. On each of these occasions, the event itself was far less important than its long-term impact on the city's physical configuration and public image. That the event was incidental to the setting could be easily shown with the help of any number of examples. But the point is readily made by referring to the unofficial guide to the city written by Carles Soldevila during the 1929 Universal Exposition. In *L'art d'ensenyar Barcelona* [The Art of Showing Barcelona], the self-styled tour guide compares himself to a *metteur en scène*. Ministering to the tourists' desire to see, he resolves not merely to show but to 'create' a city more interesting than the one available to the residents. He anticipates, in other words, the current marketing of city images.

This text reveals the onset of a split that will only grow larger as the century presses on - namely, the difference between the city of the tourists and that of the residents. What is more, it shows the former beginning to encroach on the latter. When Soldevila decides to manage the city's image, he deliberately neglects the site that was set up for the tourists and for the sake of which they had travelled in the first place: 'Your obligation is to show Barcelona. They can see the Expo on their own, as they please' (20). The problem with this zeal for authenticity is that it upsets the metonymic relationship of travel and turns the whole city into a tourist highlight, erasing the distinction between tourists and residents. Soldevila's promotion of the entire city to tourist sight helps us grasp that what unifies all the public festivals marking the growth episodes in the modern history of Barcelona is not the tribute to this or that contingent value of the day but the city-as-spectacle.

Yet the values are neither incidental nor simply instrumental. Contrary to widespread perception that the real stakes behind these macro-celebrations involve turning a profit, I contend that the deeper investment and long-term consequences relate to definition of the public sphere. Everything depends on the conditions prevailing in this sphere: the kind and intensity of the economic activity, the availability and spirit of the workforce, the smoothness or unevenness of the changes that redefine this activity. Societies apply varying means to ensure reasonable predictability of the public sphere. But whenever Barcelona is the object of study, it is crucial to keep in mind that this city's key feature is its separation from real political power. This is the clue to the wavering discourses and bizarre decisions of its leaders, and it explains the periodic return of cumbersome self-celebration.

For more than a century, modern Barcelona has absorbed migratory waves of increasing intensity and ever-more-distant origins. The result of these challenges has been an ever-deeper social segmentation and cultural heterogeneity, and consequently an ever-vaguer sense of identity as the ultimate ground of sociality. To conjure the danger posed by weakening common values, those in control of urban life have responded with rituals of community. In the nineteenth century, for instance, religious rituals such as the Corpus Christi procession engaged the population in concrete re-creation of a sense of community. During the Franco dictatorship, popular rituals such as sardana dances or activation of ancestral symbolism (as in Berga's traditional fire festival, la Patum) allowed people to rebuild their sense of 'organic solidarity' and perform 'an allegory of national death and resurrection' (Noyes: 117, 179). But in a quickly secularizing space, such rituals begin to lose their efficacy and are soon contested by counter-rituals (Kaplan). Gradually, traditional rituals were replaced by other means of visualizing self-production of a common will.

Charles Taylor links the rise of public festivals in postrevolutionary France to the republic's need to stage the transparency of the general will that was deemed to sustain the political community. In Barcelona, secular rituals were developed by the city's oligarchy as an ersatz for political representation of the collective will. In the absence of real sovereignty, public rituals proved useful as a means of projecting a space of sociality outside the political structures. In theory, the space thus constituted amounts to a public sphere, where citizens articulate values and express themselves *qua* citizens. As defined by Taylor, 'What the public sphere does is enable the society to come to a common mind, without the mediation of the political sphere, in a discourse of reason outside power, which nevertheless is normative for power' (91). Although this definition falls short of describing the complex relationship of Catalans to power, there is no denying that the discourse of reason ranks prominently in their imaginary. It attained normativity during the *noucentista* period and has remained central to Catalan politics ever since.

There is nothing essentialist about this fascination with an allegedly inherent trait. The tangential relationship of Catalan politics to power explains the centrality of *seny* (reasonableness) to its self-understanding. Being a simulation of government, the Catalan administration has always envisaged itself as a hybrid between civil society and state power. Deprived of genuine legislative prerogatives, Catalan officials seek to compensate their limited influence by relying on the public sphere. By doing so, they undermine this sphere and its democratic role as an unofficial system of checks and balances.

It is possible to trace changes in the meaning of public rituals. Although Barcelona authorities have often appealed to a tradition of urban celebrations to justify subsequent ones, it is clear that their purpose and scope has changed over time, as has the society that theoretically sponsors these events. At the end of the nineteenth century, Barcelona was still an organic extension of Catalonia, but it was already the site where Catalan society culled symbolic victories over the state. In the rough and tumble of fast social change, Barcelona was being propelled into modernity by its political marginality. Single-mindedly bent on production and exchange, the city was emerging from a century of concentrated work and painstaking accumulation of resources into a life of action and a politics of representation. Paradoxically, the self-limitation inherent in the primacy given to the economic over the political gave Catalonia the lead in Spain's modernization. The emergence of Catalanism was the mark of society's reconstitution on secular ground. This is proven *a contrario* by the efforts of the Catholic Church to hitch national energies and divert them from their worldly calling. As Taylor explains, 'The economy is the first mode of society of the new sort... a society constituted purely extra-politically and in profane time. It forms part of the background to the rise of the public sphere. It seems very plausible that the explanation of each is interlinked with that of the other' (104). This means in effect that both the Marxicizing critiques of Catalanism as tainted by bourgeois class interests and the efforts to counter those critiques by seeking lower-class origins for national consciousness miss the point. Catalanism arose within a society that was oriented towards the economy because it was hemmed in, in other respects. A ruse of history turned limitation into advantage, as the economy gradually imposed its peculiar *seny* and means–end rationality. Economic empiricism laid the basis of the public sphere, and in this regard it makes no difference whether 'conservative' or 'progressive' Catalanism gets the credit. Mere descriptors of social class, these categories do not signify what was new in this social identity. Catalanism, as a broad, transversal movement, represented the self-sufficiency of a public sphere outside the political organization of the state.

This movement grew in importance throughout the first half of the twentieth century, retaining its hegemony (regardless of political divisions) until the 19 July revolution, and then the Spanish Civil War put an end to Catalonia's democratic nationalization. The Universal Exposition of 1929, celebrated under the dictatorship of General Primo de Rivera, was the last international event before the war, because the army's revolt on 18 July 1936 precluded inauguration of the antifascist Olympics on that very day. The war arrested the Catalan government's plan for a spectacular city designed by Le Corbusier and the Group of Catalan Architects and Technicians for the Progress of Contemporary Architecture (GATCPAC) with the workers' needs in mind. Neither the so-called Macià Plan nor Catalonia's national consolidation was to be. Lost also was the self-evident complementarity of both schemes of development, the urban and the national. With good reason, Antoni Rovira i Virgili could say in his journal of the last days of Republican Catalonia that the damage inflicted on the city by the fascist air raids was a national punishment: 'The strikes against Barcelona are aimed not so much against the city as against the nation' (15). In addition to the fifteen hundred buildings destroyed by the bombs, and the thousands of casualties, the needless damage to the civil infrastructure and services, which continued into the postwar, reveals that Barcelona was made to pay for its symbolic status, because the punishment inflicted on it reverberated throughout Catalan society. Says Manuel Delgado: 'Apart from the material and psychological damage caused, generalized mass aggressions against a city serve to symbolically summon and inform it that it has been sentenced for being what it is, or rather, for being what its inhabitants have made it' (1996: 106).

Towards the Olympics

The pre-Olympic period began with the appointment of Oriol Bohigas as head of Barcelona's Department of City Planning in 1980. In 1985 he published *Reconstrucció de Barcelona*, a text that repudiates the grand projects of the Francoist era in favour of limited intervention in urban space. In this collection of practical recommendations, contextualization and respect for community contrast with the callous developmentalism of previous years. But although his watchword was 'regeneration', little in the execution of reforms did justice to the term's organic overtones. Bohigas favoured monumentalization of open spaces through architectural design of a markedly avant-garde character. With his blessing, his disciples inflicted the unpopular *places dures* on a city that was starved of green space. Bohigas's 'Mediterranean' predilection for the street as 'living space' underpinned a politics of 'urbanization' of open spaces turning over potential park sites to the architectural establishment. Whether in Albert Viaplana and Helio Piñón's Plaça dels Països Catalans, which someone has described as 'a garden of ideas in which no concession to greenery is made' (Barril and Català-Roca: 16); in the Moll de la Fusta; in the space newly opened in front of the Museu d'Art Contemporani de Barcelona (MACBA); or in the many squares reformed during this period, architects have studiously avoided any 'regression' to nature. Instead they have indulged in conceptual virtuosity, which unfortunately does little to relieve the oppressiveness of an overbuilt city.

This model, inspired by the Venetian *campi* and the squares of other Italian cities with far lower density and smaller dimensions than Barcelona, not only lives on in sculpturesque 'parks' such as Diagonal-Mar but has infected the scarce open spaces of high-density peripheral municipalities and of many medium-sized townships throughout Catalonia. But Bohigas remains adamant: 'An urban space is not a landscape, in other words, it is not an artificial or mimetic version of nature. It is architecture with all its features, adapted to architecture's own projective methods and motivated by its social and cultural objectives' (2004: 180). The consequence is clear: no room ought to be left in Barcelona for the relief afforded to Central European conurbations by magnificent parks and wise distribution of greenery throughout the urban space. Instead, space-starved Barcelonans must bow to architectural exploitation of their social habitat and resign themselves to the tyranny of 'a mineral and architectural city that rules out any landscaping fancy' (180).

It is always possible to distil meaning from decontextualized form and, depending on the degree of utopianism, claim civic virtues for elitist artwork. Pep Subirós, in an article published at the height of the *places dures* controversy, hazarded the opinion that

> in Barcelona, the formalist, often abstract character of the new public spaces and monuments reflects not only or mainly certain trends of contemporary art, but the fact that what the municipal government wants to celebrate is neither power nor glory but civility, creativity and freedom. The new monuments and spaces must represent nothing but the reconquest of the city by the citizens. (109)

The facile assertion that modern Barcelona has no reason to celebrate power or glory, but, as a civil society, must celebrate the values of bourgeois humanism smuggles in the more questionable principles on which City Hall legitimized its intrusions in urban space.

The first of these axioms is, in an odd military terminology, the notion of a popular 'reconquest' of the city, as if real estate had actually changed hands and residents were the agents rather than the resigned (or at best reconciled) users of the new public spaces, which celebrate the citizens' 'freedom' against their increasing insecurity and vocal complaints. Objectively, the only reconquest that has come about is that of commercially recycled space. In the world of facts, this is achieved by altering the uses of space and, hence, its users. Over the last three decades, an unprecedented depredation of the patrimony has generated the spaces on which the coalition of public power and private capital has most relied to act on the city's morphology (Ordiguer: 53).

The second axiom of the municipal doctrine regards the populist, rather than popular, value of abstraction in a consumer's democracy based on erasure of the traditional culture of the senses. The ravages to that culture go hand in hand with the obsolescence of the vocabulary that made Catalan a distinct language rather than a translated patois well into the Franco era, because language (*pace* Saussure) is not an arbitrary, supracultural code, but instead relates directly to experience. Thus the encroachment and devastation of a home-grown language is a sure means of replacing the mores of a people, and ultimately of replacing the people themselves.

By withholding much-needed parks and gardens in adequate number and scale, the municipal government turned its back on the Catalan tradition of the *eixida* (from the Latin *exire*, to exit). An enclosed back yard found in many small town houses, the *eixida* was a liminal space of communion with nature. Maria Jesús Buxó considers it 'a surrogate magic space for the forest, where all the elements were present', and where 'identities were recreated' (212). But in socialist Barcelona, renewal of identity - nay, identity itself - is unmentionable. Identity is what makes people and groups want to persist in their being. It resists transformation, and without transformation there is no commodification and no surplus value. The unrelenting hardness of the post-industrial city has produced a new kind of *eixida*, or 'exiting', that of weekenders leaving the city in droves to seek snippets of unprocessed landscape around the epidemic conglomerates of vacationers' homes. In the meantime, 'rural Catalonia' has become a misnomer for a subordinated hinterland that supplies the healing spaces Barcelona has outsourced to villages that once seemed picturesque. According to the Catalan Agricultural Foundation, currently each Barcelona resident is using 3.3 hectares or 21 square miles of so-called biological land, that is, forest or cultivated land necessary for renewal of carbon dioxide. If the Barcelona model of consumption were evenly applied throughout the territory, it would require a land five times the size of Catalonia (Fundació Agrícola Catalana: 25).[1]

A 'sustainable future', to use the politicians' buzzword, does not lie in further densification of Barcelona and its exploding suburbs, but in the once-feasible and now thorny integration of rural and urban. Barcelona's failure to implement this idea, which was once championed by every modern planner, has led to an unsustainable pattern of settlement involving ownership of double and even triple residences on the part of large sections of the city's upper and

---

1 Whereas in its entire modern history the metropolitan region occupied 20,000 hectares, between 1972 and 1997 it added another 30,000. If we include metropolitan facilities on the outskirts of the urban area, such as water-treatment plants, rubbish tips, prisons, golf courses, and hotel installations, then another 9,500 hectares must be counted. This does not take into consideration the land officially designated as non-urban but occupied by infrastructures such as high-voltage power lines, which occupy some 10,000 hectares. The result has led the European Environment Agency to point out that metropolitan Barcelona is among the territories with the highest concentration of problems deriving from hyperurbanization (Ordiguer).

middle classes. Barring solutions involving an acceptable density and balanced ratio of pavement to green, further urbanization will only worsen the city's oppressiveness and its pressure on the land. Yet planning remains firmly ensconced in the trend that Bohigas set 40 years ago, when in *noucentista* fashion he warned against the Northern European 'myth' of the low-density city, extolling the Mediterranean tradition of 'a life made of constant personal contacts, of stacking up, of shoving and street conviviality' (1963: 119). In 1961, Bohigas supported this opinion by reference to 'economic requirements and a situation of serious underdevelopment' (1963: 119). Four decades later, underdevelopment is hardly more than a memory for the majority of the population, while the economic exigencies (that is, the price of urban land) have increased manifoldly. Yet instead of Barcelonans bridling at construction and encouraging decentralization of services, their new affluent lifestyles and the liquidation of the traditional family lend Bohigas arguments for the compact city and for slashing the size of apartments in the money-churning business of redevelopment. This model of intense exploitation of the square metre and privatization of municipal land has metastasized to adjacent municipalities, setting a chain reaction in the gobbling up of the ecological reserves that should have yielded the metropolitan region's natural parks and gardens.

Although there is unbroken continuity with the Franco era's development policies, the chief impulse to the present overconstruction was the concession of the 1992 summer Olympics to Barcelona in 1986. The previous year, Jordi Borja, the mayor's deputy, in the course of an interview for the journal *L'Avenç* laid out City Hall's policy for the next decades. In the future, he said, only small cities could remain culturally integrated with their territory. Large cities must be open to external forces and ready to change their cultural components in order to compete on the world scale (Guillamon). This intrusive model, engineered by municipal think tanks, conceived the city as a venal commodity to be packaged and sold to an upscale international clientele. As a precondition, the city must be stripped of its historical identity, which now came to be seen as a hindrance to capitalization of the land. The result was an increasingly abstract city settled by uprooted individuals without a long-term relationship with the country, while the sharp rise in property prices sent many native youths to the periphery or into minimalist dwellings unfit for raising families. But what are overpayment and discomfort compared to the political benefits of compression and scale? Mere hitches, according to Bohigas, who, during the first rash of disorderly building in the 1960s, insisted on the upside of densification: 'For the history of Catalonia - and thus for the definitive well-being of Catalans - the present hygienic condition of rooms may be less important than [Barcelona's] potential for exerting a definitive political weight in the future' (1963: 131).

Bohigas was aware that a politically accented urbanism required the cooperation of actual political power:

> On the one hand, planning is a means to impose a social structure designed by political thought. On the other hand, it needs the assurance that a long-term political action will support the social evolution prearranged in the urban plan. In short: planning must be attached to policy, and this policy must be truly hegemonic in the country. (1963: 127)

Less than two decades later, policy rose to meet the urbanist's needs. Enter the PSC. Since 1979, the Socialist Party of Catalonia has enjoyed uninterrupted municipal power in Barcelona. During this period, its cadres have profoundly altered not only the city's physical appearance but also its social and cultural traits. For a second time since the early twentieth century, culture writ large served as an alibi for a territorial supremacism beholden to traditional priorities of command. In a chapter entitled 'Beyond Nationalism', Pasqual Maragall appropriated d'Ors's preference for a Catalonia-city over a Catalonia-nation. Implied in denationalization of the Catalan territory was the ambition to coordinate it from Barcelona, and implicitly from the institutions governed by the Socialist party (1986: 119). Brushing aside the balmy definition of Catalonia-city as a territory structured by a web of cities, Manuel Delgado puts reality into the picture: 'In practice, the chosen model was not so much a metaphysical Catalonia-city as a ravaging and absorbing Barcelona-metropolis that remains committed to the urban-imperial goals of the Franco era' (1998: 122).

Industrial Catalonia was polynuclear, with major centres of production in mid-sized towns such as Terrassa and Sabadell, which for that reason became discrete centres of modernist art and architecture. But after the textile crisis of the seventies, the expansive sectors of the culture and information society began to reorganize space according to their needs. Implementing the tertiary paradigm exacerbated the hierarchical model of space, aggravating zoning by age, education, and acquisitive power. In effect, 'the [economic] sectors that now concentrate the innovative activities which constitute the new metropolitan factory appoint themselves policemen of the territories (metropolitan regions or macro-regions) where the diffuse factory is installed' (López: 92). By 2004 this process had reached an advanced stage of development after a quarter of a century of functional assimilation of adjacent municipalities to Barcelona's area of influence. During the period, the pace of expansion grew exponentially, from an urban mesh of 62 municipalities and 1,010 km^2 in 1981 to 216 municipalities and 4,597 km^2 in 1996, in a process that will accelerate with the arrival of the high-speed train, which threatens to incorporate the Catalan provincial capitals into Barcelona's expansive dynamics (Nel·lo).

If autonomy is defined as management of the origin and goals of the mobility that is generated within municipal jurisdiction, then the consequence of Barcelona's centripetal force has been loss of autonomy for the municipalities that are caught in its orbit. In the province of Barcelona, municipalities retaining less than 50 per cent of their labour mobility (people working within the municipal limits) increased from 102 to 208 out of 310 in the ten years after Barcelona's selection as Olympic see; the trend continued at the end of the century (Nel·lo). Possibly the most spectacular increase in dependence involves the area of culture, which has become nearly a monopoly of the central city. Even affluent middle-sized towns have failed to generate the cultural amenities that one finds in smaller cities in England, Germany, and the United States. Trapped instead in the French *banlieue* model, most of these towns have blended into the grey area of the *Zwischenstadt* (Sieverts). There, people trade residential comfort for growing anomie and utter cultural dependence on the metropolitan core. This situation deteriorates dramatically as we move beyond the metropolitan area, which concentrates 83 per cent of Catalonia's scientific foundations and 77 per cent of all cultural foundations (Pedraforca). Such concentration argues for the establishment of a Greater Barcelona administration, but this step would require authorization by the Spanish government, which is always loath to increase Barcelona's political status. During the 1970s, mayor Josep Maria Porcioles's requests for the creation of a Greater Barcelona were met only halfway, with the creation in 1974 of the 'Metropolitan Corporation', which subordinated 26 satellite municipalities to Barcelona.

Officially, the purpose of the Metropolitan Corporation was to rationalize infrastructures and coordinate the transportation system, but the new entity would also have given City Hall unrestricted sway over development of a huge area in the next cycle of growth (Carreras: 472). The territorial reorganization would have brought half of Catalonia's population and most of its infrastructure under Barcelona's jurisdiction. This is no doubt the reason the Catalan government of Convergència i Unió dissolved the corporation; the Socialists responded with persistent efforts to replace the Catalan territorial model with a skeleton of conurbations in which the PSC was hegemonic thanks to the concentration of Spanish immigrants in the fifties and sixties. Continuities in planning between the Porcioles and Socialist eras cannot be gainsaid. Pasqual Maragall had, after all, been in City Hall since the days of Porcioles. City Hall, in the sixties as in the nineties, was committed to developing the larger features of the 1953 Plan General Comarcal, which included the Partial Ribera Plan, a private scheme for development of the coastline between the district of Barceloneta and the municipality of Sant Adrià de Besòs.

In 1966, the company la Ribera S.A. was constituted to promote the plan, a first instalment of which the city government approved on 2 February 1968, only to reject it two years later under pressure from organized opposition. The correction, though, was merely tactical. On 13 August 1970, City Hall approved a modified 'Plan del Sector Marítimo Oriental', which preserved the substance of the earlier plan (Martí and Moreno). Today's Barcelona is perfectly discernible in the general plans of the Franco era, whose executor the socialist administration became. Initially, those plans were called 'utopian' because of their enormous cost and the huge resistance they would encounter (Martí and Moreno). But, as these authors observe, utopia often disguises speculative inroads into the future. Barcelona has a tradition of perverting grandiose visions by the very social powers that called the visions into being. Part of the problem is that chronic lack of public financing is met by sectorial development linked to speculation, so that profits are expected to offset expenditures even before the projects are brought to completion. Public financing subsidizes the costs of infrastructure and services, while private capital reaps the commercial rewards. This murky procedure relies on legerdemain to divert attention. Since taxpayers must be anesthetized to the fact that they bear the cost of speculation and are deprived of parks and natural areas in the process, City Hall seduces them with 'ludic areas', 'equipment zones', large-scale spectacles, and the mantra of universal participation.

Planning of (the games of) planning

The 1992 Olympic games, the first post-Franco macro-festival, were Barcelona's coming of age as a world city. Planned much earlier, the Games were conceived from the beginning as an incentive for urban transformation along the lines charted by the Plan General Comarcal [General District Plan] of 1974. In the mid-1970s, Catalonia's industry was at the end of its tether, and it was apparent that the economy had to be placed on a new footing. A new general metropolitan plan, approved in 1976, created conditions for the post-industrial city as an area of intensified consumption (Tello). It was no coincidence that the original Olympic project affected primarily the Vallès district on the other side of Mount Tibidabo. The metropolitan plan targeted precisely this area, which, with a surface five times (477 km^2) that of Barcelona, hardly doubled Barcelona's population. Nor was it by chance that the Olympics finally came to Barcelona by the hand of Juan Antonio Samaranch, the president of the International Olympic Committee (IOC). Back in 1974, Samaranch was president of the Diputación (the central government's area office) of Barcelona. He also presided over the permanent commission of the Consorcio Urbanístico del Maresme, an investment group dedicated to planning infrastructures within the metropolitan area (Martí and Moreno).

With this background, placid narratives of redevelopment being 'necessitated by the Olympics' (Hargreaves: 62) seem disingenuous. The truth is the Olympics were necessitated by redevelopment schemes. If these schemes conspicuously affected the waterfront, this was not on account of the nautical competitions but because the games were a pretext to fulfil some of the objectives of the Ribera Plan, an ambitious project from the pre-democratic era. That project would come to completion only a full decade after the Olympics with the opening of Diagonal-Mar and the five-month extravaganza known as the Universal Forum of Cultures (9 May to 26 September 2004). None of this took place on virgin land. Hence, in the pre-Olympic years, the Commission for the Strategic, Economic, and Social Plan of Barcelona 'negotiated' removal of human obstacles from the affected areas. Olympic development involved urbanization of municipal land, breaking previous agreements with neighbours' associations, which demanded provision of public spaces and services. To drown the opposition under a wave of consensus, City Hall advertised its interventions with slogans such as *ciutat cara al mar* [a city turned towards the sea] - which had been coined by the Plan de la Ribera society - and similar catchphrases: *Barcelona posa't guapa* [Barcelona, doll yourself up], *Barcelona, més que mai* [Barcelona, more than ever], *la ciutat de tots* [the people's city], and so on. Such ditties were part and parcel of the manufacture of upbeat images to make capital-driven redevelopment look like a collective enterprise. They are really after-images, in that they posit their own dialectical negation: *ciutat d'esquena al mar* [a city with its back towards the sea]. These catchwords both create overdetermined contrasts in order to foster illusion and prevent their addressees from looking backstage into the methods of image production.

The Olympic games were a large-scale marketing operation based on the production of glamorous images. In his role as president of the Barcelona Games Organizing Committee (COOB), Mayor Pasqual Maragall was well aware of the stakes when, in an address to the Association of Journalists in 1991, he urged fellow citizens to stuff their eyes with images (Benach). He knew the Games were not for local consumption but for the millions of televisitors who would converge on 'the greatest TV and communications event of all time', in the words of Miquel de Moragas (Gavaldà: 4). Nor were they a self-exhausting event. Their purpose was to promote Barcelona not just as a fleeting centre of consumption but as an object of consumption in its own right. Wrapped in a sleek image, the city would sell.

The aptest symbol of the Games could well be the image of the archer shooting the flaming arrow that set the Olympic torch ablaze. This splendid image is imbued with sacredness derived from the elementary nature of fire, the solemn progress of the relay, and the archer's arresting marksmanship. A synthetic image, if ever there was one. With world TV cameras trained on the flight of the arrow and the inauguration of the Games hinging on the felicity of the archer's aim, there was no room for chance. And so the Olympic torch was ignited in synchrony with the arrow's trajectory, producing a breathtaking effect. This image condenses the entire spectacle; it is a fitting allegory of the Games.

The COOB redesigned a global sports event as a 'total event', which included deployment of the symbols of the monarchy and various levels of government in carefully calculated proportions at previously agreed moments. As a total event, the Games had to incorporate civil society. So by dexterously maximizing the ancillary rituals (such as the progress of the Olympic flame through Catalonia and Spain) the COOB was able to slot in celebrities even before inauguration day. For the anonymous mass, participation opened up with the armies of volunteers whose unpaid work contributed to organizational success. Maragall could reasonably gauge Barcelona's post-Franco culture by such participation: 'The profoundest phenomenon of [Barcelona's] cultural resurgence has gone unnoticed to the polemicists, because it has occurred precisely in the everyday world of volunteer work and popular leisure' (Maragall and Guillemet: 89). The mention of popular leisure in connection with culture is symptomatic of the new dispensation. Nationalism required a strong notion of culture centred on historical singularity and elevated enough to claim spiritual universality. It is otherwise in a period of national retrenchment, when culture becomes an object of management.

In the 1950s and 1960s, culture became the last shelter of Catalan society and politics. It was a broad strategy to *fer país* [build the nation], and the polymorphous cause of the latter's visualization, under daunting conditions. But by the 1980s and 1990s, with formal guarantees in place and a considerable decrease in social commitment, a new elite of Spanish-speaking functionaries took over the task of attacking Catalan culture. Culture was becoming an ideological weapon, which explains Maragall's allusion to 'the polemicists'. Still, used generically the word *culture* commanded universal respect. This is no doubt the reason Maragall produced a 'cultural Olympics' out of his top hat, to the delight of artists and intellectuals who pined to participate. After all, these were no longer an ordinary Olympics but a *Gesamtkunstwerk* [universal work of art]. Tenors and sopranos, theatre companies, flamenco singers, choreographers, whoever or whatever had any entertainment value, was put on display. Nothing was spared in the effort to lift the city out of its provincial cocoon into the glory of universal image. During the Games, the images most frequently broadcast on television, aside from athletic ones, showed empty lots and obsolete structures changing in a matter of seconds into the splendid buildings of Olympic Barcelona (Benach). The world was riveted by the magic.

Fill your eyes with images!

It was all about images – retinal images, to be precise. Speaking to the Association of Journalists the previous year, Maragall was aware that the value of an image lies mainly in its retention. Only images that are dramatic enough to act on the brain centres stand a chance of weathering the flood of visual stimuli unleashed by technomodernity. Lasting images of this kind are called after-images. But in a more theoretical sense, after-images are ones fraught with history; seen from a temporal perspective, they document conflict. Conflict – or, rather, awareness of it – is what Barcelona promoters wanted to prevent at all costs. Tense symbolic struggles between social groups and institutions filled the period leading up to the Games. At issue were the character and degree of visualization of the political host (Hargreaves). When the IOC selected Barcelona on 17 October 1986, Maragall told King Juan Carlos I: 'Sir, we have won. Barcelona for Spain!' (Bassa: 13). At the same time, Spanish premier Felipe González announced that 1992, would be 'the quincentennial of Spanish unity' (Bassa: 20). Barcelona was flooded with billboards advertising the Year of Spain and the Discovery of Spain. The official watchword was unequivocal: in and through the Games, wayward Catalonia would be reassimilated into Spain. When incidents took place between security forces and the population, the media looked dutifully the other way. The Guardia Civil, a hated security force, escorted the Olympic flame through Catalonia. In symbolic places such as Montserrat, in Vic and Banyoles, towns where Catalan sentiment ran high, tanks were about.

In Banyoles, anti-Olympic militants received menacing phone calls, found threats at the workplace, and saw their cars vandalized and their homes trespassed. This chain of events culminated in the sinister Operation Garzón, a pre-emptive strike against potential use of the Olympics as a billboard for Catalonia's independence.

On 29 June, one month before the inauguration, Judge Baltasar Garzón ordered nearly 40 people arrested on charges of membership of Terra Lliure, a national liberation organization that self-dissolved two years earlier without ever causing any casualties. By the end of the operation, more than 60 suspects were apprehended and deprived of constitutional rights in an action that, as later became apparent, had been planned in advance from the summit of the state. Three years after the Olympics, 25 people were arraigned and 23 sentenced to long prison terms. The court qualified the sentence with these words: 'It is true and obvious that the band Terra Lliure... was dissolved and dismantled a long time ago and its danger at the present moment may be considered null' (quoted in Bassa: 118). Something was clearly amiss because, at the same time that the court condemned the defendants as putative members of a nonexistant organization, it pleaded with the government to grant amnesty to all but two of the prisoners, recommending their immediate release. The government not only complied but also took care to amnesty the two remaining inmates a few days before the ruling party, the PSOE, lost the general elections, as forecast by every survey.

On their release, many detainees denounced their torture and mishandling while in custody, but Spanish courts failed to take legal action while Parliament refused to order an investigation even after the routine torture of prisoners in the Intxaurrondo garrison and the socialist government's responsibility in the assassination of Basque militants came into the open. When the plaintiffs took their case to the European Commission of Human Rights, it took the commission more than six months to notify the claimants that it would not bring legal action against the Spanish state. Eight years later, however, the European Court of Human Rights determined that Spain had violated article 3 of the European Human Rights Convention and sentenced the state to compensate 15 detainees for 'moral damage' (Balanzà 2004).

What makes this incident noteworthy is its relationship to the Olympic wars of representation. The mop-up of activists occurred shortly after the Office of Olympic Security announced plans to 'avoid propaganda acts by radical groups'. Later, the Ministry of the Interior claimed that its intention had been to ensure a placid Olympics. It appears now that the operation was more ambitious and had many more targets in sight, including newspapers, civic associations such as Omnium Cultural, and political parties such as Esquerra Republicana de Catalunya; in other words, the strategy was aimed against Catalan activism broadly. The Spanish media did not cover the facts and presented only the government's version of the affair. The journal *El País*, the main unofficial channel for the socialist government's propaganda, seriously breached the ethics of the press, to the point of making information indistinguishable from police work (Bassa: 155).[2]

El País was not the only medium that failed to live up to the professional ethic. The PSC pressed the Administration Council of the Catalan public consortium of Radio and Television (Corporatió Catalana de Radio i Televisió; CCRTV) to discipline those responsible for airing an interview in which Carles Bonaventura, one of the detainees on 29 June, described the torture administered by the police. Under political pressure, the director of TV3 removed Salvador Alsius, director of the midday news, and Catalunya Ràdio followed suit by removing Jordi Vendrell for casting doubt on the behaviour of the Guardia Civil. The socialists not only approved of Judge Garzón's operation, they also blocked the Esquerra Republicana de Catalunya deputies from bringing the matter up for debate in the Catalan Parliament on 14 July. The PSC's secretary, Josep Maria Sala (himself imprisoned shortly afterwards for masterminding illegal financing of the Spanish Socialist Party), declared: 'We cannot permit this small minority to stop us from taking the opportunity of showing the world in the next few weeks how tolerant and co-habiting we are' (*El País*, 19 July 1992; quoted in Hargreaves: 85). The small minority was a legal party with elected representatives in Parliament, but as Sala's language betrays, the PSC saw itself as the primary broker and chief political beneficiary of the

---

2 Heavy reliance on this journal's editorials and opinion articles vitiates Hargreaves's account of the political strategies in and around the Olympics. Under the guise of academic detachment, he furnishes a sanitized picture of the state nationalist offensive, playing up certain facts, silencing others, and in general discrediting opinions and persons associated with the Catalan cause.

Games. More compassionate, Maragall seemed to regret at least some of the costs of success when he declared, 'Some had to pay for all the unjust price of politics' (2004: 67).

The question was, would Catalonia host the Games, or would Spain? Although this question was not decided merely at the level of symbols, the struggle was especially insidious at that level. City Hall gave away complimentary city flags after changing the Catalan bars into Spanish stripes. At the door of the Olympic stadium police tore up Catalan flags, asking their bearers for identification and in some cases detaining them. But there were concessions to regional sentiment. While the COOB discouraged the national symbols, it dressed the girls making medal presentations in traditional Catalan costume (Hargreaves). Years later Maragall admitted:

> I wanted to assure the head of the Spanish government that the Mayoral Presidency of the COOB 92 understood the spirit of his words: keeping security as a priority, and working politically and in detail to ensure an image of the country which corresponded to the effort made and the enormous opportunity we had before us. (2004: 68–69)

As in a panopticon, power was a matter of visual control. What could be seen, by whom, and from where? Such questions involved high-level decisions and institutional hierarchies. Amid the war for representation, vice president of the Spanish government Narcís Serra (of the PSC) invoked tolerance as the key organizational feature, intimating that insistence on representing Catalonia by its language and political symbols would impair the welcoming of foreign visitors (Hargreaves). Maragall, more idyllically, put the emphasis on happiness. Barcelona was not a conflicted city in the pangs of a troubled historical memory, but a happy city; this was the image that it ought to give to the world (*El País*, 15 April 1992; cited in Hargreaves 72). An image synthesizing neither singularity nor political aspiration but precision and exhilaration: in the end this was the impression left on the retina of world audiences by the arrow bursting into flame at the intersection of the cosmic with visual high-tech.

A formula that works

In 1991 Maragall sought to insert the Olympic enterprise into a logic of historical necessity: 'The generation of 1992 must complete metropolitan Barcelona. This is a natural, logical, inevitable sequence which we may not give up' (*L'estat de la ciutat* 74–75; quoted in Benach: 503). It was also an expansive sequence, which may explain Maragall's recourse to teleology. He was not speaking about the city within the municipal limits that confined his political power at the time. In the 1980s, Barcelona was for all intents and purposes a finished city, so that as Ignasi de Solà Morales observed, 'More than to great expansive projects, the city must now turn to improving its own patrimony [..]. A great city pledged to its own restoration, such is the horizon to which architecture, both public and private, appears to be committed' (29). But in modern Barcelona municipal power has always gone hand in hand with urban expansion. Maragall knew this and sought to legitimate the new horizon of development by linking it up with the perspective of the turn-of-the-century bourgeoisie.

Laying claim to completion of the historical logic presented certain disadvantages, however, because it mortgaged the political future. In fact, municipal planners had already discerned that it was better if the '92 generation did not totally fulfil its historical mission. A few years earlier, J. Esteban stated: 'It is not necessarily a good idea to try to finish the city. This goal would not be achieved anyway by carelessly developing all available land, and important options for the future would be lost' (quoted in Tello: 517). This view was incorporated into the Strategic Plan Barcelona 2000, which for the first time favoured ongoing planning. The intention was not so much to renounce production of an image of the city as to reserve the freedom to generate countless images through cyclic renewal of the marriage between planning and spectacle.

The Olympics permitted the 'regeneration' and 'revitalization' of the waterfront but gave the city the *cinturons de ronda* for peripheral distribution of traffic and opened the tunnels that channelled Barcelona's demographic overflow onto the Vallès. But this was merely one stage in completing the Metropolitan Plan. Immediately the focus of attention turned northeast to the mouth of the Besòs River at the limit of Barcelona's municipality. Long derelict and settled by a marginal population, this seafront area now beckoned the planners. But how could they leap to it, amid the post-Olympic contraction and with a central government notoriously disinclined to invest in the region? After the Olympic fever, things were much as they had been in the eighties. The municipality controlled a considerable amount of public land but lacked the resources to renovate neglected areas and update infrastructures. Resorting to a classic method, City Hall 'requalified' public land and turned it over to private developers. But socialists could not do this without a 'worthy' pretext, and to create it the mayor availed himself of a proven recipe. Thus emerged the Universal Forum of Cultures.

Once more, a large-scale festival would dignify the marketing of public land, and blown-up publicity (to the tune of $US 100 million) would bring about swift appreciation of the real estate. The scale of the event would open the purse of public investment, because no administration would want to miss out on an international stunt. The idea had an additional virtue: by attracting tourists, the happening would help defray the organizational costs and fuel the leisure economy. The nature of the event was irrelevant; what mattered was making international waves. Turning to a time-honoured tradition, Maragall proposed a Universal Exposition. But there was a snag. World fairs are subject to a calendar, and none could be had in 2004. Undeterred, Maragall proclaimed that Barcelona would design its own international event. This time, the pretext was not going to be the region's bygone industrial brawn or world-class athletics. No, this time Barcelona would summon world culture for an open, friendly, egalitarian, and above all participatory dialogue. Peace, democracy, tolerance, multiculturalism, ecoconsciousness: the world's progressive values would be hosted by – indeed, they would radiate from – Barcelona.

The Universal Forum of Cultures, 'the Forum', as Barcelonans called it, was Maragall's bequest to Joan Clos, his successor in office. A grey, unoriginal administrator where Maragall is a quirky improviser, Clos summarized the goals of Strategic Plan Barcelona 2000 by repeating that cities are like businesses and must be promoted by emphasizing what they do well. What were Barcelona's assets? Clos listed a series of dog-eared axioms. It is one of people's favourite cities to live and work in (as if most people shopped for their place of residence). It is civilized, friendly, and hospitable (and, he might have added, dirty, noisy, and crime-ridden). Its climate promotes life in the street (hence apartments shrink even as their prices increase). Its squares and public objects are stylish (rather than soothing to the eye and comfortable to the body). It values public space (and privatizes it when the value reaches an irresistible level).

Maragall had already vaunted the importance of design in Barcelona, praising *modernisme*'s amorous attention to detail. Such aesthetic intensification, in his view, compensates Barcelona for the loss of status as political capital (Maragall and Guillemet). The idea of a compensatory *modernisme* is plausible only if one forgets that this 'style' was the historical achievement of the same bourgeoisie that conceived Barcelona as capital of a refounded national polity. It is impossible not to notice that *modernista* buildings overflow with references to the Catalan nation. Like it or not, Gaudí, Barcelona's uncontested architectural genius, for whose sake millions of tourists trek to this city each year, was everything City Hall socialists and their cultural retinue abhorred.

Catalanism of the early twentieth century produced a Gaudí, a Domènech i Montaner, a Puig i Cadafalch, a Jujol. Where is the Catalan architect of the socialist period whose international reputation rests on any of the buildings that have gone up in Barcelona since 1979? Sure, Barcelona is now a show window of signature works by global architects. But does this permanent exposition of roving styles reveal the city's character? During the inaugural session of the conference 'Ciutat i Ciutadans del Segle XXI', held in the Forum a few weeks before its closing, French planner Jean-Louis Cohen criticized the politicians' addiction to immediate results. Cities are made in time, not by rash political decisions, he said (*Avui*, 9 September 2004). Jean Nouvel, whose aesthetically dubious Agbar Tower features in this architectural 'Hall of Fame', asserts quite reasonably:

> What the city becomes is decided on the basis of what came before, not some hypothetical future designed by a long-term planning effort [..]. What it will become provides opportunities for the expression of a contextual and conceptual architecture that is both anchored and enriching. Change for the sake of change provides all sorts of excuses for just about anything;

in that sense, it is part of the lapse of architectural reason. (Baudrillard and Nouvel: 46)

In Maragall's discourse, modernity recurs as a value term often paired with that other rhetorical survival of the nineteenth century, the religion of progress. This bankrupt faith, which Baudelaire called 'the paganism of idiots' (quoted in Fumaroli: 240), underwrites the PSC's idea of space. Barcelona lives under the dictatorship of the modern as other cities live under the spell of religion, romanticism, or a bygone empire. Such essentialist modernism expresses itself in the prematurely obsolete high-rises that are obliterating Barcelona's distinctive horizontality. Fascination with American models of relationality - such as community-destroying suburban malls or the view-blocking shopping centre built on the breakwater - reveals the drying up of local inspiration, which in former times produced architecture combining technical ingenuity with a sense of place.

In the 1980s, modernity became the ideology of a providentialist state whose leaders replaced politics with spectacle. Under the PSOE of Felipe González, culture (and specifically modern culture) became a reason of state. Barcelona's socialists, intimidated by the huge budgets that fed Madrid's lurid *movida*, adopted a more frugal but more doctrinaire avant-garde policy, with the city's open spaces for its main theatre. Subjecting everything to the diktat of Modernity, they urged people to walk into a future without referents. But because there is no such thing as a self-referential future, an uncompromising modernity can only be a reflection of the violence required to undo traditions and blow up the emotional connection with the past. Modernity then turns its back on the lives that are secreted inside the city that others take over as a crab occupies an empty shell. Productivity - a factor of turnover speed - replaces achievement, while marketability is measured by the speed of expropriation. According to Clos, the purpose of his administration is 'to promote actions and decisions that encourage people and companies to develop new products and services, to become productive in information, art, music' (121). In the Barcelona of the new millennium, however, creativity is stimulated not with the slow yet trustworthy method of improving education and promoting self-discipline, but by nervous interventions in the spatial organization of the city. Bold strokes of the planner's pen maximize the convenience of the city as a container for technical know-how and 'innovation' flowing in from outside. Inscribed in the logic of the commodity and no longer in that of history, the future is defined by continuous overhauling of the object of consumption, driven by obsessive deployment of an adjective as devoid of attributes as 'new' is. This is no longer political discourse but the discourse of management.

Managing the territory calls for managing the population. Under democratic conditions, this objective necessitates simulation of public transparency and free exchange of ideas. That is where the Forum comes in. The Universal Forum of Cultures 2004 was the simulacrum of the public sphere that Barcelona can no longer countenance. The Forum's ideal citizen was an individual torn from his or her social group, class, or background, impotent therefore to contest the powers that rule his or her existence, and all the more eager to be drawn into representation of dissent (Vela). Massive civic rituals on behalf of obvious values replace real conflict, which is actively discouraged and sternly repressed. Basking in the sappy righteousness of the politically correct, this feel-good society thought itself to be in the vanguard of progress because it was spinning in the eddy of its own ebbing history.

El Fòrum, parlem-ne [The Forum, let's reach a deal]

If 'participation' was the catchphrase of Barcelona '92, 'dialogue' is the emblem of the new era. The city's Olympic image was tailored to promote Barcelona as a tourist destination, and in this respect the marketing succeeded beyond expectations. Three years after the Games, tourism in Barcelona had grown by 65 per cent and rose steadily thereafter (Martín Ayllón). In 2003, one year before the Forum, 23 million people visited Catalonia, contributing nearly 11 per cent of its gross domestic product (GDP), according to the World Tourist Organization (WTO) (Perramon). Many of them spent time in Barcelona. Nevertheless, the silver lining had clouds on the other side. Cheaper and more attractive destinations in North Africa, the Middle East, and Eastern Europe now challenge the primacy of the Costa Brava and Costa Daurada with better-preserved scenery and competitive prices. Could it be an accident that just when the passing bell of the tourist economy began to sound, Barcelona organized its next macro-event? Or that it centred the event on an issue that surfaced during the Olympics? The choice of culture as the object of celebration should have been cause for concern. Appropriated by the state, the word *culture*, says Marc Fumaroli, 'serves to veil the confusion of orders and the inversion of roles. No matter that it appears in the plural to better "target" its audiences and ape "freedom", the cultural state is not liberal' (20). Following Fumaroli, it is reasonable to ask if the excess of 'liberal' zeal on display in the fumbling design of this 'dialogue among cultures' was not the telltale sign of a repressive use of plurality as banal as its contents are indifferent.

A conceptually threadbare extravaganza composed of heterogeneous shows and displays, the Forum was an experiment in disrupting frail historical communities, presented as the optimal formula for politically correct globalization. Yet to criticize the Forum's vacuity, as many did, was to miss the point. It was the Forum's intention that nothing should occur there. The event was self-referential, and thus a non-event. Its consequences, if any, were supposed to be felt at a distance, as an aftereffect of the dialogues and sampling of the great human family. 'We're changing the world', asserted the propaganda, even as organizers were alarmed at the low attendance and the mayor spun a conspiracy theory. The world did not take notice; but propaganda does not concern itself with semantics, only with simulacra. The obviousness of the values celebrated (peace, diversity, sustainability) placed the Forum beyond the critical mediation that always intervenes between theory and reality.

Enforcing consensus by appealing to the *doxa* of the day was not new, but making a spectacle out of the obvious was. This was especially visible in the so-called dialogues. The Forum proposed dialogue as a discursive model for managing global society according to schemes originated in civil society. This much transpired from the official definition of these programmes as life debate sessions open to the audience's spontaneous participation. But here too, the reference to the Platonic method was unfortunate. If the dialectical method relies on equal participation through speakers' submission to universal rules of validation, and if 'extraction' of internal evidence ensures a confluence of individual freedom and public interest, the Barcelona dialogues fell painfully short of that goal. Rather than a daring model for an international public sphere, the Forum was an agora with prepaid admission and strictly limited participation, where presorted segments of civil society met to discuss what was previously agreed on. In his classic study of the public sphere, Habermas pointed out that since the eighteenth century civil society shaped a multiplicity of heterogeneous spaces of communication that had in common their independence from the official sphere. In contrast, the dialogues staged in the Forum rendered visible the dual structure of a polity of unequal citizens who meet from asymmetrical positions and hold uneven shares of a public sphere zealously guarded by the official world. The Forum was a sumptuous sound box for a discourse that simulated radical inquiry only in an indeterminate, delocalized way, while the citizens continued to resort to makeshift methods for interpellating the office holders.

Unlike the rituals of modernity, which were 'modeled on the public festival, where everyone is both performer and spectator' (Taylor: 122), the rituals of globalization no longer involve self-production of a society but participation of anomic individuals in a simulacrum of rational mediation, which remains forever intentional, like the shaking of hands in the Forum's logo. In one version of this logo, one hand was tattooed, signifying the exotic, the diverse, and the particular within the global. It was Adam's hand. The other hand is a mere outline. Blank, rarefied, and ghostly, it no longer mediates, like God's hand on the ceiling of the Sistine Chapel, between the universal and the particular, as true culture always did. Abstract and disembodied, it simulates a mediating gesture, proposing it as the emblem of the city. Maragall conceived such mediation in grandiloquent terms; the Forum was to be, in his own words, 'the third leg of Davos and Porto Alegre' (Dunning: 8); in other words, a middle way between global capital and antiglobal resistance: thesis, antithesis, and grand synthesis.

The word *dialogue* suggests a will to reach a rational decision that satisfies all, as does the pledge for 'a new modernity based on dialogue, negotiation and consensus, and not on conflict or war', made by the Organizers invoking 'the sentiment of the many citizens who have experienced and participated in this event' ('The Barcelona Manifesto',[3]). But lack of accountability to the actual community could be seen in the relationship between the themes and official participants

---

3 http://www.barcelona2004.org/www.barcelona2004.org/esp/banco_del_conocimiento/docs/declaracion_eng.pdf.

on the one hand and the interests of the organizing institutions and sponsors on the other. Many social movements refused to participate; numerous political figures and representatives of political parties and corporations furnished the intellectual references for the symposia (Martín Ayllón). Unlike the Olympic games, which were riven by symbolic struggles, the Forum did not stir representational passions.

Even so, a few 'transgressive' episodes broke through the rigid control of spontaneity and threatened to dispel the dialogical fiction. Three moments vie for the honour of bringing to light the Forum's approach to dialogue. The first turned up early on, when Mayor Clos, the official host, refused to answer a question from a journalist, prompting Mikhail Gorbachev to remind him that democracy obliges. The next occurrence saw two young women standing in front of Judge Baltasar Garzón with posters displaying questions about the fate of activists who had been detained two years earlier on Garzón's orders, accused of belonging to a national liberation organization. In a matter of seconds, the women were forced to leave the room. In the hallway, policemen were already waiting for them, while in the auditorium Judge Garzón 'dialogically' referred the issue to the courts.[4] The third incident came in July, when globalization theorist Manuel Castells angrily expelled a journalist for taking a picture inside the lecture hall. Such arrogation of disciplinary functions on the part of the speaker made it reasonable to expect an administrative apology. Yet the management's next move was to announce that the audience would no longer be allowed to ask questions for the remainder of the Forum.

As in every space of simulation, the possibility of a crisis appeared only when reality interrupted the spectacle. Prisoners taken to the Forum for the rehabilitating value of the experience pronounced edifying speeches to the delight of the authorities, before running away. The limits of the multicultural fantasy came into full view when a group of antiglobalization activists paddled their way into the enclosed area, miming the arrival of immigrants in makeshift boats. Right away, the Forum went to work to suture the tear in the mesh of illusion. Forum employees met the 'immigrants' at the beach with

---

4 The matter was resolved nearly two years later, when a judge of the Audiencia Nacional closed the case for lack of evidence of criminal behaviour (Balanzà 2006).

bottles of water to prevent the dehydration that typically affects sea crossers. 'We received them humanely', said Forum general director Jordi Oliveras. Dissent was all right, provided it reinforced the illusion of values that the Forum advertised as its raison d'être.

By committing itself to a bland, undialectical image of diversity, the Forum rendered itself helpless in the face of real conflict. Unable to process the irruption of activists who refused to become just one more feature of the spectacle, the organizers came up against the conditions of possibility of their much-boasted 'peace'. This happened when one activist threw the plastic bottle with which he had been succoured and security officers used their truncheons to cudgel protesters, who showed their disrespect for the Forum's commercial subtext by stealing food from the stands. Oliveras revealed the limits of the dialogues' practical reason by stating, 'We shall resolve it in the Forum way; only we don't know how' (Sabaté: 39).

With an overhead of €341 million ($US426 million), Forum 2004 is the largest and costliest European 'nonplace' to date - a nonplace in Marc Augé's sense, one of those postmodern spaces that spawn neither identity nor relations. Few other spaces have been planned so deliberately to be a nonplace as Jacques Herzog and Pierre de Meuron's triangular pavilion, and above all the outsized *plaça dura* designed by José Antonio Martínez Lapeña and Elías Torres, the world's largest after Tiananmen Square in Beijing. This barren surface now covers the space where Francoist victims were executed at nighttime over a period of 13 years. The sole reminder of that history is Josep Lluís Mateo's simulation of a bullet-riddled wall on his elegant International Convention Centre, an homage to the victims no doubt, but part of an aesthetic simulacrum engraved in venal space. The Forum, with its ready-made character and active erasure of history not only lacked an identity but wrote off the only identity that grounds culture in this small part of the planet.

What will the Forum's legacy, its after-image, be? The peasant people, who over centuries of hard work built garden terraces on the slopes of the mountains, changing them into 'architecture' in Eugeni d'Ors's sense: will they finally vanish into the modernity with which they became infatuated? Their culture and language, hardly visible and audible in the Forum and its associated exhibits: will they be revoked forever? The bread and circus Barcelona, epitomized in the superlative fireworks with which the Forum ended up appropriating the entire city, making it hostage to its politics: will it prevail over alternative images? A newspaper associated with this politics discerned in the neobaroque altarpiece 'Central-European precision, Mediterranean joy, oriental patience, and a musical background with ethnic tones' (Cols and Martínez), that is to say, a potpourri of the Forum's trivial multiculturalism.

It is too early to know if the resolution into smoke of the dialogues among cultures will furnish the after-image of a people divested of their history, language, and sensory culture and the repertoire of related concepts - stripped, that is, of their raison d'être as a people. No one can tell yet whether the potlatch culture promoted by the city's quarter-of-a-century-old administration will vanquish the culture of unremitting effort and long-term goals that etched this people's personality and sustained it in inhospitable times. If I were to choose a counter-image to the flaming arrow lighting the Olympic torch, it would be the sparks from welders setting the opera house on fire on 31 January 1994, just a year and a half after the Olympics. Watching the gaping crater of the Liceu, Barcelonans awoke from self-congratulatory enchantment to the cold reality of negligence. Up in smoke went the stage, stalls, and ceiling of one of Europe's great opera houses, and over a century of Catalan modernity. The Liceu was reconstructed and reinaugurated in October 1999, an ersatz whose synthetic aura is a fitting allegory of a city that has devastated its history to consume it as image. Ten years after this accident, Mayor Clos concluded the Forum with a gigantic fire festival, turning the entire city into the auditorium of the spectacle it offered to itself. Such celebratory reflexivity may be the provisional balance of nearly two decades of a politics of the image. Whether this politics will efface the city's memory and arrest its deepest vocation in a spectatorial relationship to municipal magic remains to be seen. All that may be ventured at this point is that the after-image is never the last image, only the provisional balance of an ongoing struggle for the social imaginary.

In this dialectical spirit, it seems appropriate to invert the image of Barcelona embellished by gunpowder and noise, which the Forum tried to stamp as its lasting mark on the public retina. The sheer concentration of fire that went into this image (16 tons of fireworks burned in a mere 20 minutes) bore a certain resemblance to the photograph of an air raid. Just as from the rubble of bombed cities emerges a stench of burned or decomposing flesh, Forum visitors got a whiff of the odour rising from the waste incinerator located under the esplanade. Less than an allegory of an enlightened city, the fireworks festival was a sublimation of the subterranean fire, which it displaced to the realm of consumable images. The invisible fire underground refers us to the cast-off, the redundant, and the abject, to bodies buried under tons of concrete, whose silence, not necessarily unfruitful, stands out against official self-approval. If the Forum was, in Maragall's words, 'a brutal success' ('Maragall vol un nou Fòrum'), then Barcelona is at risk of dying from its own success.

Works cited

Balanzà, Albert (2004). 'Estrasburg condemna Espanya per no investigar les tortures del 92'. *Avui*, 3 November.
— (2006). 'L'Audiència arxiva el cas dels "tres de Gràcia"'. *Avui*, 26 April.
Barril, Joan, and Francesc Català-Roca (1992). *Barcelona: la conquesta de l'espai* (Barcelona: Polígrafa).
Bassa, David (1997). *L'Operació Garzón: un balanç de Barcelona'92* (Barcelona: Llibres de l'Índex).
Baudrillard, Jean, and Jean Nouvel (2002). *The Singular Objects of Architecture*. Trans. Robert Bononno (Minneapolis: University of Minnesota Press).
Benach Rovira, Núria (1993). 'Producción de imagen en la Barcelona del 92'. *Estudios Geográficos* 54, 212: 483–505.
Bohigas, Oriol (1963). *Barcelona entre el Pla Cerdà i el barraquisme* (Barcelona: Edicions 62).
— (1965). *Reconstrucció de Barcelona* (Barcelona: Edicions 62).
— (2004). *Contra la incontinencia urbana. Reconsideración moral de la arquitectura y la ciudad* (Barcelona: Electa).
Buxó i Rey, Maria Jesús (2001). 'A Walk Through Identity in the Gardens of Catalonia', in Joan Ramon Resina (ed.), *Iberian Cities* (New York and London: Routledge), 198–217.
Carreras, Carles (1993). 'Barcelona 92, una política urbana tradicional'. *Estudios Geográficos* 54: 467–519.
Clos, Joan (2000). 'Noves estratègies per a la Barcelona del segle XXI'.

10 anys de planificació estratègica a Barcelona (1988–1998) (Barcelona: Associació Pla Estratègic), 111–23.

Cols, Carles, and Montse Martínez (2004). 'El tirón de un piromusical único brinda al Fòrum un adiós apoteósico'. *El Periódico*, sección Fòrum, 27 September: 2.

Delgado, Manuel (1996). 'La ciutat interrompuda: La Guerra Civil (1936–1939)/The City Interrupted: The Civil War (1936–1939)', in Josep Lluís Mateo (ed.), *Barcelona contemporània (1859–1999)/Contemporary Barcelona (1859–1999)* (Barcelona: Centre de Cultura Contemporània de Barcelona), 104–108.

— (1998). 'Las estrategias de memoria y olvido en la construcción de la identidad urbana: el caso de Barcelona', in Diego Herrera (ed.), *Memoria, identidad y comunicación* (Medellín, Colombia: Universidad de Antioquia), 95–125.

Dunning, Jennifer (2004). 'Barcelona Builds a Global Village'. *New York Times*, 14 March: 8–9.

Fumaroli, Marc (2001). *L'État culturel: essai sur une religion moderne* (Paris: Fallois).

Fundació Agrícola Catalana (2004). 'Per unes noves formes d'urbanitat'. *Avui*, 23 August: 25.

Gavaldà, Josep-Vicent (1993). 'El 92 en el mando a distancia'. *Eutopías* 17 (Valencia: Centro de Semiótica y Teoría del espectáculo).

Guillamon, Julià (2001). *La ciutat interrompuda* (Barcelona: La Magrana).

Hargreaves, John (2000). *Freedom for Catalonia? Catalan Nationalism, Spanish Identity and the Barcelona Olympic Games* (Cambridge: Cambridge University Press).

Kaplan, Temma (1992). *Red City, Blue Period: Social Movements in Picasso's Barcelona.* (Berkeley and Los Angeles: University of California Press).

López, Pere (1991). '1992, objectiu de tots? Ciutat-empresa i dualitat social a la Barcelona olímpica'. *Revista Catalana de Geografia* 15.6: 91–99.

Maragall, Pasqual (1986). *Refent Barcelona* (Barcelona: Planeta).

— (2004). 'Governing Barcelona', in Tim Marshall (ed.), *Transforming Barcelona* (London and New York: Routledge), 65–89.

'Maragall vol un nou Fòrum' (2004). *Avui*, 27 September: 34.

Maragall, Pasqual and Jaume Guillemet (1991). *Barcelona, la ciutat retrobada* (Barcelona: Edicions 62).

Martí, Francisco, and Eduardo Moreno (1974). *Barcelona ¿a dónde vas?* (Barcelona: Dirosa).

Martín Ayllón, Miguel (2004). 'Fòrum 2004: unes segones Olimpíades de l'especulació', in Unió Temporal d'Escribes, *Barcelona, marca registrada: un model per desarmar* (Barcelona: Virus editorial), 268–78.

Nel·lo, Oriol (2004). 'Urban Dynamics, Public Policies and Governance in the Metropolitan Region of Barcelona', in Tim Marshall (ed.), *Transforming Barcelona* (London and New York: Routledge), 27–45.

Noyes, Dorothy (2003). *Fire in the Plaça: Catalan Festival Politics After Franco* (Philadelphia: University of Pennsylvania Press).

Ordiguer, Andreu (2004). 'Enderrocs i remodelacions per a la productivitat del territori', in Unió Temporal d'Escribes, *Barcelona, marca registrada: un model per desarmar* (Barcelona: Virus editorial), 83–95.

Pedraforca, Horaci (2004). 'Barcelona: marca registrada i banderí del ciutadanisme', in Unió Temporal d'Escribes, *Barcelona, marca registrada: un model per desarmar* (Barcelona: Virus editorial), 41–53.

Perramon, Joaquim (2003). 'El mercat turístic espanyol perd pistonada'. *Avui*, 6 September.

Resina, Joan Ramon (2003). 'The Concept of After-Image and the Scopic Apprehension of the City', in Joan Ramon Resina and Dieter Ingenschay (eds), *After-Images of the City* (Ithaca, NY, and London: Cornell University Press), 1–22.

Richard, Élie (1932). *Le Volcan qui chante* (Paris: A. Fayard).

Rovira i Virgili, Antoni (1999). *Els darrers dies de la Catalunya republicana. Memòries sobre l'èxode català* (Barcelona: Proa).

Sabaté, Carles (2004). 'Els anti-Fòrum evidencien el dèficit de seguretat al recinte'. *Avui*, 19 July: 39.

Seiverts, Thomas (2003) [1997]. *Cities Without Cities: An Interpretation of Zwischenstadt*. Trans. Daniel de Lough, of Thomas Seiverts, *Zwischenstadt* (London: Routledge [Braunschweig: Vieweg]).

Solà Morales, Ignasi de (1989). 'Barcelona: construir sobre lo ya construido'. *Revista de Occidente* 97: 25–43.

Soldevila, Carles [1929] (n.d.). *L'art d'ensenyar Barcelona: manual del Cicerone amateur que vol quedar bé, tot fent quedar bé la ciutat* (Barcelona: Llibreria Catalònia).

Subirós, Pep (1989). 'Notas para una teoría de Barcelona'. *Revista de Occidente* 97: 99–110.

Taylor, Charles (2004). *Modern Social Imaginaries* (Durham, NC, and London: Duke University Press).

Tello i Robira, Rosa (1993). 'Barcelona post-olímpica: de ciudad industrial a escenario de consumo'. *Estudios Geográficos* 54: 507–519.

Vela, C. (2004). 'Apunts urbans: algunes reflexions a propòsit de la conflictivitat a la metròpolis', in Unió Temporal d'Escribes, *Barcelona, marca registrada: un model per desarmar* (Barcelona: Virus editorial), 87–109.

PART V
Literature, cinema, and the city

CHAPTER FIFTEEN

La Gran Encisera:
Three odes to Barcelona, and a film*

Josep Miquel Sobrer

Whatever else Catalonia might be, it is a macrocephalic organism, its head being the city of Barcelona. Barcelona is the biggest human conglomeration on the shores of the Mediterranean, its metropolitan area holds 83 per cent of the population of Catalonia (Mestre and Hurtado: 264). Today the city is more recognized than its country in the imaginary of an affluent and roaming international 'community'. Barcelona is 'in'. But Barcelona is also the head that devours its own body, relegating its hinterlands to the status of suburbs. Yet this rise of the city does not seem to upset Catalans in general. Having failed to build for themselves a nation-state, Catalans have transferred the focus of nationalist desire to their capital city. As Barcelona grows in population and as admiration for its architecture grows among foreigners, the aspiration for an independent Catalan nation wanes. The apparent success of the city in the international imaginary has wrestled the title of primary identity away from its haggard and laggard nation.

One of the first to pay attention to the growth of symbolic power for Barcelona was Jacint Verdaguer, the Catalan 'national' poet. In

---

* Josep Miquel Sobrer, '*La Gran Encisera*: Three odes to Barcelona, and a Film', *Catalan Review*, XVIII (2004), 1–2. © Estate of Josep M. Sobrer.

1883 Verdaguer competed, successfully, in the *Jocs Florals* (poetic competitions) with a rather bombastic poem, 'A Barcelona', which he himself defines in a footnote as an 'oda', an ode, a poem of praise. The poem, following an epigraph consisting of the well-known tribute to the city from Cervantes's *Quijote* (with no apparent consciousness of its possible irony), begins as follows: 'Quan a la falda et miro de Montjuïc seguda' (Verdaguer: 407, 1) [When I gaze on you there by the skirts of Montjuic¹]. The poem's metre is the one that Verdaguer had used in his epic success of 1877, *L'Atlàntida:* quatrains (46 in the '*Oda*') of 13-syllable verses, which are the Catalan equivalent of the French alexandrines.

Verdaguer wrote his 'Oda' in a moment of personal and collective euphoria: 'Lo teu present esplèndid' (412, 181), in the poet's own words. His triumph at the Jocs Florals of 1877 with *L'Atlàntida* marks a change in Verdaguer's vision of the city, from sinful Babylon to the red-carpet site of his literary success. For the city, the moment was also propitious: the old ramparts had been torn down (1854) and the Eixample begun in 1859. By the end of 1869 (that is to say, shortly after the revolution of 1868), the hated Ciutadella fortress had been given to the city to tear down and its land to be made into a park. Verdaguer clearly alludes to the latter event in ll. 123–24 of his 'Oda': 'la Ciutadella / per fer de jardinera ses armes trossejant'. By the 1880s the city was also acquiring electric lights and preparing for the Universal Exposition of 1888. All these euphoric developments beget hyperbole:

> Llavors, llavors al témer que el vols per capçalera,
> girant los ulls als Alpes, lo Pirineu veí
> demanarà, eixugant-se la blanca cabellera,
> si la París del Sena s'és transplantada aquí. (409, 73–76)

Parisians may breathe easy, however, as the next stanza begins with a resounding 'No'.

What makes Verdaguer's 'Oda' more notable than its literary achievement is its position in Catalan literary history, including Verdaguer's own poetic trajectory. For Verdaguer, 'A Barcelona' (the title of the ode) comprises a bridge between his two epic poems, the mythical *Atlàntida* and the historical *Canigó* (1885). The final

---

1 Unless otherwise stated, all translations are by the author.

alexandrine of the 'Oda', 'Qui enfonza o alça els pobles, és Déu que els ha creat' (412, 184) prefigures the ending of *Canigó* where the clock towers of two monastic churches recap in their dialogue the historical destiny of a Catalonia united under God.

Otherwise, 'A Barcelona' spans two literary moments in Catalan letters: the Renaixença and *Modernisme*. From its very beginning, Verdaguer's ode, with its bird's-eye view of the geography of the city, links itself to the archetypal poem of the Renaixença, Aribau's 'La Pàtria' of 1833, a composition whose author subtitled it humbly 'Trobes' [verses], but which soon acquired the title 'Oda a la Pàtria'. Like Aribau, Verdaguer refers to Montjuïc and to the mountains of the interior: Montseny, Montserrat, and the Pyrenees. Unlike Aribau, who took a personal stance in the poem, Verdaguer remains epic in scope, prophetic in tone, and direct in his allusions – to topography, church buildings, and contemporary figures. Verdaguer refers by name in the 'Oda' to the philosopher Jaume Balmes (410, 101), the sculptor Damià Campeny (410, 103), and the painter Mariano Fortuny, *père* (410, 104). Barcelona, for Verdaguer, is the crux where the chthonic, the political, the economic, and the intellectual meet and mingle amid an ever-growing population (the city more than doubled in number of inhabitants between 1857 and 1900 [Vila and Casassas: 418]). As opposed to Aribau's, Verdaguer's is truly an ode, a song of praise – of praise to the growing metropolis with enough enthusiastic copy for a tourism pamphlet, complete with references to its benign climate: 'ni eix cel que fora un dia ma tenda de campanya, / ni eix sol que fóra un dia faró del meu vaixell' (412, 171–72). At the other end of literary history, Verdaguer's 'A Barcelona' links directly with a composition by Joan Maragall, the one bearing the key word 'oda' in its title, which, like its opening verse, constitutes a clear and direct allusion to Verdaguer's work.

Indeed, Maragall's 'Oda nova a Barcelona', written in 1909, begins with Verdaguerian alexandrines, the personification of the city, and a similar admiration for the growth of the metropolis:

> –On te'n vas, Barcelona, esperit català
> que has vençut la carena i has saltat ja la tanca
> i te'n vas dret enfora amb tes cases disperses,
> lo mateix que embriagada de ta gran llibertat?
> (Maragall: 175, 1–4)

The opening dash indicates that the ode is a dialogue, and in the second quatrain Barcelona itself answers the poet:

> –Veig allà el Pirineu amb ses neus somrosades,
> i al davant Catalunya tota estesa als seus peus,
> i me'n vaig.... És l'amor qui m'empeny cap enfora,
> i me'n vaig delirant amb els braços oberts.
>
> (Maragall: 175, 5–8)

This declamatory Verdaguerian beginning, however, was soon broken. Maragall had begun composing the poem on 4 February 1909 (Benet: 97), but he interrupted the writing in the middle of l. 25. In the notebook where the first draft is preserved, after the start of the line 'Corre enllà, corre enllà', Maragall wrote: 'revolució'. One could venture that so charged a word as 'revolució' marks the death of the more placid and folkloric 'Renaixença'.

That 'revolució', most densely materialized as the 'Tragic Week' of July 1909, broke the poem as it broke the city. The placid rhythm of Maragall's 'Oda nova', with its regular alexandrines, soon turns chaotic and sour. The poet blasts the city: 'ets covarda i cruel i grollera, / Barcelona, però ets riallera'. The rhythm breaks down, as the well-composed hypotactic verses give way to the paratactic enumerations that characterize the end of the poem: 'se'n riu i flastoma i es baralla i s'esventa' (l. 90); 'que ets vana i coquina i traïdora i grollera' (l. 97). In the poem, as in the city, a motley multitude erupts and creates a new syntax, a new reality – a reality of violence and blood, of mud and fire. The frivolous, voluble city has burst out in 'riallades de sang' (l. 59).

In Maragall's view, worse than the revolt (which he did not witness first hand) is the repression, emblematized by the fortress and execution grounds atop Montjuïc:

> I tens dreta en la mar la muntanya, ai!, que venja
> amb son castell al cim,
> i amb la revenja
> mes ai! en el flanc! (Maragall: 176, 64–66)

The geological, topographical, and largely romantic views of Monjuïc by Aribau and Verdaguer no longer stand. The city is now a living, aching reality. Maragall understands healing, rather than prophesying, to be his role as poet.

An ironic detail of the Tragic Week was the benign weather it enjoyed. Enric de Fuentes, one of Maragall's informants (Maragall had been summering in Caldetes), wrote: 'I per damunt de la ciutat el sol, en un cel esplèndid de blavor ens il·lumina i ens enlluerna' (quoted in Benet: 72). The contrast between the violence in the streets and the placid clarity of the sky becomes for Maragall a sign of divine forgiveness and the inspiration for his own reaction to the events. The blue sky is at once a symbol of benevolent justice and of awareness of life. So, after seeing hope in the emerging temple of Gaudí's Sagrada Família, Maragall closes his poem with a hymn to twentieth-century Barcelona, a city to be accepted as 'ours': 'Barcelona! i amb tos pecats, nostra! nostra! / Barcelona nostra! la gran encisera!' (Maragall: 177, 99–100).

The next great poet to write an ode to the city was 'Pere Quart', the pen name that Joan Oliver used when publishing his poems. As if to go one up on the timing of his predecessors, Pere Quart's 'Oda a Barcelona' was published in 1936, at the onset of the Civil War. The poem, like Verdaguer's, was also issued as a pamphlet, but in order to mark his political distance from his two predecessors, Pere Quart's 'Oda' was printed in white ink on red paper (Turull: 49) and published by the Comissariat de Propaganda of the Republican Generalitat. The poem was re-issued the following year, but still bearing the date August 1936, in volume VII of *Hora de España* in Valencia. Pere Quart's allegiance to the Revolution, its fervour and hopes (he also wrote the lyrics for the hymn of the 'Exèrcit Popular Català'), set him apart from his predecessors, for he viewed Barcelona essentially as a politically committed citizen rather than an oracular voice.

Despite his leftist stance, the similarities with Maragall's 'Oda nova' are clear. Foremost are the frequent and direct invocations of a personified Barcelona, uttered not without paternalistic condescension. For Maragall, Barcelona was 'una menestrala pervinguda / que ho fa tot per punt' (Maragall: 176, 33–34). 'She' wears a nun's veil and a fashionable lady's outfit (176, 47), yet is fickle and morphs into a 'marmanyera endiablada', setting convents on fire only to rebuild them. At the end of the day, Barcelona is scolded by a loving Maragall: 'ets vana i coquina i traïdora i grollera', and yet, as already noted, 'amb tos pecats, nostra! nostra! / Barcelona nostra, la gran encisera!' (177, 99–100)

Maragall appointed himself the forgiving father of the prodigal daughter, but the tone employed by Pere Quart does not lie very far away. His Barcelona is also fickle, Protean, a 'monja llamenca' who struts the elite neighbourhoods in proletarian clothes. Above all Barcelona is mother, rather than daughter, but she is also the admonished object of a comminatory set of imperatives with which the poem ends:

> Treballa. Calla.
> Malfia't de la història.
> Somnia-la i refés-la.
> Vigila el mar, vigila les muntanyes.
> Pensa en el fill que duus a les entranyes.
> (Oliver, 1936: 53, 144–48)

The rhythm is irregular, seemingly broken, not unlike Maragall's. Pere Quart's poem strikes a contrast with the rest of his production – urbane and ironical. He himself, in 1949, qualified his poetry as 'aseptic, with no pathogenic elements, an automatic process of intellectual chemistry' (Oliver: 453–54).

Yet for the 1963 volume of his collected poems, *Obra de Pere Quart*, his 'Oda' was reworked considerably. He eliminated some fiery and – in the light of history – patently unprophetic lines such as:

> Seràs si vols la capital altiva
> de la petita Rússia d'Occident
> U ERRA ESSA HAC
> 'Unió de Repúbliques Socialistes
> Hispàniques'. (Oliver n.p.)

And he reorganized the poem's lines into a new set of groupings (I call them groupings rather than stanzas as they seem to obey the development of the poem's logical thought rather than anything having to do with metre or rhythm). The 1963 version was essentially repeated in the 1975 *Obra poètica de Pere Quart*, published by Edicions Proa. This latter version was dubbed definitive by the author.

Pere Quart's Barcelona is, in short, the pregnant mother of the revolution. 'Revolution' (or rather 'revolució') is what the Catalans of 1936 called what we now call the Spanish Civil War. And this 'revolution' is the protagonist of the poem that tries to portray a mixture of violence and hope. Social change – and here Pere Quart parts from Maragall – is desirable: 'el tumult és ordre' (Oliver: 49, 17). The bourgeoisie ('fills teus... enguantats, clenxinats' [50, 33–35]) have turned their backs on the revolutionary city while the revolutionaries take it over. A single image, curiously subtle for a composition of this nature, sums it up: 'les catifes comuniquen / tímides queixes a les espardenyes' (51, 64–65): the rope-soled soft *espardenya*, as opposed to the leather *sabata*, was the symbol of the working class; a poster of the time, a photomontage by Pere Català i Pic, features an *espardenya*-shod foot smashing a swastika.

Pere Quart's is an ode to Barcelona's labour, in both senses of the word: to the revolutionary working class and to the birth pains for 'el fill que duus a les entranyes' (53, 148). Indeed, the city gives birth to a new social order (both socialist and Catalanist) and to a new esthetic, of which the 'Oda' itself is a harbinger:

> Al cap d'anyades
> t'arribarà l'eco:
> sospirs, gemecs, renecs, esclats,
> sanglots, udols, xiscles, esclats!
> I ja tindràs l'himne triomfal
> sota la bandera de la quàdruple flama. (Oliver: 52, 114–19)

But of course that Barcelona – socialist and Catalanist – died giving birth. Accordingly, it is in homage to Pere Quart's – or Joan Oliver's – optimism that he included his dated and frustrated 'Oda' in all the published compilations of his poetry. Only about half a century later would the city give birth to a social reality that somewhat resembles the triumphal hymn prophesied by Pere Quart, but the broken and shrieking esthetic of the 'Oda' was to become the norm for the rest of the century.

The three odes discussed above were published, respectively, 26 and 27 years apart; that is to say, they stand one generation apart from each other. Skipping one generation – the sixties – we come, nearing this, our shiny, troubled millennium, to the imaginary of a new Barcelona, the imploded Barcelona of the Olympic games of

1992 and of Pedro Almodóvar's Oscar-winning film of 1998, *Todo sobre mi madre*, in which the Catalan language appears as mere filler, as inessential and inconsequential to life in contemporary Barcelona. The lady that vanishes is the Catalan language – or rather, the *mother* of Barcelona, its mother tongue, now vanishes: *Todo sobre mi madre, pero sin mi madre, sin mi lengua materna, sense la meva llengua materna.* The opening ceremonies of the Olympics presented to the world, through the artistry of La Fura dels Baus and other Catalan groups, an heroic vision not too distant from Verdaguer's. As in Verdaguer's epic poem *Atlàntida*, the hero therein portrayed was Hercules, but unlike Verdaguer's, here, in the Olympics, there was a silent protagonist: for, clearly, the opening ceremony in July of 1992 at the Olympic stadium in Barcelona was aimed at an international audience and was meant not as discourse but as spectacle.

In Almodóvar's *Todo sobre mi madre*, which takes place mostly in Barcelona, the Catalan language is barely heard. One of the characters, Rosa's mother (played by the consummate Catalan actress Rosa Maria Sardà) addresses her dog in Catalan, but she addresses her daughter, husband, and everyone else in Castilian. In a scene in a bar towards the end of the movie one hears a few background fragments of conversation in Catalan – and that's all, folks. Still, Barcelona has a clear and strong presence in the film. The protagonist, Manuela, escapes to Barcelona (as, she declares, she had escaped from Barcelona to Madrid 17 years before). She travels between the cities by train (but she flies to A Coruna in a brief scene), and the camera shows the train's rapid movement through a tunnel: the symbolism of a new being's delivery through the birth canal comes inevitably to mind.

Almodóvar's Barcelona is, then, a place of transformation (see *Filmography*). Interestingly, Madrid, in this film, is a static city and Barcelona the dynamic site where all change occurs. And those changes are quite radical. It is in Barcelona that two men become women, that a nun gets pregnant and is infected with AIDS, and that two other characters undergo important psychological changes before moving back to Madrid. By the same token, Barcelona is also the place where make believe becomes real and where transformation carries a price tag. In Barcelona, human personality is placed squarely in a system of economic exchange not without tergiversation. Manuela dresses as a prostitute, and is taken as one, before she can regain her lost equilibrium. Sister Rosa's mother earns her living by forging paintings by Marc Chagall. And foremost among these shifts and deceptions, we have Agrado, Manuela's transvestite friend who delivers – in lieu of a performance of *A Streetcar Named Desire* – a hilarious monologue in which each part of her body, including her breasts, is calibrated according to the pesetas she has spent. In her monologue, Manuela accepts her commodification and creates her own hagiography as, so to say, *María del Agrado, Virgen de las pesetas*. Visually too, the shots of Barcelona underscore notions of change and transformation. A multitude of prostitutes and their johns move about as busily and as tensely as a circle of wagons under Indian attack in an old Western. The *modernista* architecture and even, in one scenario, the busy wallpaper – cluttered, complex, mosaic-like, and fluctuating – completes the jarring, transformative visuals of the film. Barcelona is here a kaleidoscope.

Todo sobre mi madre is an apt portrayal of what the imploded Barcelona has become. The city is no longer *Cap i Casal*, the centre of a nation. It has turned into a place of pilgrimage, a site of personal transformation, a place where the old language is but one more of the dizzying layers of complexity, an element in its décor, a shard of tile in the city's *trencadís*. You come to Barcelona to be dazzled by Gaudí and the Rambla, by the juxtaposition of old and new, by the contrast between the grayness of a metropolis and the brightness of the Mediterranean coast. You come to Barcelona to discover yourself (whoever you might be or want to be) more than to discover it. You come to Barcelona to leave your old skin and get a new one, as shiny and complex as the most intricate *trencadís*. You come to find yourself. Barcelona is now the 'orgasmatron' of the new global soul. Joan Maragall proved to be prophetic: his city (he was born in the Ciutat Vella) has indeed become 'la gran encisera'.

Works cited

Benet, Josep (1968). *Maragall i la Setmana Tràgica* (Barcelona: Edicions 62).

Maragall, Joan (1981). *Obres completes. Obra catalana*. vol I. (Barcelona: Selecta).

Mestre i Campí, Jesús, and Víctor Hurtado (1995). *Atles Històric de Catalunya* (Barcelona: Edicions 62).
Oliver, Joan (1975). *Obres completes.* Vol. 1. *Obra poètica de Pere Quart* (Barcelona: Proa).
Oliver, Joan (1999). *Oda a Barcelona* (Barcelona: Comissariat de Propaganda).
Turull, Antoni (1984). *Pere Quart, poeta del nostre temps* (Barcelona: Edicions 62).
Verdaguer, Jacint (1974). *Obres completes* (Barcelona: Biblioteca Perenne).
Vila Dinarés, Pau, and Lluís Casassas Simó (1974). *Barcelona i la seva rodalia al llarg del temps* (Barcelona: Aedos).

Filmography

Sara Antoniazzi [2]

Todo sobre mi madre put post-Olympic Barcelona on the map of cinema, turning it into a hotspot for filmmakers, just as the 1992 Olympic Games, in the words of former mayor Pasqual Maragall (1982–1997), the grandson of Joan Maragall, 'put Barcelona on the map' as one of Europe's most fashionable cities. Since 1999, when *Todo sobre mi madre* was released, the number of movies shot in Barcelona has significantly increased, along with the international fame of the city. Many of these films depict an idealized and stereotypical Barcelona by focusing on the city's tourist landmarks – with special attention to Gaudí's heritage – and intentionally avoiding dealing with the social, cultural, and urban struggles that take place in present-day Barcelona. By uncritically portraying the city as a *modernista*, Mediterranean and multicultural metropolis they thus contribute to praise and boost both the 'Barcelona Model' of urban renewal and the Barcelona brand, that is to say, the official image of the city. The films that best illustrate this trend, besides *Todo sobre mi madre*, are *Gaudí Afternoon* (Susan Seidelman, 2001), *L'Auberge espagnole* (Cédric Klapisch, 2002), and more recently, *Manuale d'amore 2* (Giovanni Veronesi, 2007) and *Vicky Cristina Barcelona* (2008). The latter, which was co-produced by

[2] Sara Antoniazzi is a graduate student at Università Ca' Foscari Venezia. She is currently finishing a dissertation on film representations of Barcelona.

Catalan company Mediapro and partly financed by Ajuntament de Barcelona, looks like a tourist advertisement (or an infomercial) of the city, as it offers the audience a complete tour of Barcelona's must-see attractions and Gaudí's most celebrated buildings. It is worth noting that the fascination with Gaudí is nothing new: his architecture has been a constant feature of the cinematic depictions of Barcelona since the silent era. Gaudí's buildings have been portrayed in a large number of movies, such as *Gent i paisatge de Catalunya* (Josep Gaspar, 1926), *Biotaxia* (José María Nunes, 1968), *The Passenger* (Michelangelo Antonioni, 1975) and *Uncovered* (Jim McBride, 1994).

However, post-Olympic Barcelona has not been universally acclaimed. José Luis Guerín's *En construcción* (2001) and Alejandro González Iñárritu's *Biutiful* (2010) offer a striking alternative to the dominant cinematic image of a cosmopolitan, monumental, ever-charming Barcelona. By focusing on marginalized characters and neglected places, both movies reveal the gaps and the contradictions within Barcelona's model of urban regeneration. Furthermore, a critical approach to the city can be found in the documentary genre, which over the last 15 years has enjoyed increasing interest and visibility in Catalonia. Documentaries such as *De nens* (Joaquim Jordà, 2003), *A través del Carmel* (Claudio Zulian, 2006), *Raval, Raval...* (Antoni Verdaguer, 2006), *Can Tunis* (Paco Toledo and José González, 2007) and *Ciutat morta* (Xavier Artigas and Xapo Ortega, 2014), just to name a few, highlight the utter contrast between the triumphant, self-celebratory images of the Barcelona brand and the 'real' Barcelona, that is the actual city with its unattractive districts, its undesirable people, its growing inequalities.

CHAPTER SIXTEEN

The deceptive dame: Criminal revelations of the Catalan capital

Stewart King

'It is not the geography, it is not the architecture, it is not the heroes, or battles, much less so the chronicles of customs, or the fantasies conjured up by poets. No, what defines a city is the history of its crimes', claims the narrator of Brazilian novelist Alberto Mussa's *O senhor do lado esquerdo* (2011: 9) [*The Mystery of Rio* (2013)].[1] While no single genre can adequately represent a city (Resina 2008: 4), Mussa's somewhat hyperbolic justification for the social importance of the crime novel is correct in so far as crimes are culturally specific, implying the transgression of a particular society's norms. However, although crimes draw our attention to a given social order, crime fiction does much more than merely represent transgression and punishment. It also 'acts as a connective tissue within this world' because the investigation traces 'the hidden relationships crime both indicates and conceals, to bring to the surface, and show the way the city works' (Messent: 1). With this in mind, the aim of this chapter is to explore the ways in which writers use crime fiction set in the Catalan capital to reveal what one character in Manuel Vázquez Montalbán's

---

1 Unless otherwise stated, all translations are mine. The translated titles that appear in italics indicate books that have been published in English.

El delantero centro fue asesinado al atardecer (1988) [*Offside* (1995)] calls the 'palabras que [cada época] necesita para enmascararse' (105) [words that each era needs in order to mask itself]. The following discussion analyses both Catalan- and Castilian-language crime novels as well as works written in English, although due to space limitations only a select number of representative texts will be analysed.

In using Barcelona as a catalyst for analysis and comparison, this study eschews the usual literary categorization in the Catalan context that classifies texts according to the language in which they are written. In doing so, however, I do not want to downplay the importance of language. Indeed, it is worth pausing briefly to reflect on the politics of language and popular fiction in Catalonia before engaging with the ways in which the city comes to be revealed in crime novels. Due to several centuries of persistent, if uneven, Hispanicization from the fifteenth century to the Franco regime (1939–1975), many Catalans were illiterate in their own language, a consequence of which was the adoption of Castilian as the primary vehicle for most literary production and consumption in Catalonia. This in turn led to a profound cultural and identity crisis that many Catalan writers and intellectuals from the nineteenth century onwards sought to overcome by strengthening Catalan culture against the threat of Hispanicization. They did so principally in two ways. One – the dominant – group sought to maintain Catalan as a language of prestige by producing so-called literarily valuable fiction (Fernàndez: 342–43). Others, like Rafael Tasis in the 1930s, Manuel de Pedrolo in the 1960s and Jaume Fuster in the 1970s, promoted popular genres as a means of attracting barely literate readers or ones lacking in confidence to Catalan literature and away from Castilian-language works (see Pedrolo in Hart 1987: 62, 236). Thus, in the Catalan case, crime and other popular fictional forms had a specific nation-building purpose.

In drawing attention to the political role of popular fiction in Catalonia, I do not want to suggest that Castilian-language crime novels necessarily contribute to the ongoing Hispanicization of Catalan society. Crime novels are too beset by ruptures and fragmentation, ambiguities and contradictions to attribute any single worldview or function to them (Pepper: 7, 11). As the following analysis will show, there are numerous crime novels written in Castilian that seek to unsettle the nationalist discourses that promote the image of Spain as a homogenous monolingual and monocultural country. Nevertheless, any discussion of crime fiction in the Catalan capital must acknowledge the asymmetrical relationship between the two languages. Although many Catalan-language texts will be discussed in this chapter, their potential audience and, hence, their national and international reach are much reduced when compared to crime novels written in Castilian. If a city's history is made up of multiple voices (Vázquez Montalbán 1990: 7), in the case of crime fiction set in Barcelona some voices are invariably louder than others.

The crime genre developed in Barcelona, as it did elsewhere, after a period of urban expansion, internal migration and increased industrialization. According to Walter Benjamin, the social origins of crime fiction lie in 'the obliteration of the individual's traces in the big-city crowd' (43). This is true of the early attempts to produce crime stories in Catalan. Jacint M. Mustieles's *L'assassí i el compliç* [The Assassin and his Accomplice] (1924), for example, articulates anxiety about the breakdown of traditional social relations caused by increased urbanization. Here, the anonymity provided by the city is a source of fear, as the protagonist–narrator experiences a sort of Hitchcockian paranoia after being led to believe that the avuncular barbers he visits each week are in fact a twice-convicted murderer and his brother-in-law accomplice who fled their village for the fast-expanding Catalan metropolis.

Prior to the outbreak of Civil War in 1936 only a handful of crime novels set in Barcelona were published, including the parodic *Crim* [Crim] (1936) by Mercè Rodoreda, the most important Catalan novelist of the twentieth century. In many ways, *Crim* is little more than an historical curio in the development of the Catalan genre and, with the action taking place in an isolated manor house, it makes little attempt to represent the city in any detail. Barcelona is important, however, because of its subaltern position in relation to the Spanish capital – a theme that is taken up in later crime novels. In *Crim* Rodoreda reveals the asymmetrical relationship between centre and periphery through the Madrid-based Inspector Flac, who arbitrarily interferes in the lives of the cast of Catalan characters, arresting two of them even though no crime has been committed and sending them to Madrid because the legal system in Catalonia exists only to provide the illusion of justice. Power, it becomes clear, resides at the centre.

These early tentative steps in the development of crime fiction in Catalonia came to an abrupt halt with the victory of the Nationalist forces of Francisco Franco in the Spanish Civil War, when – like in Rodoreda's *Crim* – the centre imposed its arbitrary order on the periphery. The ultra-conservative regime had a profound impact on the development of the crime genre, as the publication of crime novels set in Spain became extremely difficult under a repressive regime that projected the image of a country in which 'no existían suicidas, atracadores, asesinos, policías corruptos, jueces venales, señoritas que enseñaron la liga ni cuernos de sólida implantación' [there were no suicides, robbers, murderers, corrupt police, judges on the take, women who flashed garters or longstanding extra-marital affairs], according to journalist and crime novelist Francisco González Ledesma (444).

Nevertheless, a few writers sought to circumvent such restrictions. Rafael Tasis did so by setting his detective trilogy – *La Bíblia valenciana* [The Valencian Bible] (1955), *És hora de plegar* [Quitting Time] (1956) and *Un Crim al Paralelo* [Crime on Parallel Avenue] (1960) – in pre-war Barcelona. As Patricia Hart (1989: 74) notes, the most successful of the novels is *Un Crim al Paralelo*, which despite being the last novel published was, in fact, written in 1944 during the author's exile in Paris. Set in the heart of Barcelona's theatrical and red light district – a flat, Catalan Montmartre if you will – the novel is Tasis's attempt to adapt the genre of Poe, Doyle, Christie, Hammett and Simenon to Catalan. Manuel de Pedrolo, on the other hand, was able to set the four crime novels he wrote between 1953 and 1968, including his James M. Cain influenced *Joc brut* [Playing Dirty] (1965), in Catalonia and he even managed to make discreet reference to the ongoing discrimination experienced by those on the losing side in post-war Catalonia.

Maria Aurèlia Capmany took a different path altogether by displacing the action to Albania in her 1959 novel *Traduït de l'americà* [Translated from the American],[2] in which an American private eye seeks the missing heir to a wealthy fortune who has disappeared from New York and was last seen in Albania. For a population accustomed to

---

2 The novel was retitled in 1980 *Vés-te'n, ianqui! o, si voleu, traduït de l'americà* [Yankee Go Home! Or, If You Like, Translated from the American] and again in 2005, becoming simply *Vés-te'n ianqui* [Yankee Go Home].

reading between the lines (Godsland: 160), Albania served as a thinly veiled allegory of Catalonia within Spain through which Capmany sought to explore Spanish–Catalan relations.[3] Readers would have had few difficulties identifying the two principal cities in which the action takes place – Tirana and Valona – as metaphors for Madrid and Barcelona. As the 'reducte d'una èlite reaccionària, ensopida, amb molt poca gent estrangera' [redoubt of a reactionary elite, sleepy, and with very few foreigners] (Capmany: 19), the national capital, Tirana, lives up to its tyrannical name, imposing its values on the rest of the country. On the other hand, Valona, a coastal metropolis and former capital of a medieval principality, is active, lively and outward looking through its connections to Venice and Trieste. In the novel, Barcelona is virtually superimposed on Valona, as the second Albanian city is transformed into Va(rce)lona, a metamorphosis made possible via the pronunciation of 'v' and 'b' in Catalan being indistinguishable [b] at the beginning of words. Once the two cities morph in the reader's mind, it becomes clear that the detective's revelations about place are more important than the investigation into the missing heir, as the detective exposes the regime's paternalistic rhetoric about the need to civilize those citizens who 'encara no han assimilat el nostre ordre' [have not yet accepted our order] while supporting patently uncivil, criminal practices (Capmany: 40). Indeed, the detective expresses his incomprehension at the *esperpèntic* situation of a country in which 'el contraban era legal i la poesia delicate' [contraband is legal and poetry a crime] (147).

Towards the end of the regime, more overt criticisms could be made, and a small number of writers began adopting and adapting the style, conventions and aesthetics of the American hardboiled novel to reflect local conditions. One such writer was Jaume Fuster, a pioneer writer of popular fiction in Catalan, including fantasy and science fiction. Fuster is perhaps best known for *De mica en mica s'omple la pica* [Little by Little the Basin Fills] (1972). The novel's protagonist, Enric Vidal, is a petty crook who likes to live large, but when framed for murder, he is forced to play detective and resolve the mystery to save his life. Pitting an industrialist embezzler against the workers set to lose their jobs at

---

3 For a discussion of the function of national allegories in Catalan crime fiction, see King and Whitmore.

his allegedly insolvent company, the novel represents an economically divided city in which big capital supported by a repressive regime exploits the average citizen. The novel offers little in the way of solutions, as, although Vidal can save himself, the capitalist system entraps all within it. In Fuster's own words, the novel is a rejection of the individualism of the American hardboiled because 'nunca un individuo ha resuelto el problema de la colectividad' [individuals never resolve collective problems] (cited in Hart 1987: 82).

Fuster's *De mica en mica...* and Manuel Vázquez Montalbán's *Tatuaje* [Tattoo] (1974), the first novel in his Carvalho series (discussed below), showed the genre's potential for investigating and interrogating issues of concern in contemporary society. As a result, following the dictator's demise there was a boom in the production of autochthonous crime fiction that was centred primarily in Barcelona and known in Catalan as the *novel·la negra*, or noir novel. While the transition to democracy was ostensibly a period of liberalization and progress to be celebrated, crime writers were more pessimistic, employing 'the tools of detection by the modern state at the service of uncovering the criminality of this very state and/or those who most benefited from it: politicians, businessmen and well-respected professionals' (Balibrea: 36).[4]

The violent, divided and competitive Barcelonan society that Fuster had first depicted became a standard feature of crime novels during the Transition, particularly so in the novels of Andreu Martín, the most prolific author of crime fiction in Spain today. Writing in both Castilian and Catalan, Martín uses the genre to draw attention to the exploitation of society's most vulnerable citizens: the poor, women, the elderly, the hopeless and immigrants. His first novel, *Aprende y calla* [Learn and Shut Up] (1979) follows the pattern of Fuster's classic, but here the victims are immigrants from North Africa who are trafficked illegally and forced into a form of labour bondage in Barcelona before being shipped on to the promised land of France and Germany. Martín returns to the link between immigration and criminality, in this case among the growing Chinese community, in his 2013 *Societat Negra* [Secret Society]. In his early masterpiece, *Prótesis* [Prosthesis] (1980), a gothic novel of urban terror, the dividing line between civilization and barbarism collapses, as there is little difference between political

---

[4] For a detailed history and analysis of the Spanish crime genre, see Colmeiro.

and legal institutions and the criminal underworld. In Martín's view, both are locked in a Darwinian struggle for power, control and the accumulation of wealth at the expense of ordinary citizens.

The first two novels of Eduardo Mendoza's parodic crime series – currently comprising 5 novels that span 35 years of the city's history – reach similar conclusions about the connection between power and privilege, the Catholic Church and the criminal underworld in the Catalan capital. In *El misterio de la cripta embrujada* [The Mystery of the Enchanted Crypt] (1979) and *El laberinto de las aceitunas* [The Olive Labyrinth] (1982) the police release the unhinged, unnamed and picaresque-inspired protagonist from the psychiatric institution where he usually resides to assist them with their investigations. Unravelling almost all the flaws of the new democratic Spain, the unnamed protagonist is rarely aware of the full implications of what he uncovers. For readers, however, it is clear. Through his often humorous, deranged ravings and the absurd situations in which he repeatedly finds himself, the novels show that the world within the psychiatric hospital is not so different from that beyond its walls. In both, the authorities do all they can to control and subjugate their 'charges'.

The general disillusionment with contemporary Barcelona – and, by extension, Spain – is a central feature of Vázquez Montalbán's Carvalho series, comprising 18 novels and 6 short story collections, the most famous of which was the 1979 Planeta Prize-winning *Los mares del sur* (1979) [*Southern Seas* (2000)]. Vázquez Montalbán is the most internationally recognized crime writer from Barcelona, and his work is intimately connected to the Catalan capital, so much so that in 2006 the Barcelona Town Council instituted a major international crime fiction award, the Premio Pepe Carvalho, after the series' eponymous protagonist. Vázquez Montalbán had originally begun his literary career as a writer of experimental avant-garde fiction and poetry, but he turned to crime fiction as a means of taking his 'crónica de una sociedad compleja, conflictiva, competitiva, urbana, una sociedad como la española de los años setenta' [chronicle of a complex, conflictive, competitive and urban society like the Spanish society of the seventies] to a larger readership (Vázquez Montalbán 1998: 145).

The reader's guide to this complex society is the ex-communist, ex-CIA agent and now private eye, Pepe Carvalho, for whom 'los detectives privados somos los termómetros de la moral establecida' [we private detectives are the thermometers of the moral order] (Vázquez Montalbán 1979: 15). Through his various investigations from the early 1970s until the turn of the millennium, Carvalho charts the changes that were taking place on the political, social and cultural landscape in transitional and democratic Barcelona. Carvalho is a product of the working-class Barrio Xino, but he now lives in Vallvidrera, a salubrious suburb overlooking Barcelona, from where a taxi driver states you can see 'la mierda flotante [...] en esta ciudad' [the floating shit in this city] (Vázquez Montalbán 1979: 79). While the series promotes itself as a study of the city from its upper echelons to its underworld, Mario Santana has perceptively pointed out that 'Carvalho's Barcelona does not aim to be a portrait of the city as such, but rather a representation of those areas that remain hidden to public view and social discourse'; that is, those areas 'in danger of being concealed – either because of marginality (the immigrant areas), secrecy (the high bourgeois clubs, offices and homes), or loss of memory (the reluctance [...] to confront the past)'. (542) While this is true of many of the novels, *Los mares del sur* typifies the way in which Vázquez Montalbán traces the criminal connections that link peripheral working-class suburbs, like Bellvitge and La Pau, which in the novel are transformed into the fictional San Magín, to the wealthy suburbs of Sarrià and Sant Gervasi. Crimes may be committed in less well-off areas, but as Carvalho reveals their motives are conceived in those spaces frequented by the rich and powerful.

Joan Ramon Resina has criticized the series for its depiction of Catalans, arguing that in transposing the American hardboiled genre to a Spanish/Catalan context, Vázquez Montalbán ascribes to the Catalan bourgeoisie the criminality which Hammett, Chandler and others attributed to the American capitalist class. Moreover, he is critical of the way in which criminality is further associated with the Catalans through the representation of the victims, most of whom belong to Barcelona's immigrant communities or are Spaniards who happen to be passing through (Resina 1997: 91). However, as I have argued elsewhere (King 2013), Resina's argument is problematic because rather than treating them as two distinct linguistic and cultural communities, the Carvalho series collapses the neat division between Catalans and Spaniards in Barcelona by redefining traditional understandings of belonging through cultural *mestizaje*, or hybridity.

The vision of the city depicted in the novels is one of solidarity through multicultural and multilingual diversity, which is often threatened by those, often wealthy, cosmopolitan-minded citizens concerned exclusively with their own economic and political self-interest.

As the series progresses, the erosion of the city's history through the process of urban renewal and regeneration becomes the dominant theme of many books (Wells). As Biscuter, Carvalho's secretary-cum-chef, laments 'la gente ha perdido la memoria y no quiere recuperarla' [people have lost their memory and they don't want to get it back] (Vázquez Montalbán 1988: 32–33). In particular, *El delantero centro fue asesinado al atardecer* [*Offside*] criticizes the land speculation in the name of the so-called Barcelona Model that results in the destruction and rebuilding of whole suburbs and the erasure of memories and histories they contain. By the time the series reaches *El hombre de mi vida* (2000) (*The Man of My Life* [2006]), the last true detective novel before Carvalho and Biscuter embark on a journey around the world in the posthumously published *Milenio Carvalho* [Millennium Carvalho] (2004), Carvalho has become increasingly disoriented by the changes that have taken place to the city's urban landscape since the awarding of the 1992 Olympic Games. The post-Olympic redevelopment of the city's waterfront and the urban beautification programme, 'Barcelona, posa't guapa' [Barcelona, make yourself beautiful], has destroyed the physical and social face of the city of his childhood, leaving him with little more than 'paisajes de la memoria' [landscapes of memory] (Vázquez Montalbán 2000a: 176).

Biscuter's eulogy for the passing of memory was premature, however, as a new generation of crime writers have been drawn to the past as a setting for their novels. Such novels are not mere exercises in nostalgia. They recount aspects of the city's past that have been largely forgotten and also use the past to engage in very contemporary debates. Forensic scientist and novelist Marc Pastor's *La mala dona* (2008) [*Barcelona Shadows* (2014)], set in the winter of 1911–1912, retells the story of the real-life Enriqueta Martí, the wicked woman of the Catalan title. Known as the vampiress of Ponent Street in Barcelona's sleazy Raval district, Martí was a prostitute who later turned her hand to kidnapping and prostituting children. She also killed them, using their body parts to make salves, remedies and ointments that were allegedly sold to Barcelona's wealthiest citizens. Pastor recovers the gothic tradition of crime fiction, as his Barcelona is 'una dama vella d'ànima esgarrapada que ha estat abandonada per mil amants, però que no ho vol reconèixer' (2008: 32) [an old lady with a battered soul, who has been left by a thousand lovers but refuses to admit it]. This city, inhabited by maimed and disfigured victims of Spain's futile colonial wars, diseased and poverty stricken immigrants, as well as a grotesque array of body snatchers, foreign quacks and pickpockets, reminds readers of an unsavoury and violent past that has been largely erased by the city's gentrification under the Barcelona Model.

Jordi Sierra i Fabra's 'Miquel Mascarell' series also engages in very contemporary issues; in his case, the vociferous debates concerning historical memory and transitional justice in democratic Spain as well as the calls for Catalan independence from Spain since the turn of the millennium. The first novel in the series, *Cuatro días de enero* [Four Days in January] (2008), opens on 23 January 1939, four days before the city was occupied by Franco's forces. Mascarell is the last remaining police officer of the Catalan government, his colleagues having fled to the French border. Mascarell interprets the city's impending occupation through cultural memory. Addressing the Francoists, he says 'No os conformaréis con ganar [...]. Vais a arrasar Barcelona, Catalunya entera, a matar a todo aquel que no comulgue con vuestras ideas, a reprimirnos hasta que derramemos la última gota de sangre, como en 1714' [You're not going to be satisfied with just winning [...]. You're going to lay waste to Barcelona, all of Catalonia, to kill everyone who doesn't agree with your ideas, to repress us until we shed our last drop of blood, like in 1714] (Sierra i Fabra 2008: 145), the year in which the city was occupied by the forces of Philip V in the War of Spanish Succession and Catalonia became politically integrated into Spain. Mascarell's prediction becomes reality in the following novels of the series when he returns to Barcelona after having spent eight years in jail for supporting the Republican government. On his return, not only has the small apartment he had shared with his recently deceased wife in the Poble Sec district been occupied by supporters of the regime, but also Barcelona's Catalanness has been palimpsestically erased and overwritten by the markers of a monolingual, monocultural and unified Spain. Nevertheless, like the palimpsest, the erasure of the city's Catalan identity is incomplete. Although faint and barely legible, it can still be read beneath the official, outwardly conformist,

Spanishness imposed under the regime: 'no todas las mujeres sonreían, ni todos los hombres caminaban con la cabeza erguida, ni todos los niños exteriorizaban alegría. Había algo, latente, a flor de piel, que solo él y los que eran como él podían percibir' [Not all the women smiled, nor all the men walked with their heads held high, nor did all the children radiate happiness. There was something, latent, skin deep, that only he and those like him could perceive] (Sierra i Fabra 2010: 22).

A similar separation between victors and vanquished, Spaniards and Catalans is depicted in Lluís Bosch's *Aire brut* [Dirty Air] (2013). Here, however, language marks the dividing line between the public, Spanish face of the city and the hidden, Catalan community, as the narration occurs in Catalan, but almost all the dialogue takes place in Castilian. By linking malfeasance to prominent Francoists, novels such as these serve not only to criminalize the regime but also to tell a story of continued resistance to centralist oppression.

Perhaps unsurprisingly, the relationship between centre and periphery is also present in the Barcelona-centred novels written by non-Catalan Spaniards. For example, in Lorenzo Silva's *La reina sin espejo* [The Queen without a Mirror] (2005) and *La marca del meridiano* [The Meridian Line] (2012), his Civil Guard protagonists, Rubén Bevilacqua and Virginia Chamorro, travel from Madrid to Barcelona to resolve mysteries of national importance. In both novels most of the Civil Guard characters are intolerant of expressions of Catalan identity, seeing themselves as the last bastion of Spanishness in hostile – Catalan – territory. Bevilacqua, however, is seemingly cut from more progressive, tolerant cloth and he argues in favour of Barcelona's Catalanness within the limits of the Constitution's recognition of Spain's cultural and linguistic diversity. Rather than promote difference, the novels advocate the mutual benefits of cooperation when the local Catalan police force, the Mossos d'Esquadra, collaborates with the Civil Guard to resolve crimes in record time. Here, Barcelona is very much still a Spanish city, albeit one that maintains its Catalan flavour.

Much early crime fiction set in Barcelona was a decidedly masculine affair. Women, when they did appear, tended to conform to generic stereotypes as either victims or femmes fatales that threatened the autonomy of the typical male, heterosexual gumshoe. The masculinity of the genre has been challenged by women writers, the most well known of whom are Maria Antònia Oliver, Alicia Giménez Bartlett and Lola Van Guardia. These authors not only question the genre's gender politics but they also narrate a very different relationship between the detective and the city.

While male detectives seemingly move with ease through the urban mean streets, the relationship between the city and women detectives is far more complex. This is the case of Lònia Guiu, the Majorcan-born, Barcelona-based, private detective of a trilogy by Maria Antònia Oliver. As the first novel of the trilogy, *Estudi en lila* (1986) [*Study in Lilac* (1987)], progresses, Lònia feels increasingly asphyxiated by the city's spaces, including her own apartment, and the novel draws attention to the dangers the city represents for women. In one of the two cases she takes on, Lònia is instructed by an antiques dealer, Elena Gaudí, to find three men she claims had cheated her of money. The allegorical link between Barcelona and women is rather obviously made through the client's surname, Gaudí, connecting her to the famous architect whose buildings are the international face of the city. Lònia's investigation reveals that Gaudí was raped by the three men in the Plaça Sant Jaume, the city's symbolic and administrative centre. The novel does more than highlight women's marginalization and repression; it also represents the attempt to wrest back control of urban spaces by women, a common trope of feminist crime fiction. Lònia, for example, notices the lilac-coloured graffiti appearing on buildings 'contra violació castració' (Oliver 1991: 191) [against rape, castration], a form of justice that Gaudí enacts after Lònia unknowingly passes on the identities of the three men she assumes to be middle-class crooks.

The exclusion experienced by women is situated in its historical context in Rosa Ribas and Sabine Hofmann's *Don de lenguas* (2013) [*The Whispering City* (2015)], a novel set several weeks before the 35th International Eucharistic Congress in 1952. Featuring an unlikely crime-fighting duo, young journalist Ana Martí and her philologist cousin, Beatriz Noguer, the investigation into the death of a prominent socialite reveals the corrupt practices of the regime that is typical of historical crime fiction set during the dictatorship. However, unlike many of the other novels examined here, the crime and its motive are not geographically dispersed between the wealthy and less well-off suburbs. Instead, they are contained primarily in the well-heeled Sarrià and Sant Gervasi districts, thus suggesting that the principal source of the city's ills resides among the regime's wealthy supporters. More importantly, however, the novel also draws attention to the institutionalized sexual discrimination enforced by the Franco regime, as Ana and Beatriz encounter numerous hurdles in their attempts to pursue meaningful careers.

The marginalization felt by investigators like Oliver's Guiu or Ribas and Hofmann's Ana and Beatriz is perhaps in part a consequence of their position outside the city's official power structures. Alicia Giménez Bartlett offers an alternative to this in her series of novels featuring police inspector Petra Delicado, including *Ritos de muerte* (1996) [*Death Rights* (2008)], *Día de perros* (1997) [*Dog Day* (2006)] and *El silencio de los claustros* [*The Silence of the Cloisters*] (2009). Critics have argued that Giménez Bartlett has 'an intimate and sympathetic understanding of the Barcelona of the marginalized, the delinquent, and the dispossessed [..] and a keen familiarity with the language deployed by both the police and the criminal fraternity' (Godsland: 37). While the novels undoubtedly demonstrate the author's social awareness and attention to the language of crime, this series set in Barcelona displays a general lack of engagement with the city's complex cultural and linguistic context. If the police institution acts as a metaphor for the 'wider social milieu' (Godsland: 39), then the cultural politics of this series show the degree to which the Spanish National Police Force is representative of a generic Spanishness, as the Catalan social and cultural environment in which the novels are set is almost entirely erased in the early novels.

Furthermore, the novels play down the gradual replacement of the Spanish National Police in Catalonia by the Catalan Mossos d'Esquadra, a process which began in 1994, two years before the first Petra Delicado novel was published, and which was completed in 2008. When the Mossos are mentioned in the early novels, their area of influence is reduced to more banal policing responsibilities, such as finding lost dogs and keeping tabs on religious sects, thus trivializing the work of the Catalan police force. Both Castilian- and Catalan-language writers have, however, embraced the new police force – Teresa Solana in *Negres tempestes* [*Storm Clouds*] (2010), Toni Hill in *El verano de los juguetes muertos* (2011) [*The Summer of Dead Toys* (2013)] and Carme Riera in *Natura quasi morta* [*An Almost Still Life*] (2011), to name just three – and, in so doing, they contribute further to the normalization of the Catalan government as a source of authority and justice in Barcelona.

If women are often marginalized in crime fiction, gay and lesbians are in the main invisible. When they do appear, such as in early novels of Vázquez Montalbán and Martín, they are often constructed in terms of criminality and deviance, and their deaths indicate their exclusion from the social body. A radical shift in the way the city is represented appears in *Plumas de doble filo* [Double-edged Feathers/Pens] (1999) by Lola Van Guardia, the pseudonym of Isabel Franc. In many ways, *Plumas de doble filo* is the extreme realization of the reclaiming of the streets for women of earlier feminist crime fiction. The novel begins ambiguously: 'la ciudad parecía desposeída de toda su femeninidad' (Van Guardia: 9) [the city seems dispossessed of all its femininity], before explaining that this simply means that its citizens – all women – have abandoned the city for the summer. Nancy Vosburg (84) describes the novel as lesbian utopian because all the characters are female and often lesbian and because it challenges the universalizing masculine through the use of the generic feminine throughout, such as when the Catalan police force is marked as feminine throughout the novel as *les mosses d'Esquadra*, and not the more typical *els mossos*.

Gay detectives are also few and far between. Nil Barral, the pseudonym of an as yet unknown Catalan author, is also the name of the fat, gay detective protagonist of a trilogy of novels that opens with *L'home que dormia al cotxe* [The Man Who Slept in the Car] (2011). In contrast to the association between criminality and sexual deviance in earlier crime fiction, the trilogy presents more positive images of gay experiences in Barcelona through Barral, an ex-policeman currently working as a detective investigating insurance fraud, and his attractive, academic mathematician partner. Following the well-worn template of the genre, in Barral's fiction, minor cases of possible insurance fraud lead to more in-depth, critical investigations into social problems and institutionalized corruption. However, the most important contribution of the series is its challenge to the traditional invisibility, when not deviance, of gays in the *novel·la negra*.

The association between Barcelona and fluid sexual identities is also a feature of two English-language crime novels set in the Catalan capital. Both *Gaudí Afternoon* (1990) by American Barbara Wilson, now Sjoholm, and *The Verge Practice* (2003) by Anglo-Australian

Barry Maitland play with the notion of Barcelona as a city of façades through their reflections on the constructed nature of the city, its architecture, and the construction of sexual and gender identities through performance that are reminiscent of the work of gender theoretician Judith Butler. Although the two novels constitute a small sample, it is significant that these English-language representations of the city should emphasize surface over substance, performance over essence, a theme that is important in much recent crime fiction from the Catalan capital.

In the late 1990s the traditional *novel·la negra*, with its marginalized, tough-talking, hardboiled antiheroes who expose political corruption, had become a tired, somewhat clichéd and outdated formula. It was only in the first decade of the twenty-first century that new writers began to experiment with the genre in order to make it engage with the increasingly prosperous and globalized city. The most original of this new generation is Teresa Solana, who is best known for a trilogy of parodic detective novels. In *Un crim imperfecte* (2006) [*A Not So Perfect Crime* (2008)], *Drecera al paradís* (2007) [*A Shortcut to Paradise* (2011)] and *L'Hora Zen. Un crim refinat* (2011) [*The Sound of One Hand Killing* (2013)] Solana distances herself from the typical hardboiled world of earlier writers; instead she adopts the isolated crimes and well-to-do characters of the classic detective novels of Agatha Christie and Dorothy Sayers. The novels thus mark a shift from the working-class action of much earlier fiction to the wealthy suburbs to the north of Barcelona's Diagonal Avenue, what translator Peter Bush terms the city's 'Upper North Side' (Solana 2008: 13). This shift has occurred because new ways of representing the city at the turn of the new millennium are required to take into account the city's gentrification since the 1992 Olympics. Solana, however, draws on the classic detective formula not as a retreat from reality, but as a means of criticizing, often ironically, the characteristic concerns and obsessions of a postmodern Barcelona obsessed with image.

If in the traditional mystery the investigation serves to uncover a hidden reality, this task is complicated in Solana's novels where, it is increasingly difficult to distinguish between surface and substance in the Catalan capital. Indeed, the confusion begins with the very detectives themselves and the office in which they greet their clients. The detectives are twin brothers Eduard and Pep Martínez Estivill, although Pep goes by the very pretentious, faux aristocratic name of Borja Masdéu-Canals Sáez de Astorga in order to gain the trust of their rich clients. Their office also forms part of the deceit, as they have had two false doors built into the walls to give the image of a larger space. To explain meeting their clients in the office of their non-existent secretary, the presence of whom is hinted through a carefully arranged Loewe scarf and Chanel nail polish, the brothers invent a story about ongoing renovations. Eduard and Pep/Borja's office functions as a small-scale metaphor for the city itself. The brothers' business stands for the new, post-Olympic Barcelona, a city which in the words of Manuel Delgado has become an 'enorme cadena de producción de sueños y simulacros [..] que hace de su propia mentira su principal industria' [an enormous production line of dreams and pretences that turns its own lies into its main industry] (14). In the new Barcelona substance stands for very little; the ability to shape one's image and to manipulate the image of others is the new power. Those that cannot play this game, lose.

There is a Catalan saying, 'Barcelona és bona si la bossa sona' [Barcelona is great while the coins clink]. The saying often ends there, but it in fact continues 'però tant si sona com si no sona, Barcelona sempre és bona' [but regardless of whether they clink or not, Barcelona is always great]. Such optimism, however, is not always borne out in the crime novel. Eduardo Mendoza's *El enredo de la bolsa o la vida* [The Trouble with the Stock Exchange or Life] (2012), the fourth novel in his parodic series, for example, highlights the consequences of the 2007 global financial crisis on the city's inhabitants when his unnamed protagonist is forced to sell his bankrupt hairdressing business to Chinese neighbours so they can open a restaurant. Since his release from the psychiatric hospital where he had resided in the first two novels, he has tried to conform to society's norms. However, in the wake of the systemic failures of the capitalist system, he recognizes the need for new collective social relations and forms his own, unusual, community of misfits. Teresa Solana's *L'hora Zen* also explores the aftermath of the crisis by drawing attention to its impact on the city's theatricality she had exposed in the first two novels. In *L'hora Zen*, the elaborately constructed façades begin to crumble and maintaining the performances of various actors becomes increasingly difficult. Here, the brothers' office again becomes a metaphor for the city's changing fortunes when it is trashed by thieves who break the fake doors the brothers had installed. In trashing the office, the thieves shatter the illusion that Pep/Borja had so carefully manipulated and Solana uses the destruction of the office as a metaphor for late capitalism itself, as the dreams and simulacrum of progress are exposed as sham, as little more than empty signifiers. With her characteristic irony and caustic critique of the lies and symbols society produces in order to hide its contradictions and inequalities, Solana is the contemporary writer who best continues the critical crime fiction project initiated by Vázquez Montalbán.

If popular fiction is popular precisely because it engages with the fears, hopes and desires of the reading public (McCracken: 2), then it should come as no surprise that one of the most important contemporary concerns of the new millennium – the environment – should increasingly arise in crime fiction. Environmental issues appear early in Catalan crime fiction. Maria Antònia Oliver's first short crime story, 'On ets, Mònica?' (1983) ['Where are you Monica?' (1992)], and her second novel, *Antípodes* (1987) [*Antipodes* (1989)], make a strong connection between male violence against women and capitalism's rapacious destruction of the environment.

Perhaps the most ambitious approach to environmental concerns in Barcelona-based crime fiction appears in the series of six novels by Jordi de Manuel. Primarily set – at the time of their composition – in a not-too-distant future, the 'Marc Sergiot' series blends the crime and speculative fiction genres in order to present a dystopian view of Barcelona and to interrogate the possible causes of a future environmental catastrophe. The fourth novel in this series, *L'olor de la pluja* [The Smell of the Rain], was written in 1996, published in 2006, and set in 2017, twenty-five years after the city hosted the Olympic Games. The euphoria about the city's regeneration that the Games heralded has here been replaced by a profound pessimism in its future. There are numerous technological advances, including aerial ring roads which allow rich and important citizens to circulate in aero taxis without having to mix with the city's increasingly impoverished and marginalized proletariat. But while science makes life easier for the wealthy, it cannot solve the massive environmental problems the city and the entire country suffer, including a prolonged drought that has devastated the countryside and caused food and water shortages, an outbreak of epidemics and a massive refugee problem, as tens of thousands flee the countryside for the city. Barcelona's popular waterfront suburbs of the Vila Olímpica and Poble Nou – once the showpiece of the city's Olympic regeneration – are now occupied by refugee camps and desalination plants protected by riot police. Barcelona has become a city divided into those who have access to basic necessities and those that do not. The crime at the centre of this novel is the murder of an Israeli scientist, but Sergiot's investigation reveals an unholy alliance between several national governments and multinational pharmaceutical companies that conduct genetic experiments with catastrophic consequences. De Manuel's vision of a dystopian future offers a counter-narrative to the triumphant capitalist mantra of economic development at any cost and it calls on readers to address these issues before it becomes too late.

If in the *modernista* poetry of Joan Maragall, Barcelona is 'una gran encisera' [a great enchantress], in the typical argot of crime fiction she is a deceptive dame, a dangerous femme fatale, whose mystery and secrets can only be explained by looking beyond the surface image that she presents to the world. As we have seen in this chapter, the Barcelona crime novel seeks to make visible, if only partially, 'the spaces of darkness and trickery' that crime conceals (Certeau: 18). While the city is ultimately unknowable – its complex web of social actors who live and move across diverse public and private locations make such knowledge impossible – the sheer number of crime novels combine to (re)present the Catalan capital, its diversity and its social, cultural and linguistic fault lines. As each crime novel peels off another layer to reveal what the powers-that-be would prefer to hide, each new investigation deepens our understanding of this complex, contradictory and celebrated city.

Works cited

Balibrea, Mari Paz (2011). 'In Search of a New Realism: Manuel Vázquez Montalbán and the Spanish *novela negra*', in Nancy Vosburg (ed.), *Iberian Crime Fiction* (Cardiff: University of Wales Press), 28–50.

Barral, Nil (2011). *L'home que dormia al cotxe* (Barcelona: Ara).

Benjamin, Walter (1973). *Charles Baudelaire: A Lyric Poet in the Era of High Capitalism*. Trans. Harry Zohn (London: NLB).
Bosch, Lluís (2013). *Aire brut* (Barcelona: Alrevés).
Capmany, Maria Aurèlia (2005). *Vés-te'n ianqui* (Barcelona: Barcanova).
Certeau, Michel de (1984). *The Practice of Everyday Life*. Trans. Steven Rendell (Berkeley: University of California Press).
Colmeiro, José F. (1994). *La novela policíaca española. Teoría e historia crítica* (Barcelona: Anthropos).
Delgado, Manuel (2007). *La ciudad mentirosa. Fraude y miseria del 'modelo Barcelona'* (Madrid: Los libros de la Catarata).
Fernàndez, Josep-Anton (1995). 'Becoming Normal: Cultural Production and Cultural Policy in Catalonia', in Helen Graham and Jo Labanyi (eds), *Spanish Cultural Studies: An Introduction. The Struggle for Modernity* (Oxford: Oxford University Press), 342–46.
Fuster, Jaume (1972). *De mica en mica s'omple la pica* (Barcelona: Edicions 62).
Giménez Bartlett, Alicia (1996). *Ritos de muerte* (Barcelona: Plaza y Janés).
— (1997). *Día de perros* (Barcelona: Plaza y Janés).
— (2006). *Dog Day*. Trans. Nick Caistor (New York: Europa).
— (2008). *Death Rites*. Trans. Jonathan Dunne (New York: Europa).
— (2009). *El silencio de los claustros* (Barcelona: Destino).
Godsland, Shelley (2007). *Killing Carmens: Women's Crime Fiction from Spain* (Cardiff: University of Wales Press).
González Ledesma, Francisco (2006). *Historia de mis calles* (Barcelona: Planeta).
Hart, Patricia (1987). *The Spanish Sleuth. The Detective in Spanish Fiction* (London: Associated University Press).
— (1989). 'From Knight Errant to Ethical Hero to Flatfoot: The Development of the Detective in Catalan Fiction'. *Catalan Review* 3.2: 71–93.
Hill, Toni (2011). *El verano de los juguetes muertos* (Barcelona: Debosillo).
— (2013). *The Summer of Dead Toys*. Trans. Laura McGlouglin (London: Transworld).
King, Stewart (2013). 'Carvalho y Cataluña: la subjetividad de los márgenes'. *MVM: Cuadernos de Estudio Manuel Vázquez Montalbán* 1.1: 28–45.
King, Stewart, and Alice Whitmore (2016). 'National Allegories Born(e) in Translation: The Catalan Case'. *The Translator* 22.2: 144–56.
Maitland, Barry (2003). *The Verge Practice* (Crow's Nest: Allen & Unwin).
Manuel, Jordi de (2006). *L'olor de la pluja* (Barcelona: RBA/La Magrana).
Martín, Andreu (1979). *Aprende y calla* (Madrid: Sedmay).

— (1980). *Prótesis* (Madrid: Sedmay).
— (2013). *Societat negra* (Barcelona: La Magrana).
McCracken, Scott (1998). *Pulp: Reading Popular Fiction* (Manchester: Manchester University Press).
Mendoza, Eduardo (1979). *El misterio de la cripta embrujada* (Barcelona: Seix Barral).
— (1982). *El laberinto de las aceitunas* (Barcelona: Seix Barral).
— (2012). *El enredo de la bolsa o la vida* (Barcelona: Seix Barral).
Messent, Peter (1997). 'Introduction: From Private Eye to Police Procedural – The Logic of Contemporary Crime Fiction', in Peter Messent (ed.), *Criminal Proceedings: The Contemporary American Crime Novel* (London: Pluto), 1–21.
Mussa, Alberto (2011). *O senhor do lado esquerdo* (Rio de Janeiro: Editora Record).
— (2013). *The Mystery of Rio*. Trans. Alex Ladd (New York: Europa).
Mustieles, Jacint Maria (1924). *L'assassí i el còmpliç* (Barcelona: La novel·la d'ara).
Oliver, Maria Antònia (1983). 'On ets, Mònica?', in Ofèlia Dracs, *Negra i consentida* (Barcelona: Laia), 119–49.
— (1987). *Study in Lilac*. Trans. Kathleen McNerney (Seattle, WA: Seal).
— (1989). *Antipodes*. Trans. Kathleen McNerney (Seattle, WA: Seal).
— (1991) [1986]. *Estudi en lila* (Barcelona: La Magrana).
— (1992). 'Where are you, Monica?', in Sara Paretsky (ed.), *A Woman's Eye: New Stories by the Best Women Crime Writers* (London: Virago), 370–99.
— (1993) [1987]. *Antípodes* (Barcelona: La Magrana).
Pastor, Marc (2008). *La mala dona* (Barcelona: La Negra).
— (2014). *Barcelona Shadows*. Trans. Mara Faye Lethem (London: Pushkin).
Pedrolo, Manuel de (1975) [1965]. *Joc Brut* (Barcelona: Edicions 62).
Pepper, Andrew (2000). *The Contemporary American Crime Novel: Race, Ethnicity, Gender, Class* (Edinburgh: Edinburgh University Press).
Resina, Joan Ramon (1997). *El cadáver en la cocina. La novela criminal en la cultura del desencanto* (Barcelona: Anthropos).
— (2008). *Barcelona's Vocation of Modernity: Rise and Decline of an Urban Image* (Stanford: Stanford University Press).
Ribas, Rosa, and Sabine Hofmann (2013). *Don de lenguas* (Madrid: Siruela).
— [Sara Moliner] (2015). *The Whispering City*. Trans. Mara Faye Lethem (London: Abacus).
Riera, Carme (2011). *Natura quasi morta* (Barcelona: Edicions 62).
Rodoreda, Mercè (1936). *Crim* (Barcelona: Rosa dels Vents).
Santana, Mario (2000). 'Manuel Vázquez Montalbán's *Los mares del sur*

and the Incrimination of the Spanish Transition'. *Revista de Estudios Hispánicos* 34: 535–59.
Sierra i Fabra, Jordi (2008). *Cuatro días de enero* (Barcelona: Plaza y Janés).
— (2010). *Siete días de julio* (Barcelona: Plaza y Janés).
Silva, Lorenzo (2005). *La reina sin espejo* (Barcelona: Destino).
— (2012). *La marca del meridiano* (Barcelona: Planeta).
Solana, Teresa (2006). *Un crim imperfecte* (Barcelona: Edicions 62).
— (2007). *Drecera al paradís* (Barcelona: Edicions 62).
— (2008). *A Not So Perfect Crime*. Trans. Peter Bush (London: Bitter Lemon).
— (2010). *Negres tempestes* (Barcelona: La Negra).
— (2011). *L'hora Zen. Un crim refinat* (Barcelona: Edicions 62).
— (2011). *A Shortcut to Paradise*. Trans. Peter Bush (London: Bitter Lemon).
— (2013). *The Sound of One Hand Killing*. Trans. Peter Bush (London: Bitter Lemon).
Tasis, Rafael (1986) [1956]. *És hora de plegar* (Valencia: Eliseu Climent).
— (1994) [1960]. *Un crim al Paralelo* (Valencia: Tres i Quatre).
— (2007) [1955]. *La Bíblia valenciana* (Valencia: Tres i Quatre).
Van Guardia, Lola (1999). *Plumas de doble filo* (Barcelona: Egales).
Vázquez Montalbán, Manuel (1974). *Tatuaje* (Barcelona: José Batlló).
— (1979). *Los mares del sur* (Barcelona: Planeta).
— (1988). *El delantero centro fue asesinado al atardecer* (Barcelona: Planeta).
— (1990). *Barcelonas* (Barcelona: Empúries).
— (1995). *Offside*. Trans. Ed Emory (London: Serpent's Tail).
— (1998). *La literatura española en la construcción de la ciudad democrática* (Barcelona: Crítica).
— (2000a). *El hombre de mi vida* (Barcelona: Planeta).
— (2000b). *Southern Seas*. Trans. Patrick Camiller (London: Serpent's Tail).
— (2004). *Milenio Carvalho.* (Barcelona: Planeta).
— (2006). *The Man of My Life*. Trans. Nick Caistor (London: Serpent's Tail).
Vosburg, Nancy (2011). 'Spanish Women's Crime Fiction, 1980s–2000s: Subverting the Conventions of Genre and Gender', in N. Vosburg (ed.), *Iberian Crime Fiction* (Cardiff: University of Wales Press), 75–92.
Wells, Caragh (2007). 'The Case of Barcelona in Manuel Vázquez Montalbán's Detective Fiction'. *Romance Studies* 25.4: 279–88.
Wilson, Barbara (1990). *Gaudí Afternoon* (Seattle, WA: Seal).

CHAPTER SEVENTEEN

A *Biutiful* city: Alejandro González Iñárritu's filmic critique of the 'Barcelona Model'*

Benjamin Fraser

Introduction

La buena parte del urbanismo moderno nunca ha dejado de animarlo –en Barcelona también– la intención de constituir una ciudad perfecta, es decir, una contra-ciudad advirtiendo que quizás la vocación última de cierto urbanismo acaso sea la de desactivar para siempre lo urbano.

[The greater part of modern urbanism has not ceased to be motivated by the intention – Barcelona is no exception – to construct a perfect city, that is, a counter-city suggesting that perhaps the final goal of a certain urbanism may be to disactivate the urban forever.]

Manuel Delgado Ruiz, *La ciudad mentirosa: fraude y miseria del 'modelo Barcelona'*/The Deceitful City: The Fraud and Misery of the 'Barcelona model' (2007a: 17)

---

* Benjamin Fraser, 'A Biutiful City: Alejandro González Iñárritu's Filmic Critique of the "Barcelona Model"'. *Studies in Hispanic Cinemas* 9(1) (2012): 19–34. © Benjamin Fraser.

After so many years of international applause for Barcelona's monumental and spectacular built environment, at long last Alejandro González Iñárritu's *Biutiful* (2010) shows, as this essay explores, not a dystopic future Barcelona but the dark underbelly of the Barcelona that already exists. Opposed to the city's traditional casting as a beautiful backdrop – as arguably represented in Woody Allen's *Vicky Cristina Barcelona* (2008) – here we have not the acclaimed 'model' Barcelona but the 'real' Barcelona (in the sense of the term as employed by Slavoj Žižek, see the 'Introduction' in Kay 2003) – that is, the drab, grimy city full of labour inequality, the collusion of police with multinationals, the reality of sickness (cancer) and the lack of real possibilities for the immigrants who come from abroad hoping to make a better life for themselves and for their families. Just like this article's epigraph penned by Barcelona-based critical urban theorist Manuel Delgado Ruiz (1956–), the filmic image of the Catalan capital presented in Iñárritu's film[1] calls attention to the distance between self-congratulatory discourses of Barcelona as the modern city *por antonomasia* on one side, and the injustices faced by so many of its urbanites on the other (Delgado 2007a: 17).[2] *Biutiful* manages this at the levels of both content and form: by focusing on immigrant and marginalized

---

1 Importantly, the film remains quite faithful to a strain of Spanish literature that has dramatized Barcelona as explicitly reshaped by touristic and capitalistic forces: Vázquez Montalbán's *Sabotaje Olímpico* (1993, about the preparation for the 1992 Games); *Los mares del sur* (1997, in which a detective plot highlights the ills of urban speculation); and Juan Goytisolo's *Señas de identidad* (1976, about the 1929 World Fair, as well as the accelerating tourism of the dictatorship in the 1960s). Eduardo Mendoza's *La ciudad de los prodigios* (2003) is of interest for its presentation of the 1888 Expo in Barcelona as well.

2 When Delgado writes of how the attempts to forge a 'perfect Barcelona' will 'desactivar para siempre lo urbano [disactivate the urban forever]' (2007a: 17), the reader familiar with his work understands not only that urban design is today more synonymous than ever with attracting tourism and international business but also that it is more and more geared towards reducing the possibilities for spontaneity and even democracy. This is, in fact, for some a legacy of modern urban planning in general: as Choay points out with reference to the case of Haussmann, 'the Emperor [of France], wanted to put an end to riots by destroying the medieval structure of Parisian streets and replacing them with broad arteries along which the police could assemble and charge' (15); this critique may be applied also to the broad arteries of Cerdà's Eixample.

characters throughout the film; by largely frustrating the viewer's predictable expectation of glimpses of the city's triumphant and monumental architecture; by privileging interiors throughout; through subtle yet poignant camera movements that shift attention from the 'model' city back to the 'real' city; by mobilizing a wealth of props that depict images of sea life, a way of compensating for and simultaneously drawing attention to the viewer's lack of visual access to the Mediterranean; and, ultimately, even by the integration of a spiritual/ supernatural narrative arc that captures the protagonist Uxbal's gradual crossing over into the beyond – a storyline that ultimately serves also to reinforce the theme of urban immigration/marginalization. During the discussion of each of these elements, this article emphasizes that it is the primary urban theme of the film that brings together its disparate secondary characters and subplots.

From this perspective, the choice of Barcelona as the diegetic setting for *Biutiful* and as the location of its filmic production must be understood as being in no way casual. In extra-filmic discourse, the intriguing case of Barcelona is today widely invoked by both sides of a very polemical conflict over what cities should be – many planners and architects label the 'Barcelona model' a triumph of urban design while various urban critics see it as a product of what Henri Lefebvre has denounced as capitalist modernity's 'enthusiastic (triumphant and triumphalist) consciousness' (1995: 3). Lefebvrian critic Manuel Delgado's insistence in his recent work on the 'Barcelona model' (2007a) – a concept cleverly respun by Mónica Degen in her labelling of Barcelona as the 'top-model' city (2004a, 2004b) – voices a disdain widely held by those who see an enormous gap between triumphalist and majestically touristic images of contemporary cities and the class differences, social inequalities and even the quotidian suffering requisitely hidden by the slick images promoting what many call intercity competition (see Harvey 1996). To see how *Biutiful* paints a picture at odds with the triumphalist idea of the 'modelo Barcelona', it is helpful to ground a reading of the film's formal qualities and content in the urban criticism of Delgado – which specifically addresses topics ranging from the urban built environment itself to immigration and difference. The present approach (which I will call 'urban cultural studies') may seem 'too urban' for traditional film critics and too 'cultural' for many scholars working in the more quantitative and historical field of urban studies proper. Nonetheless,

I insist that in seeking to understand Iñárritu's most recent film, it is necessary and perhaps even unavoidable to force a confrontation between these two discourses. The present Delgado-inspired urban reading of the film thus underscores that *Biutiful* is, throughout and in the final analysis, a compelling and unique film foregrounding the human costs of spectacular urban modernity.

The lived spaces of *Biutiful* Barcelona and the human costs of modernity

It is significant that director Alejandro González Iñárritu himself has said that *Biutiful* has 'little to do, at least in conceptual and structural terms' with his earlier films *Amores perros* (2000), *21 Grams* (2003) and *Babel* (2006) (qtd in Deleyto and del Mar Azcona 2010: ix; also 121–40). Although the context for this comment is a discussion of *Biutiful*'s linear storyline and its focus on the main character's subjectivity (as contrasted with the complex narrative structures of those previous films[3]), another difference is that the city is now not only a backdrop for human struggles but also an inextricable part of the film's urban critique.[4] There has been much written, of course, on the relationship between film and cities.[5] Rather than dialogue more extensively with this tradition as I have elsewhere, here I prefer to delve further into Delgado's theory of the urban itself and reconcile it with a close textual reading of the film.[6] Larry Ford's general assertion – that 'the role of cities in film gradually changed over time from serving as mere

---

3 Deleyto and del Mar Azcona 2010; see also Podalsky 2011; Paul Julian Smith 2006; Tierney 2009.
4 On the urban setting of *Amores perros*, see D'Lugo 2003, Gregori 2006, Kantaris 2008 and Thornton 2003.
5 The volumes edited by Stuart Aitken and Leo Zonn (*Place, Power, Situation and Spectacle: A Geography of Film*, 1994) and by David B. Clarke (*The Cinematic City*, 1997) are foundational in this regard (see also Webber and Wilson 2008; Mennel 2008).
6 See my previous work, which includes an article in *Studies in Hispanic Cinemas* (Fraser 2006; also Fraser 2008a, 2010; I discuss Delgado Ruiz in greater depth in Fraser 2007, 2008b, 2010 and 2011a). See also Degen 2000, Delgado Ruiz 2001, Delgado and Cruz 2008.

background scenery to acting as the equivalent of major characters in many stories' (1994: 119) – is of great relevance. With this in mind, it is easy to see that Barcelona is undeniably recognizable as the film's co-protagonist, along with Javier Bardem's lead character named Uxbal.

One of the film's strengths is that, despite a consistent focus on Javier Bardem's character, there are numerous secondary characters whose subplots become closely and carefully intertwined with Uxbal's necessarily urban experience – one reviewer summarizes *Biutiful* by writing, 'Uxbal and his morally suspect brother Tito (Eduard Fernández) are a pair of halfbaked hoods who profit from Barcelona's black market, taking money from Chinese sweatshop owners and Senegalese street vendors to pay off the city's corrupt police officers' (Feaster 2011: 36). Uxbal's contacts with such secondary characters as sweatshop co-owners (and lovers) Liwei (Jin Luo) and Hai (Taisheng Cheng), sweatshop worker Lili (Lang Sofia Lin), Senegalese street vendor Ekweme (Cheikh Ndiaye) and his wife Ige (Diaryatou Daff) are particularly emphasized as Iñárritu allows each character's experience to reflect the greater dehumanizing forces of capitalist urban modernity in Barcelona. These experiences are tragic, indeed: Liwei and Hai's business comes to an abrupt end, precipitated by Uxbal's gregarious purchase of what are nonetheless faulty gas heaters for the workers; Hai eventually murders Liwei in a hotel room after the business fails and after his wife and family have likely become aware of his extramarital affair; Lili, her child and a score of other Chinese immigrant workers die from gas inhalation, locked in the factory where they sleep nights in cramped conditions; Ekweme is beaten and arrested by the police, being eventually deported and separated from Ige, whom he urges to remain behind; and even Uxbal himself struggles to juggle his roles as father and separated husband with the bribes and black-market business ventures undertaken with his brother, ultimately falling to an end-stage cancer in the film's final sequences.

In *Biutiful*, these seemingly disparate human tragedies acquire a cumulative force as manifestations of a decidedly urban problematic where the value of human relationships is consistently subordinated to the rule of exchange. Urban theorist Delgado has written of Barcelona as being 'un artículo de consumo con una sociedad humana dentro' [an article of consumption containing a human society] (2007a: 11), and in this light, the film crafts a critical view of the reified and consumed city as product, this time as seen from the inside of the packaging. The director relies heavily on interiors, which dominate throughout the film as a way of underscoring the small-scale stories of the immigrants and street vendors who struggle from day to day just to make ends meet. We are frequently shown, for example, the locked and cramped basement room where Lili and her child sleep with other Chinese immigrants to awaken regularly at 6:30 a.m. for a demanding day's work at an underground sweatshop, just as the insides of apartments predominate (those of Uxbal, of Tito, of Uxbal's estranged wife Marambra, of his spiritual mentor Bea and of the small space Ekweme and Ige share with numerous other immigrants). When exteriors are indeed shown, the scenes alternate between still shots of empty street corners at dusk (e.g., in the area of the Chinese sweatshop) and vibrant daytime pavements crowded with people. Regardless, shots of the streets during the day (of Uxbal, the children and Marambra) are often shot at such an angle so as to crop out the sky. The vibrant pavement scenes play an important role – as when Ige picks up the children from school, for example. The crowds of people moving to and fro during the day offer a complement to the desolate night street corners, thus emphasizing the human city, the practised city – implicitly in line with the emancipatory notions of the pavement ballet/'eyes on the street' that famed antiurbanist Jane Jacobs (1992) wrote about in her book *The Death and Life of Great American Cities* (1961).[7]

Delgado has himself linked Jacobs' vision of the life of the streets with his greater critique of contemporary urban design.[8] In his

---

7 A similar evocation of Barcelona occurs in José Luis Guerín's film *En construcción*; see Loxham 2006.

8 Delgado writes of Jacobs in his own work: 'My readings of *The Death and Life of Great American Cities*, by Jane Jacobs ([published in Spanish translation by] Península, Barcelona, 1973), and *The Fall of Public Man*, by Richard Sennet [*sic*] (Península, Barcelona, 1974), were for me revelations, and the present book [*El animal público/*The Public Animal] would neither seek to, nor could it, hide this fact' (Delgado Ruiz 1999: 19; my translation). In *Sociedades movedizas/*Mobile Societies, he explores the 'life of the sidewalk', similarly pronouncing that *Death and Life* is 'a fundamental text' (Delgado 2007b: 245), and once again invoking and unpacking Jacobs' metaphor of street activities as dance (2007b: 135–36) (my translations). For Delgado, the importance of the metaphor of the sidewalk ballet seems to lie in its potential to account for difference and multiplicity in the representation of urban spaces and activities.

prizewinning book *El animal público* [The Public Animal], he goes so far as to claim the street is 'la patria de los sin patria' [the country of those with no country] (1999: 209), invoking Hannah Arendt, while suggesting that the exile and the foreigner are those who best express civic values (1999: 209, significantly enough, on the book's concluding page). It is in the street where every moment sees the production of

> [t]he integration of incompatibles, where the most effective exercises of reflecting about one's own identity can be carried out, where the notion of political commitment as a consequence of the possibilities of action makes sense and where social mobilization allows one to know the potential of the currents of sympathy and solidarity among strangers. (1999: 208, my translation[9])

Walking the city streets, in Delgado's view (just as for Jacobs and Michel de Certeau before him), defies symbolically, and often in practical terms, the necessarily static poses of much identity politics. Delgado evokes the pedestrian as a transient, uncodified, 'stateless' being whose shifting from place to place makes him or her hard to pin down and identify. Although *Biutiful* makes it equally clear that this 'statelessness' enjoyed by the transient pedestrian is necessarily ephemeral (e.g., through the scene of the police raid in the Plaça de Catalunya that rolls down the Ramblas and ends in Ekweme's deportation), the life of the streets shows through as the basis for a potential alternative urbanism that might humanize the city, embracing difference and once again asserting the priority of the city as use-value over the bourgeois legacy of the city as exchange-value.[10]

---

9 In the original Spanish: 'la integración de las incompatibilidades, donde se pueden llevar a cabo los más eficaces ejercicios de reflexión sobre la propia identidad, donde cobra sentido el compromiso político como consciencia de las posibilidades de la acción y donde la movilización social permite conocer la potencia de las corrientes de simpatía y solidaridad entre extraños'.

10 Also, in line with a tradition of urban criticism that has questioned the existence of a 'public space' that is not won through struggle (see Mitchell 2003; Lefebvre 1996; Staeheli 1996), Delgado advances a sceptical view of the notion of public space, one that is helpful in understanding *Biutiful*'s contribution to discourses of the urban (2007a: 225–26; also 2006).

Biutiful's persistent focus on interiors and on the ephemerality of street life – the human city, what Delgado (1999, 2007b) and Lefebvre (1991, 1996) call the 'lived city' – presents a stark contrast with the triumphalist view of Barcelona as a monumentally architectural and touristic Mediterranean destination. The dehumanizing experiences of these marginalized secondary characters – working in sweatshops or on the streets, living in poverty and under exploitative conditions – point to the characteristic fate of a greater number of urbanites trapped inside a city that is essentially a product for sale to tourists and multinationals.[11] Iñárritu's film is thus important not only for the interior sets on which it chooses to focus but also for the specific type of exterior it largely eschews. The viewer is generally frustrated in his or her expectation to see pleasing general shots of what is possibly one of the most photographed and 'beautiful' European cities. The most notable or recognizable public spaces of Barcelona, if they appear at all in the film, are significantly portrayed only as 'sites of conflict' (Delgado writes that 'el espacio urbano es ante todo espacio para el conflicto' [urban space is above all a space of conflict], 2010: 138).

For example, the monetary arrangements between Uxbal and the municipal police prove to be of little importance when a raid is made on Senegalese street vendors selling their wares in a particularly touristic area of the city. A shot relatively early in the film effects a subtle camera tilt downward from the Nike logo on the store window to the vendors below, set up outside the multinational's shop located in the capital-rich Plaça de Catalunya. This movement directly underscores the contrast between the city as exchange value and the city as use-value which is so important to Lefebvre (1996) and later Delgado (2007a; 2007b). Later, the dramatic police-raid sequence makes it clear that this seemingly 'public' space in the city is partial to a certain definition of the public – that a more democratic notion of public is always already subject to the uneven laws of capitalist competition. The sequence is notably filmed with disorienting hand-held cameras as a way of capturing the danger and violence of the hunt as police chase down the vendors – using brutal

---

11 As such, the film might be grouped alongside the critical urban vision of Bilbao-born Álex de la Iglesia, whose *El día de la bestia* (1995), *La comunidad* (2000) and *Crimen ferpecto* (2004) were also somewhat well-received denunciations of urban shifts in Spain (see Compitello 2003).

force. One part of the chase highlights Ekweme, who, while trying to escape, is hit in the face with a baton as he rounds a corner. A subsequent mobile close-up of his feet only (point of view – Uxbal), as his limp body is dragged away initially, leaves it open to interpretation as to whether he has been knocked unconscious or perhaps even killed. Although part of this chase sequence takes place as the vendors run down Barcelona's famed Ramblas, departing from the Plaça de Catalunya, this touristic staple of the Catalan capital is purposely obscured on screen through an excessive travelling frame and a dizzying hand-held camera, such that little visual appreciation of the area's characteristic painted performance artists or sanctioned vendor stalls is possible. In this sequence, the Ramblas and the Plaça de Catalunya are used not as touristic spectacles but instead, in line with Delgado's view of the city, as first and foremost a 'site of conflict' – whether understood in terms of immigrants versus police, multinational corporations versus street vendors, or more appropriately, both at once.

Just as importantly, the film's images of Barcelona's triumphant and characteristically 'modern' architecture are either non-existent or else marred by references to human tragedy. Establishing shots of recognizable parts of the city are few and far between, amounting collectively to a minute's duration at most in a film that lasts over two hours. Late in the film, for example, we see a brief high-angle shot of nineteenth-century urban designer Ildefons Cerdà's Eixample district illuminated at dusk with lights of car-traffic visible.[12] Another important but brief establishing shot of a familiar if touristic and monumental Barcelona similarly occurs late in the film: a pan initially

---

12 Even this shot might be interpreted as a reference to the way in which nineteenth-century cities – and Barcelona in particular – were redesigned over all else to promote the flow of traffic (even if not yet automobile traffic) and goods through the streets. The Plan Cerdà, for example, echoed the changes made by Haussmann in Paris in the construction of broad avenues and the widening of intersections with truncated corners (i.e. the *xamfrà*; see Cerdà 1867; Resina 2008: 22) – all to facilitate traffic (on Haussmann's Paris see Harvey 2006). In fact, Cerdà's 1867 two-volume treatise, which he called the *Teoría general de la urbanización*, put forth a novel theoretical understanding of the city as evolving through stages that were dependent on the form of locomotion prioritized in each: *locomoción pedestre, locomoción ecuestre, locomoción rastrera, locomoción rodada (ordinaria y perfeccionada)*.

Figure 17.1 The Torre Agbar and Sagrada Família as seen from Uxbal's hospital window (pan–left)
© *Studies in Latin American and Spanish Cinemas*

capturing the recently constructed Torre Agbar building,[13] and Antonio Gaudí's still unfinished Sagrada Família and moving left to rest finally on the rightward gaze of Javier Bardem's Uxbal, who sits in a hospital chair gazing through a window as he receives a cancer treatment (Figure 17.1). This subtle but poignant pan-left functions as a cinematic redirection, allowing the viewer to contrast the city's monumental architecture and triumphalist touristic skyline with the quotidian human stories of marginality and illness that form the basis of Iñárritu's film. Similarly, Barcelona's famed Olympic village (see McNeill 1999) can be seen briefly and likewise late in the film – but even then, as will be discussed in the next section of this essay, in a way

---

13 The Torre Agbar, designed by French architect Jean Nouvel, opened in 2005 and lies at the boundary of the Poble Nou neighbourhood, a district that has received much attention for being a hub of urban renewal schemes in the Catalan capital (see McNeill 1999).

that explicitly points to the human tragedies that are the hidden cost of urban renewal in international cities such as Barcelona. *Biutiful*'s aforementioned crucial camera movements – both subtle (the tilt, the pan) and not so subtle (dizzying mobile frame and handheld camera) – function to force a filmic confrontation between two widely divergent conceptions of the modern city. Manuel Delgado writes extensively on these two perspectives (in the process explicitly following urban theorist Henri Lefebvre's distinctly spatial reappropriation of Marx's reflections on the nature of capital).[14] In an essay titled 'La ciudad levantada' [The City in Revolt] Delgado writes that the city has – throughout the twentieth and into the twenty-first century – become so controlled by exchange value and so neglectful of use value that the

> city dramatizes, then, the perennial conflict between two models of urban society. One is that encarnated by the bourgeois city, ideally and exclusively inhabited by a self-satisfied middle class who detests conflict [...] a city that refashions itself according to the requirements of the phase of capitalist development in which it finds itself at any given moment and that is disposed to integrate itself into the great shifts of urban modernization [...] The other city lies on the other shore of the river where one finds the exploited and the excluded. (2010: 139–40; my translation[15])

Iñárritu's *Biutiful* persistently dramatizes the distance between these two opposing forces: on the one hand, the bourgeois Barcelona intent

---

14 Delgado continues Lefebvre's emphasis on the nineteenth-century shift that saw the triumph of exchange value and, just as his influence, inflects this idea with a distinctly urban perspective (see Lefebvre 2003). This shift, outlined by Karl Marx in *Capital* (1977), was for Lefebvre reflected in the uniquely modern construction of the city as an image to be consumed and visually possessed, and in the creation of needs to be satisfied through patterns of production and consumption (1996: 67–68).

15 In the original Spanish: 'ciudad dramatiza, pues, el contencioso interminable entre dos modelos de sociedad urbana. Uno es el que encarna la ciudad burguesa, habitada idealmente y en exclusiva por una clase media autosatisfecha que detesta el conflicto [...] Una ciudad que se amolda dócil a los requerimientos de la fase del desarrollo capitalista en que se encuentra en cada momento y se muestra dispuesta a incorporarse a las grandes dinámicas de modernización urbana [...] Del otro lado, al otro lado del río, los explotados y los excluidos' (Delgado 2010: 139–40).

on securing a spot as a destination city for both tourism and capital within the international market; and on the other, the Barcelona of 'the exploited and the excluded' (Delgado 2010; my translation) – the workers and immigrants who are withheld access to this dream (cf. Castells and Mollenkopf 1991; Riis 1890).

This dualistic contrast between Barcelona as a bourgeois 'model' city and as a city of the exploited can also be understood in terms of a more theoretical framework: Delgado's Lefebvrian stress on the importance of the 'practised city' over the 'planned city'. This opposition between the city as it is lived on the ground and as it is designed from above in the interests of capital accumulation comprises the key thrust of Delgado's urban critique (1999: 182). It is the practised city that holds the potential to combat the compromised (with respect to capital) perspective of contemporary urban designers and also to help craft a more inclusive city, one more attentive to the needs, realities and heterogeneity of its inhabitants. Delgado writes that

> The model of the politicized city is that of a pristine and splendorous city, a city of dreams, a city-utopia, comprehensible, polished, ordered, watched over day and night in order to avoid any possibility that would alter its perfected stillness. On the other hand, the truly urbanized city – not in the sense of being subordinated to urbanism, but in that of being completely open to the very movements that constitute the urban – would evoke what Michel Foucault, at the outset of *The Order of Things*, calls a 'heterotopia', that is an entangled human community, in which hybridities[16] have been generalized and in which the incongruent becomes the fuel for an unlimited vitality. (Delgado 1999: 182; original emphasis; my translation[17])

---

16 Hybridities in Iñárritu's earlier film *Amores perros* have been addressed recently by Brent Smith (2010).
17 In the original Spanish: 'El modelo de la ciudad politizada es el de una ciudad prístina y esplendorosa, ciudad soñada, ciudad utópica, comprensible, lisa, ordenada, vigilada noche y día para evitar cualquier eventualidad que alterara su quietud perfecta. En cambio, la ciudad plenamente urbanizada – no en el sentido de plenamente sumisa al urbanismo, sino en el de abandonada del todo a los movimientos en que consiste lo urbano – evocaría lo que Michel Foucault

Just as the planned city is opposed to the practised city, so too is the bourgeois city opposed to the city of the exploited, and the dehumanizing capitalist city to the city as a lived space. *Biutiful* carries the spirit of Delgado's critique to the screen, illustrating that the vital human essence of the city such as that found ephemerally in the streets is nonetheless persistently 'subordinated to urbanism' (Delgado 1999; my translation). Maintaining an emphasis on Delgado's urban theory, the next section of this essay turns to the film's nuanced presentation of the Mediterranean (and thus its subversion of the touristic image of Barcelona) before folding its supernatural aspects in with its capitalist critique in a reading of the first and final sequences of the film.

Barcelona as Mediterranean destination city: From the sea to the beyond

Numerous books and articles published over the years make reference to the perennial refashioning of the city by an urbanism that Joan Ramon Resina has recently (2008) called *Barcelona's Vocation of Modernity*. Scholars have frequently commented on the ills of Barcelona's urban planning – in reference to the nineteenth-century plans of Ildefons Cerdà, who designed the city's Eixample in 1859, just as to preparations for the 1929 World's Fair and the creation of the Olympic City for the 1992 Games.[18] Notwithstanding, the 'modelo Barcelona' is applauded as part of a view that prioritizes the concept of what Delgado (2007a) denounces in his introduction as 'La ciudad-negocio' [The City-as-Business]: he writes that

> Quien ansía ocupar Barcelona y avasallarla es, hoy, un capitalismo financiero internacional que aspira a convertir la capital catalana

llama, nada más empezar *Las palabras y las cosas*, una heterotopía, es decir una comunidad humana embrollada, en la que se han generalizado las hibridaciones y en la que la incongruencia deviene el combustible de una vitalidad sin límites'.
18 On Cerdà and the Eixample, see Cerdà 1867; Epps 2001, 2002; Fraser 2011b; Goldston 1969; and Resina 2003, 2008. Regarding the 1929 World's Fair, see Epps 2001; Fraser 2008c; and Vázquez Montalbán 1990. On the Olympic City, see McNeill 1999, 2002; and Degen 2008. See also Corominas i Ayala 2010; Hall 1997; and Hughes 1992.

en un artículo de consumo con una sociedad humana dentro. (Delgado 2007a: 11)

[What anxiously desires to occupy and subdue Barcelona is, today, an international financial capitalism that aspires to convert the Catalan capital into an article of consumption with a human society inside it].

An important component of Barcelona's international fame and marketability as a destination city is, of course, its proximity to the Mediterranean Sea.

To fully appreciate how Iñárritu's on-screen presentation of a decidedly bleak urban environment approximates Manuel Delgado's denunciation of a 'model' Barcelona – as an article fit for consumption – it is necessary to turn to the film's nuanced dialogue with the Mediterranean: which, although persistently denied on-screen representation, is presented indirectly through frequent ocean imagery on props and sets, and also through its association with the film's mobilization of the colour blue (the colour most often associated with water). These stylistic decisions on the part of the director nonetheless point to the conspicuous absence of the Mediterranean Sea, heightening the significance of its appearance in a crucial sequence late in the film and eventually intersecting even with the theme of worldly death and, necessarily given the plot circumstances, of supernatural connection with the world beyond.

The meaning of the film's rich formal aspects (props, sets and colour palette) cannot be considered in isolation from *Biutiful*'s primary emphasis on the human costs that undergird the perceived success of the 'modelo Barcelona'. For example, Iñárritu's film employs an often drab palette, perhaps to emphasize the lack of opportunities that exist for his marginalized urban characters – and yet, within the context of that often drab palette, the colour blue acquires a special resonance, heightening the film's sympathetic portrayal of its marginalized and even tragic immigrant characters. Blue objects haunt the film: the cabinets in the medium Bea's apartment, and the stones she gives to Uxbal; the blue bag brought to the train station by the Senegalese immigrant Ige when she thinks of leaving Spain; the underwear worn by Liwei – the younger lover and business partner who is later tragically and brutally murdered (presumably by Hai or by his order) in a hotel room – and not least of all, the blue sweatshirt worn by Uxbal as his own death grows nigh. In this way, the colour becomes synonymous with social marginalization just as it is a poetic way of redefining Barcelona as a city of 'others' – a city, as all cities, defined by either difference in the sense of a diverse community or the implicit contrast with the presumably more homogeneous structures of life outside urban areas.[19] The colour blue, of course, enjoys a rich history as the symbol for deep sadness and melancholy such as that experienced by *Biutiful*'s numerous secondary characters, and it is perhaps fortuitous in this sense that Iñárritu himself has remarked in an interview conducted during the production of his 2010 film that '*Biutiful* is like the blues: a long, melancholy note' (qtd in Deleyto and del Mar Azcona 2010: 126, translation by the authors). It would be short-sighted, however, to ignore that the colour draws its signifying power also from the proximity of the Mediterranean Sea itself. And if the director's comments are any indication, the sea does not just symbolize an escape from generalized earthly woes, but – for him – more specifically an escape from the spatial territorialism of advanced capitalism. In that same interview Iñárritu remarks,

> When I go to the seaside, what I find hypnotic about the sea, what is truly relaxing, is that there's no property. If an idiot decided to build a brick wall in the sea, if the technical possibility existed, I'm sure all the G-8 countries would erect a barrier in the sea. (Qtd in Deleyto and del Mar Azcona 2010: 139; translation by the authors)

(Compare the Lefebvrian dictum that capitalism has survived throughout the twentieth century by 'producing space, by occupying a space' [Lefebvre 1976: 21]).

The sea appears on screen more often in *Biutiful* as a motif than as a filmed image – in props/sets including the large fish sticker in Uxbal's shower, the aquarium nightlight in his children's room, the painting

---

19 On diversity and urban community, see Esposito 2009; Harvey 1996, 2009; and Jacobs 1992; on the relationship between rural and urbanized consciousness, see the now classic work, *The Metropolis and Mental Life*, by Simmel (2010); and Wirth 1938.

of the boat jarringly (but diegetically) shot early in the film, the fish stickers on the cabinets in Marambra's kitchen and the exterior wall art of a large slick shark devouring what appears to be older graffiti. These references to the sea – and thus to freedom from property, the rule of exchange-value and the misery experienced by Barcelona's immigrant underclass – serve as an intermittent reminder that a better life lies just outside the reach of the film's secondary characters. The children Mateo and Ana, as Marambra says so poignantly, 'Nunca han salido de este barrio' [Have never left this neighbourhood]; and similarly, Uxbal says that the bipolar Marambra has never heard 'el ruidoso mar' [the noisy sea] despite Barcelona's location on the coast of the Mediterranean itself. The filmgoer's visual experience of on-screen Barcelona parallels this lack of access to the beach, and thus drives home the film protagonists' collective lack of hope. Simply put, *Biutiful* largely frustrates the viewer's predictable expectation to see the Mediterranean – with one important exception.

This exception occurs late in the film. After the Chinese workers die from gas inhalation while asleep, locked in the basement room of the sweatshop, we learn that their bodies have been taken out to sea and dumped offshore so as to avoid repercussions that might harm Hai's business deals. Nonetheless, the cadavers soon wash up on shore – as we learn from an intercalated news report. We then witness a cut to a tranquil sea-line and a mobile frame passing ethereally over the rhythmic waves to a sandy beach where the bodies recall beached whales seen on television by Uxbal earlier in the film.[20] Perhaps the most memorable scene of the film (with the exception of the images comprising the beginning and end of the film's ring composition, discussed below), this one holds true to Iñárritu's decision to show not Barcelona as an architectural triumph and Mediterranean destination-city but Barcelona as a façade draped over human tragedy. A view of what might otherwise be a symbol of hope, freedom, escape and course leisure – the Mediterranean Sea itself – is thus delivered instead as a jarring reminder of the daily tragedies underscoring urban life.

As stated in the Introduction, I regard the distance between the 'modelo Barcelona' and the 'real' Barcelona, one which in reality

---

20 This type of parallel between humans and animals occurs also repeatedly in scenes where both moths and dead souls crawl on the ceilings of interiors.

makes the city's success possible, as the primary theme of the film. And yet there are secondary themes that complement this one – a fact that makes it so much easier to regard *Biutiful* as a complex film. The distance between the two Barcelonas (whether pristine image vs. underbelly; planned city vs. practised city; the bourgeois city vs. the city of the exploited) parallels (1) the neo-baroque interplay between appearance and essence highlighted by the film's ring composition, just as it does (2) the contrast between life and death as seen through the supernatural aspects of the film.

Those sequences with which the film begins and ends (comprising its 'ring composition') highlight the opposition of outer beauty and inner essence – just as does the title *Biutiful* itself, of course. The first words the viewer hears in *Biutiful* are spoken by Uxbal's daughter Ana, who asks, '¿Es de verdad?' [Is it real?] as we see a close-up of her hand touching the ring on that of her father.[21] The dialogue foregrounds the question of the 'reality' of beauty, just as the camera juxtaposes the human hand – through labour, the source of all wealth in capitalist societies – with the ring, a symbol for the products of that capitalist labour. Here, we see the hands, the ring, but no faces, no shots of either Ana or her father – a decision that has imbued the scene with a certain subjective, and even poetic, effect. If the shot is indeed a point-of-view (POV) shot, then it may be Ana's, Uxbal's or perhaps even a shared POV (an interpretation that is more plausible given the supernatural slant of the film as a whole, and the finale in particular).

The final sequence of the film returns to and re-imagines this same initial dialogue and question ('¿Es de verdad?'), although from a different perspective, one that is (not unproblematically) more objective. As opposed to the film's beginning, in the final sequence we see not a close-up but instead contextualized mid/mid-long shots of father and daughter resting in bed, while Ana touches the ring. At the side of the bed sits Uxbal's double, indicating that he is passing on into death. This passing is itself intriguing, and is rendered poetically by Iñárritu, who fuses previous moments in the film together on screen – a poetic amalgam of Uxbal's memory of his own father spawned by a photo, his son's interest in owls and previous discussion of a trip by his wife and daughter to the snow-covered Pyrenees. Along with the visual

---

21 We later learn that the ring was bought for Ana's mother, Marambra.

presentation of these images, the final and initial sequences of the film both include audio of what might very well be the sounds of the 'ruidoso mar' [noisy sea] itself. The effect of the shift made from the beginning of the film (a disjointed close-up POV) to the ending (the contextualized, more objective mid/mid-long shots) in the portrayal of what is actually a single moment in time is to highlight the human story behind the hands we initially see. The ring itself, while indeed still an object and symbol of 'biuti', requires less of our attention as we focus instead on the human relationship between Ana and her father Uxbal. In this sense, the film's ring composition parallels the film's urban preoccupation: its emphasis on the human relationships behind the shimmering myth of the Barcelona model – human relationships that, of course, through labour, have made that very myth possible.

The supernatural aspects of the film must be similarly understood in relation to *Biutiful*'s primary denunciation of urban inequalities. Just as with the mentor-character of Bea, Uxbal is himself a medium of sorts, capable of seeing the dead who have not yet passed on to the other side – for example, earlier in the film he visits the bodies of three dead children and coaxes one to move on; after the death of the Chinese sweatshop workers he sees their bodies floating in the air; at the end of the film he sees himself in a mirror and then on the ceiling just before we see him sitting at his own bedside in preparation for his departure from this earthly realm. Moreover, three extremely subtle but significant and compelling instances of asynchrony in the film resort to digital modification of aspects of the screen image in order to poetically convey the growing distance between Uxbal's earthly existence and his spiritual counterpart: (1) Uxbal's reflection moves independently of his character while sitting in front of a small dresser-top mirror; (2) while beside a car waiting outside a building with a full-length reflective window; and (3) after returning from the nightclub, the movement of his fork does not match its projected shadow (this last instance is perhaps the most noticeable for first-time viewers of the film – although without the other two it may risk being taken for a representation of his drunkenness).

And yet given the primary urban theme of the film, its opposition death/life is, by and large, subordinated to a greater discourse of 'borders'. *Biutiful* is not merely a supernatural story but an urban film highlighting the interplay of national borders by way of its nation-straddling characters (the Senegalese street vendors and the Chinese sweatshop immigrants) and even the seemingly trivial reference to the Pyrenees (above) – which conjures up images of the French/Spanish border and that is arguably echoed via the snow-laden 'beyond' experienced in death by Uxbal. Moreover, the prevalence of the theme of death and the 'beyond' in a sense also constitutes a wider exploration of the theme of immigration and exile as, like *Biutiful*'s protagonist Uxbal, we are all immigrants of sorts, merely passing through this world, and destined for another. In this way, the supernatural elements of the film allow Iñárritu to position the dead themselves as yet another kind of marginalized subjectivity (e.g. as have Jo Labanyi [2000] and Cristina Moreiras-Menor [2008] in their essays). For Iñárritu, the numerous lost souls helped by the spiritual medium Uxbal are merely the supernatural counterpart to the marginalized urbanites of Barcelona: not only the central immigrant and marginalized characters described above but also, for example, the homeless man Uxbal sees one day while looking out of his window onto the street below. Dead souls and living urbanites alike are lost in the midst of a larger city in which they do not matter.

The theme of death also foregrounds the notion of belonging, which is in turn so central to Delgado's contemporary urban criticism. The lost souls, and eventually Bardem's Uxbal, do not belong to the world of the living anymore, just as Ekweme, Ige, Liwei, Lili and her child presumably do not belong in a Barcelona that nonetheless profits from their labour. The fleeting sense of community established between Uxbal and Lili/Li, and between Uxbal and Ige, and the volatile portrayal of the family relationships between Ana/Mateo and Marambra, between Uxbal and Marambra, and between Uxbal and Tito – all of these are nothing in contrast to the portrayal of a Barcelona that does not tolerate difference and discourages a sense of belonging to place. Significantly, a number of the film's climactic scenes foreground so-called 'no-places' – for example, the hotel where Liwei is murdered and the train station where Ige struggles with the decision whether to return to Senegal or to remain in the Catalan capital.[22] The central characters of *Biutiful* are subject to this particular

---

[22] As Zygmunt Bauman has argued, no-places are those characterized by the absence of difference 'the comforting feeling of belonging – the reassuring

capitalist refashioning of city-space, in which under the illusion of homogeneity – effecting the 'absence of difference' – marginality is policed in the modern city so that space may be sold as a tourist destination or as an attractive business location.²³

In this context, lacking an identity – going unidentified – becomes a way of momentarily evading the codification that aids in the selling of city-space. Delgado writes of the urban pedestrian's 'right to anonymity', wherein the apparent lack of identity is, in fact, a protection of sorts that, in theory, makes it possible for individuals to momentarily evade the systems of control that increasingly play a role in the reproduction and vigilance over the shared spaces of the city.²⁴

> For example, the 'immigrants' or those making up cultural, ethnic or religious 'minorities'. All of these are subject to conceptualizations that do not reflect an objective reality, but that are rather derogatory attributes applied with the goal of signalling the presence of someone who is 'different', who is 'the other' in a context in which everyone in the world is – or should be – recognized as different or as the other. Those persons who are labelled 'ethnic' or 'immigrant' are systematically obliged to give explanations, to justify what they do, what they think, what the rites they perform are, what they eat, what their sexuality is, what religious sentiments they have or what their vision of the universe is. (2007b: 192; my translation²⁵)

impression of being part of a community' (2000: 99). See also Augé 2005; cf. Delgado 2004).

23 On this, see Philo and Kearns 1993; Harvey 1996; Fraser 2010; and Lefebvre 1991.

24 In *Sociedades movedizas*, building explicitly on Erving Goffman's idea of 'desatención cortés' [polite inattentiveness] Delgado (2007b: 189), writes of the seeming lack of identity enjoyed by the urban pedestrian, referencing as a refusal: 'Esos seres han renunciado a proclamar quiénes son. Se niegan a identificarse' [Those beings have declined to proclaim who they are. They refuse to be identified] (2007b: 188; my translation).

25 In the original Spanish: 'Por ejemplo, los "inmigrantes" o los components de "minorías" culturales, étnicas o religiosas. Todos ellos reciben conceptualizaciones que no reflejan una realidad objetiva, sino que son atributos denegatorios aplicados con la finalidad de señalar la presencia de alguien que es "el diferente", que es "el otro", en un contexto en el cual todo el mundo es – o debería ser

With this in mind, synthesizing the urban and supernatural aspects of *Biutiful* – in both cases foregrounding questions of marginality and beings who do not belong in the urban spaces of Barcelona – suggests that there are only a handful of ways to escape the excessive codification of identity, the concomitant cleansing of city-space and of course also the modes of social exploitation to which the city's urbanites are routinely subjected. Uxbal's passing into the other world – and the fate of the film's Chinese immigrants – intimates that the city's persecution of marginality may end only in death. Another alternative is shown through the narrative arc of Ekweme, who is forced to accept deportation as a solution to the struggles he encounters in the Catalan capital. And Ige faces an uncertain future in Uxbal's apartment in which she may even take on the not-unproblematic role of mother to his children Ana and Mateo. In the end, whether it is seen as a stunning human story or as a supernatural narrative, all readings of *Biutiful* must grapple with the dehumanizing effects of what Joan Ramon Resina (2008) calls *Barcelona's Vocation of Modernity*.

Works cited

Aitken, Stuart C., and Leo E. Zonn (eds) (1994). *Place, Power, Situation and Spectacle: A Geography of Film* (Lanham, MD: Rowan & Littlefield).

Augé, Marc (2005). *Los no lugares. Una antropología de la sobremodernidad.* Trans. Margarita Mizraji (Barcelona: Gedisa).

Bauman, Zigmunt (2000). *Liquid Modernity* (Malden, MA: Polity).

Castells, Manuel, and John Mollenkopf (1991). *Dual City: Restructuring New York* (New York: Russell Sage).

Cerdà, Ildefons (1867). *Teoría general de la urbanización.* 2 vols. (Madrid: Imprenta Española).

Choay, Françoise (1969). *The Modern City: Planning in the 19th Century.* Trans. Marguerite Hugo and George R. Collins (New York: George Braziller).

– reconocido como diferente y otro. Estas personas a las que se aplica la marca de "étnico" o "inmigrante" son sistemáticamente obligadas a dar explicaciones, a justificar qué hacen, qué piensan, cuáles son los ritos que siguen, qué comen, cómo es su sexualidad, qué sentimientos religiosos tienen o cuál es la vision que tienen del universo'.

Clarke, David B. (ed.) (1997). *The Cinematic City* (New York: Routledge).
Compitello, Malcolm Alan (2003). 'Del plan al diseño: *el día de la bestia* de Álex de la Iglesia y la cultura de la acumulación flexible en el Madrid del postcambio', in Edward Baker and Malcolm Alan Compitello (eds), *Madrid de Fortunana a la M-40. Un siglo de cultura urbana* (Madrid: Alianza), 327–52.
Corominas i Ayala, Miquel (2010). Los orígenes del Ensanche de Barcelona: suelo técnica e iniciativa (Barcelona: UPC).
Degen, Monica (2000). 'Manuel Delgado, capturing public life'. Review of *El animal público, Space and Culture*, 7/8/9.
— (2004a). 'Barcelona's Games: The Olympics, Urban Design and Glocal Tourism', in John Urry and Mimi Sheller (eds), *Tourism Mobilities: Places to Play, Places in Play* (London: Routledge), 131–42.
— (2004b). 'Passejant per la passarel·la global: ciutats i turisme urbà'. *Transversal* 23: 30–32.
— (2008). Sensing Cities: Regenerating Public Life in Barcelona and Manchester (London and New York: Routledge).
Deleyto, Celestino, and María del Mar Azcona (2010). *Alejandro González Iñárritu* (Urbana: University of Illinois Press).
Delgado Ruiz, Manuel (1999). *El animal público* (Barcelona: Anagrama).
— (2001). *Memoria y lugar. El espacio público como crisis de significado* (Valencia: Ediciones Generales de la Construcción).
— (2004). 'La no-ciudad como ciudad absoluta', in Félix de Azúa (ed.), *La arquitectura de la no-ciudad* (Navarra: Universidad Pública de Navarra), 121–54.
— (2006). 'Espacio público'. *El País*, 29 May. www.elpais.com
— (2007a). La ciudad mentirosa: fraude y miseria del 'modelo Barcelona' (Madrid: Catarata).
— (2007b). Sociedades movedizas: pasos hacia una antropología de las calles (Barcelona: Anagrama).
— (2010). 'La ciudad levantada: la barricada y otras transformaciones radicales del espacio urbano', in Josep Muntañola Thornberg and Marcelo Zárate (eds), *Hacia un urbanismo alternativo*, International Conference, Architectonics, Mind, Land and Society, 19/20; (Barcelona: UPC), 137–53.
Delgado Ruiz, Manuel, and Manuel Cruz (2008). *Pensar por pensar: conversaciones sobre el mundo y la vida*. Prologue Gemma Nierga (Madrid: Aguilar).
D'Lugo, Marvin (2003). '*Amores perros/Love's a Bitch*: Alejandro González Iñárritu, Mexico, 2000', in Alberto Elena and Marina Díaz López (eds), *The Cinema of Latin America* (London: Wallflower Press), 221–29.

Epps, Brad (2001). 'Modern Spaces: Building Barcelona', in Joan Ramon Resina (ed.), *Iberian Cities* (New York and London: Routledge), 148–97.
— (2002). 'Barcelona and the Projection of Cataluña'. *Arizona Journal of Hispanic Cultural Studies* 6 (Special Section): 191–287.
Esposito, Roberto (2009). *Communitas: The Origin and Destiny of Community*. Trans. Timothy Campbell (Stanford: Stanford University Press).
Feaster, Felicia (2011). 'Life Isn't *Biutiful*: Alejandro González Iñárritu Turns Barcelona into Gomorrah'. *Charleston City Paper* (9 February): 36.
Ford, Larry (1994). 'Sunshine and Shadow: Lighting and Color in the Depiction of Cities on Film', in Stuart Aitken and Leo Zonn (eds), *Place, Power, Situation and Spectacle: A Geography of Film* (Lanham, MD: Rowman & Littlefield), 119–36.
Fraser, Benjamin (2006). 'The Space in Film and the Film in Space: Madrid's Retiro Park and Carlos Saura's *Taxi*'. *Studies in Hispanic Cinemas* 3.1: 15–33.
— (2007). 'Manuel Delgado's Urban Anthropology: From Multidimensional Space to Interdisciplinary Spatial Theory'. *Arizona Journal of Hispanic Cultural Studies* 11: 57–75.
— (2008a). 'Reconciling Film Studies and Geography: Adolfo Bioy Casares's *La invención de Morel*'. *Mosaic: A Journal for the Interdisciplinary Study of Literature* 41.1: 153–68.
— (2008b). 'Toward a Philosophy of the Urban: Henri Lefebvre's Uncomfortable Application of Bergsonism'. *Environment and Planning D: Society and Space* 26.2: 338–58.
— (2008c). 'A Snapshot of Barcelona from Montjuïc: Juan Goytisolo's *Señas de identidad*, Tourist Landscapes as Process, and the Photographic Mechanism of Thought', in Eugenia Afinoguénova and Jaume Martí-Olivella (eds), *Spain Is (Still) Different: Tourism and Discourse in Spanish Identity* (Lanham, MD: Lexington Books), 151–84.
— (2010). *Encounters with Bergson(ism) in Spain: Reconciling Philosophy, Literature, Film and Urban Space*. Studies in the Romance Languages and Literatures, #295. (Chapel Hill: University North Carolina Press).
— (2011a). Henri Lefebvre and the Spanish Urban Experience: Reading the Mobile City (Lanham, MD: Bucknell University Press).
— (2011b). 'Ildefons Cerdà's Scalpel: A Lefebvrian Perspective on Nineteenth-Century Urban Planning'. *Catalan Review* 25: 181–200.
Foucault, Michel (1970) [1966]. *The Order of Things* (New York: Pantheon Books).
Goldston, Robert (1969). *Barcelona: The Civic Stage* (London: Collier-MacMillan).

González Iñárritu, Alejandro (2010). *Biutiful*. Perf. Javier Bardem, Eduard Fernández, Luo Jin, Maricel Alvarez (Menage Atroz/Focus Features International).

Goytisolo, Juan (1996) [1966]. *Señas de identidad* (Madrid: Alianza [Mexico: City: Editorial Joaquín Mortiz]).

Gregori, Eduardo (2006). 'Geografías urbanas: La representación de la ciudad de México en *El sitio* y *Amores perros*'. *Espéculo: Revista de Estudios Literarios 33*.

Hall, Thomas (1997). *Planning Europe's Capital Cities: Aspects of Nineteenth-Century Urban Development* (London: E and FN SPON).

Harvey, David (1996). *Justice, Nature and the Geography of Difference* (London: Blackwell).

— (2006). *Paris, Capital of Modernity* (New York and London: Routledge).

— (2009). *Cosmopolitanism and the Geographies of Freedom* (New York: Columbia University Press).

Hughes, Robert (1992). *Barcelona* (New York: Knopf).

Jacobs, Jane (1992) [1961]. *The Death and Life of Great American Cities* (New York: Vintage [New York: Random House]).

Kantaris, Geoffrey (2008). 'Lola/Lolo: Filming Gender and Violence in the Mexican City', in Andrew Webber and Emma Wilson (eds), *Cities in Transition: The Moving Image and the Modern Metropolis* (New York and London: Wallflower Press), 163–75.

Kay, Sarah (2003). *Žižek: A Critical Introduction* (Cambridge, MA: Polity).

Labanyi, Jo (2000). 'History and Hauntology; or, What Does One Do with the Ghosts of the Past?: Reflections on Spanish Film and Fiction of the Post-Franco Period', in Joan Ramon Resina (ed.), *Disremembering the Dictatorship: The Politics of Memory since the Spanish Transition to Democracy* (Amsterdam and Atlanta: GA: Rodopi), 65–82.

Lefebvre, Henri (1976). *The Survival of Capitalism*. Trans. Frank Bryant (London: Allison & Busby).

— (1991). *The Production of Space*. Trans. Donald Nicholson-Smith (Oxford, UK, and Cambridge, MA: Blackwell).

— (1995). *Introduction to Modernity*. Trans. John Moore (London and New York: Verso).

— (1996). *The Right to the City*, in Eleonore Kofman and Elizabeth Lebas (ed. and trans.), *Writings on Cities* (Malden, MA, Oxford, UK and Carlton, Australia: Blackwell), 63–181.

— (2003). *The Urban Revolution*. Trans. Robert Bononno (Minneapolis: University of Minnesota Press).

Loxham, Abigail (2006). 'Barcelona under Construction: The Democratic

Potential of Touch and Vision in City Cinema as Depicted in *En construcción*. *Studies in Hispanic Cinemas* 3.1: 35–48.

Marx, Karl (1977). *Capital: Volume 1*. Intro. Ernest Mandel, trans. Ben Fowkes (New York: Vintage).

McNeill, Donald (1999). Urban Change and the European Left: Tales from the New Barcelona (London and New York: Routledge).

— (2002). 'Barcelona: Urban Identity 1992–2002'. *Arizona Journal of Hispanic Cultural Studies* 6: 245–62.

Mendoza, Eduardo (2003). *La ciudad de los prodigios* (Barcelona: Seix Barral).

Mennel, Barbara (2008). *Cities and Cinema* (London and New York: Routledge).

Mitchell, Don (2003). The Right to the City: Social Justice and the Fight for Public Space (New York and London: The Guildford Press).

Moreiras-Menor, Cristina (2008). 'Nuevas fundaciones: Temporalidad e historia en *La comunidad* de Álex de la Iglesia'. *Modern Language Notes* 123.2: 374–95.

Philo, Chris, and Gerry Kearns (1993). 'Culture, History, Capital: A Critical Introduction to the Selling of Places', in Chris Philo and Gerry Kearns (eds), *Selling Places: The City as Cultural Capital Past and Present* (Oxford: Pergamon), 1–32.

Podalsky, Laura (2011). 'Migrant Feelings: Melodrama, *Babel* and Affective Communities'. *Studies in Hispanic Cinemas* 7.1: 47–58.

Resina, Joan Ramon (2003). 'From Rose of Fire to City of Ivory', in Joan Ramon Resina and Dieter Ingenschay (eds.), *After-Images of the City* (Ithaca, NY: Cornell University Press), 75–122.

— (2008). Barcelona's Vocation of Modernity. Rise and Decline of an Urban Image (Stanford, CA: Stanford University Press).

Riis, Jacob (1890). *How the Other Half Lives* (New York: Charles Scribner's).

Simmel, Georg (2010). 'The Metropolis and Mental Life', in Gary Bridge and Sophie Watson (eds), *The Blackwell City Reader* (Malden, MA, and Oxford, UK: Wiley-Blackwell), 103–10.

Smith, Brent (2010). 'Re-Narrating Globalization: Hybridity and Resistance in *Amores perros, Santitos,* and *El jardín de Edén'. Rupkatha: Journal of Interdisciplinary Studies in Humanities* 2.3: 268–81.

Smith, Paul Julian (2006). *Spanish Visual Culture: Cinema, Television, Internet* (Manchester, UK: Manchester University Press).

Staeheli, Lynn (1996). 'Publicity, Privacy and Women's Political Action'. *Environment and Planning D: Society and Space* 14.5: 601–19.

Thornton, Niamh (2003). 'Finding a Place in a Megalopolis: Mexico City in *Amores perros*'. *Film and Film Culture* 2: 43–50.

Tierney, Dolores (2009). 'Alejandro González Iñárritu: Director without Borders'. *New Cinemas: Journal of Contemporary Film* 7.2: 101–17.

Vázquez Montalbán, Manuel (1990). *Barcelonas*. Trans. A. Robinson (London: Verso).

—— (1993). *Sabotaje Olímpico* (Barcelona: Planeta).

—— (1997). *Los mares del sur* (Barcelona: Planeta).

Webber, Andrew, and Emma Wilson (2008). *Cities in Transition: The Moving Image and the Modern Metropolis* (New York and London: Wallflower Press).

Wirth, Louis (1938). 'Urbanism as a Way of Life'. *The American Journal of Sociology* 44.1: 1–24.

www.ingramcontent.com/pod-product-compliance
Lightning Source LLC
Chambersburg PA
CBHW061702300426
44115CB00014B/2536